READING MATTERS

READING MATTERS

FIVE CENTURIES OF DISCOVERING BOOKS

MARGARET WILLES

YALE UNIVERSITY PRESS
NEW HAVEN AND LONDON

Published with assistance from the Annie Burr Lewis Fund

First printed in paperback 2010

For information about this and other Yale University Press publications, please contact:

U.S. Office:	sales.press@yale.edu	www.yalebooks.com
Europe Office:	sales@yaleup.co.uk	www.yaleup.co.uk

Set in Minion by J&L Composition Ltd, Filey, North Yorkshire
Printed in Great Britain by Hobbs the Printers Ltd, Totton, Hampshire

Library of Congress Cataloging-in-Publication Data

Willes,Margaret.
    Reading matters: five centuries of discovering books / Margaret Willes.
        p. cm.
    Includes bibliographical references and index.
    ISBN 978-0-300-12729-4 (ci : alk. paper)
    1. Book collectors–Great Britain. 2. Book collecting–England–History.
    3. Book collectors–England–Biography. 4. Private libraries–England–History.
    5. Book collectors–United States. 6. Book collecting–United States–History.
    I. Title.
        Z987.5.G7W55 2008
        002.075–dc22

                                                            2008015557

A catalogue record for this book is available from the British Library.

ISBN 978-0-300-16404-6 (pbk)

10 9 8 7 6 5 4 3 2 1

For Victor, and to the memory of Jane Blackstock and Carole Mills

CONTENTS

List of Illustrations   *viii*

Introduction   *xiii*

Chapter 1   Books Do Furnish a Room: The Books of Bess of Hardwick and the Cavendish Family   1

Chapter 2   Enjoyment of all that's Worth Seeking After: The Books of Samuel Pepys   28

Chapter 3   Distance Learning: Three Provincial Libraries   56

Chapter 4   A Founding Father: The Books of Thomas Jefferson   83

Chapter 5   Building a Library: The Books of Sir John Soane   109

Chapter 6   A Little Light Reading?: Fact and Fiction in Georgian Britain   136

Chapter 7   Rare and Curious: The Books of Charles Winn   168

Chapter 8   The Common Reader: Books for Working Men and Women   193

Chapter 9   Children of the Revolution: The Books of Denis and Edna Healey   233

Appendix: Equivalent Values of the Pound   *263*

Notes   *264*

Further Reading   *276*

Index   *283*

ILLUSTRATIONS

Plates

I   Left panel of the 'Great Picture' attributed to Jan van Belcamp, depicting Lady Anne Clifford (reproduced by courtesy of Abbot Hall Art Gallery, Kendal, Cumbria)

II   The Library at Dunham Massey, Cheshire (NTPL/Andreas von Einsiedel)

III The Book Room at Wimpole Hall, Cambridgeshire (NTPL/Andreas von Einsiedel)

IV   'Advantages of a Modern Education' by Charles Williams, 1825 (V&A Images)

V   Selection of Gollancz books (from the libraries of Lord Healey and Joanna Goldsworthy)

VI   Selection of Penguin books (from the libraries of Jane Blackstock, Stephen Kent, Victor Morrison and the author)

VII Ralph Steadman's poster for the Cheltenham Festival of Literature, 1994 (courtesy of Ralph Steadman)

Figures

1   Portrait of Bess of Hardwick by an unknown artist, Hardwick Hall (NTPL/Angelo Hornak)

2   Appliqué needlework panel showing Penelope, Perseverance and Patience, Hardwick Hall (NTPL/Brenda Norrish)

3   Alabaster overmantel of Apollo and the Muses, Hardwick Hall (NT/Robert Thrift)

4   Engraving of Apollo and the Muses by Frans Huys (Copyright the Trustees of the British Museum)

5 Botanical octagonal canvas work of the lily of the valley (NTPL/Robert Thrift)

6 Lily of the valley from the 1572 edition of Pier Andrea Mattioli's *Commentarii* (British Library Board. All Rights Reserved (456f5, f.489))

7 *Allegory of Commerce*, woodcut by Jost Amman, 1585 (Bibiliothèque royale, de Belgique, Cabinet des Estampes, S II 4990 max)

8 The Kedermister Library, St Mary's Church, Langley Marish, Berkshire (Lucinda Lambton/arcaid.co.uk)

9 Portrait of Arbella Stuart by Rowland Lockey, 1589 (NTPL/John Hammond)

10 Portrait of Samuel Pepys by Sir Godfrey Kneller, *c.*1685 (Pepys Library, Magdalene College, Cambridge)

11 Detail from Wenceslaus Hollar's panorama of London, 1647 (Guildhall Library, City of London)

12 John Ogilby presenting his book of subscribers to Charles II, detail from *London &c. Actually Survey'd* by William Morgan, *c.*1681–2 (British Library Board. All Rights Reserved (Maps Crace Port 2 58))

13 Detail from the Anthony Roll of the Tudor navy (Pepys Library, Magdalene College, Cambridge)

14 Title page of Pepys's copy of the 1489 edition of Caxton's *Reynard the Fox* (Pepys Library, Magdalene College, Cambridge)

15 Woodcut from *Make Room for Christmas*, chapbook, *c.*1680 (Pepys Library, Magdalene College, Cambridge)

16 Advertisement for coffee powder showing a London coffee house, *c.*1700 (John Johnson Collection, Bodleian Library, Oxford)

17 Drawing of Pepys's Library in York Buildings, London, 1699 (Pepys Library, Magdalene College, Cambridge)

18 A shelf of Pepys's books (Pepys Library, Magdalene College, Cambridge)

19 Front page of John Dunton's *Athenian Mercury*, 1 January 1695 (NT Historic Properties Photographic Archive)

20 Portrait of George Booth, 2nd Earl of Warrington and his daughter Lady Mary, by Michael Dahl, 1695 (NTPL/John Hammond)

21 Sutton Nicholls' satire of a book auctioneer in Moorfields (Guildhall Library)

22 The Fire House at Townend, Troutbeck, Cumbria (NTPL/Rob Talbot)

23 Title page of *Mr Ogilby's and William Morgan's Pocket Book of the Roads*, 1689 (NTPL/Geoff Morgan)

24 Old Ben Browne's diary for 1731, kept in an almanac (Cumbria Record Office, by permission of NT)

25 A page from the 1768 catalogue of Dunham Massey Library (NT Historic Properties Photographic Archive)

26   Volumes by Dr Isaac Barrow, from the library at Townend (NTPL/Graham Edwards)

27   Catalogue of the library at Harvard College, Cambridge, New England, 1723 (NT Historic Properties Photographic Archive)

28   Bookplate of the Society for the Propagation of the Gospel in Foreign Parts, 1704 (American Antiquarian Society)

29   Thomas Jefferson's library at Monticello (Monticello/Thomas Jefferson Foundation, Inc.)

30   Portrait of Thomas Jefferson by Mather Brown, 1786 (National Portrait Gallery, Smithsonian Institution)

31   Cartoon of John Stockdale by Thomas Rowlandson, 1784 (by kind permission of James Raven)

32   A selection of Jefferson's books in the Library of Congress (Rare Books and Special Collections Division, Library of Congress)

33   Ink drawing of the Library of Congress by Alexander Jackson Davis and Stephen Henry Gimber, 1832 (I N Phelps Stokes Collection, Miriam and Ira D Wallach Division of Arts, Prints and Photographs, The New York Public Library, Astor Lenox and Tilden Foundations)

34   Title page of John Bell's edition of the poems of Edmund Spenser, 1778 (Courtesy of The Lewis Walpole Library, Yale University)

35   A printed version of Thomas Jefferson's last letter (Library of Congress, Prints and Photographs Division, LC-USZ62-40879)

36   Portrait of John Soane by William Owen, 1804 (Sir John Soane Museum)

37   A trade card of the London Booksellers, c.1800 (Bodleian Library, John Johnson Collection)

38   Interior of James Lackington's Temple of the Muses (Bodleian Library, John Johnson Collection)

39   Exterior of the Temple of the Muses from Lackington's catalogue (Bodleian Library, John Johnson Collection)

40   Bill-heading for London bookseller, James Asperne (Sir John Soane Museum)

41   Bill-heading for London bookseller, John Williams (Sir John Soane Museum)

42   'A Book Auction' by Thomas Rowlandson, c.1810–15 (Yale Center for British Art, Paul Mellon Collection)

43   Receipt from Sir John Soane, 1831 (Sir John Soane Museum)

44   Watercolour of the Soane family in the breakfast room at 12 Lincoln's Inn Fields by Joseph Gandy (Sir John Soane Museum)

45   *John Freeth and his Circle* by Johannes Eckstein, 1792 (Birmingham Museums & Art Gallery)

46 James Hulett's engraving of Wright's Circulating Library in London (Bodleian Library, John Johnson Collection)

47 Trade card for Bettison's Library in Cheltenham, Gloucestershire (Bodleian Library, John Johnson Collection)

48 Title page for Edward Cave's *The Gentleman's Magazine*, March 1749 (Guildhall Library)

49 *Before*, an engraving by William Hogarth, 1736 (Andrew Edmunds, London)

50 *Woman Reading*, engraving after John Collett by Robert Pranker, *c.*1763–5 (Yale Center for British Art, Paul Mellon Collection)

51 The library at Calke Abbey, Derbyshire (NTPL/Andreas von Einsiedel)

52 *Tales of Wonder!* by James Gillray, 1802 (NTPL/John Hammond)

53 *Four Specimens of the Reading Public*, a print after Alfred Crowquill by George Cruikshank, 1826 (Copyright The Trustees of the British Museum)

54 Portrait of Charles Winn (by kind permission of the NT and Lord St Oswald)

55 Frontispiece of the Harley sale catalogue, engraving taken from a drawing by John Vertue, 1742 (Collection Tim Knox and Todd Longstaffe-Gowan)

56 *Sir Rowland and Lady Winn in the Library* by Hugh Douglas Hamilton, 1770 (NTPL/John Hammond)

57 Medal cabinet designed by Thomas Chippendale *c.*1767–8 (NTPL/Andreas von Einsiedel)

58 Horace Walpole seated in his Gothic Library, drawing by J.H. Muntz, late 1750s

59 Sale catalogue for a mid-nineteenth-century bookseller (by kind permission of Robert Baldock)

60 Illustration by George Cruickshank from Dickens' *Oliver Twist*, 1837

61 Woodcut of Fountains Abbey by Thomas Gent, from *Yorkshire Chap-books*, edited by Charles A. Federer, 1889

62 'Swallow-tailed Kite' by John Gould, 1837 (Blickling Hall, The Lothian Collection (The National Trust), NTPL/John Hammond)

63 The Billiard Room at Nostell Priory (NTPL/Andreas von Einsiedel)

64 Book label for Mudie's Select Library

65 The W.H. Smith station bookstall at Blackpool North, 1896 (Penguin Archives, DM1294/Photo Box 3/Bookshops and Stalls)

66 Printer's proof for a 'yellowback' (Bodleian Library, John Johnson Collection)

67 Title page of the 1897 Everyman edition of Montaigne's *Essays* (by kind permission of Lord Healey)

68 American cartoon of Charles Dickens, 1868, from *Dickens in Cartoon and Caricature* (The Pepys Library, Magdalene College, Cambridge University Library, S727.c.92.182)

69 Page from the borrowers' register for Innerpeffray Library, Perthshire (with permission of Innerpeffray Library)

70 Bookplate for the Leadhills Miners' Library, Lanarkshire (by kind permission of the Leadhills Reading Society)

71 Frontispiece to Thomas Greenwood's *Free Public Libraries*, 1886

72 The Cotgreave indicator reproduced in Greenwood's *Free Public Libraries*

73 The Cotgreave indicator reproduced in Greenwood's *Free Public Libraries*

74 Advertisement for *A General History of Quadrupeds* by Thomas Bewick, 1788 (Newcastle Libraries and Information Service)

75 Advertisement for William Sugg & Co., in Greenwood's *Free Public Libraries*

76 'Education's Frankenstein' from *Punch*'s almanac for 1884 (Punch Library)

77 Denis and Edna Healey

78 Front page of the *Observer* Christmas Literary Supplement, 1931 (by kind permission of the Orion Publishing Group)

79 Allen Lane with his Penguincubator, 1937 (Penguin Archives, DM 80 1294/Photo Box 2/Bookshops and Bookstalls)

80 Advertisement for the Boots Booklovers Library (Bodleian Library, John Johnson Collection; used with the kind permission of The Boots Company PLC)

81 Advertisement for wartime Penguin Specials (Penguin Archives, DM 1294/Photo Box 2/Penguin advertisments)

82 Marks & Co. from *84 Charing Cross Road* (Brooksfilms/Columbia/The Kobal Collection)

83 Cover for first instalment of Hutchinson's 'Story of the British Nation', *c.*1920

INTRODUCTION

This book sets out to examine how people bought and acquired books over the past five hundred years, thus combining two of my favourite activities, shopping and reading. It is important to remember that books have until very recently been luxury items – and some indeed remain so. Therefore literate men and women who could not afford to buy books have had to borrow, share, acquire second-hand, inherit. Those who were not literate simply had no access apart from the oral tradition.

Books, however, are different from other consumer goods. They carry an extra factor, the provision of knowledge, and, as the philosopher Francis Bacon pointed out, 'Knowledge itself is power'.[1] This was clearly signalled by a statute issued in 1543 by Henry VIII that forbade the reading of the English version of the Bible by a whole range of people, from women to servants. There is even an echo from recent times, when Mervyn Griffith-Jones, the Senior Treasury Counsel in the trial of D.H. Lawrence's *Lady Chatterley's Lover*, asked members of the jury whether they would allow their wife or their servants to read the book. Successive governments first in England, and then in Great Britain sought over the centuries, along with the Church and other institutions, to control the power of knowledge through censorship, through monopolies enjoyed by the Stationers' Company, and through financial and legal curbs such as the 'terror' of William Pitt the Younger at the end of the eighteenth century. These, and the battles of those who sought freedom of access to knowledge and learning, have had their effects on the ownership of books and journals.

The two main groups of readers singled out by Henry VIII's legislation, women and the lower orders, are the subjects of two general chapters, 'A Little Light Reading?' and 'The Common Reader'. It came as quite a shock to discover the attitudes in the past towards women reading, and the virulence with which works of fiction, and the apparently innocuous circulating libraries, were viewed in the eighteenth century. Economic and social restrictions imposed on those perceived as belonging to the lower orders also make for sober reading, and I can only view with admiration the men and women who struggled to secure decent education, and access to books and journals. Many of these obstacles have been removed, but snobbery is the hardest to eradicate. Jonathan Rose in his chapter entitled 'What Was Leonard Bast Really Like?', with reference to the clerk from E.M. Forster's *Howards End* who was crushed and killed by his books, provides a whole host of vivid examples of twentieth-century attitudes in *The Intellectual Life of the British Working Classes.*[2]

Looking back at my own life, I realise that it has been very bookish. Like Jaques in Shakespeare's *As You Like It*, my experiences can be assigned to seven ages: reader; student; librarian (briefly); editor; bookseller (again briefly); publisher; and now author. Since having completed my studies in the 1960s, two great changes have been the huge development in access to information and the explosion of interest in the study of the book. The first has proved an invaluable tool, the second a challenge. In 1990 Robert Darnton in *The Kiss of Lamourette* wrote, 'The history of books has become so crowded with ancillary disciplines that one can no longer see its general contours. How can the book historian neglect the history of libraries, of publishing, of paper, type and reading? . . . It is enough to make one want to retire to a rare book room and count watermarks.'[3]

I have, indeed, retired to the Rare Book Room of the British Library, but counting watermarks has not been my fate. I have tackled the huge and multidisciplinary subject by concentrating on case studies. These have been selected to demonstrate ownership of different kinds of books, from chapbooks and practical books to rare incunabula and fine editions, and the different kinds of book owners, from country-house aristocrats to yeomen farmers, from Regency ladies of leisure to hardworking professionals. Wherever possible, I have found examples of collections of books that have survived, supplemented by records of ownership, acquisition and what the reader thought about their books. I have also described how people accommodated their collections. I look not only at the customer, but also at the provider, the publishers, booksellers, auctioneers, reviewers and those involved in marketing.

My time frame begins with the sixteenth century, when the printed book became generally available. I have chosen as part of my first case study Bess of Hardwick, not because she was a great book lover, but because with her increasing wealth and her marriages to cultured men she had access to books beyond the Bible, psalms and devotional works that were the reading fare of most literate women in the Tudor period. Moreover, as the matriarch of a large family, Bess was responsible for the early education of her own children

and of stepchildren and grandchildren. The achievements of future generations both dynastically and culturally are due to her determination that they
should prosper in the world. My last chapter brings the acquisition of books
and information about books right up to the present day. I have chosen here
Lord and Lady Healey, whose lives have spanned most of the twentieth
century and reflect the great changes that have been wrought during this
period. I am very grateful to them for allowing me to interview them and to
provide me with access to their considerable collection of books.

I have tried, whenever possible, to trace various aspects of publishing and
bookselling to their historical roots. Thus, I have looked at the earliest book
reviews from the mid-eighteenth century. Although footnotes, or, rather
marginalia, have always been a feature of books, the arrival of the select
bibliography is more difficult to pin down, partly because the word 'bibliography' has meant different things at different times. Kevin Jackson in *Invisible
Forms* makes a rapid journey through its history, identifying the Swiss
naturalist Conrad Gesner as the father of the bibliography, when he set
out with his *Bibliotheca universalis*, published in 1545, to list every religious
book published to date.[4] Thomas Frognall Dibdin not only made famous
the term 'bibliomania', but also wrote *The Bibliographical Decameron* in 1817.
Nevertheless, select bibliographies were not a usual part of books throughout
the nineteenth century, as shown by the three-dimensional example kindly
provided for me by Douglas Matthews. When Charles Dickens was writing
A Tale of Two Cities, he asked Thomas Carlyle, the author of the great work on
the French Revolution, for a list of books on the subject. Carlyle's response
was to have a barrow-load of books sent round to Dickens from the London
Library. This rather cumbersome solution suggests that reading lists were not
available in the 1850s.

Whenever possible I have given the prices of books, and at the end of the
book there is a table of the equivalent value of the pound over the centuries.
This has to be a rough and ready calculation as the buying power of the pound
has varied so greatly: I have therefore tried also to provide the earnings of
various levels of society.

* * * *

My learning curve in researching the great range of the subject has been
almost vertical, and I have been very dependent on the good nature and
generosity of many experts. While it is invidious to single out individuals, I
have to give particular thanks to Giles Mandelbrote at the British Library,
whose encyclopaedic knowledge I have tapped all too often. I hope in the
future he will be able to venture through the Rare Books and Music Library

without fear of intervention. The Libraries Advisers at the National Trust have also proved invaluable, especially in their guidance to the appropriate collections in their care. Mark Purcell has revolutionised the provision of information about these collections, putting them into their social context. Edward Potten, while at the National Trust, generously allowed me access to his research on the Booth family at Dunham Massey in Cheshire and on Charles Winn at Nostell Priory in Yorkshire. It has been especially helpful to visit these and other libraries, and so I am very grateful to the Bibliographical Society for awarding me the Royal Oak Award with a contribution from the National Trust to enable me to travel around Great Britain.

The staff of many libraries and archives have helped me in my research: Andrew Peppitt and Stuart Brand at Chatsworth; Muriel Kemp at the Kedermister Library; Dr Richard Luckett and Sarah Anderson at Pepys Library, Magdalene College, Cambridge; John Hodgson at the John Rylands Library in Manchester; David McClay at the John Murray Archives in the National Library of Scotland, Edinburgh; Susan Palmer and Stephen Astley at the Sir John Soane Museum; Gerry Healey at Linenhall Library in Belfast; John Doherty at Edzell Library; Harry Shaw and Mary Hamilton at Leadhills Reading Society; and Anne Edgar and Colin Miles at Innerpeffray Library. The National Trust staff at the various houses have been invariably welcoming and helpful, including Nigel Wright at Hardwick Hall, Margaret Stone at Dunham Massey, Patricia and Alistair Law and Roberta Rea at Springhill, Katie Lord at Calke Abbey, Felicity Stimson, and Hugh and Gill Dixon. In my search for pictures, I have been helped by Jeremy Smith at the Guildhall Library, Sheila O'Connell at the Department of Prints and Drawings in the British Museum, Julie Anne Lambert at the John Johnson Collection in the Bodleian Library, and Guy Penman at the London Library.

Many years ago, I edited Anthony Hobson's *Great Libraries*, and his knowledge and wisdom have reappeared to help me in many different areas. I am also grateful to my old college friend Christina Mackwell for deciphering and identifying references to books in the account books of Sir William Cavendish – she is a veritable Hercule Poirot. Thank you too to David McKitterick, Richard Barling, Stephanie Pickford, Thirza Morrison, Jeremy Devlin Thorp and Christine Pugh, Alan and Sue Warner, Phoebe Phillips, Mark Llewellyn, Oliver Garnett, Tim Knox, John Saumaurez Smith, Michael Goff, Gill Coleridge, Liz Sich, David Way, John Armstrong, Joanna Goldsworthy, Kate Pocock and Rachael Lonsdale. Finally I am grateful to Robert Baldock for having faith in me, and to the Morrison family for their patience during the writing of this book.

CHAPTER 1

BOOKS DO FURNISH A ROOM

The Books of Bess of Hardwick and the Cavendish Family

A twentieth-century Labour politician once described Joseph Stalin as just a working man making his way in the world.[1] Bess of Hardwick could likewise be characterised as just a Tudor housewife doing the best by her family. Bess was born in late 1527 into an old established Derbyshire family that had fallen into a state of genteel poverty. Her father John Hardwick died when she was only a few months old, leaving the modest sum of £26 13s 4d to each of his four daughters, and a few hundred acres and the rather rundown medieval manor-house of Hardwick Hall to his only son James.[2] From these modest beginnings, Bess built up her personal fortune through her four marriages and by her astute and careful husbandry. When she died, at the advanced age of eighty-one in February 1608, she was the richest woman in England.

Although her early life was financially straitened, exacerbated by the constant litigation that characterised Tudor England, Bess was well connected. Through cousins she was related to Henry Grey, Marquess of Dorset and great-grandson of Edward IV's Queen, Elizabeth Woodville, and her family had friends at court. Her early education would have been provided by her mother, Elizabeth – this is borne out by her handwriting which is not in the fine Renaissance italic hand of women such as Elizabeth Tudor or Lady Jane Grey who had the benefit of tutors. When she was twelve, Bess was sent to the Zouche family at Codnor Castle in Derbyshire to undertake the typical training of a well-born woman, and continued her education under the supervision of Lady Zouche, who before her marriage had been a lady-in-waiting to Henry VIII's second queen, Anne Boleyn.

When the Zouches travelled down to their London house, Bess went too, and made her first brief marriage to Robert Barlow, who died on Christmas Eve 1544. The young widow then became waiting woman to Frances Brandon, the King's niece, married to Bess's distant kinsman Henry Grey. This was the ideal milieu for a young lady thirsting for the good things of life. She became close to all the Greys' daughters, but she seems to have been particularly influenced by the intellectual fervour of Lady Jane and her famous tutor, Roger Ascham. Through the Greys, Bess met her second husband Sir William Cavendish, Treasurer of the King's Chamber, marrying him in 1547. Cavendish was one of the Tudor 'New Men', not from an aristocratic family, but well-educated and able. Both he and his older brother George began their careers in the household of Thomas Wolsey. Bess and William Cavendish had eight children: two daughters, Lucretia and Temperance, died in infancy, but the other six (three boys, three girls) grew up to adulthood and fulfilled Bess's ambitions as a dynast. When Cavendish died in 1557, Bess married Sir William St Loe, an intellectual, described by his tutor John Palsgrave as 'the best sped [accomplished] child of his age'.[3] Like his great friend Robert Dudley, he was favoured by Queen Elizabeth, becoming Captain of her Personal Guard at her accession. Once more Bess was at the centre of court and cultural life.

Bess, like many successful women, has not enjoyed a good press historically. Her wealth and ambition have rankled, and she is usually described as formidable. But her second, third and fourth husbands all married her for love and she was clearly a lady of great beauty and charm. Although she had no children by St Loe, he treated his stepchildren as his own. The accounts at Chatsworth record his purchase of books in 1560 for them: French grammars by his former tutor Palsgrave, two cosmographies of the Levant, psalms in French, an almanac and a book of pronunciation. When the elder boys Henry and William went to Eton, he bought them classical texts and the fables of Aesop.[4]

This happy family scenario ended in 1565 with the sudden death of St Loe, possibly poisoned by his brother. Two years later, Bess married her fourth husband, George Talbot, Earl of Shrewsbury, one of the leading noblemen of the realm. The union has been likened to the merging of two companies, for at the same time Bess's eldest son Henry married Grace, the Earl's daughter, and her daughter Mary married the Earl's heir, Gilbert. At first the marriage between Bess and Shrewsbury flourished, but then the captive and captivating Mary Queen of Scots came into their lives when Shrewsbury was made her custodian. As the Queen's wearisome captivity stretched from months to years, Bess came to suspect her husband of falling under Mary's thrall, while he developed a form of paranoid illness which made him quarrel with everybody, and nobody more so than his wife. It is an indication of the affection that Queen Elizabeth held for Bess that she, along with leading courtiers such as Robert Dudley, now Earl of Leicester, and William Cecil, Lord Burghley, attempted to reconcile the warring couple. In the end, nothing could mend matters, save the death of Shrewsbury in 1590.

1 Portrait of Bess of Hardwick painted by an unknown artist in the 1550s, probably when she was married to Sir William Cavendish. This painting was later incorrectly inscribed as 'Maria Regina' or Mary Tudor.

Bess was an indefatigable builder, and Lord Shrewsbury's death enabled her to embark on a major new phase. With Sir William Cavendish she had created the great house at Chatsworth in Derbyshire that still exists as the core of the present Baroque mansion. In 1583 when her feckless brother James was declared bankrupt, she acquired her birthplace, Hardwick Hall, and began to enlarge and refurbish it. In 1590 she stopped this work and, with the money now at her disposal, began at once to build a completely new and very grand house, the New Hall, just yards from the Old. Hardwick New Hall survives as one of the finest examples of Elizabethan architecture in England, with the decorative schemes and many of the furnishings installed by Bess. The quarrels between Bess and Shrewsbury often focused on their belongings and, as a result, give us a lot of information about them. In addition, she drew up in 1604 an inventory of Chatsworth, and the Old and New Halls at Hardwick. Frustratingly, details of her personal plate, jewellery and general book collection were omitted. Inventories of this period are notorious for the absence of books, but there are clues to what she might have owned.

Five books only are recorded as being in Bess's bedchamber. For any modern reader, such bedtime reading would prove a tough proposition. All the identified books are religious in subject matter: a book of meditations, 'Saloman's proverbes'; 'Calvin upon Jobe' (covered in russet velvet); and a book entitled 'Resolution'; the other two are unspecified. From these rather vague descriptions, scholars have concluded that 'Saloman's proverbes' refers to one of the books illustrated by Bernard Salomon for the publisher Jean de Tournes in Lyons – a popular title was *Quadrins Historiques de la Bible*, dating from 1553 with an English translation, *The true and lyvely historyke purtreatures of the vvoll Bible*. 'Calvin upon Jobe' is *Sermons of Master Iohn Calvin, upon the Booke of Iob*, an English translation made by Arthur Golding and first published in London by Harrison and Byshop in 1574. This again was a popular title, going into reprint the same year, with several subsequent editions.

The third title, 'Resolution' masks a complicated publishing history, but one which is revealing about the state of religion in England at the time. The original book was by a recusant Catholic priest, Robert Parsons, sometimes known as Persons, who developed it from *The Exercise of a Christian Life* by an Italian Jesuit, Gaspar Loarte. Parsons' full title was *The First Booke of the Christian Exercise, appertaining to resolution*, and as a recusant, he had it · published in Rouen in 1582. Loarte had managed to rise above the war of words between Catholics and Protestants to concentrate on inspiring individual spiritual renewal. So popular did it prove as a devotional work that a Yorkshire Protestant minister, Edmund Bunny, produced a book with almost the self-same title, cutting out references to purgatory and free will, but retaining ninety per cent of the original. His first edition was published in London in 1584, and went through many editions: by 1600 the ratio of Bunny to Parsons was twenty-four to one. The copy belonging to Bess is probably the 1599 edition published by Thomas Wight, which was in the library at Chatsworth until 1958.[5]

The fact that all the books listed in Bess's bedchamber were devotional emphasises the very important role that religion played in the daily life of

Tudor men and women. Indeed, women were enjoined to concentrate on religious books and not to waste their time on fripperies such as romances. Lady Margaret Hoby was a Yorkshire gentlewoman who kept a diary from 1599 to 1605. The entry for Tuesday, 8 January 1599 reads as follows:

> After prayer, and that I was readie, I went about and took order for divers things, then I prayed and, after I had eaten a little, I went to church and heard a sermon. After I came home, I prayed, dined, took my leave of Mr Hoby, and so went again about the house till 5, and then went to public prayers and examination of the sermon . . . after, heard Mr Rhodes read prayers, and went to bed.[6]

This entry was not for the Lord's Day, nor is it untypical – indeed the constant reiteration of her prayers and reading of the Bible makes the diary rather dull fare. Margaret Hoby had been brought up in a household verging on the Puritan, but her devotion to her religion would have been shared by most women of the period.

Two paintings of the Virgin Mary are recorded in the 1604 inventory, raising the possibility that Bess had Catholic sympathies. Hindsight has made us divide the population of Elizabethan England into Protestants and Catholics, but in reality the situation was much more complex. Although Bess had been born into pre-Reformation England and brought up to use the Roman liturgy, later in her life her circle of friends was largely Protestant. When Bess and Cavendish were choosing godparents for their children, most were of the Protestant persuasion, such as the Greys, the Seymours, the Dudleys and Princess Elizabeth, but they also hedged their bets, asking Queen Mary Tudor and her Catholic Bishop of Winchester, Stephen Gardiner, to stand as godparents to their third son, Charles. Bess's most likely stance was the 'middle way' adopted by Queen Elizabeth, and her devotional books would have reflected this. She certainly had no compunction about cutting up medieval ecclesiastical copes and robes, acquired from the Dissolution of the Monasteries by her husbands, for use in some of her appliqué embroideries.

The much-used adage, 'books do furnish a room', is literally true as far as Bess is concerned. The decorative schemes that she instituted at Chatsworth in the 1560s and 1570s, in Hardwick Old Hall in the 1580s, and at the New Hall in the 1590s were based on literary sources. A series of inlaid and painted panels, originally made for Chatsworth but now hanging at Hardwick, are derived from woodcuts by the artist Jost Amman from a picture bible printed in Frankfurt in 1564. One of the panels is based on his depiction of the palace of King Solomon in Jerusalem, and Anthony Wells-Cole has proposed the theory that Bess intended the whole spectacular design of Hardwick New

Hall, with its rectangular body and six 'towers', to reflect Solomon's palace, signalling that Bess was like the wise king of the Old Testament.[7]

Jost Amman's illustrations were also used as the basis for a painting that still hangs at Hardwick, of the return of Ulysses to his wife, Penelope. This was painted for Bess in 1570 by one of the craftsmen who worked for her on a long-standing basis, John Baclehouse (known as John the Painter because his Flemish name was difficult). The story of faithful Penelope was a favourite, for Bess identified with her desire to be a good and loving wife, even if sorely tried. A tapestry set relating the History of Ulysses hangs in the High Great Chamber at Hardwick, while in a magnificent series of appliqué hangings Bess included Penelope, and it is thought that the heroine's features are based on her own, a theory supported by surviving portraits.

Bess owned several sets of appliqué hangings, but perhaps the most dramatic are those of five famous women of the Ancient World: Penelope, Cleopatra, Lucretia, Zenobia and Arthemesia. She may well have conceived the idea of these from Geoffrey Chaucer's *The Legend of Good Women*, for an inventory taken in 1547 records a copy of Chaucer in the parlour of Northaw, one of the houses belonging to Sir William Cavendish. Santina Levey has suggested that this may have been an edition of his complete works compiled by William Thynne and first published by Thomas Godfray in 1532.[8] In the prologue to *The Legend*, Cupid, the god of love, orders Chaucer in a dream to write accounts of nineteen women who suffered or died as a result of devotion to their lovers. In the event, Chaucer completed only eight of the pieces, writing of Cleopatra and Lucretia, but never getting to Penelope. Each of Bess's famous women are accompanied by appropriate virtues, so that Penelope is flanked by Perseverance and Patience, Cleopatra by Fortitude and Justice (this hanging is known only from fragments), Lucretia by Chastity and Liberality, Zenobia by Magnanimity and Prudence, and Arthemesia by Constancy and Piety. The story of Lucretia, the wife of a Roman nobleman who committed suicide after being raped by Tarquin the Proud, was another favourite of Bess, and she named her youngest daughter after her. When the hangings were made in the 1570s, they were to be hung round the walls of one of the chambers at Chatsworth, and therefore have a strong architectural element. Bess took the details for the classical pilasters that enclose each group from John Shute's *First and Chief Grounds of Architecture*, published in London in 1563.

An alabaster overmantel made for the Muses Chamber at Chatsworth in the 1570s and now in the Withdrawing Chamber at Hardwick shows Apollo surrounded by the Muses. This scene is based on an engraving made by Frans Huys after Frans Floris and published by Hieronymous Cock in Antwerp in 1565. The works of Flemish painters such as Floris and his brother Jacob,

2 Appliqué needlework panel showing Penelope, the long-suffering wife of Ulysses, flanked by Perseverance and Patience. This is one of a series of hangings made in the 1570s, probably based on Geoffrey Chaucer's *The Legend of Good Women*. The architectural details are taken from John Shute's *First and Chief Grounds of Architecture*, published in London in 1563. Bess particularly identified with Penelope, and it is believed that the heroine's features are based on her own.

Maarten de Vos and Maarten van Heemskerck come up again and again as the sources not only for overmantels, but also for plasterwork in the High Great Chamber at Hardwick, created in the 1590s, and for embroideries and textile designs throughout the decades. Books illustrated with woodcuts, and sets of engravings using copper plates, came at the top of the price range and almost without exception would have been imported. Most folio books cost around 10 to 12 shillings, while the most expensive engravings supplied by the Antwerp printer/bookseller Christopher Plantin cost 16 stuivers.[9] These sources could have belonged to the craftsmen who worked for Bess, though this is doubtful given that John Baclehouse, her highest paid craftsman, received an annual salary of £2. Bess could well have owned them herself, for she certainly had the money to buy them. A third possibility is that they were lent to her by other members of the Elizabethan court.

The Flemish artists mentioned above were the source of designs for embroideries and textiles, but there were others. Bess was a skilled

3 & 4 Above: an alabaster overmantel depicting Apollo and the Nine Muses. Made in the 1570s, it was originally installed in the Muses Chamber at Chatsworth, but was moved to the Withdrawing Chamber at Hardwick New Hall in the nineteenth century. Below: An engraving by Frans Huys after Frans Floris, published in Antwerp in 1565.

embroiderer, who spent many hours at work with another superb needle-woman, Mary Queen of Scots, during the early and happier years of the latter's captivity. Their works, and those of professional embroiderers employed by Bess, have survived in the remarkable collection of textiles still at Hardwick, and elsewhere. Among these are many with a botanical theme, based on the woodcut illustrations made for Pier Andrea Mattioli. The Italian botanist and physician, who spent twenty years in service to the Hapsburgs in Prague, wrote *Commentarii* on the work of Dioscorides which he published in 1565 in a magnificent illustrated edition in Venice, adding many plants that he had identified through his own travels and in correspondence with a wide circle of botanists, including new species from Turkey. The octagonal flower 'slips' now on display at Hardwick are framed with Latin tags that Bess must have taken from the *Adages* of the humanist philosopher, Erasmus. Other embroideries of birds and fish are based on French sources, possibly from books belonging to Mary Queen of Scots rather than Bess herself. When Bess was looking for sources for the wonderful collection of animals and flowers that populate the great plaster frieze in the High Great Chamber at Hardwick, she used hunting prints engraved by Philips Galle after designs by the Flemish artist Johannes Stradanus, first published in 1578.

How did Bess obtain these books and prints? From the 1540s, when she was in the service of the Zouche family, she travelled from Derbyshire to London on a regular basis, and her last three husbands owned or rented a series of houses in the capital. Indeed Sir William Cavendish's house in Aldersgate Street was situated close to St Paul's Churchyard, the area populated by the various trades that made up England's publishing heartland – printers, booksellers, engravers, binders, print sellers and mapmakers.

In the sixteenth century, both printers and booksellers were responsible for publishing, and came under the general title of stationers, a term which is thought to refer to their permanent status as opposed to itinerant tradesmen. On 4 May 1557, during the reign of Mary Tudor, the Stationers' Company became a royally incorporated fellowship, with their hall in Ave Maria Lane, just off Paternoster Row by St Paul's Churchyard. Earlier there had been a mystery or trade guild of stationers with a brotherhood instituted in 1403, before the invention of printing. Even after this there was a need for the production of manuscripts, and professional scriptoria continued until at least the end of the seventeenth century. However, the royal incorporation enabled stationers to refine and develop their trade by owning copyrights and limiting productive capacity by regulating their numbers. In 1583, for example, there were 23 printing houses, equipped with 53 presses. Many of these were located in St Paul's Churchyard itself, either in shops forming an irregular rectangle around the yard, or in lock-ups against the cathedral walls

5 & 6 Above: Botanical octagonal canvas work with an image of the lily of the valley (below), taken from Pier Andrea Mattioli's commentary on the herbal written in the first century AD by the Greek doctor, Pedanius Dioscorides. This edition was published in Lyons in 1572. The motto surrounding the flower in the embroidery, *per publicam viam ne ambules* ('stray not upon the highway'), came from a collection of the moral adages of Erasmus.

between the buttresses. At one stage they ousted a chantry chapel and sermon house, and a common privy, much to the discomfort of the local residents and scholars from St Paul's School.[10] The bookshops often had a stall-board projecting from the front of the building with a second board, a penthouse. Both boards could be folded back against the wall when not in use.

One of the best known printers and booksellers was John Day, who was probably born in Dunwich, then a prosperous East Anglian port, now a mysterious 'lost town' beneath the waves of the North Sea. He came to London in the 1540s in the service of a physician-cum-printer, Thomas Raynalde, but joined the Stringers' Company, which made bowstrings for archers, rather than the brotherhood of Stationers. By 1549 he had set up his own printing house, in the gatehouse of Aldersgate. This was an exciting time for publishers and printers. The accession of Edward VI in 1547 had brought Protestantism to the fore, and the opportunities to produce the work of reformers such as John Calvin were ripe for development. Day seized these opportunities, and no fewer than 130 books are attributed to his press during the Edwardian period. He employed many foreign craftsmen and opened a shop in Cheapside in 1550. Granted the lucrative monopoly to publish John Ponet's *Brief Catechism*, he prospered greatly, much to the annoyance of other booksellers. He was prevented from acquiring a pre-fabricated shop in St Paul's Churchyard, and in 1573 was obliged to seek the protection of the Earl of Leicester when he and his family were nearly murdered by 'one Asplin', either an aggrieved apprentice or a rival printer.

The profit earned from publishing Protestant catechisms and psalters enabled Day to take on the major publishing venture of the sixteenth century, John Foxe's *Actes and Monuments*, familiarly known as *The Book of Martyrs*, the record of persecution of Protestants by 'Bloody Mary' Tudor. During her reign, Day kept a very low profile, while Foxe went into exile. But with the accession of Elizabeth, Foxe returned to England, and began working with Day on the project. It was huge. Running to over 1,800 pages, it involved different typefaces, columns and margin notes, to which the author kept on adding as more information was provided to him. On top of this, there were fifty woodcut illustrations, probably being produced in the Netherlands, and evidence suggests that they arrived late, generating the nightmare that is all too familiar to modern illustrated book publishers. The first edition appeared in March 1563, and work began immediately on the second, which required three presses to run simultaneously. It has been estimated that Day would have had to invest the staggering sum of £1,000 in the venture.[11]

In the end, it was all worth it: the book was a runaway success and John Day made a fortune. It was ordered that every cathedral church had to have a copy, and many parishes followed suit. Every Protestant household that could afford to do so bought a copy and sometimes displayed it in their hall as a public statement of their faith.[12] Foxe argued that the technology of printing was part of God's providential design: 'the blessed wisdom and omnipotent power of the Lord began to work for his church; not with sword and target to subdue his exalted adversaries, but with printing, writing and reading: to convince darkness by light, error by truth, ignorance by learning.'[13] His title page showed both men and women listening to the Word with bibles in their laps, and *The Book of Martyrs* was a particular favourite of women, who often bequeathed their copy in their wills. A folio copy of Foxe in two volumes, dating from 1597, is in the library at Chatsworth.

The native English publishing business was, however, only part of the story. Books that were imported from outside 'the obedience' of the King or Queen formed part of the Latin trade. This applied to any foreign book or print – Latin, after all, was the *lingua franca* of the time. An act dating from 1534, during the reign of Henry VIII, stipulated that those books from abroad must arrive without bindings of board, leather or parchment, to protect the interests of the English binding industry. Alien booksellers were limited to buying books abroad wholesale and carrying them to the port of London. This too was to protect native interests, but it also meant that foreign booksellers would be used where the talents lay, in buying from Continental publishers, and in pricing the books competently. In fact, a lot of alien booksellers gained denization so that they could continue with their trade, and once the Stationers' Company had been incorporated, they joined as Brothers. Trade in foreign books and prints was largely centred in Duck Lane and Little Britain, just south of Smithfield.

Booksellers and book buyers found out about the latest publications from broadside lists and catalogues. The Swiss physician and naturalist Conrad Gesner wrote in 1548: 'Most printers and booksellers, especially those furnished with the more learned sort of books, have broadsides and lists of books which they have printed or have for sale, and some of these have actually been printed as booklets'.[14] He went on to list the various European printers and publishers who did this. Broadsides were not designed to be read or kept as a book, but rather were fixed on the wall of a bookshop or behind the counter for the shopman's reference. Some publishers employed travelling salesmen, who on arrival in town would put up at an inn and post up the broadside, particularly canvassing the local clergy for orders. They would also visit local fairs, offering stock to stationers at a special price. Octavo catalogues were developed in Paris in the sixteenth century by Robert Estienne, described as an outstanding printer by Gesner. He divided his catalogues into Hebrew, Greek and Latin, beginning within the divisions with editions of the alphabet, followed by grammars, dictionaries and texts. With this catalogue Estienne promoted books by retail through his own shops, in correspondence with customers who lived a distance from Paris, and for wholesale sales to other booksellers, but because it was so difficult to fix standard rates, prices were not included.

The great European trade fair for books was held – as it still is – in Frankfurt. Now it takes place in October, but in the sixteenth century it occurred twice a year, at Lent in spring and at Michaelmas in autumn. Frankfurt's 'unique selling point' was that as an Imperial free city it did not have the complicated tolls and regulations that bedevilled so many of the German states, and it also offered religious tolerance to both Catholics and Protestants. It was accessible from all parts of Europe; booksellers, publishers, binders and paper merchants, scholars and potential authors could travel there from Italy, Spain, France, Germany, the Low Countries and England, often going by road as far as Cologne and thence by water. The first week was spent buying and selling books and swapping the latest news, the second finalising and settling accounts, using Rhenish gold florins as the common currency or letters of credit and promissory notes, with credit being extended from fair to fair. There was even a special 'Frankfurt rate' organised between publishers as a special deal – a phenomenon still encountered by publishers at the modern Frankfurt Buchmesse. Booksellers would leave surplus supplies in their agents' depots, which then became outlying branches of their trade, open all the year round.

The first printed catalogue for the Frankfurt Bookfair was produced in 1564 by George Willer of Augsburg, 'For the convenience and use of booksellers elsewhere and all students of literature'.[15] Printers would send their lists to Willer to coordinate and put in subject order. The 1564 catalogue contained 256 books, printed in nineteen cities, including Coimbra in Portugal and Budapest in Hungary. As the catalogue expanded in size, so imitations were made until the city council stepped in and produced the first official Frankfurt catalogue in the autumn of 1598. The mystic Dr John Dee, a great book collector, is the first recorded owner of a Frankfurt catalogue in England. To have a book published at the time of the fair could be a great advantage. The sensation of the 1587 fair, for instance, was *Historia von D. Johann Fausten*, which was translated into English in 1592 and became the basis for the play by Christopher Marlowe.

The biggest players in the Latin trade into England were the Birckmanns, an old established family from Cologne. As well as importing wholesale, they sold books at their shop in St Paul's Churchyard. These would arrive at the Port of London in barrels and baskets, to be noted in port books for the purpose of charging petty customs. Port books provide a fascinating source, with the name of the ship, port of origin, cargo and the name of the merchant. The unbound folios would be wrapped in waterproof bales and packed in maunds (baskets) or dryfatts (barrels): a maund was conventionally valued at £4, attracting customs duty of 12d, while a dryfatt was reckoned to be half a maund, with a duty of 6d. The waiters or searchers at the ports were not only after customs duty: they were also concerned about seditious literature. In 1564 injunctions were issued against trade with the Low Countries. Shortly afterwards, Sir William Cecil made a special plea on behalf of Arnold Birckmann and his factor Conrad Molyar, who were about to dispatch to England five fatts and two maunds of books from the Frankfurt Fair via Antwerp. He asked that they might quietly discharge the books – and four or five boxes of green ginger for his own use. Ironically, Cecil, as Lord Burghley, was later responsible for the control of book imports. The Surveyor of the Customs, Richard Carmarden in the 1590s refers to a command from Burghley that his waiters should 'look narrowly after all books that come into this port from foreign parts'.[16] Catholic recusant presses knew how to dodge this system, landing their books at unpoliced places in Kent such as Margate or the Isle of Sheppey.

Another large importer of books into England was Christopher Plantin, who set up his printing works in Antwerp in 1555, at the Sign of the Golden Compasses. His house and works are still to be seen, and the records that he and his successors kept are invaluable. A typical order from the London bookseller Nicholas England consisted of a substantial number of small-format classics, such as fifty copies of the selected letters of Cicero, and some large format books in ones or twos.[17] Christopher Plantin's shop, or 'bouticle', was separate from the printing works. The only detailed record of it dates from the mid-seventeenth century but gives a good indication of the working conditions of bookshops at this period. The assistants, who lived on the premises, began their day at 5:30am, attending church before starting work at 7:00am. Their lunch hours were expected to be spent in 'honest pastime', learning to write, or to study Latin, Spanish or French, or to count. Work ended at 8:00pm and they retired to bed at the same time as their master. Plantin not only sold his own products in his shop, but those from other publishers, and ran a delivery service to institutions and private individuals. Casks of Rhenish wine and beer were kept on tap to entertain foreign merchants.

The shops where Bess and her family bought their books were centred around St Paul's Churchyard and Paternoster Row. However, the sets of engravings from Continental artists used as reference for their craftsmen could have formed special orders through agents in Antwerp or Cologne. Both William St Loe and Lord Shrewsbury had close trading links with the Continent: the latter had a ship called *The Talbot*, which regularly took heavy goods from Hull to London and Northern Europe, returning with luxury

7 Jost Amman's woodcut of 1585, the *Allegory of Commerce*, praising Antwerp as a centre of international trade. On the upper level are depicted the coats of arms of the great trading cities of Europe surrounding Mercury, the god of commerce, who holds a set of scales in which credit and debit accounts are weighed. Below are the various professions of the city, including printing and publishing.

items such as spices and wine. When Bess spent longer periods in Derbyshire, away from the royal court and London, she would have had to make all her purchases by agency.

An insight into buying at one remove is provided by Sir Thomas Knyvett of Ashwellthorpe in Norfolk. Knyvett was born about twelve years after Bess – and like her, was long lived, dying in 1618. Like Bess, too, he was well connected, but Sir Thomas was much more interested in his books than seeking fame and fortune, preferring to stay in Norfolk and build up a collection, which reached a total of 70 manuscripts and 1,400 books at his death.[18] It was his brother Henry, a courtier and lawyer, who acted as his agent in London, not only getting him books, but sorting out his wardrobe too. In 1583, Henry wrote to his brother: 'If therefore it may please you to send me your measure for a doublet, and also what coloured cloth and of what fashion you will have your cloak, I will send you them both very shortly. You shall receive the books which you sent for very shortly, but I have sought for Hesiodi (ερμα και ημεραι) and cannot find it'.[19] Knyvett made a careful note of the price of his books. The most expensive were 10s, but most of his acquisitions cost him around 4s, though he got a bargain, possibly second hand, for 1s 8d. He also noted the contents of his library. This in itself is interesting, as rooms set aside as libraries were comparatively rare in late Elizabethan England. In his library, Thomas Knyvett kept antiquities, another of his collecting passions, a pair of globes by the great mapmaker Gerard Mercator, pictures and portraits.

Knyvett's library may well have been in a small study or closet, to which he could retire to read and contemplate. Such rooms dating from the early 1600s have almost all disappeared or been radically altered, but one has survived intact, not in a country house, but in a church. In his will of 1631 Sir John Kedermister left his collection of three hundred volumes, almost all works of theology, to the church of St Mary, Langley Marish in Berkshire, with his wife, Dame Mary as its administrator. The library is reached via the family pew in the church, but once through the door into the study, the visitor steps into a seventeenth-century domestic interior, with a fireplace surmounted by an ornate overmantel decorated with Kedermister's arms, grotesques and a depiction of the Virgin Mary. The books are kept in shelved cupboards, the doors of which are covered with paintings, including portraits of Sir John and Dame Mary, and local scenes such as Windsor Castle and the Thames. All the library furniture has survived, including a table, forms, pews and a set of steps. It seems likely that Sir John transferred his library lock, stock and barrel from his house at Langley Park to this little room, cutting down the panels where necessary.

8 The library of Sir John Kedermister, now in the church of St Mary, Langley Marish in Berkshire. Behind the painted panels are the shelves for the books, which would probably have been displayed with their fore-edges facing.

No library is described as such in Bess of Hardwick's inventory, although it is known that one existed in Hardwick Old Hall in the seventeenth century. In her bedchamber, however, are recorded a whole series of desks and of chests which could have contained her books. The inventory drawn up in 1632 for Henry Percy, 9th Earl of Northumberland at Petworth House in Sussex referred to over sixty chests of books. Robert Smythson, who worked with Bess on the building of Hardwick New Hall, drew a design for a closet or study, *c.*1600. This shows four elevations fitted out with shelves in compartments, with built-in desks. Some compartments are indicated for maps, loose papers, writings and ink, and the rest were presumably for books and papers.

Books at this period were not displayed spine out, nor did they have title labels. Sir John Kedermister's books all have plain spines, with his coat of arms impressed on the covers. Sir Thomas Knyvett added titles in manuscript to the fore-edges that faced anybody studying the shelves. Volumes were acquired unbound, in cheap protective pasteboard, or in vellum wrappers so that customers could adapt the binding to their own taste. Henry Percy, Lord Northumberland, and Robert Dudley, Lord Leicester, both had their own stamp impressed on the bindings of their books. Knyvett was more discreet in his use of ornaments, with double horizontal lines and small flowers on his spines, and two pairs of green ties to join together the fore-edges.

A pictorial record of books in a library is provided by *The Great Picture* of Lady Anne Clifford. Born in 1590, Anne was the daughter of George Clifford, 3rd Earl of Cumberland and Lady Margaret Russell. She became their sole heiress with a potential inheritance of large estates in Westmorland and Yorkshire, though she spent much of her life fighting for her lands. In 1646 she commissioned *The Great Picture* to celebrate her family; it now hangs in the Abbot Hall Gallery in Kendal. It takes the form of a triptych; in the central panel are portrayed Anne, her parents and her elder brothers who died young, with pictures of her aunts pinned on the wall. On the left-hand panel she is shown aged fifteen with her lute and portraits of her tutor and governess (Plate I). On the right-hand panel she is portrayed in her fifties, with portraits of her husbands, Richard Sackville, 3rd Earl of Dorset, and Philip Herbert, 4th Earl of Pembroke. Books are shown in all three panels, but perhaps the most fascinating are in the youthful portrait. Twenty-six volumes are displayed, some on shelves, others on the floor, and include 'all the works of Chaucer and Spenser', Sir Philip Sidney's *Arcadia*, Gerard's *Herball* and Camden's *Britannia*. Some are shown spine out, in leather bindings, with their titles indicated by paper labels. Others display their fore-edges, with the titles affixed to them, as recorded by Sir Thomas Knyvett.

* * * *

In Tudor times, the task of teaching children to read and write fell to mothers, so it was Bess who would have had charge of the primary education of her sons and daughters and of the little stepdaughters that she acquired with her marriage to Sir William Cavendish. This education was started young – as Erasmus advised, 'Press wax while it is softest; model clay while it is still moist; pour precious liquids only into a jar that has never been used before; and only dye wool that has just arrived spotless from the fullers.'[20] Children were provided with a hornbook, a single sheet of paper pasted to a wooden board with a handle, and covered with skin or horn for protection. At the top the alphabet was set out in upper and lower cases. Below came the Lord's Prayer and possibly the Ten Commandments. As the teacher, Bess would furnish herself with learning-to-read texts, with individual letters in a variety of type-faces, indications of vowels and consonants, and lists of syllables. All these would have a distinctly religious content, for as the schoolteacher Richard Mulcaster pointed out, 'Reading, if for nothing else it were, as for many things else, it is very needful for religion.'[21] After the Lord's Prayer, children moved on to other prayers, metrical psalms and excerpts from the Proverbs, and even abbreviated versions of Foxe's *Book of Martyrs*, though some of the illustrations might have been expected to give nightmares to the more sensitive.

In 1582 Bess took on the education of yet another child, when she took charge of her orphaned granddaughter, Arbella Stuart. Eight years earlier, Bess's daughter Elizabeth had met and married Charles Stuart, Earl of Lennox. It was a match that must have thrilled the ambitious Bess, for Charles had a claim to the English throne, but the union also roused the suspicions of Queen Elizabeth and was, in the end, to cause endless grief and difficulty for Bess and her family. In 2003 a member of the National Trust's conservation team found a book of catechism behind the panelling in the room that had been Bess's private dining chamber at Hardwick. The dry conditions had preserved it amazingly well, so that with some conservation it has emerged as bright and beautiful as the day it disappeared behind the woodwork. *The Christian's ABC, with the mirror of youth* was printed and published in 1583 by Thomas Vautrollier, a French Protestant who had settled in Blackfriars in London twenty years previously. He was particularly known for the beauty of his type, and for the quality of his illustrations, including his device of an anchor held by a hand issuing from clouds, with two sprigs of laurel and the motto 'Anchora Spei', all enclosed in an oval frame. The Hardwick catechism shows all this, together with a fine brown calf binding decorated with gold fleurs de lys and green silk ribbons. It is possible from the date that this was originally bought for Arbella Stuart, and dropped by her or one of her cousins in the 1590s during a bored moment at dinner.

Bess's elder sons, William and Henry, were sent first to Eton College, armed with books bought by their stepfather St Loe, and then later had tutors: one of these disgraced himself by spreading slander about their mother. Meanwhile, Bess would have continued with the education of her daughters, Frances, Mary and Elizabeth, and of her stepdaughters. This probably consisted of a combination of further learning and of practical training for their future role in running households. The most influential guide to the education of women *The Instruction of a Christian Woman* was written by Juan Luis Vives, adviser to Henry VIII's first Queen, Catherine Aragon and first appeared in English in 1529. At a time when most men were afraid of encouraging learning in women, Vives adopted a liberal approach, as did his translator, Richard Hyrde. In his address to Queen Catherine in the introduction to *Instruction*, Hyrde expressed his exasperation that women 'in every country' were not taught to read Latin nor was it translated for them, so that they could enjoy a good education, and thus overcome the complaints that men made about their ignorance. This argument was put even more forcibly over a century later by Margaret, wife of Bess's grandson William Cavendish, Duke of Newcastle, in a complaint to the universities of Oxford and Cambridge: 'We are become like worms that only

9 Portrait of Arbella Stuart, painted in 1589 when she was thirteen, by Rowland Lockey. A noted scholar, she is shown with a pile of books.

live in the dull earth of ignorance, winding ourselves sometimes out, by the help of some refreshing rain of good educations which is seldom given us.'[22]

It is impossible to tell whether this chimed with Bess's own views, but the fact that her eldest daughter Mary was an outstanding intellectual, who produced three very learned daughters, suggests she would have applauded these very enlightened sentiments. The status of Arbella motivated her grandmother to provide her with an education fit for a future queen, and she had a whole series of tutors, including a Mr Morley who has been proposed as Christopher Marlowe.[23] Whether or not the great dramatist was her teacher, Arbella responded by showing great intellectual skills. Sir John Harington, one of her close friends, described how at thirteen she 'did read French out of Italian, and English out of both', a style of teaching that Roger Ascham had practised for Elizabeth Tudor and her cousin, Lady Jane Grey.[24] Like the Queen, Arbella could dictate Latin extempore and when Harington read her part of his translation of Ariosto's *Orlando Furioso*, she provided him with a critique.

In addition to being the educator of her children Bess had a household to manage. From the age of about twenty, she looked after a series of houses, sometimes several at once, a complicated balancing act, and all the evidence is that she was very good at it. Of course she had a host of servants to help her. In the kitchen she would have had a male cook – in the 1590s at Hardwick his name was, appropriately, Henry Cook. Such a man had rudimentary reading and writing, learning his craft by training, so that cookery books were not a necessary part of the household. The task of carving meat and fish, however, could not be left to the cook, but was one of the skills that marked out a gentleman just as much as his ability in swordplay and making an elegant leg on the dance floor. The book that would have provided Sir William with this information, as well as educating the sons of the house, was *The Boke of Kervynge,* first published in 1508 by Wynkyn de Worde. De Worde had worked with the man who introduced printing to England, William Caxton, and after the latter's death moved his print works from Westminster to the Sign of the Sun by St Bride's Church in Fleet Street. This significant move meant that thenceforward, the printing and publishing industries were set in the City, not the royal court. De Worde's *Boke of Kervynge* includes instructions for carving a bewildering variety of animals and fish, each with their own Norman-French verb, so that one 'untached' a curlew, 'taymed a crab' and 'traunched a salmon'. This book was such a seminal work that it went through several editions during the sixteenth century.

While the cook might reign supreme in his kitchen, the still-room was the domain of the lady of the house, assisted by her daughters and maids. It was here that medicines were prepared, as well as the dishes and drinks that were to be served as 'banquetting stuffe', the banquet being the special final course that had developed from the custom of eating sweet food and drink at the end of a medieval meal. Sugar represented the most important ingredient of the banquet, put in pastes, jellies, cakes and distilled drinks. Grown in North Africa, sugar was brought to England on spice ships from Venice and Genoa, and was therefore an expensive item, to be kept locked up like spices and used carefully. The first substantial guide for ladies in how to produce the sweet-meats, comfits, distilled drinks and sugar-work in the still-room was the *Secretes* of Alexis of Piedmont, translated from the Latin by W. Warde and published in English in 1562. The title is significant, for the secrets are medical, and therefore not to be shared with the ignorant but are instead for the eyes of the lady of the household, who had care of her family and servants. As Bess began to run her own household in 1547, she might well have owned a Latin edition of *Secretes*. She certainly taught the skills well, for her daughter Mary Talbot was known for her mastery of distilling, brewing and preserving. The medical cures and recipes practised by Mary's daughter Elizabeth, who became Countess of Kent, were published after her death in 1651 as *A Choice Manual* or *Rare Secrets in Physick and Chirugery*, while her sister Alethea, who became Countess of Arundel, published *Natura Exenterata*, in which chemical experiments were set alongside traditional recipes and advice.

When Bess planned the building of Hardwick New Hall, she had a banqueting house constructed in the garden, and another installed in the south turret on the roof. This was probably the work of Robert Smythson, who had built similar 'prospect towers' at Longleat in Wiltshire for Sir John Thynne and at Worksop Manor in Derbyshire for Bess's husband, the Earl of Shrewsbury. The one at Hardwick can still be reached by a staircase in the north turret and a walk across the leads of the roof to a little room richly decorated with plasterwork. Here Bess's favoured guests could sample succades (orange and lemon slices preserved in sugar), comfits flavoured with aniseed and fenugreek and other sweet delights, washed down with hippocras (sweet spiced wine), while they admired the formal patterns of her gardens laid out below.

Bess was clearly keen on her gardens, as she had them laid out at Hardwick before the building of the Hall was complete. For knowledge of plants, she would have used herbals. Mattioli's *Commentarii* has already been noted as a source for her embroideries. The first herbal to be published in English was Henry Lyte's translation of the *Cruedeboek* by the Flemish Rembert Dodoens, which appeared in 1578 as the *Niewe Herball* or *Historie of Plantes*. Today, the best known herbal of this period was that published by the barber surgeon John Gerard in 1597, illustrated with woodcuts of the flowers that he purported to grow in his garden, and dedicated to William Cecil, Lord Burghley, for whom he worked at Theobalds in Hertfordshire.

Cecil was part of a high-powered circle of courtiers that included Robert Dudley, Earl of Leicester, Sir Christopher Hatton and Bess herself. All were close to Queen Elizabeth, and therefore with political power, which they sought to enhance by impressing their monarch and persuading her to accord them the ultimate (and costly) honour, to stay at their houses on the royal progresses that took place each summer. To entertain the Queen they built fine houses and laid out elaborate gardens. Cecil not only built Theobalds, but also Burghley House in Northamptonshire; Hatton eventually bankrupted himself with his great schemes at nearby Holdenby and Kirby Hall; Leicester added new apartments to his medieval castle of Kenilworth in Warwickshire. Other courtiers engaged in extensive building works included Sir John Thynne at Longleat and Sir Francis Willoughby at Wollaton in Nottinghamshire. These builders swapped ideas and craftsmen, so we find Robert Smythson first working as master mason for Thynne at Longleat in 1568, for Willoughby as 'architector' – the first use of the term in England – or surveyor of the work at Wollaton in the 1580s, and surviving drawings suggest he also carried out design work for Shrewsbury at Worksop and Bess at Hardwick Hall. These drawings showed that he knew and used Serlio's *Architettura* and possibly Palladio's *I Quattri Libri*, as well as the works of the Flemish designer Vriedman de Vries. Bess may have owned the works of Serlio and Palladio, but more likely is that Smythson had his own copies or that they were passed among the circle of patrons. Likewise, Hatton, Cecil, Leicester and Bess looked at the designs for each other's gardens and swapped plants and books. In 1591 Bess went for one long, last visit to London and the royal court. Impressed by the gardens at Greenwich Palace, she was presented with strawberries, her favourites, by the gardeners. On the way back northwards, she visited the gardens and house at Holdenby and at Wollaton.

Bess confined her travels to England and never ventured abroad – although the journey that she made many times from Derbyshire to London could well be described as an adventure as it took seven days in a lumbering, unsprung coach. It would have been in character for her to have taken an interest in travel. Listed in her inventory at Hardwick is a painting of the four continents known at the time, and she owned objects from Turkey, Persia and China. In 1560 William St Loe recorded in his accounts the purchase of two copies of a 'Cosmography of the Levant in French' for his stepsons, William and Henry Cavendish. This book has been identified as *La Cosmographie du Levant* by André Thevet, a copy of which is still in Chatsworth Library.[25] Published by Jean Richart in Antwerp in 1556, this is no illustrated travel book, but a densely written text which clearly inspired the boys. William was one of the first investors in Virginia, co-grantee of the Bermuda Islands, and put money into the Russia and East India Companies. Henry not only went on a grand tour of the Continent in 1571, but also made an expedition two decades later, to Constantinople via Germany, Austria, Venice and the Balkans. This was written up by his servant Fox in one of the earliest known accounts of such a journey. Fox, a man of limited education and almost certainly a Protestant, reacted to his adventures with fascination and humour. He would record how one night they would sleep in a hen roost, the next on benches in a dragoman's house and the third, 'we got a good store of hay and lay like kings'. In fact, the most disappointing part of his account is of Constantinople itself: he describes the inhabitants as 'rude and roud and very malicious towards Christians' and is relieved that their stay lasted for only fourteen days.[26]

* * * *

After her last visit to London over the winter of 1591/2, Bess chose to remain in Derbyshire. Although she was in good health, she was in her sixties, a great age for the time, and some of the business of running her estates was passed to her second and favourite son, William, whose household accounts for the years 1597 to 1601 have survived.[27] A cultivated man, William was to appoint the philosopher Thomas Hobbes as tutor for his son, also William, and his book purchases are to be found in the parts of the accounts headed 'foreign charges', that is, made beyond Derbyshire.

William had retained his early interest in travel and the wider world. His most expensive purchase was Richard Hakluyt's *Principal Navigations* costing the considerable sum of 22s. This work, published between 1598 and 1600, came in three folio volumes, illustrated with maps, hence the high price. At the other end of the scale, he bought a quarto pamphlet, costing less than 3d, by Edward Webbe, 'The rare and most wonderfull things which E. Webbe hath seene in the landes of Jewrie, Egypt, Grecia, Russia, and Prester John', published in 1590. Other travel books include the journey of Sir Anthony Sherley to Persia, published in 1600, the account of 'eight ships of Amsterdam' on their voyage to the East Indies, published in 1601, the voyages of the Seigneur de Villamont, Knight of St John of Jerusalem in French, published in Tournai in 1596, and an account in Latin of the Jesuit missionaries in India, published in Mainz in 1601.

Cavendish was also interested in his own country and its history. He bought William Camden's great work *Britannia,* a little book on the monuments of Westminster, and Richard Carew's *Survey of Cornwall.* Carew, a contemporary of Camden at Oxford, was a scholar and antiquary who wrote a whole range of books, including a humorous rendering of Sir Philip Sidney's *Arcadia*, but his great achievement was his survey, 'Long since begun, a great while discontinued, lately reviewed, and now hastily finished' that was published in 1602: it was to be the prototype for all future topographical accounts of counties. In contrast to the historical subject matter, Cavendish also acquired William Gilbert's pioneering account of magnetic attraction, *De Magnete*, published in 1599.

As befitted a gentleman, he bought books on etiquette. The accounts refer to the binding up of 'Civil Conversation', probably the 1586 translation into English by George Pettie of Stefano Guazzo's *La Civil Conversazione*, which dealt with issues of courtly fashion. The most famous, and earliest book of etiquette available in England was Baldassare Castiglione's *Cortegiano*, translated into English by Sir Thomas Hoby and published in 1561. Cavendish bought the Latin translation by Bartholomew Clerke that appeared in 1593. Also part of this group was 'Memorable Conceits', an account of the behaviour of 'divers noble and famous personages of Christendom' by Gilles Corrozet, published in 1602.

These books are all non-fiction, and this preponderance reflects the attitude of the period, for books that excited 'the pleasures of the imagination' were regarded with suspicion, especially for ladies. Here, as in so many areas, status moderated this suspicion. Sir Philip Sidney's *Arcadia*, written originally for his sister Mary's private entertainment and only published in 1590, was considered suitable for ladies, as was Edmund Spenser's *Faerie Queene*, dedicated to Queen Elizabeth and the women of the court. Both these books are recorded not only in Lady Anne Clifford's *Great Picture* but also in the diary that she kept from 1616 when she was married to the Earl of Dorset and living at Knole in Kent. She makes clear in this diary that she liked having people read to her, including her female servants: 'Rivers used to read to me in Montaigne's Plays and Moll Neville in the Fairy Queen'.[28] In October 1601 Cavendish's accounts record the purchase for 5d of the 'sixth book of Lazarillo deforms in English'. This refers to *La Vida de Lazarillo de Tormes*, attributed to Diego Hurtado de Mendoza, and first published in Spain in 1554. The picaresque novel, painting a picture of Castilian life through the adventures of a poor squire, took the world by storm, being translated into English by David Rowland of Anglesey in 1586. Its form was much imitated, for instance in the writings of Miguel de Cervantes, *Don Quixote* (1605) and *Novelas Ejemplares* (1613). Perhaps Lazarillo's exploits were read to Bess at Hardwick.

Several of the publications are pamphlets, such as an account of the pageant of the Lord Mayor of London, priced at a penny, and five copies of 'the arte of setting of corne', costing 3d each. This booklet was written by Sir Hugh Platt, agriculturalist and inventor extraordinary, and might have been intended for distribution amongst the farmers on the Cavendish estates. Items were also bought for other members of the family so the purchase of 'paper books', blank stationery for his niece, Arbella Stuart, was recorded. The singing book, costing the substantial sum of 11s might also have been for her, as she was an accomplished musician: her composer cousin, Michael Cavendish, dedicated a book of songs and madrigals to her. William later recalled how Hardwick at Christmas was filled with music and revels with musicians borrowed from the households of the Earls of Rutland and Essex, and the Nottingham waits.

On a purely practical level, the accounts record sending books to the binder, adding a significant amount to their expense. There are also entries for the making of hampers in which to send the books up from London to Derbyshire. Just one bookseller, Mr Norton, is identified by name, but on several occasions, suggesting that he acted as an agent for William Cavendish in acquiring works from other booksellers. The Nortons were a considerable publishing family, at one stage setting up the Officina Nortonia. Bonham Norton, with his premises in Blackfriars, could be the man, but it is more likely to be his cousin John, based in St Paul's Churchyard, for next to an entry referring to Norton comes a payment of 6d to the poor of Ludgate. John Norton ran a very considerable business, and his shop was a social centre for book collectors and literary men, and so would have appealed to William Cavendish.

A significant entry in the accounts, in 1602, records the purchase of a catalogue of books for 6d. This might be the catalogue of English books compiled in 1595 by the Lothbury bookseller Andrew Maunsell, 'Seeing that men desirous of such kind of Bookes, cannot aske for what they have never heard of, and the Booke-seller cannot show that he hath not'. It is, however, more likely that this publication was a Frankfurt Bookfair catalogue, enabling the Cavendish family to follow all the latest publishing across Europe. John Norton made regular journeys to the Fair, advertising nearly forty of his own titles in the catalogue, and conducted much trade with the Continent, especially with the Officina Plantina in Antwerp.[29] Some of the books that are noted in Cavendish's accounts were published by the Frankfurt house of Claude Marni and John Aubri, successors to Andrew Wechel, and these surely came to Derbyshire via Norton.

According to his accounts, William Cavendish was avidly buying books, especially in the months leading up to Christmas, and many of the titles were newly published. They were to form part of the considerable library that was kept at Chatsworth when he came into his inheritance. Thomas Hobbes combined his duties as tutor to Cavendish's son with acting as librarian, and his handwritten catalogue compiled in 1620s of the collection, which by then numbered over 2,000 titles, remains at Chatsworth. Almost all the books mentioned above, together with the three books identified as belonging to Bess in the 1604 inventory, are contained in this list.[30]

In 1608, five years after the death of Queen Elizabeth, Bess of Hardwick was laid to rest with appropriate splendour in Derby Cathedral. Her life had passed through difficult periods, but was one of great achievement. Dynastically she was the founder of four ducal families. She had built great houses, several of which are still with us. And now her well-read, cultured and creative grandchildren were to become some of the leading lights of the Stuart court.

CHAPTER 2

ENJOYMENT OF ALL THAT'S WORTH SEEKING AFTER

The Books of Samuel Pepys

Part of Samuel Pepys's diary entry for 10 April 1668 runs, 'So to piper's. And Duck-lane and there kissed the bookseller's wife and bought *Legend* – 14s'.[1] The piper was Drumbleby, the maker of flageolets; the bookseller with the attractive wife was William Shrewsbury, who traded in Duck Lane, one of the centres of the Latin or foreign book trade in London; and the purchase was *The Golden Legend*, a collection of lives of medieval saints by the thirteenth-century Dominican, Jacques de Voragine. In these brief notes Pepys encapsulates some of his passions: music, sex, shopping, London, and books.

Samuel Pepys was born in Salisbury Court, just south of Fleet Street in the parish of St Bride's on 23 February 1633. His home may have been close to the heartland of London publishing and printing, but his family was not bookish. His father ran a tailor's shop serving lawyers and was barely literate, his mother was a former laundrymaid and probably could not read or write at all. But Samuel had more promising relatives. His cousin John was a successful lawyer, while his great-aunt Paulina had made a very good marriage, to Sir Sidney Montagu, producing a son, Edward, who was to become a powerful friend and patron to Pepys. With the help of his family and grants, Pepys enjoyed an excellent education. First he attended the grammar school in Huntingdon, where Oliver Cromwell had received his education. Though he may have learnt some Greek and Hebrew, Latin was the dominant subject, still the *lingua franca* for European scholarship, with more books published in Latin than English until the beginning of the eighteenth century. Pepys made good use of his Latin, not only to read widely, but also to converse with a Dutch admiral and on occasion to write about his sexual exploits in his diary.

He went on to St Paul's School in London, probably in 1644 at the very beginning of the Civil War. The school was situated next to the cathedral and England's publishing heartland. Its Surmaster was Samuel Cromleholme, an

10 Sir Godfrey Kneller's portrait of Samuel Pepys, *c.*1685, which hangs in the Pepys Library at Magdalene College, Cambridge.

enthusiastic book collector, so when Pepys went up to Magdalene College, Cambridge he was fortified with a love of books. At university he officially studied logic, philosophy and rhetoric, but unofficially enjoyed playing games with anagrams, learning Thomas Shelton's system of shorthand, making music with friends 'upon violin and basse' and writing part of a romantic novel *Love a Cheate*, which never saw the light of publication as he destroyed it ten years later.

On his return to London in 1654 he became clerk to his cousin and rising star Edward Montagu, who coped cleverly with the topsy-turvy world of the time, becoming Earl of Sandwich and a leading member of the Stuart court with the Restoration of Charles II. Pepys was to remain loyal to his cousin, serving his family even after Montagu's death at the naval battle of Sole Bay in 1672.

During his early days as a clerk, Pepys had no home of his own, but 'perched' in Edward Montagu's lodgings in the shambling palace of Whitehall in Westminster. At this time he earned about £1 per week, and would spend his money on letting down his hair with his fellow clerks in the local taverns and coffee-houses. Coffee drinking had been introduced by the Levant merchants from Turkey in the 1620s, and the first public coffee-house in the City (and indeed in Christendom) was opened as a market stall in an alley running past the churchyard of St Michael's Cornhill. Although the diarist John Evelyn disapproved of this innovation, complaining in *A Character of England* of the 'deplorable' habit of 'drinking of a muddy kind of *Beverage*', it took off as a pastime.[2] Samuel Pepys used to frequent the Turk's Head Coffee-house in New Palace Yard in Westminster, where in 1659 he also joined the Rota Club. This group was founded by James Harrington, author of *The Commonwealth of Oceana*, who proposed a republic with a rotating senate, an extended franchise and limitations on property ownership. An oval table was specially constructed, around which members could stand or sit while the coffee-house proprietor, Miles, dispensed coffee and tobacco by way of a passage along the middle. This political debating society set the pattern for London coffee-houses of the future, where newsbooks and newspapers could be read and the topics of the day discussed, although come the Restoration of the monarchy, the Rota was far too dangerous to continue.

Any visits to coffee-houses would have been made alone, for respectable women were not expected to attend such venues. Samuel Pepys had married Elizabeth Marchant de St Michel on 1 December 1655 at St Margaret's Westminster: a love match, and quite a rash decision on the part of the normally careful Pepys. His bride, just fifteen when they wed, was the daughter of impoverished French Protestants. She was clearly a beauty, and although not very well educated, she was intelligent, quick, and interested in books. Pepys's biographer Claire Tomalin wonders whether they met in a bookshop. After three years sharing Samuel's perch at Whitehall, the couple moved into a house in Axe Yard in Westminster.

We know so much about Samuel Pepys, of course, because of his diary, which he kept from 1660 to 1669. It is fortunate that he chose to cover such exciting times. Through him we can witness at close quarters the final days of the Commonwealth, the entry of Charles II into his restored kingdom and his coronation. We are in London with Pepys when the city was visited by the Great Plague of 1665 and the cataclysm of the Fire of 1666. We meet the great people of the day, including the King himself, his brother James, the Duke of York – Pepys's ultimate naval boss, Queen Catherine of Braganza and the King's many mistresses. But the diary is more than this. It is also a record of the minutiae of life, the inner thoughts of Pepys himself, the things he bought and enjoyed, the taverns, coffee-houses and theatres, the supper parties and trips on the river. And for a study of books, it is a delight – he tells us what books he acquires and reads, where he gets them from, what they cost, and how and where he keeps them. He rose at four in the morning to read his 1582 Venetian edition of Cicero, and burned his candles right down last thing at night with a book. He browsed in bookshops, had a book propped up while eating, read while travelling by boat on the Thames and in a coach, and even tried to concentrate while walking through darkened streets with a link boy.

Last, and not least, his diary is the record of a marriage. We probably know more about the domestic life of Samuel and Elizabeth than we do of any other couple in history – or at least, the domestic life as seen by Samuel. Elizabeth is the silent woman, although many people have sought to give her voice. It is a marriage full of strife and emotion, with Samuel pulling her nose and slapping her, Elizabeth retiring to bed in a sulk or taking out her temper on her servants. The very first entry, on 1 January 1660, opens with a combination of the arrival of General Monck and his army in London as a prelude to the Restoration and details of Elizabeth's menstrual period: Pepys was forever in hope that she might conceive, though sadly the hopes were all dashed and there were to be no children. Despite the quarrels and disappointments, however, this was a marriage that succeeded.

Nobody knows why the diary was begun in the first place, only that Pepys took a boat down the Thames from Westminster to the City and bought a paper-covered book from John Cade, stationer at the sign of the Globe in Cornhill. Ruling neat margins in red ink down the left hand of each page and across the top, he began to write in black and brown ink with a quill, using longhand for names, places, and some words, but the main body of the diary was in Thomas Shelton's system of shorthand that he had learnt years before in Cambridge. Keeping a diary was recommended by Puritan divines, but most of the results make ineffably dull reading. More promising are those of two of Pepys's friends, the scholar and courtier John Evelyn, and the scientist and architect Robert Hooke. Yet even these lack the vitality and charm and the intimate detail that make Pepys's diary unique.

Samuel Pepys had started to buy books as an undergraduate from William Morden, the Cambridge bookseller. However, London provided him with an unprecedented range of sources. When he was living in Westminster, Miles and Ann Mitchell were his local booksellers. They operated out of Westminster Hall, the great hall of the Norman kings and the place where Charles I was tried and condemned to death in 1649. Courts of law, such as Chancery and the King's Bench, operated at one end, while 'moveable shops' or stalls were set up at the other. Shoppers in the Hall from the 1660s were faced with the disconcerting display of the exhumed bodies of Oliver Cromwell and his generals, Ireton and Bradshaw: they were removed twenty years later when they had thoroughly rotted. Obviously Pepys was made of strong stuff, for he does not refer to these, but describes how he ate bread at

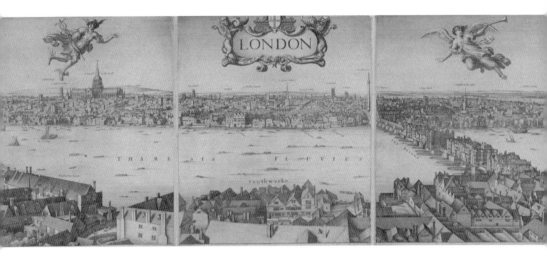

11 Detail from Wenceslaus Hollar's panorama of pre-Fire London, made in 1647 and published in Antwerp. The artist use
as his viewpoint the roof of what was later to become Southwark Cathedral, looking down upon London Bridge where Samu
Pepys bought many of his chapbooks. The heartland of the printing, publishing and selling of books lay around St Pau
Cathedral, which dominates the skyline on the left.

the Mitchells' stall to keep going when he attended the coronation of Charles
II in 1661. From the Mitchells he bought newsbooks and political pamphlets.

In 1660 Edward Montagu secured for Samuel Pepys the job of Clerk of the
Acts to the Navy Board at a salary of £350 per annum. With this came a house
in Seething Lane, just west of Tower Hill within the City of London. Now
Pepys was much closer to the printers and booksellers and stationers who
clustered around St Paul's Churchyard and Fleet Street. His main source of
books in the early 1660s was Joshua Kirton, who traded out of the Churchyard
itself. On 23 December 1661 he describes going to Kirton's shop and by
chance meeting up with his former schoolmaster and book collector, Samuel
Cromleholme. Three years later, again in December, he writes of going 'to my
booksellers' to order 'several books against New Year's day, I resolving to lay
out about 7*l* or 8*l*, God having given me some profit extraordinary of late'.[3]

Joshua Kirton was one of the people ruined by the Great Fire that destroyed
so much of the City in September 1666. When the fire broke out on the 2nd,
Kirton and his fellow booksellers had put their stock for safekeeping in
Stationers' Hall off Ludgate Hill, and in the churches of St Faith and
Christchurch in Newgate Street. St Faith's, fondly described as the 'babe in the
mother's womb', was situated within the crypt under the choir of the old cathedral of St Paul's, and the massive stone walls were considered more than
adequate protection from the flames. Tragically they were not, and all the buildings perished, along with the stock. Pepys, in his diary entry for 26 September,
reckoned that £150,000 worth of booksellers' stock had gone up in flames –

John Evelyn put the figure even higher, at £200,000. 'My poor Kirton', Pepys wrote, died the following year, 'I believe of grief for his losses by the fire'.[4]

Others lived to fight another day. After the Fire, Pepys moved his custom to John Starkey who sold books at the sign of the Mitre in Fleet Street. By this time Pepys had become a sharp-eyed collector, as shown by his diary entry for 8 April 1667: 'So I away to the Temple to my new bookseller's and there I did agree for Rycaut's late history of the Turkish Policy [Paul Rycaut, *The Present State of the Ottoman Empire*, 1667] which costs me 55s; whereas it was sold plain before the late fire for 8s, and bound and coloured as this is for 20 – for I have bought it finely bound and truly coloured, all the figures; of which there was but six books done so, whereof the King and Duke of York and Duke of Monmouth and Lord Arlington had four – the 5th was sold and I have bought the 6th'.[5]

Pepys patronised other bookshops including that of William Shrewsbury in Duck Lane, though here his search may have been for Mrs Shrewsbury rather than desirable books. His first visit came on 10 April 1668, when he bought *The Golden Legend* and kissed the lady. Two weeks later he examined some of the books that had belonged to the disgraced French finance minister, Fouquet. His superb collection of 30,000 volumes had been confiscated by Louis XIV and are now in the Bibliothèque Nationale. Some were sold, and Pepys was able to purchase a Spanish book, *Summa de varones illustres* by Juan Sedeno, published in Toledo in 1590. At the same time he describes in the language that he used for sexual exploits how he 'did find [Mrs Shrewsbury] sola in the boutique, but had not la confidence para hablar a ella. So lost my pains – but will have another time'.[6] This assertion proved false – no doubt the lady kept away when she saw Pepys approaching. The last time that he saw her, she was pregnant, and he ungallantly pointed out that 'ella is so big-bellied that ella is not worth seeing'.[7]

Once the book trade recovered itself, St Paul's Churchyard resumed its place as the centre of the London trade, with Duck Lane and Little Britain just to its north. Significant groups of booksellers returned to the rebuilt Royal Exchange and continued to trade from the area of Fleet Street and Temple Bar. Some migrated westwards to the New Exchange, a 'shopping centre' on the Strand, and later to Covent Garden, while open stalls, often selling second-hand books, were set up in Moorfields. Business hours were usually from six o'clock in the morning in summer, and eight in winter, until eight or nine in the evening in summer and nightfall in winter. Most shops had shutters hinged at the base so that they could be folded down and supported to form a counter during trading hours. Pepys noted that the shops that had been rebuilt in the Royal Exchange after the Fire had fixed windows, enabling the display of goods.

Inventories taken after the death of tradesmen give some idea of what the interior of bookshops may have looked like. James Allestree, one of the great booksellers of his day, lost his shop in St Paul's Churchyard as a result of the Fire and took up temporary premises in Duck Lane, where Pepys visited him in November 1667. Like Pepys he was lucky with his relatives, for his cousin was Richard Allestree, Regius Professor of Divinity at Oxford and one of the best-selling writers of the seventeenth century. His most famous book, *The Whole Duty of Man*, was published anonymously in 1658 for political reasons.[8] It is estimated that more than ten per cent of households owned a copy in the seventeenth century, and the book remained in print throughout the eighteenth. Cousin James never produced an edition of *The Whole Duty*, but was able to recover his business after the Fire with the help of Richard's books of sermons, and moved back into a new house in the Churchyard in 1670. When he died shortly after, the inventory describes fairly grand living quarters above a ground floor dedicated to business, with a counting house at the back, and a shop in front, furnished with presses and shelves. A decorative partition, made up of a double arch with two doors, provided an inner sanctum where Allestree could entertain prospective authors and important customers, including members of the Royal Society for whom he was printer.

James Allestree was clearly a man of means and the inventories show that others did not prosper so well, for publishing then, as now, was a risky business. Relatively few London publishers produced books in Latin, and therefore their turnover was small compared to their European counterparts. When they printed in English rather than Latin – and an increasing number were doing so by the end of the seventeenth century – their market was restricted, even though the book trade countrywide was expanding, and there was a small market overseas with the growth of British colonies in North America and the West Indies. In order to minimise risks, all kinds of marketing ideas were therefore tried.

One of the most ambitious publishing ventures took place in the 1650s with the publication of the Polyglot Bible. This project, involving the most learned scholars at Oxford, produced printed texts in nine languages and six large folios. To get the project off the ground, subscribers were invited to make gifts to the project or to advance money, being repaid by copies of the work at £10 per set. Those who did subscribe found their investment paid off, for Pepys noted in his diary that many sets had perished in the publisher's warehouse in the Great Fire, and it was reckoned that surviving copies would now be worth £40.

Another marketing ploy was to run a lottery. This was a speciality of John Ogilby, one of the most colourful figures of the seventeenth-century book trade. According to John Aubrey in his *Brief Lives*, Ogilby started his career by

12 John Ogilby presenting to Charles II and Queen Catherine of Braganza in 1682 a book listing the subscribers to his project surveying London for his post-Fire map. In the background on the left can be seen Pepys's boss, James, Duke of York; the King's illegitimate son, the Duke of Monmouth; and his cousin, Prince Rupert of the Rhine. On the right are Mary of Modena and her two stepdaughters, Princess Mary and Princess Anne.

paying off his father's debts in a lottery managed by the Virginia Company in March 1612, though this claim has to be taken with a pinch of salt as he would have been twelve at the time. A man of many parts – dancing master, theatre owner, poet and translator – in the 1660s he became the King's Printer as well as a compiler of geography books and atlases. Pepys records in his diary entry of 19 February 1666 attending a book lottery where he acquired two of Ogilby's books – a translation of Aesop's *Fables*, and his account of the coronation of Charles II. As both these books were finely illustrated, the first by David Loggan and the second by Wenceslaus Hollar, the tickets cost 40s each, and there was only one blank. By this means Ogilby was able to offer 500 copies of Aesop, and 225 of the coronation. Pepys avoided the blanks and triumphantly brought the books home in their white vellum bindings.

Pepys must have found out about the lottery through the newspaper, *The Gazette*. One advertisement for a lottery in 1668 runs 'Mr Ogilby's lottery of books opens on Monday, the 25th instant, at the Old Theatre between Lincoln's Inn Fields and Vere Street, where all persons concerned may repair on Monday, May 18, and see the volumes, and put in their money'. Lotteries and raffles were also used by Joseph Moxon, a science instrument-maker based at the Atlas in Warwick Lane, from whom Pepys bought a pair of terrestrial globes in September 1663. Moxon ventured into the publishing world, producing the first manual of printing, *Mechanick Exercises*, which came out in monthly instalments between 1677 and 1684. Maps were so expensive to produce that Moxon not only employed the idea of instalments but also pooled his resources by working in ad hoc partnerships with other producers of atlases.

This sharing of risk and pooling of capital was adopted by booksellers in general, and can be seen on the title page of certain books, where the listing takes on the representation of a map of the book markets of London. Thus an illustrated *History of the Old and New Testaments* published in 1691 announces at the bottom of the title page: 'printed for and sold by Richard Blome, at Mr Notts in the Pal-Mal, by Mr Saunders in the New Exchange, Mr Wilkinson and Mr Freeman in Fleet street, Mr Clavel and Mr Brome at the West-end of S.Pauls, Mr Horn and Mr Southby by the Royal-Exchange, Mr Richards Bookbinder in Stanhope street by Clare Market, and by other Booksellers in London and Westminster'.

∗ ∗ ∗ ∗

If the year 1666 was to prove a watershed for the book trade, 1669 was to be the same for Samuel Pepys. On the last day of May he suddenly announced the end of his diary-keeping. On account of his eyesight, he felt that he could write his shorthand no longer, poignantly ending 'And so I betake myself to that course which [is] almost as much as to see myself go into my grave – for which, and all the discomforts that will accompany my being blind, the good God prepare me'.[9]

In fact, Pepys did not go blind. In June of that year he took a Continental holiday with Elizabeth. It was rather a busman's holiday as he planned to tour the shipyards in Holland, but the visit to Paris was very much for recreation, with detailed recommendations on the libraries, galleries, engravings and print shops provided by his friend John Evelyn. On the journey home, Elizabeth Pepys fell sorely ill, and died on 10 November. Samuel was devastated and surely this was one of the reasons he never seriously took up his diary quill again.

More trouble was to follow. The excitement that greeted the return of the Stuarts in 1660 had now turned sour with the profligacy of Charles II and his court. Despite his many children by mistresses, he had no legitimate heir by his Queen, so the heir apparent was Pepys's boss, James, Duke of York, and his conversion to Roman Catholicism in 1668 plunged the nation into political turmoil. When Pepys himself was elected to Parliament he was questioned in the House of Commons about owning papistical books – a charge that he denied, no doubt with his fingers crossed, as he certainly owned some suspect literature. Seething Lane had escaped the ravages of the Great Fire, but on 29 January 1673 one of Pepys's neighbours began a conflagration in her closet, and his house was destroyed. Remembering how his old schoolmaster Samuel Cromleholme had lost one of the best private libraries in London, he made the rescue of his books and papers a priority, though everything else went up in flames.

Pepys found a new home with his loyal servant William Hewer in York Buildings in Buckingham Street, near the Thames, south of Charing Cross. He also found a new companion in Mary Skinner, whom he met in 1670. She probably moved in with Pepys when he acquired a house of his own in Buckingham Street, and remained his companion for the rest of his life. They never married, although some of his friends referred to her as his wife, and it is remarkable that the relationship was respected. In 1673 Pepys was appointed Secretary of the Admiralty Commission, an important job that brought him status and a substantial income. His political troubles, however, were never far away – at one stage he was committed to the Tower of London on suspicion of treasonable correspondence with France – but he survived to become the King's Secretary for the affairs of the Admiralty, serving Charles II for a short time, and from 1685 his long-standing boss James II. When the latter was driven from the throne in the Glorious Revolution of 1688, Pepys retired from public life.

Despite the lack of his daily record, we continue to know a lot about Pepys's books through his correspondence. His range of booksellers increased over the years, and he also used friends and occasionally agents to acquire books for him at home and abroad. He may well have used catalogues that were produced by London booksellers from 1668, known as term catalogues because they were issued to coincide with the legal terms of the year, Michaelmas, Hilary and Trinity. The bookseller Robert Clavell, for instance, would reprint in his cumulative catalogues the broadside lists produced by John Playford, so that Pepys had the opportunity to keep up with his music publisher's latest works.

Publishers also inserted their lists in the books themselves, after the table of contents or at the end of the printing. Samuel Pecke used the last page of his *Perfect Diurnal* published in May 1650 to advertise four books by other publishers. This was satirised in a news-sheet, *The Man in the Moon*, in which John Crouch poked fun at Pecke for letting out 'to the Stationers, for six pence a piece, to place therein the Titles of their Books, the most famous *History of Tom Thumb*, *Long Meg of Westminster* or *Mr Cooks Dream*, and are to be sould

[by] *John an Oakes*, at the signe of the *Three Loggerheads*, in Pudding-py Lane'.[10] Despite the mockery, publishers were quick to see that this was a good way to get their titles known, and to take advantage of advertising free in their own publications. Timothy Garthwaite, publisher of Richard Allestree's *Gentleman's Calling* in 1660, listed details of four books 'newly printed' at the end of the prelims: the first known use of the term. He set his 'advertisement' in a variety of typefaces to catch the eye of the reader, something that Victor Gollancz was to exploit in his twentieth-century book marketing (p. 238).

With his increased means, Pepys was able to add substantially to his collection, which reached over five hundred books by 1668. Once retired, he moved happily into a higher gear, so that at least half of his collection was gathered in the last thirteen years of his life. The various categories that make up the collection reflect Pepys's personal interests. Given his distinguished career in the Navy, it is scarcely surprising that he owned a very fine collection on maritime matters, and that the bindings of many of his books were impressed in gold on the upper cover with a mantled shield recording in Latin his service as Secretary to the Admiralty. Later he had bookplates with his initials, two crossed anchors and his motto.

In 1694, Pepys explained to his friend, Dr Charlett of University College, Oxford that he had no time for 'lookeing-out of Curiositys' on any subject except the sea. He owned manuscript descriptions of great voyages including Edward Fenton's account of his travels with Martin Frobisher, which was given to him by John Evelyn. One of his treasures was part of the Anthony Roll, a gift from Charles II. Anthony Anthony had recorded in 1546 the forty-six ships of Henry VIII's navy, including the only representation we have of the ill-fated *Mary Rose* that had sunk in Portsmouth Harbour the previous year. At one time Pepys possessed Henry Tudor's pocket calendar, but discarded it once he had acquired that of Sir Francis Drake. He was fascinated by the Spanish Armada, so had pictures of the movements of the battle and the book of charts used by English ships in the action, Waghenaer's *Speculum Nauticum* in English, Latin and Dutch editions. These were known familiarly by sailors and by Pepys himself as 'waggoners' and he anguished about their fate during the Great Fire.

But he was not only interested in naval history, owning no less than seventeen volumes of current Admiralty letter-books, which he took home with him on retirement and kept despite appeals by his successor for their return. He collected books on navigation and ship-building, and had an important collection of some 1,100 maps, charts and plans now considered the best organised of the period. The catalogue, probably begun in 1695, showed his meticulous approach, with three main categories – land, sea and miscellaneous – and grids drawn out in manuscript for each map, alphabetically

13 Detail from Anthony Anthony's illustrated roll of Henry VIII's navy, given to Pepys by Charles II and one of his most treasured possessions. Anthony compiled the record of the Tudor navy in 1546 and included the *Mary Rose*, even though it had foundered in Portsmouth Harbour the previous July during a battle with the French.

indexed to facilitate finding places. Critical of the standard of compilation, in 1693 he commissioned at his own expense the chartmaker John Thornton to look at what existed and point out errors. As a result Trinity House, the authority for regulating lights and lighthouses, had the British coast surveyed anew. The difficulty about this area of publishing was the cost involved. Pepys made this clear in conversation with a master-mariner: 'This work is never well to be done at the charge of private people, it being too chargeable and what will never answer their expense and care'.[11]

There were about fifteen 'map shops' in London by the beginning of the eighteenth century. Pepys continued to buy from Joseph Moxon, the instrument-maker at the Atlas, acquiring from him *Sacred geographie or scriptural mapps*, published *c*.1671. Moxon was not a stationer, but a member of the Weavers' Company, and where he led, his apprentices followed. So, in the world of maps there were not only waggoners but weavers too. The book and atlas seller that Pepys particularly respected was Richard Mount, who provided Thames-based ships' masters and mates with waggoners and almanacs from his shop on Postern Row near the Tower of London. On 14 May 1695 Pepys recorded a conversation with Mount, in which he was told that the 'Dutch have such a Vent [sale] for all their Books of Navigation & Coasting. That besides those known ones of their Lighting-Column ... which are ordinarily sent-over hither and sold here: they have printed several other Books of Navigation, even in English, which they vend to our own Countrymen coming-in there'.[12]

In 1665 Pepys was elected to the Royal Society of London for Improving of Natural Knowledge. The Society had begun as a series of informal meetings in Oxford and London from 1645, receiving its charter from Charles II in 1662. In line with the current desire to develop knowledge through practical experiment, it was even suggested by the Society's historian Thomas Sprat that there should be no library for the institution. In the event, a library was created and Sprat described his colleagues as, 'Read', 'Travell'd', 'Experienc'd and Stout'.[13] So Pepys and the other Fellows attended experiments at the weekly meetings of the Royal Society at Gresham College, adjourning to the Grecian Coffee-house in Threadneedle Street.

Fellows also devoted time to the receipt, reading and distribution of written materials because they recognised the importance of disseminating the results of experiments in a credible manner throughout Europe. They were obliged to submit any work they planned to publish, and this would be 'presented' to the Royal Society at their meetings. One or two Fellows would take the text away and report back a week or two later, the work being duly registered in a manuscript volume, the one way that an author's work could be protected from usurpation. So distinguished were the Fellows of the Society that publishers were able to sell scientific books in the English language in Europe – the Latin trade in reverse. The most successful publication was the periodical *Philosophical Transactions* launched by the Society's Secretary, Henry Oldenburg, in 1665, which circulated the institution's work throughout Europe, and is still going today.

However, book projects often involved illustrations and thus were very expensive to produce. Subscription was used by the Royal Society to persuade reluctant publishers to undertake their production. When Martin Lister wanted to publish his book on insects, for instance, the Society helped to pay for the impression by buying fifty copies for its virtuosi and a further hundred copies for other recipients. The Society was usually able to use its imprimatur along with this form of guaranteed subscription to get stationers to take the financial risks, but on one occasion tried to support an entire publication itself – Francis Willoughby's book on fishes, *Historia Piscium*. The result was dire: the book has been described as 'expensive to produce, aesthetically unimpressive, slow to sell and of imperceptible scholarly impact'.[14] In 1684 Pepys was made the Society's President, no doubt because of his administrative skills, for he never contributed experiments or papers. Thus it is his name that appears on the title page of Isaac Newton's groundbreaking *Principia Mathematica*, published for the Royal Society in 1687.

One of Pepys's favourite recreations was to go to the theatre. It has been estimated that he watched performances no less than seventy-three times between 1 January and 31 August 1668. Often he took his wife Elizabeth with him, at other times his friend Deb Willett, thus countering the myth that only aristocratic women or whores went to see plays. Pepys was also an inveterate buyer of collections of plays, and read up a script in preparation for his visit to the theatre. In his diary, he makes a clear distinction between the effectiveness of plays read and of plays seen. When he went to watch *Catiline* by Ben Jonson, he judged it 'a play of much good sense and words to read, but that doth appear the worse upon the stage'.[15] He read a translation of Corneille, *Le Cid*, with great pleasure, but when he saw it performed as *The Valiant Cidd* on 1 December 1662 at the Cockpit in Whitehall, he thought it 'a most dull thing acted' – the King and Queen agreed, not smiling once throughout.[16]

In the 1660s the leading publisher and bookseller of poetry, drama, prose romances and classical translations was Henry Herringman: indeed his list virtually defined contemporary literature. After the Great Fire, he established his shop at the Blue Anchor in the Lower Walk of the New Exchange, which soon became a resort of the literary world. He was the publisher of the dramatist John Dryden, who had been at Cambridge with Pepys. In June 1668 Pepys records visiting Herringman's shop and being warned that Dryden himself regarded his latest play, *An Evening's Love*, as fifth-rate. If Pepys wanted to see Dryden in person, he would go to Will's Coffee-house in Covent Garden. Here Dryden would draw around himself 'all the wits of the town'.[17] The tables would be covered in manuscripts and printed papers, so that those interested could catch up on all the latest literary developments.

Elizabeth enjoyed reading French novels, and Pepys describes how she sat up after he had gone to bed because she could not tear herself away from *Polexandre*. This was the story of a queen inhabiting an inaccessible island and sending her knight to punish aspiring suitors, but it was hardly an easy read, for the author Marin Le Roy de Gomberville managed to spin it out into five volumes. Elizabeth was clearly made of stern stuff because Pepys also records buying for her *Ibrahim or L'illustre Bassa*, a fashionable romance by Madeleine de Scuderi, in four volumes, and in the same year, 1668, *Cassandra* by La Calprenède, this time in ten volumes. Pepys's own taste in French literature was for Racine, Corneille and Molière, and for the philosophers Pascal and Descartes. This is very respectable fare, but he also admits to his diary the acquisition of a pornographic book *L'Escholle des Filles*, a conversation between an experienced woman and a virgin. This had first appeared in Paris in 1655, and caused such an outrage that the author, Michel Millot, was condemned and the book burned. Originally Pepys went to the bookseller, John Martin in the Strand, intending to buy the book for his wife to translate, but when he discovered the contents, he bought it in a plain binding 'because I resolve, as soon as I have read it, to burn it, that it may not stand in the list of books, nor among them, to disgrace them if it should be found'.[18]

For 'modern' literature, works from the 1590s onwards, he preferred the latest editions, so he replaced Shakespeare's Third Folio of 1663/4 with the Fourth Folio when it appeared twenty years later. For the 'antique', however, he went for earlier examples, making swaps where necessary, because Pepys was fascinated by the transition from script to printing, a fundamental factor that lies behind various parts of his collection. His appreciation of the works of Geoffrey Chaucer remained with him for the whole of his life. In November 1666, he records reading from the poet's works to his wife and brother after supper 'with great pleasure'. Many years later, having recommended to Dryden that he should translate the Parson's Tale, he invited the playwright to discuss Chaucer over a meal of cold chicken and salad. The work by Chaucer mentioned in the diaries is probably a printed edition by Thomas Speght published in 1602, but Pepys went on to own Chaucerian poems in manuscript 'whereof some never printed'. If he was able to acquire a manuscript version of a printed edition, he would keep both – the only duplication that he permitted in his collection.

Pepys's collection of incunabula – the term comes from the Latin for swaddling clothes and refers to the infancy of printing, reckoned to be before 1501 – is very fine. He defined his criteria in a table, *Of the Origine & Growth of Printing in England*, that he bound into a copy of Moxon's *Mechanick Exercises*. This was based on advice received from his own observation, from Moxon himself, and from John Bagford. Bagford is yet another fascinating character in the world of seventeenth-century books. Born in Fetter Lane in London in 1650/1, he trained and worked as a shoemaker. Despite his lack of academic education, by 1686 he was engaged in the book trade around Holborn collecting early printed editions for a history that he planned to write. At the same time he was looking out for incunabula for some of the leading collectors of the day, including Robert and Edward Harley and Sir Hans Sloane, founding fathers of the British Museum Library, and for Samuel Pepys when old age made him less mobile. Pepys's collection contained six books published by William Caxton, including a very rare copy of the second edition of *Reynard the Fox*, seventeen examples of the work of Caxton's assistant, Wynkyn de Worde, among them *The Golden Legend of Voragine*, bought from William Shrewsbury in 1668, and work from the presses of other early printer-publishers such as Pynson, Machlinia and St Albans.

14 The title page of Pepys's copy of William Caxton's *Reynard the Fox*. This is the second edition of Caxton's translation from the Dutch, published at Westminster in 1489. Manuscripts did not have title pages as such, but were usually introduced by *incipit*. As printed books might be stored before binding and selling, the pages needed some kind of identification and protection, so title pages developed as a result. This is an early example, with Caxton's imprint writ large, above the title of the book.

Pepys's interest in printing and typography also lies behind his collection of ballads and chapbooks. By the time of his death, Pepys had built up a collection of over 1,700 ballads, constituting the largest single collection of its kind. Ballads were single sheets printed with the words of songs usually accompanied by a picture, sold for a penny or two on the streets. From casual references made by Pepys in his diaries, we know that he bought these sheets and that he would sometimes perform the songs, but probably then threw away the paper or copied the words into a commonplace book. However, he started to make his collection because this was the period when black letter printing (Gothic) with pictures began to give way to white letter (Roman) without pictures. It was a remarkably prescient thing to do, because the ephemeral and fragile form of the ballads meant that they have often perished, and over half the items in his collection are the only known copies in existence. Paper at this period was at a premium, used to wrap cheese, light pipes, by pastry cooks to line their pie dishes, and trunk-makers to line their trunks. Sir William Cornwallis recorded that he kept 'pamphlets and lying stories and two-penny poets' in his privy to be read there – and then used as lavatory paper.[19]

Alongside these ballads, Pepys also built up a collection of 215 chapbooks. A chapbook was a book of around 4 to 24 pages, roughly printed on cheap paper and sold at under 6d. Pepys owned some in quarto format, but the majority were smaller, in octavo and duodecimo. In his passion for categorisation, he divided them into Vulgaria, Penny Merriments and Penny Godlinesses. His collection contains the whole range of chapbooks, including almanacs, what we might call 'penny dreadfuls', histories and practical books, among which are some cookery titles, and a few pious booklets.

These 'downmarket' publications were produced and sold by a specialist group of booksellers based in West Smithfield and on London Bridge and known as Ballad Partners. The latter is a rather misleading term as the ballad part of their business was decreasing, and probably derived from the fact that they kept their stock in a building traditionally known as the Ballad Warehouse. London Bridge at this time was a teeming thoroughfare, the only

15 'Come who buys my New Merry Books', a woodcut showing a chapman selling his wares to a young countryman. The illustration is in one of Pepys's 'Penny Merriments', published *c.* 1680 and entitled *Make Room for Christmas*. Such books were printed on cheap paper, hence the 'see-through' from the next page.

bridge across the Thames and the main exit southwards to Canterbury and the Channel ports. The piers were so narrow that boatmen and their passengers took their lives in their hands when they tried to 'shoot the bridge' during high water: an average of fifty watermen perished each year in this hazardous occupation. Above, land was at a premium, so the shops and houses rose dizzily to several storeys. Samuel Pepys must have been familiar with all the noise and drama as he visited Josiah Blare at the Looking Glass or John Back at the Black Boy to buy his 'Merriments and Godlinesses'.

Downmarket their products may have been, but business could be good. A probate inventory taken in 1664 on the property of Charles Tias at the Three Bibles on the Bridge shows that he owned considerable stocks. Books, reams of books and ballads were stored in the shop, with more in a lower chamber on the street, the hall, the garret and even on the stairs. Altogether there were just under 10,000 books ready to go out, most priced at under 6d, but with bibles at 10s and 4s, and the equivalent of 37,500 ballad sheets. When Josiah Blare's inventory was taken in 1707, he had over 31,000 'great and small books'. One of the most profitable lines was almanacs. It is estimated that in the 1660s over 300,000 were produced annually, the equivalent of one for every three families in the kingdom, and Blare alone had one chapbook in his shop for every forty-four families.

In 1686 John Back included in the back of one of his books, *Danger of Despair*, a trade list of further publications that he had available – a custom still practised by paperback publishers. He also announced that he 'Furnisheth any Countrey Chapmen with all sorts of Books, Ballads, and all other Stationary-Wares at reasonable Rates.' The Ballad Partners operated out of London Bridge and West Smithfield as this was near where their distributors lived and could gain access to the main roads leading out of London. Chapmen, hawkers and pedlars would load up with their books and ballad sheets, often pre-packed for their convenience, and set off across the country. In fact, books would only form a small part of these packs; they carried rolls of cloth, medicines, pins, ribbons, and looking glasses too. Shakespeare conjures up just such a figure in Autolycus in *The Winter's Tale*. In his collection, Pepys has a 'merry book' with an illustration of a country youth buying wares from a chapman. Not all these were cheap – a bible at 10s represented considerable outlay, and pedlars would also have 'upmarket' goods for the gentry, such as perfumes and poking sticks for ruffs. The trade was two-way, with chapmen buying hair from country girls to bring back to London and supply the wigmakers.

John Bunyan, author of the great seventeenth-century classic *The Pilgrim's Progress*, was strongly influenced by cheap print. He was born in 1628, the son of a cottager in Elstow in Bedfordshire whose nine acres of smallholding were scarcely sufficient for subsistence so that he eked out a living by tinkering. Despite their poverty, Bunyan's parents sent him to the village school so that he could learn to read and write. In 1666, looking back at his childhood, Bunyan confessed in *A Few Sighs from Hell* to the sin of preferring chapbooks, bought at his cottage door or from market, to the Holy Scriptures. The books that he specifically mentions are ballads, newsbooks, *St George on Horseback* and *Bevis of Southampton*. The last two are what were described as 'penny and pleasant' histories – medieval chivalric romances with plenty of blood and thunder. When Bunyan began his own writing, he realised that his readership would be familiar with the stuff of chapbooks – giants, lions and dragons, as well as the language of the Bible.

Bunyan may have regarded the reading of these books as a sin, but they were enjoyed by a wide range of people. On long winter evenings in town and country they would have been read aloud in homes, workshops and alehouses as a form of shared entertainment. The gentry read cheap print for amusement and relaxation, and so did schoolboys. The bookseller Francis Kirkman, son of a London merchant, described in 1673 how he forked out sixpence to buy popular tales, 'and reading *Montelion Knight of the Oracle*, and *Ornatus* and *Artesia*, and the Famous *Parismus*, I was contented beyond measure and (believing all I read to be true) wished my self Squire to one of these Knights'. He extended his range by swapping and bartering with his school-fellows.[20] We have no record of what Samuel Pepys read as a child, but there is no doubt that among his collection of Vulgaria were memories of his own youthful reading, before he moved on to the more serious works of history.

Two more forms of cheap print were newspapers and newsbooks. The Thirty Years War that tore Europe apart in the early seventeenth century created demand for information and, as a result, corantos came into existence. These were half-sheets printed in black letter type, produced in Amsterdam from 1618, with translations appearing in London two years later. The half-sheet format developed into quarto, and newsbooks began to hit the streets and the alehouses. When England withdrew from the wars in Europe, the demand faltered, but the outbreak of Civil War revived public desire. The government, which regarded news as the property of the state and had meted out severe punishment for unauthorised information, was now in no position to stop it. The first domestic newsbook appeared on 29 November 1641, entitled *The heads of several proceedings in this present Parliament*. By 1649, fifty-four different periodicals had been published.

After Charles II was restored to the throne, an attempt was made by the government to return to state control. The original spokesman for the Crown was Henry Muddiman, but in 1663 he gave way to the extraordinary Sir Roger

L'Estrange. An aristocrat and a Cavalier of the old school who hated Dissenters, Whigs and what he described as Trimmers, in the twentieth century L'Estrange might have contributed happily to the editorial columns of the *Sunday Express*. He thought as he spoke, using italics to add force to his arguments. Installed in an office above the shop of his bookseller Henry Brome in St Paul's Churchyard, he maintained total authorial control over what was produced. Writing in one of his newspapers, the *Observator* on 17 May 1683, he defended his use of Brome's printer: 'first he is *Near* me, upon any Occasion of *Altering*, or *Correcting*. 2ly He is *Carefull* of my *Work*. 3ly I'le Ask no *Pragmaticall Fopps* leave, what *Printer* I am to *Employ*.' His text must have been a nightmare to set up in type.

L'Estrange began producing the *Intelligencer* and the *News* at the end of August 1663. The former appeared on Mondays, the latter on Thursdays, both priced at half a penny. Samuel Pepys records in his diary for 4 September 1663, 'by water to White-hall and Westminster-hall, and there bought the first news-books of Lestrange's writing, he beginning this week; and makes methink but a simple beginning'.[21]

Two years later the *Oxford Gazette* was introduced: it later became the *London Gazette*. Adopting the format of the corantos of the 1620s, and of contemporary Continental periodicals, it decisively changed the face of news publication. Always on the ball, Pepys recorded the first day of publication in London, 22 November 1665, comparing it favourably with L'Estrange's work: 'This day the first of the *Oxford Gazettes* came out, which is very pretty, full of news, and no folly in it – wrote by Williamson'.[22] Williamson was secretary to the minister Lord Arlington, and was probably the supplier of the news, which was then actually written by Henry Muddiman. In the Pepys Library there is a series of the *Gazette* running from November 1665 to January 1704, in uniform binding. These, along with L'Estrange's publications, could be distributed within the metropolitan area by Docwra's penny post, but also by 'flying stationers' and 'mercuries', often women, who ran through the streets crying and selling. Further afield they were carried by chapmen. Coffee-houses and alehouses all over the country would have copies of newspapers and newsbooks available for customers.

L'Estrange ceased his newsbooks in 1666, but took up his journalistic pen again with the *Observator* in 1681 following the hysteria roused by the Popish Plot. This plot had been concocted by the fertile mind of Titus Oates, who accused Jesuits financed by the Pope and Louis XIV of planning to murder Charles II and put his brother James on the throne. By this time, the periodical press had diversified, with specialised journals such as the Royal Society's *Philosophical Transactions* in circulation. More downmarket were the Old Bailey sessions papers, *Inquest after Blood*, published from 1670: crime has

Will's Best Coffee Powder at Manwarings Coffee House in Falcon Court over against St Dunstans Church in Fleet Street

16 A London coffee house, from an advertisement for Will's coffee powder, *c.*1700. Two of the customers are reading newspapers, probably the *London Gazette* and the *Post-Man* which was produced specially for coffee houses.

always proved a good seller. The Popish Plot triggered off a whole rash of other news-sheets. Whigs produced *Protestant News*, Tories *Loyal*, while L'Estrange was satirised in the *Snotty-Nose Gazette* as Towzer the dog, with a broom (his bookseller Henry Brome) tied to his tail. Although James II in particular tried to suppress the press, the genie was out of the bottle.

Other ephemeral parts of Samuel Pepys's collection are not as crude or cheap in their production, but were gathered for similar reasons: his interest in printing and design. He bought copy or calligraphical books, explaining in the introduction to his collection that they included examples of handwriting from the previous thousand years, and the 'Performances of all the Celebrated Masters of the Penn (now Extant and Recoverable) whether Domestick or Foreign, by Hand or Burin, within the Past & Praesent Age'.[23] One of the contemporary examples bought by Pepys is Mr Gery's copy-book, engraved in 1665 by William Fairthorne and printed and sold by John Garrett 'at his shop, as you go up ye stayres of ye Royall Exchange in Corn-hill, who sells all sorts of maps and coppy books'. When Pepys became frail, he sent his nephew John Jackson to find foreign copybooks, which would then be numbered and collated by his clerk Paul Lorrain, a gifted calligrapher.

John Garrett's address indicates how difficult it was to pinpoint the location of a shop or place of business in the years before street numbering, let alone postal codes, as shown by Pepys's collection of London trade cards. Only one of these is for a bookseller, Roger Tucker, 'at the signe of the Golden Legg, at the corner of Salisbury Street in the Strand'. It is not known if Pepys used Tucker as a bookseller, but he probably acquired the card for the design and typography. Booksellers' cards were rarely as flamboyant as those of other tradesmen because of their 'dignified profession' and lack of decorative possibilities – the sign of the Bible was common choice, as was the head of a literary figure. David Mortier, for instance, was a bookseller specialising in French and Latin books at the turn of the eighteenth century; his shop in the Strand had the sign of Erasmus's Head.

One of Samuel Pepys's great friends was James Houblon, member of a large clan of French Protestants who had fled from religious persecution to London in the 1590s. In the seventeenth century the family was able to build up a trading and shipping business that covered the known world, and got to know Pepys through the Navy Board. James entertained Pepys in style at his house close to London Wall, and after a good dinner in November 1690 Pepys wrote in a letter to John Evelyn that none of the food or drink besides the bread and beer came from anywhere nearer than Persia, China and the Cape of Good Hope. Pepys would have intended this as a compliment, as he loved the idea of the exotic. He had taken up not only the drinking of coffee but also tea, recording in his diary how, in the middle of his working day, 'he did send for a Cupp of Tee (a China drink), of which I had never drank before'.[24] When he had his portrait painted by John Hales in 1666, he chose to wear an Indian gown, an informal silk garment cut like a kimono, and he furnished his house with Indian cottons. It is scarcely surprising therefore to find the exotic among his book collection, including a Slavonic book of hours, an example of Chinese block printing, and an empty Turkish notebook.

Hales's portrait showed Pepys in his 'Indian gown' holding a copy of his own composition, a motet, *Beauty Retire*. Pepys's passion for music was lifelong. In a letter in November 1700 he wrote that music was a 'science peculiarly productive of a pleasure that no state of life public or private, secular or sacred: no difference of age or season; no temper of mind . . . nor . . . distinction of quality, renders either improper, untimely or unentertaining'.[25] His collection of music contains about seventy volumes, though he probably owned many loose sheets of his 'practical music' that he later discarded. Most are printed, and date from the seventeenth century, but there are some fifteenth- and sixteenth-century manuscripts, again reflecting his interest in the development of the technology of publishing.

Much of his contemporary music was bought from his friend John Playford, who traded out of the west porch of the Temple Church. Playford first appears in Pepys's diary in February 1660, when he bought from him a great book, probably *Select Ayres and Dialogues*, published the previous year. Despite Oliver Cromwell's disapproval of dancing, which smacked of Frenchness, Playford wrote and published the first edition of his immensely successful *Dancing Master* in 1652, providing instructions on steps arranged in sequences of orderly progressions. A copy of this was purchased in November 1662 by Pepys to appease his wife, who was annoyed that he had attended a dancing school in Fleet Street. In turn Pepys became jealous of her dancing master, 'a pretty neat black man' called Pembleton, and quarrels over dancing fill the diary for months after.[26] Away from the problems of the dance floor, Pepys bought Latin motets for two and three voices accompanied by an organ. Later, he had his own household musician, Cesare Morelli, who transposed songs for him in bass voice. Pepys also owned a collection of psalm books with settings for domestic enjoyment, and John Evelyn wrote of private concerts where operatic songs might be performed, including pieces from Luis Grabu's *Albion and Albanius*, with words by John Dryden.

* * * *

Samuel Pepys had a passion for collecting from an early age. In one of the books that he owned while an undergraduate at Magdalene College in Cambridge is an inscription. This is unusual in itself, as Pepys rarely marked his books. But it also records that the book is from the 'musaeo Samuelis Pepys', in other words part of a collection of interesting objects, often known as a cabinet of curiosities.[27] Well-educated men, referring to themselves as virtuosi, collected coins and gems, books and globes, pictures and engravings, and in some cases examples of natural history or antiquities, keeping them in their private studies or cabinets. Did the young Pepys hope one day to have his own cabinet of curiosities? In the event he moved in another direction, building up a significant library, which he kept and recorded meticulously, just as a curator should manage his museum.

In the summer of 1666, finding that his books were 'growing numerous, and lying one upon another on my chairs'[28] he commissioned Thomas Simpson, one of the joiners from the Thames-side dockyards, to make up for him two bookcases in oak to his designs. These could be taken to pieces for easy carriage, and had glazed fronts – the earliest extant examples of such furniture. Each press held about 250 books, with folios at the bottom, and octavo and quarto volumes ingeniously stepped on some of the other shelves to maximise the space. Once the bookcases were acquired, Pepys drew up an alphabet and a few months later, a catalogue or shelf-list. As the pace of book acquisition accelerated, so more cases were made, culminating in twelve. Seven of these are to be seen in drawings made of the library in York Buildings in 1699. A long, panelled room looks out towards the Thames with the presses standing against the walls. Above, hang portraits, among them his friends

17 Pepys's Library in York Buildings, a drawing made in 1699. The glazed bookcases constructed for him by the naval joiner, Thomas Simpson, are lined up against the walls, while large folios were probably kept under the draped table. A map, along with portraits of his friends and his patron James II hang on the walls.

John Evelyn and Robert Boyle, and over the fireplace, James II. A low draped table in the centre probably held folios too large for bookcases.

In 1692 Pepys decided to review and reorganise his collection, withdrawing to the country for three months to put his papers in order.[29] The following year, he was ready for his 'Adjustment' of the books. They were marshalled in strict order according to size. If one did not match, then out it went, unless a favourite, in which case it was made up to size with a wooden plinth disguised in gilt leather. There were three catalogues, one by name, a second by alphabet and third by subject. The three together were called 'Suppellex Literaria' (literary furniture). Pepys's love of Latin names came to the fore: 'Consutilia' for volumes of pamphlets, 'Repertorium Chiro-Typicum' for facsimile signatures of famous people.

The 1690s were a time of intense bibliographical activity, but also for reflection. In 1695 Pepys wrote a memorandum encapsulating the principles that had guided him in the construction of his collection. He made clear that he wanted it to be quite different from the 'Extensive, Pompous and Stationary Libraries of Princes, Universities, Colleges and other Publick-Societies'. Instead, he was aiming for 'the Self-Entertainment onely of a solitary, unconfined Enquirer into Books', and that it should comprise 'in fewest Books and least Room the greatest diversity of Subjects, Stiles, and Languages its Owner's Reading [would] bear'. Able administrator that he was, he wanted the

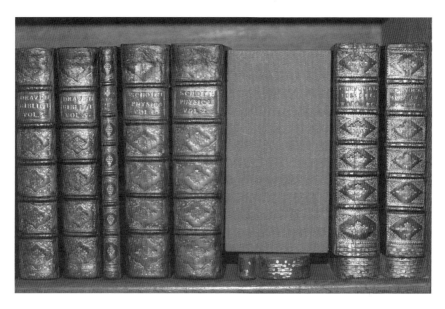

18 Following the major 'adjustment' of his library, Pepys ensured that books were all of the same height on a shelf by having wooden bases made for the smaller volumes.

catalogue to display 'Clearness, Comprehensiveness and Order', and the bindings to reflect 'Decency and Uniformity'.[30]

Generous in his loyalty, Pepys also enjoyed loyalty from others, and was able to gather around him a group of assistants. Mary Skinner did some scribing, but perhaps given that her spelling has been described as of the picturesque school, her contribution was limited. His clerk Paul Lorrain became Ordinary (chaplain) of Newgate Gaol in 1698, where one of the lucrative aspects was to take down the last speeches of those about to be executed at Tyburn and publish them in ballad form, so he shared an interest in ballads. Despite his position in the prison, Lorrain continued to act as a library assistant (sometimes called footman). Perhaps the person closest to Pepys was his nephew John Jackson, whom he treated as his heir, sending him off on the Grand Tour of Europe in 1699. Arriving in Rome in time for the celebrations marking the new century, Jackson duly sent back books and manuscripts, sonatas by Corelli, and guidebooks and engravings of Roman monuments. As Pepys grew frailer, so he made increasing use of friends and agents to buy books and other publications on his behalf. His godson Dr John Shadwell sent frontispieces from Paris where he was the English Ambassador's physician. His friend Dr John Montagu, the Dean of Durham, went so far as to cut fragments from two manuscripts in the Cathedral Library so that Pepys could contemplate their 'Character and Antiquity'. When the Chapter wanted them back, Pepys protested that they surely understood 'the Curiosity of One of my Gusto in these matters?'[31] James Houblon used his dealers to pick up rare volumes in Europe. Every Saturday fellow members of the Royal Society would come to dine, and no doubt bring the latest publications as well as news and gossip.

Pepys was both a lender and a borrower of books. One of his principal correspondents was John Evelyn, and the warmth between the two diarists grew with the years. When Pepys returned him a package of books and papers in 1692, he had to own up to damaging one work. To aid his poor eyesight he had enlisted 'an unskilful hand' to wash the prints with a thin stain to cut down the glare from the paper. Like all good book borrowers, he had tried to find another copy, but auctions had produced nothing, and the bookseller Robert Scott could only produce a poor substitute, so he ruefully decided 'it more religious to restore it to you now as it is than leave you to expect it in the same pickle 7 years hence from God knows who'.[32]

With the encroaching years, Pepys became martyr to all kinds of illnesses and pains. It is indeed a miracle that he survived as long as he did, for he alone among his many siblings made it to old age. Moreover he suffered agonies from stones in the kidneys and bladder, and underwent the horrific experience of being cut for the stone in 1658, an operation undertaken without anaesthetic. Extremely lucky to have survived this ordeal, for many years he held a celebration on 26 March to mark the anniversary, but problems with the stone reappeared in 1700 and he began to suffer from an ulcerated kidney. His physician was Hans Sloane, with whom he shared his books and his passion for them.

William Hewer, Pepys's loyal assistant from decades earlier, had moved westwards out of London to Clapham, then in the countryside. Pepys would often stay with him for long periods, but in 1702, with his health deteriorating significantly, it was decided that he should move to Clapham permanently, taking his library with him. Thomas Simpson's bookcases were easily taken apart and transported to their new home in a large and handsome room. Double-sided pictures were set in panels on the walls, the two globes were installed on pulleys and Pepys's collection of model ships displayed in cases. A visitor to the house soon afterwards left a description of the library, noting that 'the books [were] so well order'd that his Footman [Paul Lorrain] (after looking the Catalogue) could lay his finger on any of 'em blindfold'.[33]

Sadly, Pepys was so ill that he could not enjoy his new home for long. Realising that death was near, he added two codicils to his will concerning the future of his collection. His nephew John Jackson was to enjoy it for his life-time, and was instructed to 'complete' the library by adding missing volumes or sets. On Jackson's death, Pepys intended that the collection should go to his old Cambridge college, Magdalene. However, he stipulated that it should be kept in a separate room, *Bibliotheca Pepysiana*, and remain unchanged in perpetuity, without addition or subtraction. Should this stipulation be broken, then the library should go instead to Trinity College.

In the event, Magdalene kept to the terms, and on Jackson's death in 1723 the collection of approximately 3,000 volumes went to the college, together with the twelve presses, to be installed on the first floor of a seventeenth-century building. A German visitor who saw it in 1728 made the gloomy prediction 'After some time the whole lumber may grow out of date, the little gold blackened, and the use of the library [will] vanish'.[34] How wrong he was! To be fair, he was not to realise that the *Bibliotheca Pepysiana* concealed a time-bomb: the six volumes of the Diary, written in Shelton's system of short-hand. The first part, transcribed by a poverty-stricken young academic, the Revd John Smith, was published by Lord Braybrooke in 1825. Although severely bowdlerised, it made Samuel Pepys well known once more, and the library revelled in his glory. Amazingly enough, Pepys's diary had to wait until the 1970s before its full and wonderful form was revealed to the world by Robert Latham and Professor William Matthews.

Samuel Pepys died on 24 May 1704. An autopsy was performed on his body by two fellow members of the Royal Society, Hans Sloane and John Shadwell, with the surgeon Charles Bernard. They were following John Jackson's wishes 'for our own satisfaction as well as public good', though, with his respect for scientific research, Pepys would have most probably approved. The autopsy report revealed how stoic he had been in the last years of his life. His great friend John Evelyn immediately wrote a tribute, but perhaps the most fitting words had been penned in his letter to Pepys back in 1692: '*O Fortunate Mr Pepys!* Who knows, possesses, and injoyes all that's worth seeking after. Let me live among your inclinations and I shall be happy.'[35]

CHAPTER 3

DISTANCE LEARNING

Three Provincial Libraries

One of Samuel Johnson's most famous observations was: 'When a man is tired of London he is tired of life, for there is in London all that life can afford.'[1] In the late seventeenth century London was the centre in England for both intellectual life and for the acquisition of luxuries, and thus for publishing and bookselling.

How then did the book-lover who lived outside the capital find out about the latest books and obtain them? A vivid picture is provided by Sir William Boothby who resided at Ashbourne Hall in Derbyshire, approximately 150 miles from London, a journey on horseback of four or five days.[2] Boothby was a moderately wealthy member of the Derbyshire gentry who bought Ashbourne Hall from the poet Sir Aston Cokayne in 1671. He was part of a local literary circle, and one of his great friends was another poet, Charles Cotton. In his diary he recorded a week-long visit in November 1676 to Chatsworth where his host was William Cavendish, 3rd Earl of Devonshire. The Earl had been tutored in his youth by the philosopher Hobbes, who had also been in charge of his library, and although Boothby mentions in his diary only his days out hunting with Cavendish, he must have also enjoyed his fine collection of books. In a letter written to Cotton on 21 July 1685, Sir William describes books as 'the Great Joy of my Life'. His collection is now dispersed, although one of his personal diaries and copies of outgoing letters have survived, recording his communications with his booksellers.[3]

Boothby was purchasing many works of theology, but the range of his collection goes far beyond this, including atlases, dictionaries, prints and maps. He certainly liked illustrated books – 'Bookes with Cutts [engravings] must be considered' – and one of his purchases was Dr Nehemiah Grew's *Anatomy of Plants*, published in 1682. In this important book, Grew, a Coventry physician and botanist, established the sexuality of plants for the first time, and Boothby was quick to purchase it, in a folio edition, produced with the best paper. His interest in books *per se* is shown by his acquisition of Gabriel Naudé's influential treatise on how to form a library, translated into English by John Evelyn as *Instructions concerning erecting of a library*, and of Joseph Moxon's manual of printing, *Mechanick Exercises.*

Boothby's literary taste is very interesting. He bought the discourses and poems of John Milton and the plays of John Dryden, but he also kept up with the latest works of female writers, the poems of Aphra Benn and Jane Barker's 'Poeticall Recreations'. Although he refused to buy the latest volume of the works of the eccentric and flamboyant Margaret Cavendish, Duchess of Newcastle, his reason was not prejudice. He already owned three volumes and 'because her works are very deare', returned to the bookseller her *Philosophical Letters* that carried the hefty price of 11s.

Several booksellers in London provided Boothby with his books. Some were from the City, others from the expanding trade westwards, including a French bookseller in the Strand. His principal bookseller, however, was Richard Chiswell in St Paul's Churchyard. Chiswell was expected to provide a variety of services beyond supplying books, as made clear in the letter that Boothby wrote to him on 21 May 1684:

> We do not come up to London as we designed (at present). I have returned you some moneys from [name illegible], so soon as it comes to your hands, let me hear. I hope you receipt my last sent with the bookes by the carrier. May send me the last terme catalogue and continue the pamphlets with care (which I take much delight in). Pray buy me a quarter of pound of tee of the best, though deare, for I cannot drinke bad. Faile not to send it this next week for I have not to send me a weeke (designed to come up myself) and fear I cannot live without it.

Tellingly it is signed 'Your friend'.

The term catalogues mentioned in this letter were mainly produced by Robert Clavell, one of Chiswell's neighbours in the Churchyard and another of Boothby's booksellers. Not only did Clavell issue term catalogues, he was also an early example of a bookseller who energetically exploited the provincial book market. Clavell had been a clerk in the Post Office under the administration of Lord Arlington after the Fire of London in 1666. In this capacity he was able to collect from local postmasters all over the country names and addresses of provincial booksellers and to dispatch to them parcels of title pages about to be published, which he acquired, together with a fee for the service, from London publishers. He justified sending these parcels free of charge on the grounds that they would ultimately increase the revenue of the Post Office. This practice was challenged by a rival bookseller, John Starkey, 'since Country Booksellers usually write by their Carryers, and post-masters do not much concern themselves with Bookes'. Starkey brought out a news-paper, *Mercurius Librarius* at Michaelmas 1668, at 6d a copy, where he included advertisements from publishers but did not charge them. Clavell was rattled by this, for he could see that a single-sheet paper would be more convenient to send than a parcel of title pages, and via Arlington suggested to Sir Roger L'Estrange, the licensor of the press, that he, Clavell, should have sole licence to print catalogues of new books. L'Estrange diplomatically proposed that Starkey and Clavell should run *Mercurius Librarius* in partnership, and so the third edition that appeared at Easter 1669 carried both names. However, given the commercial potential of the market, the quarrel between the two booksellers rumbled on for many years.[4]

Boothby demanded much from his booksellers. He was particularly concerned about costs, thus writing on 15 August 1683, 'The 8° Books are so to[o] deare That I desire them Either in quiers or stich'd – and yr other Books are Dearer that I can have them at my own Doore.' The following year, on 10 October, he wrote dramatically to Chiswell that he should ensure the accounts were clear to avoid 'running the greatest hazard if you should die, and myself also (as we are both mortal)'. The process of ordering from a distance also proved frustrating when Boothby found books arriving with faults in the binding, pages not cut or cut narrow, and leaves misplaced. On one occasion, a parcel of books had been broken by the carrier, damaging the books and requiring them to be rebound.

At the end of 1688 James II fled the country and the throne was taken by his elder daughter Mary, and her consort, William of Orange. In these tumul-tuous weeks Boothby's isolation in Derbyshire became more marked. By this time Joseph Watts, another bookseller in St Paul's Churchyard, had become his principal London supplier. In a letter of 2 December 1688, following a petulant complaint to Watts about his neglect, he wrote, 'I believe you are in great disorder and disturbance in London, as we are in the Country, many great men, and others being up. But my Allegiance and Religion According to ye principles of the Church of England keeps me Joyning with them'. Two months later in a letter began on 26 January, his desire for news and for every kind of current newsletter, pamphlet and proclamation burst out in another complaint to Watts: 'you have omitted sending the weekely Intelligences . . . the above are in most Gentlemens hands and in Coffy houses Long ago', and he gave a list of the missing issues of the various newspapers.

He was right to cite coffee-houses as being the centres of news and gossip, for they were a vibrant part of London life. One author compares the coffee-house culture of this period with walking into the internet, opening up culture and information, unlike institutions such as schools, the Church and clubs which were exclusive by nature.[5] Scientists from the Royal Society gathered at Garraway's in Exchange Alley off Cornhill, and sometimes conducted experiments there. The Temple Coffee-house in Fleet Street was the location for the Botany Club, formed by a nucleus of members of the Royal Society, such as Hans Sloane and Nehemiah Grew, who met and debated with amateur botanists, practising nurserymen and gardeners.

The haunts of booksellers and printers were the Chapter Coffee-house in Paternoster Row and Child's in Warwick Lane, although an innovation in the world of publishing was founded at Smith's Coffee-house in Stocksmarket, an area later cleared to make way for the Lord Mayor's residence, the Mansion House. Here in 1691 the bookseller John Dunton initiated the *Athenian Gazette*, later changed to *Athenian Mercury* to 'oblige Authority'. Readers were invited to send their queries on any subject to a club of self-styled learned men, who were in fact Dunton and his two brothers-in-law, Samuel Wesley (father of John and Charles) and Richard Sault. They answered a diverse range of questions from the biblical, 'What became of the waters after Noah's Flood?' to the basic, 'Why a horse with a round Fundament emits a square Excrement?' The periodical also included literary pieces, such as the early verse of Jonathan Swift, proving very successful among both male and female readers and paving the way for the *Spectator* and the *Tatler*.

To find out the latest literary gossip in Pepys's day, the visitor had to go to Will's at the corner of Russell and Bow Streets in Covent Garden, where the dramatist John Dryden held court. On his death in 1700 the literary torch passed first to Tom's in Russell Street established by Captain Thomas West, and then in 1712 to Button's just across the way. The latter was run by Daniel Button, an ex-servant set up in business by Joseph Addison following the success of his journal, the *Spectator*. The poet Alexander Pope described how Addison went every day to Button's, spending hours there at a stretch and assembling around him a circle that included Richard Steele.

Addison and Steele had met as schoolboys in the 1680s at the Charterhouse in Clerkenwell, and had both gone up to Oxford. Steele became a writer for the official government newspaper, the *London Gazette*, but in 1709 he started his own paper, the *Tatler*, consisting of a folio sheet printed on both sides and folded once to create four pages, which was produced three times a week and cost a penny. Taking the alias of Isaac Bickerstaff, Esq, Steele declared his intention was 'to expose the false arts of Life, to pull off the Disguises of Cunning, Vanity and Affectation, and to recommend a general Simplicity in our Dress, our Discourse, and our Behaviour'.[6] He promised to describe the various coffee-houses, such as Dick's in Fleet Street, White's Chocolate House in St James's, and Will's in Covent Garden. This was a canny choice, for they were all locations of a

19 The front page of John Dunton's *Athenian Mercury*, 1 January 1695 edition. This is part of a collection of early periodicals made by John Hervey, 1st Earl of Bristol who, like Dunton, was an enthusiastic supporter of the Protestant Succession.

relatively elite culture; none had commercial interests such as Lloyd's Coffee-house in the City, or radical politics.

The *Tatler* lasted for two years, selling well right across England, and beyond to Europe and North America. In its place in 1711 came the *Spectator*, which sold even better under the joint editorship of Steele and Addison. Dispensing with the Bickerstaff *nom de plume*, 'Mr Spectator' wrote of the club of men and the aim to urbanise philosophy. On 12 March 1711 he declared, 'It was said of Socrates, that he brought Philosophy down from Heaven, to inhabit among Men, and I shall be ambitious to have it said of me, that I have brought Philosophy out of Closets and Libraries, Schools and Colleges, to dwell in Clubs and Assemblies, at Tea-Tables and in Coffee-Houses.'[7] A large letter-box was installed in the shape of a lion in Button's so that customers might furnish their own material for the journal.

Among Sir William Boothby's requests to his London booksellers were catalogues of forthcoming auctions, which were often held in coffee-houses and taverns. Auctions had been used since the sixteenth century, chiefly for forced sales following quarrels over inheritance or non-payment of rent, but these were mostly of household and farm goods, with books making a rare appearance. The first identified use in England of an auction specifically for books came in 1676 when the London bookseller William Cooper produced a sale catalogue and auctioned the library of Dr Lazarus Seaman, former Master of Peterhouse, Cambridge. The sale proved highly successful, as Cooper noted in the preface to the catalogue for his next sale to 'the great content and satisfaction to the Gentlemen who were buyers'.[8] He had placed advertisements in the *London Gazette* and specified that the selling would be by outcry, an idea that had been introduced from the Netherlands. This was to provide the pattern for future book auctions. Newspaper advertisements would list a whole series of bookshops and coffee-houses where catalogues might be obtained, to ensure maximum coverage for the sales. The catalogues were often specifically printed on large paper to provide spaces for prices and buyers' names to be added. If they were not big enough, an extra strip was pasted along the fore-edge. If the books to be auctioned were pornographic in content, then they were paid for by ready money and names were not recorded.

In 1682 Richard Chiswell conducted the auction of the library of Richard 'Obituary' Smith. The sale was spread over weeks, starting on 23 March and finishing on 15 June, and across various locations, where different categories of books were offered. The last sale, for instance, was of pamphlets. Book buyers often did not attend sales in person but sent agents to bid on their account. John Dryden, for example, used an agent, Mr Orme, who bought fifty-four books for him from the Smith sale on 15 May. Boothby commissioned Chiswell to act for him in such circumstances.

The sale of private libraries by auction was to snowball in frequency as the eighteenth century progressed, providing connoisseurs, scholars and book collectors with the opportunity to acquire rare books at moderate prices. The development of this market is discussed in Chapter 7, but there were other types of book auctions. In order to preserve their control over the market, and in particular the distribution of popular books, an elite group of London booksellers known as 'congers' (thought to derive from conger eel, in that they swallowed up smaller fry) met regularly in the 1690s at the Chapter Coffeehouse to hold private auctions at which books were sold wholesale. Another form of private auction was the trade sale in copyrights. Any author whose book was to stand a chance of success had to sell their copyright to members of this invited group, which usually excluded provincial booksellers. This stranglehold was loosened in principle by the Copyright Act of 1710 which limited copyright to existing publications to twenty-one years for books already in print, and fourteen years for new books. Nevertheless in practice the situation remained messy and contentious for many years thereafter.[9]

Publishing and selling books had, since the sixteenth century, been centred on London with some production from the university printers in Oxford and Cambridge. Mary Tudor's grant to the Stationers' Company in 1557 enabled booksellers not only to control publishing but also to secure copyrights by entry into the company registers. This monopolistic situation collapsed with the political storms of the mid-seventeenth century and printers were able to bypass booksellers and open printshops. Although the Stuarts sought to reverse this with the Restoration, the die was cast, and with the lapse of the Licensing Act in 1695 printed material no longer had to be registered with the Stationers. There had always been some booksellers in towns scattered throughout England, supplied from London and also by publishers in Dublin and Edinburgh, beyond the restrictions of the Stationers' Company. Now, these provincial booksellers could significantly expand their trade. So Sir William Boothby was able to buy from booksellers in Coventry, Oxford and Lichfield. The last, just 25 miles south of Ashbourne, was one of three shops owned by Michael Johnson, father of Samuel. Johnson senior, born in 1656, had been apprenticed to a London bookseller, Richard Simpson. It is not known exactly when he set up business by himself, but he was corresponding with Boothby by April 1683 when the latter's quarterly account was established.

In August of the following year Boothby placed a very substantial order with Michael Johnson, having perused his catalogue – over forty titles are recorded. Among the works ordered were two books by the freethinker Charles Blount, his *Anima Mundi* and *Great is Diana of the Ephesians*, which Boothby requested to be bound together. These were Blount's two major deist works: the former caused a great clamour when published in 1678 and precipitated the Bishop of London into ordering it to be burnt. What was Boothby, an avowed member of the Church of England, doing with such inflammatory material? The answer may lie in the first part of his letter to Johnson, in which he mentions that he had seen one of the volumes in the author's study, for Blount had an estate, Blount's Hall, in Staffordshire, not far from Ashbourne. In addition to the order for books, Boothby requested a copy of 'Mauncell's catalogue'. This was the catalogue of English books compiled in 1595 by Andrew Maunsell (see p. 26) which remained a valuable handbook for bibliophiles nearly a century later.

As with his London booksellers, Boothby used Johnson for a whole range of services, treating him as a postal agent, and asking him to find a chaplain and tutor for his household and to search out lodgings in Lichfield. He subsequently complained that the latter were too near the choir school and therefore noisy. Johnson also undertook the binding of books, and taught the craft to his son. Boothby, who was very fussy about his bindings, stipulated exactly how he was to use the family arms and crest. At one stage he dreamt up a scheme whereby Johnson should hire a bookbinder to undertake wholesale binding of his library at Ashbourne, where he, Boothby, could keep a firm eye on the quality control. This ambitious idea, fraught with potential problems, never materialised.

In addition, Johnson acted as an initiating publisher. His first recorded venture was Sir John Floyer's ΦΑΡΜΑΚΟΒΑΣΑΝΟΣ *or, The Touch-stone of Medicines . . . in Two Volumes.* On the title page he records, 'Printed for Michael Johnson, Bookseller: And are to be sold at his Shops at Litchfield and Uttoxiter, in Stafford-shire; And Ashby-de-la-Zouch in Leicester-shire'. A variant imprint says that the book is to be sold by Robert Clavell at the Peacock in St Paul's Churchyard, and Clavell cooperated on several books with him, so this was possibly the source of Boothby's introduction to his London booksellers. Others with whom Johnson shared imprints included John Back on London Bridge, who provided Samuel Pepys with some of his godlier chapbooks. Four of Michael Johnson's 'authors' were Staffordshire clergymen, who must also have been his customers, along with the local gentry. The interaction between the bookseller and his customers-cum-authors could be mutually beneficial financially, as the author would buy a number of copies at discount and be given further copies in payment for his manuscript. He would then distribute these free to ensure his printed words circulated among his congregation.

Michael Johnson enjoyed a reputation for learning, but this could lead him into some pickles. In 1706, he bought up the library of the 9th Earl of Derby, a massive investment of nearly three thousand volumes, including Patristics and French history, many of which must have been virtually impossible to sell. Samuel was dismissive of his father's business methods and abilities, although he was proud of being able to appreciate a good binding. In 1779 he wrote to the bookseller Thomas Cadell complaining that he had supplied a book bound in sheepskin, 'a thing I never saw before. I was bred a Bookseller, and have not forgotten my trade'.[10]

Sadly Sir William Boothby's library, which by his death in 1707 totalled about six thousand volumes, has been dispersed. The style and appearance of his library, however, can be recreated from one that survives remarkably intact, that of the Booth family of Dunham Massey in Cheshire. Although later generations made additions, the core consists of the books belonging to Henry Booth, 1st Earl of Warrington (1652–94), his son George, the 2nd Earl (1675–1758), and George's only child, Mary (1704–72), who became Countess of Stamford.

Henry Booth was a Presbyterian who supported the Exclusion that aimed to prevent James, Duke of York as a Roman Catholic succeeding to the throne on the death of his brother, Charles II. Although Booth's uncompromising views landed him in the Tower of London, accused of high treason, he was acquitted after the case was unproven. No doubt aware that he had used up some of his nine lives, he retired to Cheshire. The nightmare scenario feared by the Exclusionists became a reality in 1688 when a healthy son was born to James, now king, and his queen, Mary of Modena, thus ensuring a Catholic dynasty. Unlike Boothby, who chose to watch from the sidelines, Henry Booth leapt into action, raising troops in support of William of Orange, and when William ascended the throne with his wife Mary, he was appointed Chancellor of the Exchequer. His unbending style caused him all too soon to fall out with his colleagues and he was dismissed from royal service in 1690 with the compensation of the earldom of Warrington and a pension of £2,000, little of which was ever paid. Retiring once more to Dunham, Henry Booth died in 1694, leaving his young son George a debt-ridden estate.

Detective work by Edward Potten has recently identified many of the books at Dunham that belonged to Henry Booth: it is reckoned that he had a substantial collection of between 400 and 500.[11] Some are mentioned in a treatise of advice that he composed for his sons in September 1688 after his release from the Tower, when he thought he was likely to be 'swept away in the common Calamity'. Along with general advice on how to behave privately and publicly, he points out that, 'These directions, and what else can be given you, will not much avail without your own improvement of them, which must be done by reading and observation'.

Booth's particular recommendations of books to his children coincide with his own fundamental belief that, 'God has not appointed the World any form of Government, but left every Nation and People to chuse such a model as best liked them'. 'Worth its weight in gold' is his description of Nathaniel Bacon's *An Historical Discourse of the Uniformity of the Government of England,* first published in 1647 and regarded as one of the most influential works in support of the Parliamentarian cause. So dangerous did this publication appear to the government that when the radical bookseller John Starkey produced a new edition in 1689, he was prosecuted and forced to flee to Amsterdam. Booth also commends the *Institutes* of the eminent seventeenth-century lawyer, Sir Edward Coke, who placed the source of law in popular custom and wisdom rather than in royal command, tracing Parliament back to Anglo-Saxon times and the great council of the kingdom. For further reading, Booth advises *De Laudibus Legum Angliae* by the fifteenth-century political theorist Sir John Fortescue, who likewise championed the concept of the continuation of British ancient law. Next to law, Booth felt it was necessary for his children to read English history, the lives of kings, but also of famous men and chronicles of other countries. Plutarch's *Lives* are especially recommended, *De Jure Belli et Pacis* by the Dutch humanist Grotius, which he describes as 'allowed by all to be one of the best Books that ever was writ', and the writings of Machiavelli, 'not withstanding the clamour'.

Rash in his politics and ill-advised in his financial affairs, Henry Booth proves to be sagacious and moderate in his advice on reading. Most, if not all of the books that he recommends he says are to be found in his study. He promises his sons that the books of law should take no more than a few months to digest, and then they can move on to other reading. But, he counsels moderation: 'be sure to drive the nail only as you find it will go', don't go on too long with your reading because you will lose the taste and won't remember things properly. And, he allows that 'to read a Play or Romance now and then for diversion, may do no hurt'.[12]

We know what books Henry Booth owned, and why, but cannot say where they were bought. With the exception of a handful from Oxford and Cambridge, the imprints are all from London or the Continent. His London contacts must have been excellent, for he regularly attended Parliament first in the House of Commons, and later in the Lords, and of course, he resided on occasion in the Tower of London at His Majesty's Pleasure. As Custos Rotulorum and Lord Lieutenant of Cheshire, he had a town house in the city of Chester, a particularly active centre for bookselling and some printing.

It may be that Booth's Presbyterian principles led him to do business with booksellers of similar outlook, such as John Starkey, the radical bookseller in Fleet Street. After Joshua Kirton lost his business in the Great Fire Samuel Pepys was also one of Starkey's customers, although they would not have agreed in their politics, and Starkey proved a doughty challenger to Robert Clavell. He was the publisher, with two Fleet Street colleagues, of the works of Machiavelli mentioned by Booth and still on the shelves at Dunham Massey.

John Dunton, the bookseller who produced in printed form Henry Booth's advice to his children, was likewise of Presbyterian views. In 1694, trading at the Black Raven opposite Poultry Counter, he co-published with John Lawrence *The Works of the Rt. Hon Henry, late L. Delamer and Earl of Warrington*, probably at the instigation of John de la Heuze, the French Huguenot tutor to the Booth children. Dunton is a larger than life character, who published in 1705 his autobiography, *The Life and Errors of John Dunton*, the first of an English bookseller. Born in 1659 the son of the Rector of Graffham in Huntingdonshire, he had been apprenticed to a Presbyterian bookseller in London, Thomas Parkhurst. In the autumn of 1685, shortly after James II's rout of Monmouth's army at the Battle of Sedgemoor, he departed for New England. The voyage westwards was the more perilous, and Dunton's experience proved hellish, as he nearly perished from starvation after four months at sea. His description remained remarkably good-humoured: 'myself and four more of the Passengers belong'd to the Captain's Mess, but very often, when we were soberly sat down to Dinner, one Blast of Wind wou'd lay all our Provisions in Common'. In Boston he established a bookstore and warehouse; among his customers were one of the Fellows and some of the students of Harvard College.

In his autobiography, Dunton gives accounts of the people with whom he did business on his return to London. These have proved an invaluable source for the business of publishing and selling books at the end of the seventeenth century. Of William Shrewsbury, whose wife was such an object of desire for Pepys, he records, 'He merits the Name of *Universal Bookseller*, and is familiarly acquainted with all the books that are extant in any Language – He keeps his Stock in excellent Order, and will find any Book as ready as I can find a Word in the *Dictionary*'. With reference to the dangerous publication of Bacon's *Historical Discourse*, he describes John Starkey as 'a brave Assertor of *English Liberties* to his last Breath'. Dunton was not always flattering, however. A bookseller named John Salusbury certainly crossed him, for he is described as 'a desperate Hypergorgonick *Welchman* – He wou'd dress as it were in Print, only to have the Ladies say, *Look what a delicate Shape and Foot that Gentleman has* – He was a Silly, Empty, Morose Fellow – He had as much Conceit, and as little Reason for it, as any Man that I ever knew'. Perhaps the reason for this animosity was that Salusbury started up a periodical, *The Flying Post*, in competition with the *Athenian Mercury* and was suspected of trying to steal Dunton's texts.

Dunton also recorded biographical sketches of printers, bookbinders, and even his authors. Henry Booth is described as 'a very great Man, and one that deserved well of his Country: he asserted the English Liberties with Noble Zeal, and never carry'd his Point by Noise and Tumult, but by Prudence and the Strength of Argument'.[13] Henry's son George, 2nd Earl of Warrington, might well have begged to differ with the choice of the word prudence. When he inherited Dunham in 1694, it was described as 'in rotten condition and very barely furnished with worn-out goods', while the whole estate was crippled by debts. Thereafter he decided to avoid public office and to expend his energies on reviving the fortunes of Dunham for the sake of future generations.

In 1702 George Booth married Mary Oldbury, the heiress of a London merchant who brought him a fortune of £40,000. Marriage between City wealth and landed families was relatively unusual at this period, and this particular experiment in social integration turned out to be disastrous. One witness to the marriage recorded that 'they lived in the same house as absolute strangers to each other at bed and board'. Despite this, they did produce one child, Mary, who became the apple of her father's eye and the founder of the dynasty that he so desired. According to Warrington, his wife taunted him with her coarse behaviour, driving at breakneck speed through Altrincham Fair and upsetting the stalls, and attending athletic games and 'cracking rude jokes with the young men'. His contribution to the literary world was to publish anonymously in 1739 a book snappily entitled *Considerations Upon the Institution of Marriage, With some Thoughts Concerning the Force and Obligation of the Matrimonial Contract. Wherein is Considered, how far Divorces may, or Ought to be Allowed. By a Gentleman* . . .

George Booth used his wife's dowry to rebuild in plain Georgian style the existing Tudor house at Dunham Massey, and laid out the surrounding parkland in the formal geometric style pioneered by Le Nôtre, Louis XIV's gardener at Versailles, in the course of which he planted over 30,000 trees. In the south-west corner of the first floor of the house he created a private suite consisting of the Library, an ante-room known as the Instrument Room, and a reading room, the Oak Room (Plate II). This is an intimate, cabinet-style library, harking back to the seventeenth century, when men would retire into their private domain to read, write letters and attend to business, as opposed

20 George Booth, 2nd Earl of Warrington, with his only child and heir, Lady Mary Booth depicted in a double portrait by Michael Dahl. Lady Mary Booth is holding a piece of music by Purcell.

to the grand, much more public room such as that designed by Robert Adam at Kedleston Hall in Derbyshire.

To enter the Library at Dunham is to be shot back to the first half of the eighteenth century. The books belonging to the 1st and 2nd Earls and Mary Booth are lined up on the oak shelves, with their leather and gilt bindings, and the monogram and earl's coronet stamped on their spines. Here and there are books still in their paper wrappers, as they would have been displayed in a bookshop, before being bound for the individual customer. On display are three astronomical instruments: an orrery, an armillary sphere and a reflecting telescope, made for Lord Warrington by Thomas Wright, instrument-maker to George II. All these components might be found in the library of a gentleman of scientific bent, but above the fireplace hangs something unique – a carving of the Crucifixion after Tintoretto by the great wood-carver, Grinling Gibbons. He was working on this, his earliest known piece, in a cottage in Deptford when he was discovered by the diarist John Evelyn in 1671, and his fortune was made. George Booth must have acquired it some time in the 1730s and, given his Protestant principles, placed it in the Library rather than the Chapel.

In his dedication to the writings of George Booth's father, John de la Heuze wrote of his pupil:

> You have become in a little time a great Master of several Languages, and most of Philosophy, and I may say without flattery, that your Lordship hath Genius, Learning and Piety enough to make one of the Best and most Accomplish't Gentlemen in England; But yet more Quality requires something more; for it is not enough for one in your Lordships High Station to be a Humanist, Geographer, (and I may add) a Good Man too; he must also be a States-man and a Politician.[14]

Flattery aside, George Booth, 2nd Earl of Warrington was clearly well read and his books reflect this. When an inventory was drawn up at his death in 1758, the compiler recorded that the Library contained, 'A Great Number of Usefull Books'. The choice of the term 'usefully' is interesting; a distinction was drawn between books that were practical and those that were curious. The Duchess of Northumberland did just this when she visited the library at Kedleston in 1766, describing in her diary the books there as well chosen rather than curious. Curious or rare books were the domain of book collectors such as Sir Hans Sloane, and Booth's near neighbour, Samuel Egerton of Tatton Park, who travelled the Continent in quest of fine antiquarian books.

As in many libraries of this period, religious and devotional books make up a high proportion of the collection at Dunham, with titles such as Jeremy

Taylor's *The Worthy Communicant*, 1686, Thomas Comber's *Short Exercises on the Common Prayer*, 1701, and John Kettlewell's *Death made Comfortable*, 1722. This last title contains the bookplate of Mary Booth, who appears to have been pious in much of her reading matter. Among her devotional books is a 1700 edition of Richard Allestree's very popular *Art of Contentment*, and William Beveridge's *Private Thoughts upon Religion and a Christian Life*, 1715, with a note in the front that it was given to her by her mother, an interesting contrast to Booth's caustic characterisation of his wife. There are many bibles in the Library and elsewhere in the house, including Brian Walton's massive Polyglot Bible of 1657.

The Booths, long established in the locality and acquiring Dunham in the fifteenth century, were very conscious of their place in Cheshire society. The 1st Earl owned a copy of Sir William Dugdale's *Baronage of England*, 1675–6, which includes the Booth family pedigree that was probably compiled on one of the author's occasional visits to Dunham as Norroy King of Arms. Sir Peter Leycester, who had a substantial book collection at his house nearby, spent much of his time on the history of Cheshire, and his *Historical Antiquities*, published in 1673, is at Dunham, alongside Daniel King's *The Vale Royal of England or County Palatinate of Chester,* 1656. There are books on heraldry, including John Guillim's *A Display of Heraldry*, 1633. The law is well represented: landowners at this period needed to be well-versed in property rights, but in addition George Booth was highly disputatious, quibbling over his father's will and immersing himself in the finer points of matrimonial contract in order to write his book. He would therefore have had plenty of use for the folios of statutes and books of civil and common law that fill two presses.

The presence in the Library of the 2nd Earl's scientific instruments show his interest in geography. Among his books is John Harris's *The Description and Use of the Globes, and the Orrery,* 1731, containing annotations, presumably by Booth himself. Perhaps the most magnificent book is the massive set of Blaeu's *Geographica* published in Amsterdam in 1662, with hand-coloured maps and plates of the observatory of the great Danish astronomer, Tycho Brahe. Another sumptuously illustrated book from Amsterdam is Andreas Cellarius's *Harmonia Macrocosmica*, 1661. The Booths were lords of the manor of Warrington in Lancashire, the home of Warrington Academy, established in the eighteenth century, which gained the reputation of being one of Europe's seats of learning, in effect England's third university, teaching science as opposed to the classical education offered at Oxford and Cambridge. The Academy was a Dissenting institution, with teachers such as Joseph Priestley returning after receiving their education abroad. Warrington was also the centre for probably the most important eighteenth-century academic press outside London and Oxbridge, that of William Eyres.

However, this was almost certainly lost on the Booths at Dunham because of the religious divide.

Some of the 'Usefull Books' in the Library could be associated with the 2nd Earl's recreation of the house, gardens and parkland at Dunham. For architecture, he had Colen Campbell's *Vitruvius Britannicus,* 1717–25, and Giacomo Leoni's edition of Palladio, 1715, plus bird's-eye views of other gentlemen's houses with Joseph Smith's *Nouveau Théâtre de la Grande Bretagne,* 1724. For the garden, he had T. Langford's *Plain and Full Instructions to Raise all Sorts of Fruit-Trees,* 1696. For the estate, he owned a hardy perennial, Sir Hugh Platt's *Diverse New Sorts of Soyle not yet Brought into any Publique use, for Manuring both of Pasture and Arable Land,* 1594, and slightly more up to date, Sir Richard Weston's *Discourse of Husbandrie used in Brabant and Flanders,* 1652.

Mary Booth seems to have been interested in cookery; in the Library is a copy of Charles Carter's *The Complete Practical Cook,* published in 1730. Illustrated with the most elegant engraved table plans of the period, it shows how entire meals can be laid out *à la française* – all the dishes for one course produced at the same time. Although Carter called it 'practical', the emphasis of the book was upon entertaining in style, and was aimed at the mistress of the house rather than the cook working in the kitchen. Mary also kept her own recipe books in superb hand, and these too date from the 1730s. The recipes are sophisticated and show an interest in the latest culinary fashions. There are, for instance, Indian recipes: 'for the Exact Composition for Pickled Mangoes, as practised in East Indies, which serve for Cucumbers'; and 'A pickle in Imitation of Indian Bambook', where elder stooks could substitute for bamboo shoots. The Georgians had a passion for puddings, and one recipe uses green tea as a flavouring for creams, another is for ice-cream, flavoured with fresh fruits. In unromantic contrast comes the copy of *The Universal Directory for Taking Alive and Destroying Rats,* published in 1768 by Robert Smith, 'Rat-Catcher to the Princess Amelia'.

Because the Dunham Library is such a remarkable survival, it is maddening that we do not know the identity of the booksellers, or where they were located. As Earl of Warrington, George Booth regularly attended the House of Lords, over the years renting various lodgings in Soho and around Piccadilly, and thus had access to the capital's bookshops. His account books record his London expenses – the amount of tips he gave the doorkeeper of the House of Lords, purchases of tea and sugar, the cost of hiring sedan chairs, but no trace of books.

Booth could as easily have purchased his books through an agent based in London, or from booksellers closer to home, for times were changing. The capital's publishers were dependent on provincial booksellers to make commercial sense for their ventures, and the expansion of the English language market, helped by increasing levels of literacy, was important for their survival. Apprentice stationers would come up to London to be trained, returning to set up as booksellers in their own towns and using their former masters as their contact for the books which their customers had ordered, or which they required for stock. These books would be supplied to them at trade rates. Samuel Johnson set down the kind of discount given to a country bookseller in a letter written in 1776 to the Vice-Chancellor of Oxford concerning a London agent for the university press. For a book published in London, the warehouseman would expect 5 per cent of the published price, the wholesaler 7.5 per cent, the country bookseller would then take 17.5 per cent, and absorb the transport costs rather than pass them on to the customer. Bookselling has always been a precarious business, so many country tradesmen spread their risk by also selling insurance, lotteries, stationery and medicine. For example Robert Whitworth, printer of *Whitworth's Manchester Magazine*, inserted the following advertisement on 24 June 1740:

> where only is to be had, the Right Daffy's ELIXIR, the best sort of which was never sold under 15d a bottle; and where also may be had the Right STOUGHTON's Elixir, BATEMAN's Pectoral Drops and Plain Spirits of Scurvy Grass, Bibles and Common Prayer Books, Maps and Pictures, Stamp'd paper and parchment, paper and pocket books for Devotion and the Sacrament, and all sorts of Bookseller's and Stationer's Wares; Books bound; money for libraries or small parcels of books, and the best Spanish and Scots snuffs, of such flavour as to please the most nice.

By the early eighteenth century London publishers were producing catalogues that served both country booksellers who needed information about new books, and private book buyers. John Worrall made this clear in his *Annual Catalogue* of 1738, writing in the preface that it was 'principally intended for those Gentlemen, Ladies & who live remote from London, or seldom see the multitude of Newspapers wherein Books are advertised'. In 1763 Thomas Mortimer compiled the first trade directory of London, abandoning the original idea of specifying publishers' chief books under their name and address because of the complexities of the copyright system. Thus when John Murray, founder of the great dynasty of publishers, bought the business of William Sandby in October 1768 and set himself up at 32 Fleet Street, there was a well-established network for trade between the capital and the rest of the country.

Murray hailed from Edinburgh and his first career was in the marines, providing him with a wide network of contacts. When he set up as a bookseller he offered himself as an agent to provide country customers with books, and as a 'correspondent' for provincial booksellers, to search out titles ordered by their customers. These contacts are revealed in the letter-books that survive from the 1770s and 1780s. He wrote to the Manchester bookseller John Haslington in 1779, asking him to set up an account via Mr Clarke and advising him that he had sent the books ordered from his catalogue 'by wagon from the Blossoms Inn'.[15] He did much business with booksellers in Scotland, not only finding London books for them but also exchanging published titles. Thus he wrote to William Creech in Edinburgh in 1782, 'If you are inclined for an exchange, I am willing to give you the following books for some equally good'.[16] The appended list included James Thomson's *Seasons*, 3s, the poems of Thomas Gray, 2s 2d, and William Boutcher's *Treatise on Forest-Trees*, 10s. Two years earlier, Creech had frustrated Murray by publishing a translation of the pioneering book of natural history by the French Enlightenment author, the Comte de Buffon, without considering him as a partner. To the translator of the book, William Smellie, Murray wrote, 'It is surprising that my friend Mr Creech did not fix upon a publisher in London for Buffon. It is also more wonderful that there should be any difficulty fixing this point.'[17]

Vital to the development of the provincial book trade was the spread of coffee-houses. The first recorded outside London opened in Oxford in the 1650s – indeed it has been claimed as earlier than any in the capital. Many early examples were located in seaports, as they provided ideal places for the exchange of news on arrival: Exeter, Plymouth, Yarmouth, Harwich, and Bristol all had coffee-houses in the seventeenth century. Dublin was particularly rich in them according to the bookseller John Dunton, so too was Chester. The first record for Liverpool comes in the diary of Squire Blundell, who bought a periwig in the Exchange Coffee-house in 1707. The earliest coffee-house in North America was established by Boston merchants in 1670, soon followed by others, including the London Coffee-house opened in 1690 by the Puritan Benjamin Harris. He had run a bookshop next to the Royal Exchange in London, so combined the selling of imported books and coffee with publishing almanacs. He also started a monthly newspaper, *Public Occurrences*, which was soon suppressed by the Governor because he lacked a licence. The first coffee-house in New York appeared in 1696, opened by John Hutchin at the Sign of the King's Arms on Broadway just north of Trinity Church. He took the London model, a large room lined with booths, commanding views over the river and harbour.

As the web of coffee-houses spread across Britain and America, so provincial newspapers and journals followed, stimulated by the lapse of the Licensing Act in 1695 and the migration of printers from London. The *Leverpole Courant* was founded in Liverpool in 1712, seven years later Manchester got its first newspaper, *News from Abroad, or the Manchester*

Weekly Newsletter, Containing the Freshest Advices; both Foreign and Domestick. By 1730 there were about twenty provincial papers in England; by the end of the century this had risen to forty-nine. Almost all the news was taken from London papers, with publishing days tied to the arrival of mail coaches. London publishers recognised that these journals provided an excellent vehicle to publicise their wares in the form of advertisements.

Coffee-houses were also the venue for public auction sales, where booksellers took the opportunity to sell off their stock of both old and new titles. John Dunton, for instance, sent over to Dublin 'ten tuns' of books in July 1698 for three distinct sales in Dick's Coffee-house, causing embittered squabbles to break out among competing Irish booksellers. In London in the early part of the eighteenth century these sales usually started at 8 o'clock in the morning, running through to 6 o'clock or when all the books had sold. Reflecting the calendar of commercial activity of luxury trades, they tended to be concentrated in the winter season. In mid-summer sales were often held outside the capital; perhaps the most famous was at the Sturbridge Fair near Cambridge, which dated back to the Middle Ages and was described by John Bunyan as 'Vanity Fair' in *The Pilgrim's Progress*. Trading took place in crops, wool and textiles, but also in luxury items such as perfumes, millinery and books. The bookseller Edward Millington was particularly skilled at conducting auctions and was celebrated for his patter. An auction held at Cook's Row, Sturbridge Fair in 1704, is described by 'London Spy', cleverly parodying Millington's style, so that his voice echoes over the centuries:

> Here's an Old Author for you, Gentlemen, you may Judge his Antiquity by the Fashion of his Leather-Jacket; herein is contain'd for the Benefit of you Scholars, the Knowledge of every thing Written by that Famous Author, who thro' his Profound Wisdom, very luckily discover'd that he knew nothing. For your Encouragement, Gentlemen, I'll put him up at Two Shillings, advance three Pence; Two Shilling once: What, no Body Bid? . . . Knock, and now you've bought him, Sir, I must tell you, you'll find Learning enough within him to puzzle both Universities. And thus much, I promise you further Sir, when you have Read him Seven Year, if you don't like him, bring him to me again, in Little Brittain, and I'll help you to a Man shall give you a Shilling for him to cover Band-Boxes.[18]

The book auctions at Sturbridge no doubt flourished because of its proximity to Cambridge and the university, but sales were held all over the country. Often they were arranged to coincide with the meeting of the Assizes, when gentlemen were in town, for the gentry and clergy were inevitably the best potential customers. In Liverpool in February 1758, the press of people

21 Sutton Nicholls' early eighteenth-century satire of a book auctioneer in the guise of an advertisement announcing a book sale. This was to be held in Moorfields, an area of open ground just to the north-east of the City of London. Among the titles offered here is *Mr Ogilby's Book of Roads*, a book purchased in London by Young Ben Browne of Townend (see p. 78).

attending the auction of 'A Valuable Collection of Books' was so great that the floor gave way under their feet, with everybody except the auctioneer plunging into a deep cellar. The auctioneer saved himself by holding on to a Welsh dresser attached to the wall, and when rescued still had a copy of *Sherlock on Death* (William Sherlock, the prolific producer of sermons) clutched in his hand. Luckily nobody was seriously hurt and the sale took place the following week.

Michael Johnson not only had his bookshops in Lichfield, Uttoxeter and Ashby, he also took stalls for use on market days in Birmingham and Uttoxeter. In James Boswell's *Life*, Samuel Johnson recalled with shame how as a self-conscious boy he refused to help his father on his stall. Selling books at market was an important part of the provincial book trade, and London booksellers took to the road to sell direct to retail customers and to deal wholesale with other sellers, a practice that gradually fell off presumably as the provincial trade gained in strength and opportunities decreased. John Dunton in his autobiography singles out William Shrewsbury as the 'only *Bookseller* that understands *Fair-keeping* to any advantage'.[19]

Book auctions were not confined to towns, however. On 30 April 1707 at Low Fold, a farm at the southern end of Troutbeck, a village then in Westmorland in the heart of the Lake District, a sale was held of the effects of James Cookson and Christopher Birkett, recently deceased. This included all kinds of works from light reading to serious devotional works. Christopher Birkett was the father of Elizabeth, second wife of Benjamin Browne of Townend in Troutbeck. That day Benjamin bought twenty-three books, including five of sermons, six in verse, and a sharp satire on Mary of Modena, the Roman Catholic Queen of James II, entitled *The Amours of Messalina*.

The Brownes were a statesman family, not in the political sense but as estatesmen or yeomen farmers, holding land by 'customary tenure', a system peculiar to the Border counties and giving an unusual degree of independence. The first member of the family recorded at Townend was George Browne who was living there by 1525; the last, Clara Jane, of the thirteenth generation, died in 1943 and the house passed to the National Trust. As a result of this continuity the books collected by the Brownes over the centuries have survived in the house, while family papers, including details about their purchase, are now held in the record office in Kendal. This in itself is remarkable, but so too is the fact that the library at Townend represents not the collection of a rich bibliophile or an aristocratic family, but of middle-ranking farmers and later solicitors, clergymen and doctors.

This part of England was certainly remote, for it usually took a week to travel to London. However, it was not remote as far as education and book learning were concerned. When Lady Anne Clifford endowed a hospital for twelve ladies in Westmorland's county town, Appleby, in 1653, she appointed for their maintenance not only a 'mother' but a 'reader' too. This tradition continued: in the eighteenth century, the benefactors' book of the Appleby grammar school library shows that people possessed books to read and recognised the importance of supporting the library. The Westmorland village of

22 The Fire House, or main living room, at Townend in the Lake District village of Troutbeck. Here the Brownes probably read their books by the light of the fire, and with glass bowls filled with water to reflect the candlelight – some of these survive in the house.

Bampton, although small, also had a famous grammar school, which was probably where Richard Hoggart, born in the early 1660s the son of a farmer, was given his good classical education. With his two friends, Thomas Noble and Edmund Gibson, he made the long journey south. Noble and Gibson attended Oxford and prospered, Gibson becoming Bishop of London. Hoggart changed his name to Hogarth, and set up an establishment in the gatehouse of the former priory of St John in Clerkenwell, with this advertisement appearing in a coffee-house newspaper in 1704: 'At Hogarth's Coffee House ... there will meet daily some learned gentlemen, who speak Latin readily, where any Gentleman that is either skilled in that Language or desirous to perfect himself in speaking thereof will be welcome.'[20] Sadly the gentlemen of London were not ready for such an esoteric concept and the coffee-house failed, but Richard did produce a famous son, the artist William Hogarth.

Perhaps Richard Hogarth should have remained in his native county, for coffee-house book groups flourished there, an establishment in Kendal opening in 1760, followed by others in Carlisle, Appleby and Penrith. These normally had a small membership, usually less than twenty, paying an annual subscription. After every member of the group had read a book, it would be auctioned off. Sometimes these groups called themselves literary or reading societies and could restrict themselves to a specific group such as clergymen or physicians. The later eighteenth-century Brownes may well have belonged to such a group. At Townend there is also a catalogue of the circulating library at Kendal, offering about five hundred titles, dating from the 1750s.

The families of Troutbeck sent their sons to their little grammar school, where they too would have received a basic classical education. One of the books at Townend is a Latin textbook: apart from this and a few other school-books, the library consists of works in English. Mark Purcell has identified many of the books that belonged to Benjamin Browne (1664–1748), known as 'Old Ben', and of his son, also Benjamin (1692–1748), 'Young Ben'.[21] The most numerous are religious in nature, reflecting the central importance in daily life of belief. They include popular titles such as Jeremy Taylor's *The Rule and Exercises of Holy Living*, 1680, and Edward Boughton's *A Short Exposition of the Catechism of the Church of England*, 1675. The Brownes were firm Anglicans, hence the purchase at the 1707 auction of the anti-Catholic *Amours of Messalina*, and the presence in the library of *The Reasonableness of the Church of England's Test*, published in 1688 and advocating the exclusion of Dissenters. Richard Allestree's best-selling *Whole Duty of Man* is represented in two editions.

Many of the books are of a practical kind. Young Ben acquired a copy of *The Complete Parish Officer*, published in the Savoy, 1720, which he must have used when serving on the magistrate's bench. In 1706, inhabitants of Border counties would have found of concern the union of the kingdoms of England and Scotland, hence the *Journal of the Proceedings of the Lds Commissioners of Both Nations in the Treaty of Union*, 1706, bought for a penny. For their travels, the Brownes would have undoubtedly used *Mr Ogilby's and William Morgan's Pocket Book of the Roads*. Their edition, published in 1689, provided detailed maps of the main routes out of London to all parts of the country. Old Ben's wife, Elizabeth Birkett, kept a commonplace book, in which she transcribed recipes as well as remedies and aphorisms.

At some time before 1719 Young Ben travelled to London to be apprenticed to a lawyer, copying documents. While he was living in the capital he bought himself several books of literature. An edition of Shakespeare's plays dating from 1714 was bought in 1734. Richard Steele's *The Funeral; and the Tender Husband: Comedies*, 1712, has a note that it was bought by Ben in August 1734. Steele's associate, Joseph Addison, is represented by *Miscellaneous Works in Verse and Prose*, 1726. Ben also acquired an early edition of Montaigne and a 1718 London imprint of the *Arabian Nights*. He also made purchases for his family and neighbours in Troutbeck. For instance, in April 1725 he reported to his father: 'I have gott you a Wood's Institutes of the Comon Law and a Littleton's Dict. 2d. hand but really could not get any that were tollerable

23 The title page of the 1689 edition of *Mr Ogilby's and William Morgan's Pocket Book of the Roads*, from the library at Townend.

under 12s. or 13s. Yet I thought that wich I have sent you is as good as any Now Out for a School Boy they both come in Mr Rowlandsons Box and you have the prices here under written'.[22]

Mr Rowlandson was Richard, Ben's employer in London, and his box appears to have been the means for transporting all kinds to various people in Troutbeck and the neighbourhood, for his brother Thomas was Mayor of Kendal. On 9 September 1725 Browne wrote to his father: 'The many things I have sent in the box I have directed to Mr Thos. Rowlandson vizt. a Book for Lady Fleming and a Toy for Dan and a Silver Thimble for Bridget Atkinson'.[23] The trade was not all one way. In one letter Young Ben asks his father that once Thomas Cookson, a Troutbeck neighbour, has finished with the Psalm Book that he had lent him, to send it up to London with a pair of his stockings. He also asks for the return of another psalm book from Bob the fiddle player, so that he can get it copied and pricked 'Exactly as they Sing in all Churches in London'.[24]

The lending and borrowing was vital for a community that did not have a huge amount of books at hand. Old Ben compiled a list in 1731 of all the books that he had recently loaned to his neighbours, in particular law books that were often used in this litigious area of the country. So, Mr Brigs borrowed 'Hooks Institutes' and Cousin Cumpton took 'Lex Constutionalis'. Robert Cookson and William Benson both borrowed a book on the trial of the regicides, signatories to the execution of Charles I whose fates were particularly gruesome. Mr Greenwood and Cousin Cumpton borrowed 'Culpeper School of Physick & Dr Smith's receipts'.[25]

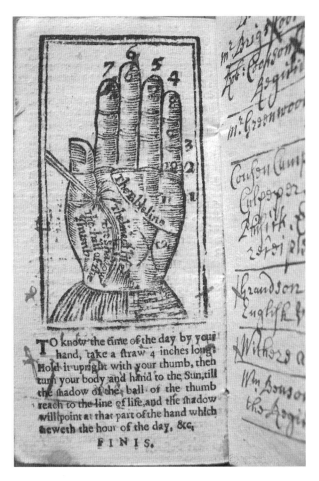

24 Old Ben Browne's diary for 1731, kept in an almanac. The left-hand page suggests a way of using the hand as a sundial, useful for telling the time out in the fields with no benefit of a pocket watch. Browne used the right-hand page to list the various people to whom he lent books, including 'Cousin Cumpton'.

Kendal, fifteen miles away, had two booksellers, Miles Harrison and Thomas Willan, operating from the 1660s, and after the lapse of the Licensing Act of 1695, the town became a significant centre of provincial printing. Thomas Cotton, an Irishman, set up as a music printer and seller, but he also started a local newspaper, *The Kendal Weekly Courant*, in 1731. Three years later, Thomas Ashburner, 'Bookseller in the Fish-Market' introduced a rival, *The Mercury*. These two papers not only extracted news from the London papers but also promoted local culture, such as plays and horse-races, and advertisements for their bookshops. A copy of one of Ashburner's bookselling catalogues is in the Browne papers, and lists both new books for purchase and 'Ready Money and Books in exchange for Libraries or Parcels of Old Books'. Nearer to Troutbeck was Ambleside, and the Brownes bought books there too, for a volume of accounts compiled by an unidentified tradesman between 1701 and 1709 is included in the archives.

Auctions like the Low Fold sale continued to be a source of purchases. One of the books in the library at Townend, John Downame's *Lectures upon the Foure First Chapters of the Prophecie of Hosea*, published in London in 1608 contains a note to the effect that John Cooperthwaite bought the book for 4d on 27 December 1723 at John Griscoll's sale of books, and then had it bound by William Langholm, Minister at Troutbeck, at the cost of 6d. Catalogues of auctions later in the century show that other yeomen owned libraries similar in size and range.

The books at Townend are now accommodated in the Bower, the sleeping room at the back of the house, where a nineteenth-century Browne installed carved oak bookcases. It would seem, however, that books were not kept on shelves in the eighteenth century, but in the chests and cupboards listed in an inventory produced for Old Ben in 1731. Many of the earlier books have inked titles on their fore-edges, in the style to be seen in *The Great Picture* of Lady Anne Clifford (Plate I). This way of storing books would have been regarded as very old-fashioned by the likes of more sophisticated library owners, such as the 2nd Earl of Warrington and his daughter Mary.

Among the records and papers of Dunham Massey is a catalogue of the library compiled in 1768.[26] It is divided into two parts: the first provides a shelf-list with format, author, title, place and date of publication; the second a list of the books in alphabetical order. In the beautiful copper-plate hand of the period the provenance of the books is rolled out before the reader – the overwhelming majority are from London, with a few here or there from Oxf for Oxford, Cantab for Cambridge, Antwerp, Amsterdam, Paris, Venice and so on. The only English provincial city to be mentioned is Birmingham, for an edition of Virgil by the famous type-founder and printer, John Baskerville. Just one bookseller's invoice has survived among the family papers, dating

(23)

Quarto.

Abregé de la Philosophie de Gassendi — — — — — — Paris 1675.
Bibliotheque des Auteurs Eccles.astique, par Du Pin: 3ᵉᵐᵉ edit.
12 tom relié en 6. Paris 1693.
Magna Britannia: or a Survey of Great Britain. 6 vol. Lond: 1738
Ballard's Memoirs of eminent Ladies — — — — Oxf: 1752.
Enquiry into the Nature of the Human Soul. — — — Lond:
Young's Night-Thoughts &c — — — — — — 3 vol. Lond: 1743
Thompson's Poem on Sickness — — — — — — — Lond: 1745

Octavo.
Mason's Poems — — — — — — — — — Lond: 1764
Cooper's Poems — — — — — — — — — Oxf: 1761.
Wheatley's Observ. on modern Gardening — — — Lond: 1770.
Miscell: Tracks on Education — — — —
Smollet's Travels thro' France & Italy. 2 vol. Lond: 1766.
White's Cases in Surgery — — — — — — — Lond: 1770.
Miscell: Tragedies — — — in the Gallery Room — 4. vol. Lond: 1772.
Miscell: Comedies — — in the Gallery Room. — — 4. vol.
Miscell: Comic Operas — — — — — — — —

Quarto.
Lord Lyttelton's History of King Henry II. — — — — 4 Vol. Lond. 1767
Watson's History of Philip II. King of Spain — — — 2 Vol. Lond. 1777
Philip III. King of Spain — — — — 3 Vol. Lond. 1769
Robertson's History of the Emperor Charles V. — — 2 Vol. Lond. 1777
— — — — of South America — — — — 4 Vol. Lond. 1763
Mrs Macaulay's History of England — — — — 2 Vol. Lond. 1759
Robertson's History of Scotland — — — — — 2 Vol. Lond. 1776
Sir David Dalrymple's Annals of Scotland — — — 2 Vol. Lond. 1764
Swinburne's Travels in the two Sicilies — — — Lond. 1770
Xenophon's History of the affairs of Greece; translated by J. Smith. — Lond. 1770
Manstein's Memoirs of Russia — — — — — Lond. 1770
Rome's abridgment of the History of England — — 8vo Lond. 1795
Hooke's Roman History — — — — — 4 Vol. Lond. 1738
Watson's History of Philip III. King of Spain — — Lond. 1783.
Sheridan's General Dictionary of the English Language — 2 Vol. Lond. 1780.
Falconer's Remarks on the Influence of Climate &c — Lond. 1781.
Marsden's History of Sumatra — — — — — Lond. 1780.
Irwin's Voyage up the Red Sea — — — — — Lond. 1780.
Burgoyne's Expedition — — — — — Lond. 1780.
Cox's Russian Discoveries — — — — — Lond. 1780

25 A page from the 1768 catalogue of the library at Dunham Massey, with the book titles and their imprint details. Later hands have noted additions in the late eighteenth and early nineteenth centuries.

26 Volumes from the library at Townend, with their author, the theologian and mathematician Dr Isaac Barrow, and his titles marked in ink on their fore-edges.

from the autumn of 1759 and addressed to Mary Booth, Countess of Stamford.[27] It was issued by the bookbinder John Leech, for supplying a bible and prayer-books, and for binding William Robertson's *History of Scotland* and an edition of *The Life of Edward Earl of Clarendon*, both published that year. Despite its solitary character, this invoice is significant, for John Leech was a bookseller based in the local town of Knutsford. Other hands have added subsequent acquisitions of the late eighteenth and early nineteenth centuries to the Dunham catalogue, and here too local imprints begin to appear – Newark, Chester, Warrington, Liverpool, Manchester. The provincial book-trade was now in full production.

CHAPTER 4

A FOUNDING FATHER

The Books of Thomas Jefferson

'I cannot live without books', Thomas Jefferson told John Adams.[1] In his lifetime he assembled no less than four libraries. The first was destroyed in a fire at his house, Shadwell, in 1771; the second was sold to the government for the Library of Congress in 1815, and his letter to Adams announced his resolve to start anew; the third was collected up to his death in 1826; and the fourth was developed with his advice in the 1820s for the newly established University of Virginia.

Yet living without books was what Jefferson's forefathers were obliged to do. When he was born on 13 April 1743 at Shadwell in Albemarle County, Virginia, he was part of the fourth generation of his family in America. His great-grandfather, therefore, must have arrived in the colonies some time in the mid-seventeenth century, and Thomas recorded that he came from Snowdonia, in North Wales. Whether he was a gentleman, an indentured servant or a professional of some kind is not known, though the probability was that he fitted into the second or third of these categories.

The frustrations faced by book-lovers living in provincial England in the late seventeenth century are vividly evoked by the correspondence of Sir William Boothby, yet Derbyshire was a stone's throw from London in comparison with the English settlements of North America. When the bookseller John Dunton made his journey to New England in 1685, the voyage westwards took four months with many perilous adventures on the way. London booksellers trying to do business with the colonies had to cope with longer terms of credit, and complicated payment systems. The colonists meanwhile were living in scattered, isolated settlements strung out down the Atlantic coast from New England through the 'middle colonies' to Chesapeake Bay in the south, with a population of Europeans amounting to only 55,000 in 1670. These men and women in their struggle to survive both physically and economically tended to have more things on their minds than reading.

Nevertheless, the determination to acquire books was strong. The New England states were shaped by Protestant ideas and practices that put great emphasis upon revelation through the scriptures and a thorough knowledge of the Bible, so that by 1700 Boston had become the centre of book production and distribution in North America. Book production was at a minimum: almost all the books sold in America at this period were supplied by European booksellers, and almost all of these by London. One of the most prominent booksellers in this field was Richard Chiswell, at the Rose and Crown in St Paul's Churchyard, who also supplied Boothby with some of his books. With the invoices for books shipped out to the Boston merchant John Usher, Chiswell would enclose free copies of term catalogues, thus informing bookbuyers in New England of the latest publications.

There had been an important transfer of learned culture into New England through a generation of clergymen ordained in the Church of England, in particular a group of graduates from Emmanuel College, Cambridge. Realising that more clergymen were needed, Harvard College in Cambridge, Massachusetts, was founded in 1636 and two years later named in honour of John Harvard, a graduate of Emmanuel and a wealthy young minister who left at his death half his estate and all his books to the college. One of the central requirements of the young college was a mastery of Latin, Greek and Hebrew, another a detailed knowledge of the scriptures. This curriculum was recreated in Connecticut at Yale sixty years later by Harvard graduates. However, no seventeenth-century New England printer or bookseller issued any of the learned schoolbooks used in the grammar schools or at Harvard. Students had instead to rely on handwritten texts and borrowed books from patrons, or from overseas. Little wonder, then, that John Dunton made a visit to Harvard from Boston during his stay in the New World in 1685 to try to sell his books and leave his catalogues with the fellows and students.

The original members of the Virginia Company, arriving in Chesapeake Bay in the early 1600s, brought with them bibles and practical books, but the supply then dried up through the lack of a network of entrepreneurial printers and booksellers. It has been estimated that, in all, 20,000 volumes were carried to Chesapeake in the seventeenth century and dispersed among a thousand or more households. Examination of probate inventories of three counties, Surry and York in Virginia, and St Mary's in Maryland, show that most household libraries were small, on average containing between 20 and 100 volumes, and that the larger collections belonged to clergy or doctors. More than half did without books altogether, while many had just the Bible and one or two other volumes, probably religious in subject matter.[2] These patterns show higher book ownership than those pertaining in some parts of England, but lag behind New England.

27 Catalogue of the library at Harvard College in Cambridge, New England, published in Boston in 1723. The production of such a publication had a two-fold purpose: to provide a record of the books already acquired, and to seek out further titles and funds. This copy was sent to Sir Richard Ellys of Nocton in Lincolnshire (see p. 173) probably in the hope that he might leave his fine library to the College. He did not rise to the bait: indeed, the catalogue remained uncut.

Acquiring these books within the southern colonies was no easy matter. Some general stores carried blank books, primers and hornbooks for children attending the 'small schools', but for those who wished to add to their collections, the best hope was to be the recipient of a bequest, to borrow and exchange, or to ask the tobacco merchants who dominated the trade to Europe to bring back specific titles. As in New England, a kickstart was provided by the foundation of a college. In fact the institution had been planned early in the century, even before the foundation of Harvard. James I had ordered his English bishops to raise funds so that the Virginia Company might build a college at Henrico on the James River, just below Richmond. This project was brought to a violent end by an Indian uprising in 1622 that left 347 colonists dead, including the man in charge of the development, and the site annihilated. It was not until 1690 that Anglican clergy proposed a college of three schools, of grammar, philosophy and divinity, with financial support from Virginia merchants. The college of William & Mary duly received its charter from the joint sovereigns on 8 February 1693, and the state capital was moved from Jamestown to Middle Plantation, renamed Williamsburg, six years later.

At the same time, the southern colonies were benefiting from the work of the indefatigable Revd Thomas Bray, founder of the Society for Promoting Christian Knowledge. When he was appointed commissary in Maryland by Henry Compton, Bishop of London in 1698, he learnt of the poverty and isolation of clergy in America, and founded the Society for the Propagation of the Gospel in Foreign Parts. Parochial libraries with collections of about two

28 Bookplate, 1704, of the Society for the Propagation of the Gospel in Foreign Parts. The figure being welcomed with rapture may be the Revd Thomas Bray, who provided many libraries for the North American colonies in the early eighteenth century.

or three hundred books, paid for by English donors, were shipped over to the colonies, supplemented by larger shipments, described as 'provincial libraries', to towns like Annapolis and Charleston. In the course of time the latter became the Charleston Library Society. A similar scheme had been instituted for England and Wales, and although these libraries on both sides of the Atlantic were primarily intended for clergy and consisted mainly of religious books, they were also used by lay people. A delightful bookplate from the Society for the Propagation of the Gospel shows a clerical figure, presumably Bray himself, arriving in America to the joy of the colonists who rush to the shore to greet him.

One of the early students at William & Mary College was Thomas Jefferson's maternal grandfather, Isham Randolph, who became a sea captain. After the death of his first wife, Randolph went to London to find another. Jefferson's mother, Jane, was the eldest child of eleven by this second marriage, born in 1720 in Shadwell, one of the marine hamlets on the north bank of the Thames downstream from the Pool of London. When the family returned to Virginia, Isham Randolph prospered from the slave trade and was able to build a spacious house using a hundred slaves. In 1739 Jane married Peter Jefferson, a great friend of her cousin Colonel William Randolph, and a prominent member of the Virginian gentry. According to Jefferson his father had a strong mind, sound judgement and was a great reader, despite a neglected education. He was chosen with Joshua Fry, the Professor of Mathematics at William & Mary College, to run the boundary line between Virginia and North Carolina, and the map that the two men drew was published in London in 1751. Thomas Jefferson must have been enthralled by his father's tales of exploring the Fairfax Line, the limit of a huge grant from George II to Lord Fairfax, of near starvation conditions, of horses tumbling over precipices, and of killing bears.

William Randolph enabled Peter Jefferson to buy the land in Albemarle County that he coveted, and the plantation was duly named Shadwell, after Jane's birthplace in London. When William died in 1745, the Jefferson family moved to his estate at Tuckahoe on the James River in Goochland County so that Peter could act as guardian to his children, and manage the estates. Thus Thomas Jefferson was raised amid a large household, with many slaves, where he developed an ambivalent attitude toward slavery that was to remain with him throughout his life. While he went to school, his slave companions did not. Later he advocated slaves be educated to 'tillage, arts or sciences', boys until the age of 21, girls until 18, but was never to suggest integration. Jefferson was thus both ahead of his time and of his time.

Thomas Jefferson was educated first at Dover Church and then in Fredericksville, boarding during the week with an Anglican clergyman, James

Maury. Jefferson found this classical scholar both dour and pretentious – Maury claimed to be descended from the French royal family. This encounter may well have fostered Thomas's dislike of clergymen and of the established faith. However, he mastered Greek so well that he was able to read Homer in the original, and so launched his lifelong fascination for the poet. In particular, the adventures of the Argonauts captured his imagination, and Argonauts was his name for the leaders of the American Revolution. His father died in 1757, leaving Thomas his small but select library of forty-two volumes that included works by Addison, Pope, Swift and Shakespeare, Rapin's *History of England* and the account of Admiral Anson's voyage around the world. In his will, he bequeathed his eldest son and heir, 'my mulatto fellow Sawney, my Books, mathematical Instruments & my Cherry Tree Desk and Book case'.

In 1760 Thomas Jefferson entered William & Mary College, and for the first time had the opportunity to use an institutional library. Among his teachers was the Professor of Mathematics and Natural Philosophy, the Scotsman William Small. Jefferson later wrote to a friend that Small was like a father, filling up the measure of his goodness by introducing him to George Wythe, the law tutor, and to Francis Fauquier, the Governor of Virginia. A world of culture and science was being opened up to Jefferson. When Small returned to England to study medicine, he became a member of the Lunar Society of Birmingham, which included men such as Erasmus Darwin, Matthew Boulton, James Watt and Josiah Wedgwood, who would meet at each other's houses on the Monday nearest the full moon to give them the maximum light for travelling. Fauquier was said to have lost his fortune gambling with the circumnavigating Admiral Anson, who out of compassion got him the governorship. Arriving in Virginia in the middle of a hailstorm, he not only used the huge stones to cool his ice and make ice cream, but also measured them and sent an account back to London where it was published in the *Philosophical Transactions of the Royal Society*. Wythe, described by Jefferson in his autobiography as 'my faithful and beloved mentor in youth, and my most affectionate friend through life' was a fine scholar and collector of books. He gave his pupil a wide education, encouraging him to keep a commonplace book, and to collect books for himself. Jefferson persuaded the executors of his father's will to allow him to stay on after matriculation in 1762 so that he could continue with his law studies under the tutelage of George Wythe.

The source of Peter Jefferson's books is not known, but his son, while living in Williamsburg, began to buy books from the *Virginia Gazette*, the leading bookstore in the colony. This had been founded by the Englishman William Parks, born in Shropshire, apprenticed to a Worcester printer, and founder of the *Reading Mercury*. He had arrived in the Chesapeake in 1726, setting up shop in Annapolis. To maintain a living, he combined jobbing printing, binding, publishing *A Compleat Collection of the Laws of Maryland* and establishing the first newspaper of the mainland colonies south of Philadelphia, the *Maryland Gazette*. Returning to London in 1730, he bought up a whole range of books, which he advertised in the *Gazette* on 20 October: '*Lately imported by William Parks, from* London'. These consisted of a combination of spelling books and primers, bibles and prayerbooks and other religious works such as the English version of Charles Drelincourt's *The Christian's Defence against the Fears of Death* and the inevitable *Whole Duty of Man*, a selection that shows what he reckoned would appeal to his colonial customers.

In 1730 he established a printing office in Williamsburg, repeating in essence what he had developed in Maryland, including starting the *Virginia Gazette* in 1736. As well as his printing shop he also opened one or possibly two bookstores. The records of the governing board of William & Mary College noted: 'Mr Wm Parks intending to open a bookseller's shop in this Town and having proposed to furnish the students of the College with such books at reasonable price as the Masters shall direct him to send for and likewise to take all the schoolbooks now in the College and pay 35 p.cent on the sterling cost to make it [local] currency, his proposals are unanimously agreed to.'[3] He was thus buying back textbooks, which he could resell, attracting students to his store. He also built a paper mill, overcoming one of the biggest problems facing printers in the American colonies: the lack of usable paper. Benjamin Franklin, based as a printer publisher in Philadelphia, found him a builder by advertising in his *Pennsylvania Gazette* and shipped off thousands of pounds of rags to make quality paper; in return Parks supplied Franklin with paper.

Franklin also provided some of the books that Parks sold, including a hundred sets of the first American edition of Samuel Richardson's *Pamela*, but this would have been the exception rather than the rule. Franklin himself had a close association with the London publisher William Strahan who had sent his most able assistant, David Hall, out to Philadelphia to work with him. Franklin reported to Strahan that the London bookseller Thomas Osborne was 'endeavouring to open a Correspondence in the Plantations for the Sale of his books' and had sent parcels to bookstores, including William Parks in Williamsburg. Franklin adds, having seen some of the invoices, '[I] observe the Books to be very high-charg'd, so that I believe they will not sell'.[4] Nevertheless Parks did buy books from Osborne, as did his successor at the *Virginia Gazette*, William Hunter. Despite his energy and ingenuity, William Parks only just made a living, and when he died in 1750, his estate barely covered his debts. Hunter, and his successor, Joseph Royle, were both postmasters and found that their postal account along with stationery, the bindery and the sale of their newspaper contributed more in revenue than did their book sales. However, they continued to deal with London booksellers, Hunter with Samuel Birt and Thomas Waller, Royle with William Johnston and for maps and prints with Robert Sayer.

The *Virginia Gazette* daybooks that have survived from the 1760s show that Thomas Jefferson was a good customer: in 1764–5 he purchased thirty-two titles. Nine of these, not surprisingly, were law books, but also included David Hume's *History of England*, William Robertson's *History of Scotland* and William Smith's *History of the First Discovery and Settlement of Virginia*. He was teaching himself Italian, so bought a dictionary. He also acquired poetry, including the works of John Milton, Edward Young and William Shenstone.

Books from London booksellers sold in the *Virginia Gazette* bookstore were inevitably expensive. One way of avoiding this was to order directly from England, and Jefferson certainly did this later in his life. However, there is only one invoice surviving from the 1760s, sent to Jefferson on 2 October 1769 along with a letter from Perkins, Buchanan & Brown in London.[5] This reports that their ship would be in the James River the following March, and solicits Jefferson's consignment of tobacco, in return for any goods that he might require. The invoice is for books ordered and bought through his English agent, Thomas Adams, from Thomas Cadell at the Shakespeare Head in the Strand.

Tobacco merchants played an important part in general trade between England and Virginia, and even sold books through their stores. As a contemporary observer explained to his British readers, local factors had 'large quantities of all kinds of *European* and *Indian* goods, which they expose to sale in shops or house; which in the country go under the name of *stores*'.[6] The records of the comparatively modest firm of Lawson & Semple, trading between Virginia and Glasgow, have survived due to a lawsuit. They show how twice a year their ships sailed across the Atlantic from Port Glasgow to Port Tobacco in Maryland, laden with all manner of goods, including books, and made the return journey with their cargo of tobacco. In London, information about ships leaving and collection arrangements were organised through the colonial coffee-houses, the Pennyslvania Coffee-house, the Virginia Coffee-house and the Carolina Coffee-house, all close to the Royal Exchange. John Murray I, who was a sea captain before taking up bookselling and had a group of customers in North America and the West Indies, left boxes of books at the Virginia Coffee-house to be collected on behalf of Robert Miller of Willamsburg. Miller was a general merchant, with sisters in London who conveyed his orders and payments to Murray.[7]

Book buyers like Robert Miller and Thomas Jefferson would keep themselves abreast of the latest publications from London, Edinburgh and Dublin through the booksellers' printed catalogues. William Strahan sent his catalogues out to David Hall, to be distributed among customers; John Murray sent one of his to Miller, suggesting he showed it to his friends, 'who may perhaps order some Books from it'.[8] Newspapers were an invaluable source, especially periodicals that carried critical reviews. The *Gentleman's Magazine* and its rival, the *London Magazine*, were dispatched to America from the early 1730s, and the two Philadelphia printers, Andrew Bradford and Benjamin Franklin, tried to create their own home-grown periodicals with the *American Magazine* and the *General Magazine*. This fomented a vitriolic quarrel between them, but in the end neither publication prospered. However, the two London magazines, along with a growing number of other titles, supplied the all-important information on the latest books.

The books that Jefferson acquired from Thomas Cadell via Perkins, Buchanan & Brown included several that were useful to his growing political career. In 1769 the young lawyer had become a justice of the peace, lieutenant of the county militia and had been elected by the citizens of Albemarle County to the Virginia House of burgesses. Half of the books were on the history and workings of Parliament, others were works of political theory, including 'John Locke on Government'. But most, if not all of these books went up in flames the following year, when Shadwell was destroyed by fire. The destruction of Jefferson's childhood home marked a watershed. He was already building a new house for himself, on a hilltop overlooking the Shadwell estate. Originally called the Hermitage, it became Monticello, with the new name first appearing in August 1767 when he recorded the inoculation of cherry buds for his new garden in his Garden Book. The house was based on designs from Andrea Palladio's *Four Books of Architecture*, with the service quarters remaining largely unseen so that the building could appear smaller and lighter. The garden and orchard plans evoked the great gardens of England in their informality, but with touches of Italy. To Monticello, still in the process of construction, he brought his new bride, Martha Wayles Skelton, whom he married on New Year's Day 1772.

The library at Monticello was to be in a large room on the second floor of the south pavilion, directly above the parlour. Here he began to rebuild his book collection. Jefferson had been away from Shadwell when the fire broke out, and family tradition has it that his first response on hearing the news was to ask about the fate of his books. In a letter to a college friend, he wrote 'My late loss may perhaps have reached you by this time, I mean the loss of my mother's house by fire, and in it, of every paper I had in the world, and almost every book. On a reasonable estimate I calculate the cost of the books burned to have been £200 sterling. Would to god it had been the money; then had it never cost me a sigh!'[9] It has been estimated from this valuation that the library consisted of between three and four hundred volumes, a substantial collection for a young man in North America at this period.

29 Jefferson's library at Monticello. On the desk is his revolving bookstand, constructed to allow five books to be open simultaneously, probably made to Jefferson's own design.

Some idea of Jefferson's plans for his next collection of books can be seen in a letter that he wrote to his cousin Robert Skipwith on 3 August 1771.[10] Skipwith had asked for a list of books 'suited to the capacity of a common reader who understands but little of the classicks and who has not leisure for any intricate or tedious study'. In response, Jefferson provided a list of 148 titles, together with the address of the London bookseller Thomas Waller and prices to a total of over £100. It gives only some idea of his own intentions, for although it contains many books that were his personal favourites, he is taking account of Skipwith's specific request. Thus, nearly half the recommendations were for works of English literature, a far larger proportion than he would have had in his own library, and included novels by Fielding, Richardson and Smollett that Jefferson never acquired for himself. He recommends only three books of law, 'a few systematical books as a knowledge of the minutiae of that science is not necessary for a private gentleman'. The first of these is Lord Kames's *Principles of Equity* along with three other works by him (see p. 94).

Jefferson had admired the great library created by William Byrd II of Westover. Byrd, who died in 1744, was a wealthy Virginia landowner who received his education in England and become a member of the Royal Society at the age of twenty-two. His library of 3,500 volumes particularly attracted Jefferson because of its broad range, with the conventional collection of Greek and Roman classics, law, divinity and music, but also a rich collection of Elizabethan and Restoration dramatists, many books on architecture, painting, gardening, agriculture and practical works on distilling and cookery. In 1773 Jefferson noted in his Memorandum Book the number of volumes in the Westover Library, 3,482, and an estimated total price of £1,219 18s. On the next page he appears to have calculated how much money he could raise by the sale of his own books, 669 volumes valued at £219. It is astonishing that in only three years he had acquired so many. However, it was not enough to enable him to buy Byrd's library, though in the following years he did acquire individual titles from this source, and his collection was built very much along the lines of Westover.

At the same time as the changes in his private life, Jefferson's political career was rapidly developing, spurred on by the deteriorating relations between the colonies and Britain. He was not a skilled public speaker, but his erudition and eloquence with the pen brought him great respect among his contemporaries. When the First Continental Congress was called in 1774, he wrote 'A Summary View of the Rights of British America'. As he explained much later, 'The Summary view was not written for publication. it was a draught I had prepared of a petition to the king, which I meant to propose in my place as a member of the Convention of 1774. being stopped on the road by sickness, I sent it on to the Speaker, who laid it on the table for the perusal of the members. it was thought too strong the times & to become the act of the convention, but was printed by subscription.'[11] This closely reasoned statement of colonial grievances has been compared to the 95 Theses of Martin Luther in its passion. Therefore it was to Jefferson that his fellow revolutionaries turned to draft first the 'Declaration of the Causes and Necessity of Taking up Arms' in July 1775, and then the American Declaration of Independence of 4 July 1776, with its unforgettable 'life, liberty and the pursuit of happiness'.

Thomas Jefferson found great personal happiness in his marriage to Martha, the daughter of John Wayles, a prosperous slave merchant. When Wayles died in 1773, his heirs made the fatal decision to divide his estate before liquidating the claims from British merchants, which then got tangled up in the outbreak of the Revolutionary War, a move that was to cause financial problems for Jefferson for the rest of his life. Martha bore Jefferson six children, but her pregnancies were not easy and only two daughters, Martha known as Patsy, and Mary known as Maria, survived to maturity.

In June 1779 Jefferson was elected War Governor of Virginia. He was reluctant to accept, and was right to have reservations. Lacking effective constitutional powers, he failed to prevent the invasion by a British expeditionary force that drove the government out of their temporary quarters in Richmond and obliged him to take flight from Monticello. His resignation from the governorship in 1781 marked both a nadir in the state's history, and in his own career. On top of this, his wife's health was failing. At this time of despair he turned to writing his *Notes on the State of Virginia*. This was inspired by a series of twenty-two questions about the new United States posed in September 1780 by François Barbé-Marbois, secretary to the French minister in Philadelphia, and sent out to governors and dignitaries. Barbé-Marbois received only two replies, one couched in a desultory language, the other, by Thomas Jefferson, providing three hundred pages of information. A combination of guidebook, encyclopaedia, and philosophical treatise, it has been described as the agenda for the American Enlightenment.

Jefferson's interest in the writings of both Scottish and French Enlightenments is shown in the list of books he recommended to Robert Skipwith. Lord Kames features particularly strongly, including his *Sketches of the History of Man*, in which he organised history into four stages, based on his wide-ranging reading of law, history and geography. The four-stage theory that saw man developing from hunting and fishing, through pastoral and nomadic, to agricultural and commercial pursuits was taken up by William Robertson, Principal of Edinburgh University in his hugely popular *History of the Reign of Charles V*, which also features on Jefferson's list. Another title appearing there is Thomas Reid's *Inquiry into the Human Mind*. Reid, appointed Professor of Moral Philosophy at the University of Glasgow in 1764, had been shocked by David Hume's argument that human beings needed to be guided through a reality that is ultimately unknowable. As Benjamin Disraeli put it a century later, 'Few ideas are correct ones, and which they are none can tell, but with words we govern men'.[12] Reid thought that this was nonsense, and what was needed was common sense. The impact of his *Inquiry* in America was enormous, and Jefferson probably took from him the idea of self-evident truths that he put into the Declaration of Independence. One of his successes as Governor of Virginia was to overhaul the curriculum at William & Mary College, basing it on the Scottish model and discontinuing the grammar and divinity schools while establishing chairs in anatomy, medicine, law and police, and modern languages. Thomas Reid was firmly placed at the centre of the new curriculum, while David Hume was left out. Another tenet of the Declaration of Independence was the pursuit of happiness. Jefferson probably took this from the teaching of Francis Hutcheson, founding father of the Scottish Enlightenment alongside Lord Kames. As Professor of Theology at Glasgow, he had promulgated the philosophy of moral altruism, 'action is best, which produces the greatest happiness for the greatest number'. Strangely, his great work *A System of Moral Philosophy*, published posthumously in 1755, is not on the Skipwith list.

Although Jefferson was influenced and inspired by the writers of the European Enlightenment, he also disagreed with some of their theories, especially those that deduced the backwardness of the New World. In *Notes on the State of Virginia*, he took issue not only with the historical theories of the Scot William Robertson, but also with those of the French *philosophe*, the Abbé Raynal, and those of the naturalist Comte de Buffon, which maintained that America, having emerged later than other continents from the Flood, was doomed by nature to degeneracy.[13] Raynal wrote that America had never produced one good poet, one able mathematician, or one man of genius in a single art or a single science. With regard to the good poet, Jefferson responded, 'When we shall have existed as a people as long as the Greeks did before they produced a Homer, the Romans a Virgil, the French a Racine and Voltaire, the English a Shakespeare and Milton; should this reproach be still true, we will enquire from what unfriendly causes it has proceeded.'[14]

He also argued that education should be provided not on the basis of privilege and wealth, but for all. While Voltaire could write of the rabble being 'apt for every yoke' and not worthy of being enlightened, Jefferson declared in a letter to George Wythe, written from Paris in 1786, 'I think by far the most important bill in our whole code, is that for the diffusion of knowledge among the people. No other sure foundation can be devised for the preservation of freedom and happiness. If anybody thinks that kings, nobles or priests are good conservators of the public happiness, send him here. It is the best school in the universe to cure him of that folly.'[15]

Jefferson was able to observe European Enlightenment or otherwise at first hand by becoming American Minister at the French court. Martha Jefferson died on 6 September 1782, and in his grief Thomas decided to return to political life. Originally it was intended that he should join the delegation at the Paris peace talks, but this was postponed when news arrived that negotiations had been successfully concluded, and Britain recognised the independence of the United States of America. Despite the political and personal upheavals of the last decade, Jefferson had been assiduously adding to his book collection: indeed, membership of the Continental Congresses had given him direct access to the bookstores of Philadelphia. One of the attractions of accepting the diplomatic appointment in Paris was the chance of getting direct access to the bookshops of Europe too.

After a slow start, the southern colonies had become great importers of books. In 1770 more books were exported annually from England to the American colonies than to Europe and the rest of the world combined, and 40 per cent of these went to Virginia. Trade continued throughout the

Revolutionary War, albeit at a lower level. In December 1778, the Edinburgh bookseller Charles Elliot wrote to Mr Colebourn Barrel, one of his private clients in New York, to apologise for the disruption in his book order, as the ship could not sail due to 'the Rupture with France'.[16] With peace restored in 1783, the trade resumed with a flourish. There were many complexities, and the letter-books of Charles Elliot and John Murray tell of misunderstandings, confiscation of cargoes and non-payment of debts. Some clients could be very difficult; the Charleston Library Society became notorious for its demands. When in January 1786 Charles Dilly was given the unwelcome news that the Society had dismissed their London bookseller William Nicoll because he had 'not served them with that Punctuality which the Spirit of their Society required' and that he had been elected instead, his response was to decline to serve them at all.[17] John Stockdale, Jefferson's London bookseller and publisher, was later dismissed after only one attempt to serve the Society. In a letter of protest he pointed out, 'Many of the Articles tho' trifling in price, were the most difficult to procure and were only to be got by accident as they came into the trade from private persons, for this reason my Clerks and myself have traversed the streets of London from Bookseller to Bookseller I firmly believe an hundred times over at least.'[18]

Jefferson finally arrived in Paris in August 1784. Thirty years later he recalled his book-collecting activities there: 'While residing in Paris, I devoted every afternoon I was disengaged, for a summer or two, in examining all the principal bookstores, turning over every book with my own hand, and putting by everything which related to America, and indeed whatever was rare and valuable in every science. Besides this, I had standing orders during the whole time I was in Europe, on it's [sic] principal book-marts, particularly Amsterdam, Frankfort, Madrid and London, for such works relating to America as could not be found in Paris.'[19] Jefferson frequented the bookshops of the Palais Royal, but his spiritual home was the Left Bank, the traditional centre of the Parisian book trade, with its stationers, printers, engravers, as well as booksellers, many of them located along the Quai des Grands Augustins.

He particularly liked dealing with J-F. Froullé at his shop on the corner of the Rue Paveé leading from the Quai, and recommended him to James Monroe when he set out for Paris ten years later: 'I can assure you, that, having run a severe gauntlet under the Paris book-sellers, I rested at last on this old gentleman, whom I found, in a long & intimate course of after dealings, to be one of the most conscientiously honest men I ever had dealings with.'[20] But not all the booksellers in Paris satisfied him. Barrois, who traded in the Rue de Hurepoix at the far end of the Quai, wanted to publish Jefferson's *Notes on the State of Virginia*. Jefferson was always a rather reluctant author, preferring to publish anonymously, but was forced to agree in this case as a pirated edition

30 Portrait of Thomas Jefferson painted by the young American artist, Mather Brown. This is the first known likeness of Jefferson, who sat for Brown during his brief visit to London in 1786. Brown painted a companion portrait of John Adams, depicting him with Jefferson's *Notes on the State of Virginia.*

was being threatened. He found Barrois a shifty character to deal with, and there was a long dispute over the map to be included, which was based on Peter Jefferson's work of 1751, before the French edition was published in 1786.

The dispute with Barrois was made more complicated by the fact that *Notes* was being published in London too. Jefferson's publisher there was John Stockdale, whose shop was in Piccadilly, one of the highways of the eighteenth-century book trade. Benjamin Disraeli recalled his father Isaac describing how in the late 1790s 'when literary clubs did not exist, and when even political ones were very limited and exclusive in their character, the booksellers' shops [in Piccadilly] were social rendezvous. Debrett's was the chief haunt of the Whigs, Hatchard's, I believe, of the Tories'.[21] From the mid-seventeenth century, many London booksellers, who were usually also publishers, had been highly political in a complicated matrix of Tory and Whig, Established Church and Dissenters, that became even more complicated in the late eighteenth century with divided opinions concerning such issues as the revolutions in America and France, the abolition of slavery, parliamentary reform and Catholic Emancipation. Several booksellers were sympathetic to the American colonists in their grievances, and even supported their fight for independence. William Strahan, Franklin's friend and publishing partner, was based just off Fleet Street; Joseph Johnson, the radical Dissenter who published Franklin and was a prime mover in Thomas Paine's *Rights of Man*, had his shop in St Paul's Churchyard; the Dilly Brothers, Charles and Edward, who specialised in works about America, traded at the sign of the Rose and Crown, 22 Poultry. John Almon, however, opened his shop in fashionable Piccadilly, near the Pall Mall residence of his patron, Richard Grenville, Earl Temple, and the gentleman's clubs of St James. From his shop a pamphlet war was waged against the government of Lord Bute by Temple, Pitt the Elder and John Wilkes.

Almon also became a specialist in American tracts including the first London edition of John Dickinson's *Letters from a Farmer in Pennsylvania*, published in 1768. Dickinson, 'the Penman of the Revolution', went on to write *Late Regulations Respecting the British Colonies*, one of three landmark works published by Almon and printed by William Strahan; the other two were Arthur Lee's *Appeal to Justice* and Thomas Paine's *Commonsense*. So associated was Almon with the American revolutionaries that when the Duke of Grafton was asked the numbers of their forces during a debate in the House of Lords, he suggested applying to Almon for the information. From 1774 to 1780, Almon employed John Stockdale as his porter or shopman, so that Stockdale witnessed all the political upheavals at first hand. Stockdale was not a bookseller by training: his father was a blacksmith from Cumberland, hence a cartoon published by Thomas Rowlandson in 1784 showing Stockdale hammering a folio on his anvil.

At Almon's retirement in 1781, his bookshop at 178 Piccadilly passed to John Debrett, while John Stockdale took over the premises almost next door,

31 Jefferson's London publisher, John Stockdale, in a cartoon of 1784 by Thomas Rowlandson. Unlike most London publishers and booksellers, Stockdale did not serve a printing apprenticeship, but was the son of a Cumberland blacksmith, hence the volume on the anvil.

and also inherited several of his authors. One of these proved a lucky break for Stockdale. Thomas Day, a member of the Lunar Society and a barrister, wrote the very successful children's book *The History of Sandford and Merton* which was published in three volumes between 1783 and 1789. As an admirer of Rousseau, Day introduced the doctrine that many are made good by instruction and the appeal to reason in a series of episodes in which the rich and objectionable Tommy Merton is contrasted with the upright and tender-hearted Harry Sandford, the son of a farmer. Eventually Tommy is duly reformed. Day was a highly eccentric character, who determined to select a girl from an orphanage and train her to be a perfect wife. Unfortunately his Galatea married his friend John Bicknell instead. But Day and Bicknell worked together on a poem about the iniquities of slavery, *The Dying Negro*, which was republished by Stockdale.

Many Americans came to London to read for the bar, and the Middle Temple had become a centre for aspiring lawyers from the southern states. Through Day and this network, some of these got to know Stockdale and his bookshop. John Adams, albeit a lawyer from Massachusetts, was one of Stockdale's authors and when he brought his son Quincy to London, they lodged over the shop at 181 Piccadilly. When Adams became the first official American minister resident in London in 1785, he wrote to Jefferson from Grosvenor Square, 'I shall go this morning to Stockdale to talk with him about sending you the newspaper and pamphlets'.[22] Jefferson began to order books from Stockdale, including a whole consignment of books for James Madison, President of William & Mary College back in Virginia. Stockdale was here being used as an agent, getting books not only from London booksellers but also from Scotland. Many books came as a result of the voluminous catalogues issued by James Lackington, but as he did not extend credit, Jefferson expected Stockdale to sort out the account (p. 121).

In March 1786 Thomas Jefferson paid a visit to London. This, his only stay in England, lasted just over six weeks. One of his less successful forays was to the Court of St James, where John Adams was to introduce him to the King. When George III turned his back on them both, Jefferson wrote that the British 'of all nations on earth . . . require to be treated with the most hauteur. They require to be kicked into common good manners.'[23] However he visited several English gardens, and indulged in shopping, including for books. John Adams in his diary noted that he walked to the booksellers, Stockdale, Cadell, Dilly, Almon.[24] He probably meant Debrett, as Almon had retired, and although he does not specify Jefferson was with him, he was surely there.

On 20 November Stockdale wrote to Jefferson in Paris, asking him to obtain a copy of the French edition of Thomas Day's *History of Sandford and Merton*, which had been translated by Arnaud Berquin, a well-known author of children's books. He went on to report that two French gentlemen had called upon him with a copy of *Notes on the State of Virginia* with a view to having it printed. Stockdale had for some time been asking Jefferson to allow him to produce an English edition, and this finally pushed him to make a decision, again fearful of a pirated edition becoming available. Stockdale duly published *Notes* after considerable effort, for Jefferson provided him with detailed instructions: 'By the diligence of tomorrow I will send you a corrected copy of my *Notes*, which I pray you to print precisely as they are, without additions, alterations, preface, or any thing else but what is here.'[25] The English edition appeared in February 1787.

Isaac D'Israeli was right to point out the conviviality of bookshops. Joseph Johnson used to give three o'clock dinners in St Paul's Churchyard, with guests such as William Godwin, Mary Wollstonecraft, Thomas Paine and the artist Henry Fuseli. Debrett's shop was known as the gathering place in the middle of the day for fashionable people and the place for political and literary conversation. Thomas Payne, who became Jefferson's London bookseller, described his shop in Castle Street near the Mewsgate in Leicester Fields as a 'Literary Coffee House and Bookseller combined', and this tradition was continued by his assistant John Hatchard when he set up for himself in Piccadilly, with a table for newspapers by the fireside, where readers often fell asleep, and a bench provided outside for the cabmen. Booksellers thus expected to develop a friendship with their authors, and Jefferson did so with Stockdale by becoming his scout in Paris, buying Berquin's books for children so that Stockdale could publish English editions. Back in Paris, he also discussed with Pissot, Benjamin Franklin's French publisher, plans for reprinting English classics in collaboration with a Basle printer. To undercut prices in England, and even Ireland, he sent specimen pages to Philadelphia in the hope that Franklin's grandson, Benjamin Franklin Bache, might serve as Pissot's American distributor, thus also neatly helping literary relations between France and America at the expense of England.[26]

* * * *

In September 1789, just two months after the fall of the Bastille, Thomas Jefferson left a highly charged Paris to return to the United States and to a highly successful political career that saw him as Secretary of State, Vice-President to John Adams, and in 1801 becoming President himself. The seat of government was moved from Philadelphia to Washington, where President Jefferson stayed in a boarding house while the Capitol was built. As Gouverneur Morris wrote to a French friend, 'We only need here houses, cellars, kitchens, scholarly men, amiable women, and a few other such trifles, to possess a perfect city.'[27]

Over these years, Jefferson was assiduously building up his book collection. In Philadelphia he bought from a whole series of booksellers, including Dufief, Reibelt Roche and Patrick Byrne. John Stockdale was replaced by Thomas Payne as his English bookseller, but Froullé continued to provide him with books from Paris. Van Damme was his bookseller in Amsterdam, while his former assistant William Short acted as his agent in Madrid. Jefferson bought up libraries while he was in Paris, and continued to do so on his return to America. As a distinguished bibliophile, he was approached to be a subscriber, and his correspondence shows that he often took up the offer. As a man of power and influence, he was also given many books by authors, and his courteous thank-you letters also feature in his correspondence. In 1806 he received the unexpected bequest of the library of George Wythe, his 'faithful and beloved mentor'. Wythe died under mysterious circumstances, probably poisoned by a great-nephew jealous at his intention to leave some of his property to a putative mulatto son. So, by 1812 Jefferson had one of the great private libraries of the United States, with over 6,000 books.

By 1812 too, the United States under President James Madison was at war again with Britain, much to the dismay of Jefferson who had already expressed his view that 'one war was enough for the life of one man'.[28] He was doubly dismayed, therefore, when an American force set fire to the Parliament Building in York (now Toronto) in Upper Canada, destroying archives and the library, inspiring the British to seek revenge. In September 1814 the British army burned both the White House and the Capitol Building in Washington, destroying the congressional library. Jefferson's immediate reaction was to

32 A selection of Jefferson's books in the Library of Congress. In the foreground are the letters of Cicero with dual language text and a handwritten emendation by Jefferson.

suggest paying incendiaries in London to set British buildings on fire, but his more measured response was to offer his own library as a replacement, on condition that it be taken in its entirety, and that he should be paid at a price based on the valuation made by Congress.

The idea of a library for Congress had begun in 1774 when members of the First Continental Congress had secured borrowing privileges from the Library Company of Philadelphia, an agreement that continued in 1789 when the First United States Congress was provided with access to the New York Society Library. It was recognised that this could only be a temporary arrangement, and a formal foundation was established in 1800 when the capital was moved to Washington. On 24 April President John Adams signed the transfer bill that included legislation for a Library of Congress, with $5,000 assigned for the purchase of books and a suitable apartment to contain them. The library's first home was in an upper room of the new Capitol Building, and in 1802 Jefferson, now President, offered his thoughts on what it should contain to the head of the committee responsible for its establishment: 'I have prepared a catalogue . . . in conformity with your ideas that books of entertainment are not within the scope of it' and avoiding 'those desirable books ancient and modern which gentlemen generally have in their private libraries, but which can not properly claim a place in a collection made merely for the purpose of reference'.[29]

The important question was whether the new Library of Congress should be a practical working library, a 'public library' for members, like the subscription libraries to be found in cities, or a national library to serve the federal government in Washington and to act as a cultural and historical archive. In 1800, the 'public library' option was chosen. One English bookseller sent 152 titles in 740 volumes delivered in hair trunks, which he thoughtfully suggested were more useful than boxes, as they might be resold. By 1812 the library had increased to 905 titles in 3,000 volumes, almost all printed in England and sent over, although the most expensive purchase was Diderot's *Encyclopédie* in 35 volumes, bought from Paris for $216. This was the collection that was destroyed by the British in 1814.

Jefferson's motives in offering his library were undoubtedly mixed. From a purely practical view he was now seventy-one years of age, and deeply in debt. His library was counted by a committee from Congress, who estimated 6,487 volumes, valued according to size, $1 for octavos and duodecimos, $3 for quartos, $10 for folios, making a total of $23,950. When he received this sum, Jefferson used two-thirds of it to pay off his outstanding debts. However, there were also ideals involved. Jefferson felt that a new country needed a fine library, and favoured the third option offered in 1800, of a collection that mirrored the great European national libraries.

The concept of a national library grew out of the princely libraries of the Renaissance: Milan, Florence, Naples and Rome before 1500, and later, Paris, Munich, Vienna, Heidelberg and the Escorial.[30] England was slow off the blocks. In 1556 the bibliophile Dr John Dee wrote a 'Supplication . . . for the recovery and preservation of ancient Writers and Monuments' addressed to Queen Mary Tudor. He suggested that by diligent searching he could find 'the remnants of such incredible store [from the dissolved monasteries], as well of Writers Theological, as in all other liberal Sciences might be stored'. Dee offered to enrich this 'Library Royal' with printed books from Europe and manuscript copies of the best works from 'the Vaticana in Rome, S.Marci at Venice, and likes at Bonomia, Florence, Vienna'.[31] The Queen rejected it, probably on terms of cost, and instead Dee in his Thames-side house of Mortlake created his own great library, which he threw open to scholars, politicians and merchants. It can be argued that England's first 'national' library was the Bodleian in Oxford, opened in 1602. Sir Thomas Bodley's description of his foundation was 'The Publique Librarie in the Vniversitie of Oxford', and it was intended from the beginning to be generally accessible, allowing graduates and 'sonnes of Lordes' by right, and any 'gentleman stranger' might apply to study. This, of course, means that it was generally accessible to the cultured and the well born.

The same applied to the British Museum Library, which opened in 1759. Members of the public, escorted by a member of staff, could only view the collections and anybody wanting to study in detail had to obtain a ticket. Although the Keeper of the Reading Room resented the duty of attending to needs of readers, the poet Thomas Gray was a regular visitor, describing to a friend how, 'I regularly pass four hours in the day in the stillness and solitude of the reading room, which is uninterrupted by anything but Dr Stukeley the Antiquary who comes there to talk nonsense, & Coffee house news; the rest of the Learned are (I suppose) in the country, at least none of them come there except two Prussians, and a man who writes for Lord Royston'.[32] The British Museum became a very different institution with the new Copyright Act of 1814 that enforced properly the system of legal deposit, and with the donation of George III's magnificent library, given by his son, George IV, in 1823. It is a fine irony that Thomas Jefferson and George III, at odds in so many different ways, should have provided the basis for their national libraries.

Jefferson's offer of his library to Congress was received with modified rapture. Political opponents pointed out that the country was at war, and that many of the books seemed beyond the needs of a congressional library. One outspoken critic, Cyrus King, argued that Jefferson's books would help to disseminate his 'infidel philosophy' and were 'good, bad and indifferent, old, new, and worthless, in languages which many can not read, and most ought

33 A drawing in pen and ink by Andrew Jackson Davis and Stephen Henry Gimber of the Library of Congress in 1832. The Library, with Jefferson's collection, had opened eight years earlier in the west front of the rebuilt Capitol Building in Washington.

not'.[33] The vote was very close, only a majority of ten, but the House of Representatives agreed to the purchase.

Jefferson supervised the packing up of the books. By that time they were kept in a library created under the central dome at Monticello, in separate modules that could be detached to form portable bookcases. These were taken down, face boards nailed across, and loaded in one of ten wagons, before being set on a six-day journey to Washington. Jefferson had originally classified his books in a similar manner to his recommended reading lists. Thus his list for Robert Skipwith had been divided into nine headings, beginning with Fine Arts, going through to Natural Philosophy and History, and ending with

Miscellaneous. However, by the time of the transfer to Congress, he had adopted a classification based on the division of knowledge devised by the seventeenth-century philosopher Francis Bacon, whom Jefferson greatly admired. The first division was into memory, reason and imagination, and Jefferson then further divided this into forty-four subjects. The Congress librarian refined the forty-four, locking them into a printed catalogue that froze the classification system for a hundred years and created much confusion among librarians and students. On Christmas Eve 1851 a fire, not this time caused by the British, broke out in the Library, destroying two-thirds of Jefferson's collection. The Library is currently seeking to reassemble what remains of Jefferson's library as it came to Congress.

Although the Monticello library went to Washington, Jefferson was not entirely bereft of books as he had a 'petit format library' at Poplar Forest, his plantation near Lynchburg where he spent several weeks each year. While in Paris in 1786 he had dislocated his wrist, and found that books in the larger format of folios and quartos were difficult to use. In his precise instructions to Thomas Payne in 1788, he told him never to send a folio or quarto if a smaller edition existed, saying he liked a handy size, which had the additional benefit of being cheaper and taking up less room. He very much admired the little reprints of classics published by the London bookseller John Bell, collecting his editions of *British Poets* and of the works of Shakespeare (p. 206). Now Jefferson began to build up another library at Monticello, telling John Adams that the books acquired for it would be for amusement rather than practical use.[34] Adams introduced him to George Ticknor, a graduate from Dartmouth who was about to depart for Europe, and Jefferson was able to use him as his book-buying agent there. Ticknor, for instance, acquired for him the fine editions of classics produced by German publishers.

At Jefferson's death in 1826, his 'retirement library' had grown to 931 titles, consisting of some 1,600 volumes. In addition, he became involved in the foundation of the University of Virginia in Charlottesville, a long cherished project, into which he threw himself with gusto. He surveyed the site himself, laid out the stakes, and worked on the blueprints with the architects, selecting for the library a rotunda based on the Roman Pantheon. He planned the curriculum and selected the faculty, bringing in many scholars from Europe, and writing that the university would 'be based on the illimitable freedom of the human mind. For here we are not afraid to follow truth wherever it may lead, nor to tolerate error so long as reason is left free to combat it.'[35] His pride in the university was reflected in the epitaph that he wrote for himself: 'Author of the Declaration of Independence, and of the Statute of Virginia for Religious Freedom, and Father of the University of Virginia.'

34 The title page of the first volume of the poems of Edmund Spenser, 1778, in the series *Poets of Great Britain* published by John Bell. When Jefferson ordered books from his London bookseller, Thomas Payne, he particularly requested Bell's reprints, as they were cheap, small and thus took up less room, and were easy to hold with his weakened wrist.

When John Adams heard that Jefferson's library was to pass to Congress, he wrote to him, 'I envy you that immortal honour'.[36] There may have been a touch of irony in this, as the two had endured some very difficult times, falling out over both public and private matters, and Adams himself had a very fine

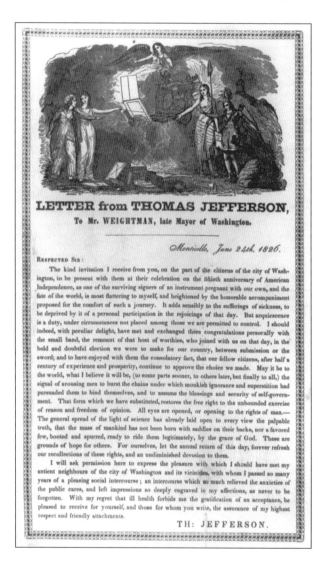

35 A printed version of Thomas Jefferson's last letter, written to the Mayor of Washington expressing regret at not being able to attend the fiftieth anniversary celebration of American Independence. Jefferson actually died on the day of the anniversary. His letter was incorporated into a broadside allegory, with Liberty showing the art of printing to the four continents. In the foreground a pile of volumes with a scroll celebrates pioneer printers.

library. However, in their last years their friendship was mended and underwent a late blossoming as they wrote to each other about their books and their views on writers from Plato to modern times. The two bibliophiles and founding fathers, Thomas Jefferson and John Adams, died on the same night, fittingly the fourth of July 1826.

CHAPTER 5

BUILDING A LIBRARY

The Books of Sir John Soane

When news of the death of Sir John Soane was announced on 20 January 1837, he was one of England's leading architects whose works included great national institutions such as the Bank of England, country houses, the exquisite mausoleum at Dulwich and his own home in Lincoln's Inn Fields. Fellow of the Royal Academy and of the Royal Society, knight of the realm, he was a man of wealth and status. But this was not how the story had begun, for he had been born plain John Soan in humble circumstances some eighty-four years before.

The *Encyclopaedia Britannica*, although a product of the Scottish Enlightenment, declared chillingly in its essay on education: 'let the youth who is born to pass his days in this humble station be carefully taught to consider honest, patient industry as one of the first of virtues. Teach him contentment with his lot by letting him know that wealth and honour seldom confer superior happiness.'[1] Soane challenged this concept of knowing one's place through his acquisition of knowledge and book learning. With his highly developed awareness of his own place in history, he built up a fine collection of not only books, but also the memorabilia connected with them, creating a unique archive that he bequeathed to the nation along with his house in London. As a result, we have an incredibly detailed knowledge of how he bought and acquired his library. But the encyclopaedia's message carried with it an Icarus-like warning about the fruits of wealth and honour, and Soane indeed reaped the harvest of quarrels and unhappiness in both his professional and private life.

John Soan was born on 10 September 1753, probably in Basildon in Berkshire, although the baptismal record has not survived. His father, also John, was a bricklayer by trade, who seems to have suffered some kind of financial crisis, plunging the family into sudden poverty. Soane, when he came to write his memoir that was published privately in 1835, was reticent about his early life, so we do not know how he came by his education, although his own generosity to the 'deserving' and implacable hostility towards the 'undeserving' suggests that he might have benefited from some kind of charity. He also reinvented himself, for in 1784 he added the 'e' to his name, and even corrected almost all his earlier signatures to conform to this.

John Soan had four surviving siblings, and examination of some of his earliest books shows that literature was circulated among them. Thus the flyleaf of George Fisher's *The Instructor or Young Man's Best Companion*, published in London in 1760, bears the inscription: 'J Soane [e added] 1767/Susannah Soane [e added] her Book./Given her by her Brother J.Soane [e added]/given him by his Sister Deborah Soan; who/died July 13, 1766 aged 22yrs 5 mo 3 days &/was buried in Upper Church Guildford/in Surry/July 27, 1767.'

It is interesting to compare John Soane's early experiences with those of William Cobbett, the political journalist and writer, born ten years later in Farnham in Surrey, the son of a modest farmer. In his autobiography, which was much more revealing than Soane's, he described how, working as a gardener at Farnham Castle, he set off to see Kew Gardens, 'with only thirteen half pence in his pocket'. In Richmond, he spotted a copy of Jonathan Swift's *A Tale of a Tub* priced 3d in the window of a bookseller: 'The title was so odd, that my curiosity was excited. I had the 3d, but, then, I could have no supper.' Buying the book, he went hungry, but read until it grew dark. Despite the Latin tags and literary allusions which flew over his head, Cobbett found Swift's satire against various Christian churches made such an impact, that it provided 'a birth of intellect' that he never forgot.[2]

We shall never know whether John Soane experienced such a Damascene moment, but he certainly had a predilection for books. His family, recognising this, set about providing him with an education beyond that enjoyed by his brother and sisters. Richard Altick, in his classic work *The English Common Reader*, paints a dismal picture of the school system, still recovering from the damage inflicted by the Civil War: 'By the end of the seventeenth century the old idea of "degree" had hardened into a rigid pattern of social attitudes, and everywhere there was an intensified awareness of status.'[3] The rich and well born could enjoy the attentions of private tutors and governesses or attend public schools. Grammar schools continued to provide a traditional classical education, but their quality varied enormously, and only the better-endowed institutions were able to send their cleverest pupils to Oxford and Cambridge. Most boys had to accept an abbreviated education in primary or petty schools, where the prevailing notion was to maintain the status quo by providing a dull regime. Daniel Defoe called this 'the great law of subordination': to tempt the poor to rise through their own efforts was both morally sinful and politically dangerous.

The bookseller James Lackington, who was to number John Soane among his customers, gives a vivid description of the kind of educational opportunities on offer to the poor in his autobiography.[4] He was born in Wellington, Somerset, in 1746, the eldest of eleven children. His father was a shoemaker who eventually took to drink, but luckily James, at the senior end of the family, was able to go to school for the sum of twopence per week. 'I was put for two or three years to a day-school, kept by an old woman; and well remember how proud I used to be to see several ancient dames lift up their hands and eyes with astonishment, while I repeated by memory several chapters out of the New Testament, concluding me, from this specimen, to be a prodigy of science.'[5] In the end he had to leave, still not able to read, because his mother could not afford even this small sum. Lackington was rescued from illiteracy by the Methodists, as were many people in eighteenth-century England. With the help of one of the sons of the shoemaker to whom he was apprenticed, he learnt his letters, improving his reading with study of the Bible and John Wesley's hymns and tracts, all read by the light of the moon as candles were not permitted.

In view of his later life, it could be argued that Lackington was exaggerating his humble origins, but the experiences of many others run in a similar vein. For instance, Soane's close friend, John Britton, described his schooling in his autobiography. The son of a Wiltshire baker, he was brought up in the little village of Kington St Michael, where he recalled no newspaper or magazine was purchased until 1780 when the Gordon Riots in London were talked about and wondered over. Recalling his various teachers, he wrote of being placed under one schoolmistress whose ostensible business was 'to teach the young idea how to shoot' although their practice was chiefly to keep children 'out of harm's way'. He learnt 'the "Chris-cross-row" from a horn-book, on which were the alphabet in large and small letters, and the nine figures in Roman and Arabic numerals'.[6] With the help of this aid that dated back to the Middle Ages, he was launched into the world.

In the light of this, John Soane was exceptionally lucky in his schooling. He was sent to a private school in Reading run by William Baker, described by a contemporary as 'of great classical and mathematical learning'. Here he certainly learnt the basics – mathematics, literature, and probably Latin too. In his collection there are two Latin textbooks, one faintly inscribed J. Soan, 1767, on the flyleaf. By coincidence, Thomas Frognall Dibdin also received some of his education from Baker and his son-in-law John Man, and recalled in his *Reminiscences* how his 'bibliomania' was inspired by the sackfuls of books available at his school (p. 169).

With the death of his father in 1768, Soane moved in with his older brother William in Chertsey. William was described by E.W. Brayley in his *History of Surrey* as an 'illiterate and ill-conditioned elder brother . . . who plodded through life as a petty bricklayer', and depicted John crouched at the foot of the ladder reading a book rather than acting as his hod-carrier.[7] This is a very unfair description of William, who may have been lacking in letters but certainly could read and write, passing on to his younger brother books on mathematics and calculation, such as John Robertson's *Compleat Treatice of Mensuration*, published in 1765. Even better, like a fairy godfather, he introduced him to James Peacock, surveyor and right-hand man of the architect George Dance the Younger, and at the age of fifteen John was employed in Dance's office. At this time, Dance maintained both his house and office on the corner of Moorfields and Chiswell Street, in the part of London now known as the Barbican. He had just inherited his father's post as Clerk to the City Works, and had become a founder member of the newly formed Royal Academy, one of five architects amongst thirty-six. Fortune was smiling upon Soane, for Dance was convivial, a good musician, and had a fine library.

It is difficult to assess exactly what John Soane's status was in the household. The main source is Joseph Farington, who was gossipy and spiteful about Soane, and claimed that his job was to clean the shoes. This may be true, as Soane must have started in a 'low capacity' but such was the thoughtful generosity of George Dance that he was soon helping him with his first commission beyond the City of London, the remodelling of Pitshanger Manor in Ealing for Thomas Gurnell. With his strong sense of history, Soane was to buy Pitshanger in 1800 from descendants of Gurnell, and deliberately retained Dance's work there to commemorate his loyalty to the man who had lifted him from obscurity.

Dance helped Soane to refine his draughtsmanship and the latter's growing confidence in his architectural drawings can be traced. Some idea of his training at the time may be deduced from a programme devised probably by James Peacock. Entitled *Essay on the Qualifications and Duties of an Architect*, and published in 1773, it was designed to exonerate Dance, who was in trouble over inferior materials substituted by a mason working on Newgate Prison. This recommended a liberal education between the ages of five and fifteen in drawing, mathematics, classics and French, followed by two or three years as an articled apprentice to an eminent architect who would teach the rules of architecture, a training supplemented by other masters in the fields of mechanics and mensuration. Some lessons in French were also proposed to help later in travels, for after initial training, it was advised that, 'the Youth now makes the Tour of France and Italy, etc., inspects all the ancient Remains

I Detail from the 'Great Picture' of Lady Anne Clifford, showing her at the age of fifteen in 1605. She rests her hand on a book of music, with a lute propped up against the table. Portraits of her tutor, the poet Samuel Daniel, and her governess, Mrs Anne Taylro, are depicted above the top shelf. Some books are on the shelves, more are piled up on the floor. Little slips of paper inserted into the fore-edges give the titles, which include religious works, Sir Philip Sidney's *Arcadia*, Ovid's *Metamorphoses*, the works of Geoffrey Chaucer and of Edmund Spenser, John Gerard's *Herball* and William Camden's *Britannia*.

II The library at Dunham Massey, with the 2nd Earl's scientific instruments in their glazed cases and, over the fireplace, Grinling Gibbons's carving of the Crucifixion after Tintoretto. The library steps date from the early nineteenth century.

III The Book Room at Wimpole Hall, Cambridgeshire, which Soane designed in 1806 for Philip Yorke, 3rd Earl of Hardwicke. The style of the room provides a strong contrast to the intimate gentleman's cabinet library at Dunham Massey, although Soane's austere lines also make it different to the relaxed family room at Calke Abbey (p. 157).

IV 'Advantages of a Modern Education' by Charles Williams, published in 1825. The cook, who should know her place and the reading matter appropriate for that place, is immersed in one of Scott's novels *The Heart of Midlothian*. On the shelf pious works such as Isaac Watts' *Hymns*, *The Whole Duty of Man*, and Bunyan's *The Pilgrim's Progress* are covered by a spider's web, while the unheeded pot boils over on the range and the household pets run amok.

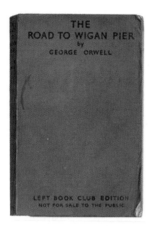

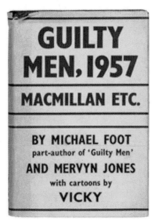

V Titles from Victor Gollancz. George Orwell's *The Road to Wigan Pier* proved a bestseller when it appeared as a Left Book Club choice in March 1937. *Whose Body?* was Dorothy Sayers' first book, published in 1923 by Fisher Unwin who were bought up by Benn, for whom Gollancz worked at the time. He worked on her subsequent books, and always felt she was 'his' author. The edition shown here is the fifteenth impression, issued in 1962.

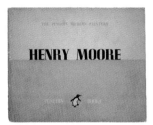

VI A selection of early Penguins, showing the wide range implemented by Allen Lane. His Penguin Modern Painters series was particularly pioneering. Under the general editorship of Kenneth (later Lord) Clark, the first title appeared in 1944 with *Henry Moore* by Geoffrey Grigson, followed by *Duncan Grant* by Raymond Mortimer and *John Piper* by John Betjeman. *Flowers of the Woods* was a 'King Penguin', published in 1946 as a reprint of a nineteenth-century text.

The Daily Telegraph

Cheltenham Festival of LITERATURE

Friday 7th to Sunday 16th October 1994

VII The Cheltenham Festival of Literature does not escape entirely from the satirical sting of Ralph Steadman's pen - even in its own advertisement. The barely discernable festivalgoer, wearing a rather jaunty hat, is literally scrambled with excitement. A staid Regency building transforms into a rollercoaster, and a quote from Beckett jostles alongside the opening of a child's story. It evokes the breadth and inclusiveness of today's literary festivals, as well as the public frenzy that star authors can now ignite.

of Architecture . . . the works of the Moderns, compares them with the ancient Works, marks their difference, and improves upon both in his own Designs'.[8]

This programme of course reflects the education enjoyed by well-connected and financed young architects like Dance himself, while John Soane was setting off from a standing start. What Soane did derive from the essay is the maxim, 'Use every Opportunity to improve yourself; let nothing curious in any of the polite Arts or Sciences escape you, that is likely to be of the least Utility'.[9] On his very small salary, Soane began to buy books, which reflected his compulsive desire for self-improvement both professionally as an architect and personally in his social life. Thus in 1769 he acquired Hawney's *The Compleat Measurer* that would help him to calculate prices and quantities of construction materials, and John Ward's *The Young Mathematician's Guide*. For the development of his intellectual tastes, he bought *The Philosophical Grammar*, a Greek grammar by Sir John Holmes, works by Virgil and Ovid, and Peter Magnant's *The French Scholar's Assistant*, inscribed with the date 1772. These were relatively inexpensive. Costly architectural treatises, some of the most expensive books on the market, must have been outside his grasp, although he did own a copy of *A Parallel of the Antient Architecture with the Modern* by Roland Fréart de Chambray.

Probably at Dance's instigation, Soane applied to become a student at the Royal Academy schools, and began attendance in October 1771. Based in Old Somerset House on the Strand, the schools were free, financed by annual exhibitions, with the King meeting any deficit. Architectural students, exempt from the academic drawing exercises, worked in the offices of their practices during daytime and went to lectures and to the library in the evenings. Sir William Chambers, as Treasurer, provided funds for the books that he felt were appropriate in the library. Soane was thus able to attend lectures on Monday evenings in winter by the Professor of Architecture, Thomas Sandby, and to use the resources of the library to transcribe passages from the architectural books that were beyond his purse.

The following year, 1772, he moved from Dance's office to that of the eminent builder, Henry Holland. According to his own account, this transfer was to provide him with the practical knowledge possessed by Holland, and was done with George Dance's 'approbation'. As was his wont, Farington put a nasty gloss on this: 'Soane the architect was foot Boy to George Dance, who encouraged an inclination He discovered in him for Drawing. The remembrance of his former situation in *Dances Office* among the young men, rendered his situation rather unpleasant. He removed to Holland the Architect and was his Clerk'.[10] In fact, this was an upward step for Soane, for he was paid an annual salary of £60, which was about the same as clerks could hope to earn in a London merchant's office. Moreover, Holland and his father-in-law, the landscape architect Capability Brown, took an enlightened interest in Soane, allowing him access to their private library, as apparently did other architects such as Robert Adam and Sir William Chambers. This was a very small world, and Soane was clearly a young man with talent. While working under Holland, Soane started to spread his wings. He began his life-long passion for Shakespeare's plays, and in 1777 acquired a volume of dramas by Sir John Vanbrugh. He bought a range of novels: Oliver Goldsmith's *The Vicar of Wakefield*, Samuel Richardson's *Clarissa*, Rousseau's *Julie ou La Nouvelle Héloise* and Smollett's translation of Le Sage's *Gil Blas*.

In 1776 Soane won a Gold Medal at the Royal Academy, making him eligible for a three-year travelling scholarship to Rome, which he gained the following year. He wrote later of his departure to Italy: 'Oh it was a bright day, it flew on wings of down!'[11] In fact his adventure could have ended before it even began, for he left England just as war was breaking out. Laurence Sterne had a similar experience, writing in *A Sentimental Journey through France and Italy*, 'I had left London with so much precipitation that it never entered my head that we were at War with France, and . . . that there was no getting there without a passport.'[12] Arriving in Rome on 2 May, Soane used contacts provided by Dance, and visited the English Coffee-house in the Piazza di Spagna. There he met Frederick Hervey, Bishop of Derry.

Hervey, who later became 4th Earl of Bristol and therefore known to posterity as the Earl-Bishop, was an extraordinary character from a family of eccentrics. Perhaps he might best be described as a tease: when a rich living fell vacant in his bishopric, he invited the fattest of his clergy to a rich dinner, then proposed they should race for the living. Not only were the unfortunates forced to run on full stomachs, but the course was along the sands. Du Prey, in his study of Soane's time in Italy, felt that Hervey held genuinely friendly feelings for Soane.[13] He gave him a copy of Palladio that bore his episcopal arms tooled in gold on the binding and Soane inscribed in it, 'From the Bishop of Derry to J. Soan [Soane later added an 'e'] at Rome, Octr 1778'. At about the same time, he also presented him with a copy of Bernardo Galliani's 1758 translation of Vitruvius's *De Architettura*.

Both these very generous gifts were motivated by a desire to instruct the young architectural student in the true ways of taste as propounded by the ancients and by Andrea Palladio. Allured by eating fresh mullet with the Bishop amid the ruins of the temple of Apollo in the villa of Lucullus during their visit to Sicily, Soane assumed that in the future he could count on his patronage. But all this pleasure was to prove a snare. When he came to write his *Memoirs*, Soane wrote, 'Experience had now taught me how much I had overrated the magnificent promises and splendid delusions of the Lord Bishop of Derry. I was keenly wounded, depressed in my spirits, and my best energies paralysed'.[14] In the event, the pretty little Mussenden Temple, perched on the north Antrim coast on Hervey's Downhill estate, was designed by an Irishman, Michael Shanahan, and his extraordinary rotunda mansion of Ickworth in Suffolk was built to the drawings of the Italian architect, Mario Asprucci. Soane lost not only the commissions but also money that he could ill afford, but he did recognise the Earl-Bishop's gesture of the books, for in a portrait painted by William Owen in 1804, Hervey's copy of Vitruvius is depicted in the background.

Other contacts made during his stay in Italy, however, were to prove fruitful as far as commissions were concerned, so that on Soane's return to England, he began to acquire an architectural practice. He also acquired a wife: on 21 August 1784 he married Eliza Smith, niece of the City builder, George Wyatt. Not only was she experienced in the ways of the building trade, but she was educated and intelligent. After her death, the *Gentleman's Magazine* carried an

36 Portrait of John Soane painted by William Owen in 1804. Soane holds his copy of Antoine Desgodets' *Les Edifices Antiques de Rome* at the page showing the Temple of Vesta at Tivoli. In the background the artist has depicted the edition of Vitruvius given to Soane by Frederick Hervey, Bishop of Derry, during his stay in Italy.

obituary describing her vivacity and literary talents – 'a letter writer scarcely excelled by a Sevigné, a Woolstoncraft or a Montagu' – as well as her ability to hold her own and offer decisive and informed opinions at the dinner table, surrounded by 'eminent artists, literati and men of science'. Moreover, 'what are usually termed the fashionable elegancies of ladies, she despised: for she justly remarked that they were merely calculated to make women the dolls or puppets of men – the playthings and not companions of husbands'.

At first the Soanes, now firmly with an 'e', lived north of Oxford Street, and two sons, John and George, were born to them. In 1789 Soane embarked on his first and perhaps his greatest project – the design of the Bank of England. The trajectory of his good fortune seemed unstoppable when Eliza's uncle George Wyatt died a year later, leaving the young couple independently wealthy. With £2,100, Soane bought the freehold of 12 Lincoln's Inn Fields and, demolishing the existing seventeenth-century house, began to design and build his own home. Lincoln's Inn Fields, located just north of High Holborn, was an ideal centre. It was close to Somerset House, home of the Royal Academy, the Royal Society and the Society of Antiquaries. Equidistant between the City and Westminster, it enabled Soane to visit his various building sites. As regular playgoers, he and Eliza could reach the theatres. Nearby too were coffee-houses and inns. The Architects' Club, which he joined in 1791, met at the Freemasons' Tavern to discuss common concerns, and he was a regular visitor to the Piazza Coffee-house in Covent Garden. Eliza's journals are full of references to shopping in and around Oxford Street, the Strand, westwards to Pall Mall, and eastwards to the City. And, of course, both John and Eliza were excellently based for forays to bookshops.

John Soane kept meticulous notes in his journal account books and his notebooks: book purchases are, for instance, sandwiched between payments to his mother's surgeon and the acquisition of sausages and an umbrella. In the 1790s he did not always specify the names of his booksellers, but after 1800 they are noted carefully, and a picture of his bookbuying can be traced. There are references to more than fifty London booksellers plus a dozen binders, printers and stationers. This, of course, covers a half century of acquisition, but nevertheless is a huge number, a source of wonder that one man should use so many bookshops, but also that there were so many of these establishments in one city. However, John Britton in his autobiography written in 1850, provides a guide to the London book trade concentrated around St Paul's Churchyard and Fleet Street, and mentions many more establishments not patronised by Soane. And of course, there were booksellers in Piccadilly, selling books to Thomas Jefferson and his friends. When William Blake arrived in London in 1800, he was astonished by the number of bookshops, declaring that they outnumbered butchers.[15] This was not quite the case, but

John Pendred in his guide to publishing, *The London and Country Printers, Booksellers and Stationers Vade Mecum*, 1785, listed over 650 businesses in London connected with publishing.

John Britton, following his unpromising start in life, came to London in the late 1780s to serve as an apprentice to a wine merchant based at the Jerusalem Tavern in Clerkenwell Green. His fortunes were changed by meeting a painter of watch-faces who became his mentor, lent and gave him books and introduced him to E.W. Brayley, librarian of the Russell Institution. With Brayley he wrote a penny ballad, 'The Guinea Pig', satirising the guinea tax imposed on hair powder. This was promptly pirated by a noted printer of ballads, who published it with an illustration of a pig by the great wood-engraver Thomas Bewick, and sold 70,000 copies. Despite this hiccup in his publishing career, Britton's partnership with Brayley blossomed, and they went on to produce a prolific number of books, including *Beauties of England and Wales* and *Architectural Antiquities*.

With his friend Thomas Rees, John Britton produced an analysis of the London book trade as it existed in 1850. Rees divided the booksellers into three categories:

> The first comprehends publishers only, whose sale of books was confined to their own property. The second might be designated book-merchants, who were chiefly wholesale dealers, and carried on an extensive and important trade with country booksellers: they were also publishers upon a large scale, both of periodicals, under the designation of magazines and reviews; and likewise works on general literature and science, of the larger and more important and costly descriptions. The third were chiefly retail traders, mostly in old books, but in some instances were publishers of pamphlets, and books of comparatively small expense.[16]

In his first category, he included James Harrison, who took to new heights the idea of dividing books into portions and issuing numbered series. Harrison started with the *Novelist's Magazine*, reprinting popular English novels in octavo with double columns, stitched up in small numbers and published weekly at the bargain price of 6d. He went on to produce *The British Classics*, taking material from journals such as the *Spectator*, the *Tatler*, the *Guardian* and the *Connoisseur*. A man with marketing flair, Harrison offered 12-inch globes to purchasers with his *General Geography*.

In Rees's second category came a familiar publishing name, Longmans, in which his brother was a partner. The firm had been founded *c.* 1726 by Thomas Longman at the Ship and Black Swan in Paternoster Row, prospering with its copyrights in Greek and Latin schoolbooks. With the generations, so

37 A trade card from *c*.1800, listing some of the London booksellers, several of whom supplied books to John Soane.

the name of the house changed – when Britton and Soane were buying their books in the early nineteenth century, it was trading as Longman, Hurst, Rees, Orme & Brown. Unusually the firm had a department of old books, but it also ran a large general wholesale trade supplying country booksellers and foreign markets. Part proprietors and London publishers of the *Edinburgh Review* and with a stable of authors such as Walter Scott, Robert Southey and Tom Moore, Longmans would give dinners and soirées in their Paternoster Row house, inviting all kinds of literary people.

Annoyed by the popularity and effect of the *Edinburgh Review,* John Murray II, with his strong religious and Tory opinions, started to publish the *Quarterly Review* in 1809 from his bookshop at 32 Fleet Street. By 1812 he had moved to 50 Albemarle Street off Piccadilly, where the publishing house continued to trade until subsumed into Hodder Headline in 2002. John and Eliza Soane bought many books from Murray's and among the ephemera in the Sir John Soane Museum are trade catalogues that were bound into some of their publications. These offered general books, such as Walter Scott's *Marmion* at 12s 'printed in the most beautiful manner by Ballantyne', medical books, 'Valuable Guidebooks for Travellers on the Continent' and 'Books of Entertainment and Instruction for Young Persons'. Like Longmans, Murray's had a distinguished list of authors, including Lord Byron and Jane Austen. According to John Britton, 'At the social and friendly board, both at home and abroad [John Murray] manifested engaging conversational powers; and it has been my good fortune to have been repeatedly amused and informed by him, in company with some of the bright literary planets'.[17]

While Longmans and Murray's were now large publishing enterprises, the booksellers in Rees's third category were chiefly retail traders, buying single or several copies of titles at trade price and selling on. The uncoupling of publishing from bookselling was now gaining apace. A bookseller included in this category was Mr William Bent, who from 1773 published an annual *London Catalogue of Books.* He is commemorated today in *The Bookseller,* 'organ of the book trade', where a regular column is provided by Horace Bent. John Walker's activities are also familiar today. He produced the *Trade Auctioneer,* a catalogue of books that had accumulated large stocks. Retail dealers were invited to meet the publishers of these books together with the auctioneer at a tavern, eat an early dinner and then hold the auction – in other words, a remainder exercise.

One of the earliest booksellers used by John Soane was James Lackington. His autobiography, first published in 1791 and taking the form of a series of letters addressed to 'a Friend', records how he, like John Britton, had escaped from rural poverty and found a passion for books. At the annual fair held in Bristol, he came upon a stall of books, including

Thomas Hobbes' translations of Homer, and spent many hours puzzling over the text. Undaunted, he proceeded to buy second-hand books and proudly lists them. Arriving in London in 1773, with 2s 6d in his pocket, he was helped by Methodist contacts to find lodgings in Whitecross Street and to start a shoemaking cum bookselling business in nearby Featherstone Street just south of Old Street on the north-east limit of the City. As with many self-made men, his account of his life emphasises the difficulties of the start: he describes how he and his long-suffering wife went without their Christmas dinner because he had bought a copy of Young's *Night Thoughts*. But soon he was doing very well – his opening stock was worth £5, within six months he had increased this to £25. He moved premises to 46 Chiswell Street, and this is where John Soane may have first bought books from him, for George Dance's office and home were in the same street. Lackington did not think much of this location, 'a very dull and obscure situation; as few ever passed through it besides Spitalfields weavers on hanging days, and Methodists on preaching nights'.[18]

In 1789 Lackington made a third move, this time to a large establishment at the corner of Finsbury Place and Square. In an advertisement announcing the opening, he described it as 'elegant and commodious . . . for such Ladies and Gentlemen as wish to enjoy a literary Lounge, somewhat more retired than a Public Shop will admit of. A communication is opened between the Shop and the ground floor of my Dwelling House'. It was huge, topped by a cupola with a flagstaff where a flag was flown when Lackington was in residence, and 'The Temple of the Muses' and 'Cheapest Booksellers in the World' triumphantly written across the façade. A trade card illustrates the interior that was so spacious that the Yarmouth mail-coach was able to drive around the circular counter that stood in the centre. Clerks are shown serving customers, and behind are staircases leading to a series of 'lounging rooms' and circular galleries under the dome. Around each gallery ran shelves; the higher the shelves, the shabbier the bindings and the lower the prices.

Lackington was clearly a shrewd businessman. In his autobiography he describes the infatuation that customers had for what they perceived as a bargain – the modern equivalent is the person who has 'saved' huge sums by going to the sales. He found that people would buy at auctions held by Christie's books that could be purchased for a quarter of the price from him. He made the bold decision not to give credit for books, and to mark 'in every book facing the title the lowest price that I would take for it, which being much lower than the common market prices, I not only retained my former customers, but soon increased their numbers'.[19] Some people were so suspicious of this that they thought something must be wrong with the

38 The interior of James Lackington's Temple of the Muses, showing the great circular counter around which the Yarmouth mail-coach was reputed to have been driven. Circular galleries can be seen rising up through the dome.

product – he was, for instance, accused of using sheep hide for binding. He attended the 'remainder' sales held by John Walker and others, recording how he had seen seventy or eighty thousand volumes, 'good, bad and indifferent' sold after dinner.[20]

Lackington produced two kinds of catalogues, the first for those within the trade, the second for the public. The print run for the latter, which was published twice a year, was three thousand, and he found it an excellent form of advertisement because people would lend their copy to friends. This was the catalogue that Thomas Jefferson used to choose his books, sending first John Stockdale and then Thomas Payne to make the purchases on his behalf (p.100). Lackington prepared the copy for these catalogues himself, reading widely – from novels by Fielding, Smollett and Ann Radcliffe to translations of classics, travels and history. This helped him to know his stock: 'A bookseller who has any taste in literature may be said to feed his mind as cooks' and butchers' wives get fat by the smell of meat'. He carefully analysed his customers and their tastes:

Here you may find an old bawd inquiring for "The Countess of Huntingdon's Hymn-book;" an old worn-out rake for "Harris's List of Covent-garden Ladies;" simple Simon, for "The Art of Writing Love-letters;" and Dolly for a Dream-book; the lady of true taste and delicacy wants "Louisa Mathews;" and my lady's maid "Ovid's Art of Love;" a doubting Christian calls for "The Crumbs of Comfort;" and a practical Antinomian for "Eton's Honeycomb of Free Justification;" the pious churchwoman for "The Week's Preparation;" and the Atheist for "Hammonds Letter to Dr Priestly [*sic*]," "Toulmin's Eternity of the World," and "Hume's Dialogues on Natural Religion;" the mathematician for "Sanderson's Fluxions;" and the beau, for "The Toilet of Flora".

The list goes on at length, bringing in the Roman Catholic and the Protestant, the fortune-teller and the old hardened sinner, ending with the philosopher who 'dips into everything'.[21]

With his acute interest in his customer base and his marketing techniques, James Lackington prospered, retiring with a fortune in 1798, leaving a cousin as head of the firm. Because he did not accept credit, no receipts for accounts have survived in Soane's archives. However, Soane did note buying a copy of Richard Burn's *Justice of the Peace* from him on 23 May 1798, the very day that he filed his qualifications as a magistrate at Clerkenwell Sessions House. This book had been published by Thomas Cadell at the Shakespeare Head on the Strand. John Britton noted in his survey of booksellers that Alderman Cadell made his money with four books whose author's names begin with 'b': Burn's *Justice*, Blackstone's *Commentaries*, Blair's *Sermons* and Buchan's *Domestic Medicine* – law, religion and medicine have been the staples of many publishers over the centuries.

Lackington's Temple of the Muses was a one-off, destroyed by fire in 1841. Most of the bookshops that John and Eliza frequented looked like the engraving on the billheading of James Asperne, bookseller at the Bible, Crown and Constitution, 32 Cornhill, who supplied Soane with issues of the *European Magazine* for many years. The shop, resembling a backdrop to a Regency drama, has a bow front with multi-paned windows in which the books could be displayed, and the shop sign on the cornice. Asperne's bookshop in Cornhill was within easy reach of the new buildings of the Bank of England, which rose slowly and dramatically from 1788 to 1808. Other booksellers used by Soane were situated very close to Lincoln's Inn Fields, in High Holborn and in the newly fashionable streets of Bloomsbury.

Soane was clearly a good customer, paying promptly. James Moyes, Soane's printer friend, wrote in a letter in 1825, 'I have let you know how much you are in <u>debt</u>. Yours is a species of anxiety which I seldom or never meet with'.

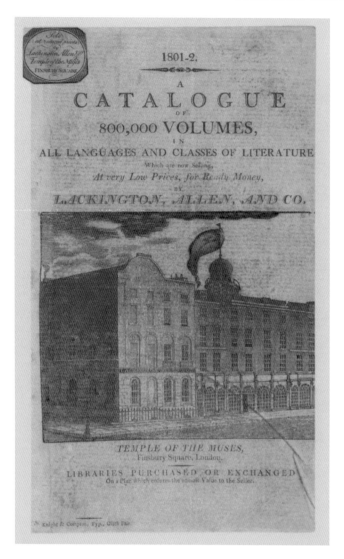

39 Exterior of the Temple of the Muses in Finsbury Square, with its cupola and flagstaff. This illustration appears on the cover of one of Lackington's catalogues. He took immense pains in compiling his catalogues both for the trade and for book-buyers. This is probably aimed at the latter, and Lackington makes clear that he supplies books only for ready money, and does not extend credit.

On one occasion Soane noted in his journal that he had called on one of his regular booksellers, Messrs White & Cochrane at 63 Fleet Street, 'the Bill not being paid, nor any notice taken of their application, I paid the same £3'.[22] It was the general practice to run accounts, and Lackington was unusual in his refusal to give credit. This could damage booksellers – for instance, Edward

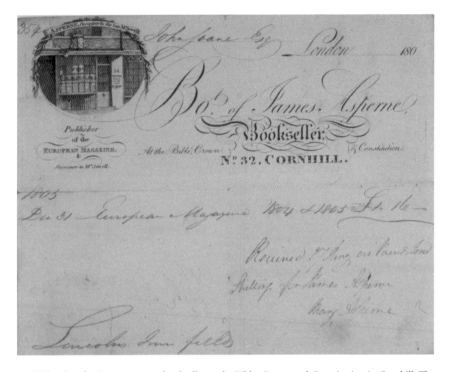

40 Bill-heading for James Asperne, bookseller at the Bible, Crown and Constitution in Cornhill. The engraving shows the front of his shop, with a bayed window in which the books could be displayed, very much the norm for any shop of the period.

Lawrence, in the Strand, who supplied Soane with very expensive books including ten volumes of the *Annual Register* on half-yearly credit, became bankrupt in 1803. There is evidence in the archives that Soane traded in books, especially in the 1790s, when settling his accounts. There is evidence too that, through contacts in the book trade, he was able to obtain discount. For example, on 10 October 1817 Moyes bought two copies of a book on the Elgin Marbles from Longmans at £1 10s, reduced from £2, passing on the 25 per cent discount to John Soane. Several years later, on 27 September 1822, Moyes wrote a personal letter to Soane warning, 'Please to burn the little account respecting the books: for if it should by any chance fall into the hands of any bookseller, the tocsin would immediately be sounded through the whole trade against me for sending them at the trade price.'[23]

Apart from the booksellers who sold him general books, Soane used specialist booksellers. From the outset he bought many of his books of architecture and design from the brothers Isaac and Josiah Taylor, whose 'Architectural Library' was situated at 56 High Holborn – a mere stone's throw from Lincoln's Inn Fields. They were his publishers, too, producing his first book, *Designs in Architecture*, in 1778. Originally this was to have been an ambitious project in folio, but it shrank to a small format, with copper-plate engravings, selling for 6s. As experts, they felt that this was the price that the market could bear for a work of 'architectural snippets' like garden seats and eyecatchers, and it would seem that they were right, for the book reprinted three times. One of their trade catalogues is to be found in the Soane archives, probably dating from 1793. It shows the range of their product: 'Theoretical ornamental Viz Books of Plans and Elevations for House, Temples, Bridges, etc. Of Ornaments for Internal Decorations, Foliage for Carvers, etc. On Perspective. Books of use to Carpenters, Bricklayers, and Workmen in general, etc., etc. Which with the best Ancient Authors are constantly on Sale.' As noted earlier, architectural books can be very expensive. At the top of the price range is James Paine's *Plans, Elevations, etc, of Noblemen's Seats*, in folio format, two volumes in sheets, priced at 7 guineas; the purchaser would have to spend at least £2 or £3 more to have them bound. Soane's second book, *Plans, Elevations and Sections of Buildings* published in 1789, comes in the middle range, at 2 guineas. At the bottom of the range is *The Builder's Price-Book*, first published by the Taylor brothers in 1776, and for over a century the standard work on costs of building materials and labour. This sold for 2s 6d.

The Taylors' catalogue also points out that they sold 'the Works of the most celebrated French *Architects* and *Engineers* of which a MS catalogue may be seen'. This would have appealed to Soane who bought prolifically both English and foreign books. As soon as the final part of Ledoux's *L'Architecture* was announced in 1804, he wanted it, and the publishers had to ask him to wait awhile as it had not yet been printed. From the early 1770s he made his own translations from the key works of French architectural theorists and historians, using the volumes in the library of the Royal Academy. Believing that architecture was essentially an intellectual art, by the time he became Professor of Architecture at the Academy in 1806, he was deeply immersed in his studies, preparing for his public lectures. In particular he identified with Jean-Jacques Rousseau, whose *Confessions* and *Les Rêveries du promeneur solitaire* were among his favourite reading, and whose intensely self-preoccupied nature was so like his own.

David Watkin paints a vivid picture of Soane sitting up night after night, studying and making notes, spurred on by his conviction that he belonged to the Gallic tradition of the encyclopedists and their concern to make lists of data and organise their information.[24] His collection of books is untypical for this period, in that it contains almost nothing pertaining to the Church, and the few devotional books that there are in the library in Lincoln's Inn Fields were most probably bought by Eliza. Instead, he subscribed to the idea of the philosophers of the Enlightenment, that truth should be attained by reason rather than faith and that problems could be solved by a return to origins. The Roman architect Vitruvius was the first to trace the origin of classical architecture to the timber construction of the huts of primitive man, and Soane owned in all fourteen copies of his *De architettura,* in twelve editions ranging in publication date from 1546 to 1826, in Latin, Italian, French and English. But the inspiration behind his pursuit of first principles was the French neo-classical theorist Marc-Antoine Laugier, whose *Essai sur l'architecture* was published in 1753 – Soane owned ten copies of this, presumably for the use of his assistants.

Another bookseller who specialised in architectural books was John Williams, who traded from 10 Charles Street, Soho Square in the 1830s. One of his bill-headings dating from 1834, with an exquisite engraving of architectural details, can be found in the Soane archives. He not only supplied Soane with books but also acted as his agent at sales, including that held on the death of the architect John Nash in 1835. For many professions it was common practice to hold sales of the effects of the dead man to provide financial help for his widow and family – a kind of benefit night. For architects this was particularly important as their business involved large sums of money and many sub-contractors. Soane himself was unusual in that he died rich and there was no need to sell his books and other possessions in order to pay off builders and other suppliers. He attended several sales of leading architects, partly as a tribute to them, and partly to acquire – many of his finest books of architecture and drawings were bought in this way. Soane's copy of the auction catalogue for the sale of Nicholas Revett's books at Christie's in 1804 indicates his interest in William Stukeley's drawings for the Bible, estimated at 18 guineas. At the sale of Robert Adam's library, also conducted by Christie's over two days in May 1818, he bought more than twenty titles, including editions of Serlio and Palladio, while the list of books from the Nash sale shows that John Williams bought twenty-three titles on his behalf.

As a prodigious buyer of books, a prompt payer and a known subscriber, Soane became well known to booksellers and publishers, who constantly sent him catalogues. An advertisement still in the library at Lincoln's Inn Fields is for Humphry Repton's *Landscape Gardening* to be published by the Taylor brothers in 1802. For an expensive project such as this, with coloured engravings and Repton's famous 'before and after' designs that were tipped in by orphans from Essex, the publishers were keen to secure advance subscriptions. Thus they specified, 'The Price Four Guineas to Subscribers, the Number of whom from the Nature of the Work, must necessarily be limited: and if any Copies shall afterwards remain, the Price will be advanced to Five Guineas. It is requested that each Subscriber will pay or remit Two Pounds at the time of subscribing.' Soane, despite his reservations about the role of landscape

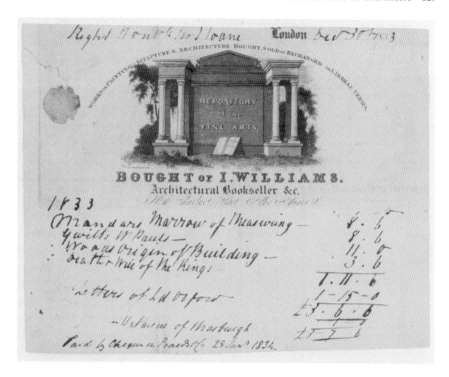

41 The elegant bill-heading of John Williams who traded from Soho Square. He specialised in architectural books, and also acted as Soane's agent at auctions.

gardening, once noting that it was 'inferior to architecture', duly paid up his four guineas, and the advertisement is enclosed within the book.

Soane also acquired books as presents. One of the first came very early in his career, when he was given a copy of *Holkham* by the architect Matthew Brettingham the Younger in 1769. Why Brettingham made this generous gesture is not known, although his nephew Robert was one of Soane's friends who went with him to Italy. Later Soane became a friend of James Christie, the scholarly son of the founder of the auction house. Christie made a study of Etruscan vases, publishing his *Disquisition* in 1806 and presenting Soane with a copy, followed in 1814 by *An Essay on . . . the Worship of the Elements*. Soane returned the compliment by presenting him with *Designs for Public and Private Buildings*.

The famous auction house of Christie's had been founded half a century earlier when James's father, also called James, arrived in London from Scotland and worked as a sales clerk in Covent Garden for the auctioneer Annesley, who took him into partnership. By 1767 he was working on his own, issuing auction catalogues from a 'Great Room' in fashionable Pall Mall.

Good-looking with agreeable manners and a fluent and witty style on the rostrum, he prospered giving dinners of venison and claret to his 'Fraternity of God Parents', which included artists such as Joshua Reynolds and Thomas Gainsborough, in return for their help with artistic judgements. Christie held his first book sale in March 1776, selling the library of John Ratcliffe of Bermondsey. His son James took over the family firm in 1803, and must have come to know Soane well through his frequent purchases at the salesroom.

Christie's great rival Sotheby's had started life as a bookseller, founded by Samuel Baker in 1733. At first Baker issued catalogues of books to be sold at fixed prices, but his first auction of books – or 'literary properties' – was probably the library of Sir John Stanley, begun on 11 March 1744. His business passed in time to his partner George Leigh and his nephew John Sotheby. It was from Sotheby's that Soane bought perhaps his greatest literary treasure, a First Folio edition of William Shakespeare's plays. For Soane, Shakespeare was the embodiment of literary genius. With Eliza he watched many of Shakespeare's plays, including performances by leading actors such as Edmund Kean, John Philip Kemble and Sarah Siddons, and with a group of friends he would meet regularly to discuss matters Shakespearean. Soane already owned copies of the Second, Third and Fourth Folios when the opportunity arose to acquire the First at a sale of the books of James Boswell the younger in May 1825. Moreover, Boswell had purchased his copy from Kemble's library, and this would have been irresistible to Soane with his fascination for books with famous associations. John Britton, who shared Soane's

42 Thomas Rowlandson's satire of a book auction, *c.*1810–15.

love of the theatre, was dispatched to the Boswell sale, and was able to report in characteristically melodramatic language that he had 'bag'd the prize' for a hundred guineas and was sending it to Soane for his 'larder', where 'it will keep, be always in good flavour, and do honour to the possessor – It will afford a perpetually standing dish on the table of genius and Talent – never to create surfeit but "increase appetite" by its almost miraculous qualities'.[25]

Another of Soane's heroes was Napoleon Bonaparte. Although he was regarded by many as a bogeyman, for Soane there was a sense of identification with a man of destiny who had risen from obscurity. When Napoleon abdicated and was sent into exile on the island of Elba in 1814, Soane, along with hundreds of others, seized the opportunity to travel to Paris where he bought all manner of Napoleonic things, including a description of the marriage ceremony of Napoleon and Marie-Louise of Austria in 1810, with handsome hand-coloured plates. Also in Soane's collection is a catalogue of the display of Napoleon's paintings, exhibited by Mr Bullock, proprietor of the London Museum (also known as the Egyptian Hall) in Piccadilly in 1816. Like Napoleon, Soane was fascinated by ancient Egypt, and bought many books on the subject, including the *Description de L'Égypte*, a monumental record in twenty volumes of thirty years of French scholarship, which was delivered to him in September 1835 shortly before his eighty-second birthday. Ten years earlier he had acquired his own ancient Egyptian monument, the sarcophagus of Pharaoh Seti I (1303–1290 BC) discovered in his tomb in the Valley of the Kings by the Italian circus strongman turned archaeologist, Giovanni Battista Belzoni. Soane bought the huge sarcophagus when the British Museum refused the price of £2,000 and celebrated its arrival in the crypt at Lincoln's Inn Fields by throwing a series of parties, with more than a thousand guests and the house lit by hundreds of oil lamps.

Soane had always bought French books, often using Dulau & Co., at 37 Soho Square, who described themselves as 'Foreign Booksellers and Circulating Library'. But once the war with France was over, he began to buy direct from Paris. His agent for this would appear to be the husband of his housekeeper, Mrs Conduitt. In the archives are a series of receipts for books bought by Edward Conduitt from the bookseller, J. Salmon. Soane himself made a second journey across the Channel in 1819, when his spending reached giant proportions. His journal records buying books old and new on architecture in shops and libraries, novels at the Louvre, and prints at salerooms. On one day, 13 September, he spent the considerable sum of 900 francs. Among the ephemera in the Soane archives is a receipt for a case of books shipped over from France in 1831. It was issued by the Cross Keys Inn in Gracechurch Street, which ran 'superior vans on springs daily to the south coast', and carries an illustration of one such horse-drawn van.

For a case of Books from France 10' Feb. 1831

CROSS KEYS INN,
Gracechurch-Street.

SUPERIOR VANS ON SPRINGS,
DAILY, TO

Portsmouth, Isle of Wight, Brighton, Cuckfield, Worthing, Arundel, Bognor, Rye, Hastings, Tunbridge Wells, Seven Oaks, &c. &c.

	£.	*s.*	*d.*
Carriage		14	2
Paid out			
Porterage		2	6
Paid JOHN STEVENTON, *Porter.*	£	16	8

†↓† Goods carted in from all parts of the Town, by addressing a line to the Book-keeper.

☞ Parcels and Luggage booked for the above Vans, at the SPREAD EAGLE Coach, Van, and Steam Packet Office, REGENT CIRCUS, Piccadilly.

43 A receipt from Soane's carrier for books bought in Paris in 1831.

* * * *

When Soane rebuilt No. 12 Lincoln's Inn Fields in the early 1790s, he combined the library with the breakfast room. A watercolour by his assistant Joseph Gandy shows the ceiling decorated with a painting of leafy trellis to give the room light and a feeling of being in the country rather than in the heart of London. Surrounded by walls lined with bookcases, John and Eliza are depicted taking breakfast while their young sons, John and George, are playing on the floor: a delightful combination of a booklover's sanctum and family room.

A decade later, Soane was creating a book room for his friend Philip Yorke. He had met Yorke during his sojourn in Italy, and this relationship proved much more fruitful than his attempt to work for the Earl-Bishop. In 1790 when Yorke inherited the earldom of Hardwicke together with Wimpole Hall in Cambridgeshire, Soane was summoned to transform the house and estate. Many of these plans never materialised, but he was responsible for designing the dramatic Yellow Drawing Room, a plunge bath, the home farm buildings and the book room. With Wimpole, Yorke had inherited a famous bibliophile house, the home in the early eighteenth century of Robert Harley, lst Earl of Oxford, and of his son Edward (see p. 170–2). To accommodate the huge

44 Joseph Gandy's watercolour of the Soane family in the breakfast room cum library at 12 Lincoln's Inn Fields. The ceiling, with its leafy trellis painted by John Crace, and the potted plants on the wall outside the window created a rural impression at odds with the very urban site of the house.

collection of books amassed by both Harleys, James Gibbs designed a magnificent double cube with arcaded bookcases. With Edward Harley's spectacular bankruptcy, Wimpole was bought by the lst Earl of Hardwicke, himself a book collector, so the shelves that had been emptied with the sale of the estate were soon refilled, and his grandson needed further room for his own books. In 1806 Soane designed for him an elegant room with arches decorated with plaster rosettes springing from the projecting bookcases (Plate III). Plaster urns made to look like black Wedgwood basalt – fashionable accoutrements for libraries at this time – stand atop each bookcase.

Almost simultaneously, Soane was designing a country-house library for himself, at Pitshanger Manor in Ealing. He repeated the idea used in Lincoln's Inn Fields of painted trelliswork for his library, but at Pitshanger it was more like a study. Most of his books were kept upstairs, in the drawing room, where visitors could admire his collection that included many architectural folios.[26] Pitshanger was extensively refurbished by Soane not only as a country house for himself but also, as he wrote later, 'to make . . . as complete as possible for the residence of the young architect'. The young architect in question was his son John, then aged fourteen. Unfortunately these hopes were to be dashed, for the happy family scene depicted by Gandy in the breakfast room in Lincoln's Inn Fields proved a false dawn. John, who suffered from constant ill health, lacked the compulsive drive of his father and would not settle on any profession. His younger brother, George, inherited Soane's energy but not in a direction that was approved of. In 1808 George announced his interest lay in literature, so Soane set him the task of cataloguing his library. George duly completed the task, but signed off by throwing a tantrum, flinging ink and inkstand across the floor. His taste was for the dramatic, and he was already gravitating towards the prolific playwright James Boaden whose daughter he was to marry.

Gothic was very much the fashion of this period. Soane created a monk's dining room in the basement of Pitshanger, encrusted with real Gothic fragments, lit by stained-glass and, according to him, inhabited by a resident hermit. This fantasy was visited in 1804 by 'Monk' Lewis, author of the famous bestseller *The Monk*, and by James Boaden, whose play *Aurelia and Miranda* was based on the novel. However, Soane did not approve when his son George produced a Gothic novel of his own, *The Eve of S. Marco*, published in three volumes, the first appearing in 1811. Where Soane might adopt whimsy when describing the hermit in his dining room, he spared his son nothing. Writing to him on 18 May 1812, he declared: 'I have read your two publications [the first two volumes] – such productions will neither add to your fame nor . . . your fortune.'[27]

By this time Pitshanger had been sold. There is no indication that Eliza warmed to the house, and his son John was showing no signs of becoming an architect. The sale was conducted by James Christie in 1809. Meanwhile, Soane had bought up the lease on 13 Lincoln's Inn Fields and began to remodel the house in conjunction with No. 12. To accommodate his Pitshanger books, he converted his drawing office into a library cum study.

Throughout his architectural career, Soane had his critics – in 1796 *The Modern Goth*, an anonymous satire on his work was published and, to Soane's fury, comments such as 'pilasters scor'd like loins of pork' were read out by James Wyatt to a room of architects. However, nothing hurt him as much as a vicious attack that appeared in September 1815, in *The Champion*, a recently founded Sunday newspaper. His library in Lincoln's Inn Fields was described as 'a satire upon the possessor, who must stand in the midst of these hoarded volumes like a eunuch in a seraglio; the envious . . . guardian of that which he cannot enjoy'. Realising that the author must be none other than his own son George, Soane kept the articles from Eliza, but she eventually read them. According to Soane, her reaction was that George 'has given me my death blow. I shall never be able to hold up my head again'.[28] Eliza had been troubled by stress for several years over the disintegration of the family, but now she complained of severe pains, and she died on 22 November. Soane had little doubt that George was the major contributor to her death, framing his 'Death Blows' and hanging them in the drawing room at Lincoln's Inn Fields.

It was a terrible bereavement, and Soane began to identify with Shakespeare's King Lear, living with the sharp serpent's tooth of ungrateful children, and with Le Sage's Gil Blas, a figure continually undermined by circumstance. As his eyesight deteriorated, his former assistant George Wightwick would read to him from his favourite novel, and recorded how Soane would cry, 'p-o-o-r Gil!'. One way of dealing with his unhappiness was to buy books prodigiously, and he did so, ceasing only in 1835 when he purchased the twenty-three books at the sale of John Nash's library. By this time his library was combined with the dining room, in pride of place on the ground floor of 13 Lincoln's Inn Fields. There the books were kept in glazed bookcases, not a good idea as this deprived them of air, but with his interest in the effects of lighting, he wanted the room to glitter as he entertained his guests to dinner. Even so, not all his books could be accommodated there, so they were kept in recesses and under windows in every room and passage, and piled up on tables.

Due to his break with his sons and their families, Soane decided that his house in Lincoln's Inn Fields should become a museum and library in the administration of trustees. He wanted the library to be open for study at least two days per week as a national architectural academy. This had to be done through a private Act of Parliament, the third reading of which was held on 1 April 1833. On that day, William Cobbett, recently elected as MP for Oldham in Lancashire, presented a petition against the bill on behalf of George Soane. His rhetoric was, as always, very effective. Declaring that he had never met Soane or his son until four days before, he quoted St Paul: 'if a man take not care of his own house, he has denied the faith, and is worse than a heathen'. This was extremely ironic, as Cobbett was a noted radical not known for his recourse to the Bible, who, moreover, enjoyed tumultuous relations with his own wife and children. On top of this, Soane had to suffer a debate about who should control the house and collection. Sir Robert Peel suggested that the British Museum was the appropriate institution to administer the collection. Soane opposed this as he predicted that the museum would cherry pick, that the Belzoni sarcophagus would to go to the Emperor of Russia, his collection of Hogarth prints and paintings to the King of Holland and coins to the King of Bavaria. The debate then developed into a discussion about public accessibility, and the difficulties encountered when visiting the British Museum, especially for labourers and tradesmen obliged to observe working hours: an interesting discussion, but one that must have infuriated Soane. In the end, both Cobbett's petition and the British Museum concept were dismissed, and royal assent was given on 20 April.

Soane provided the endowment, stipulating that the curator should be an English architect who had distinguished himself or gained an academic prize: in fact, Soane nominated his chief clerk, George Bailey, in his will. Meanwhile his housekeeper, Mrs Conduitt, on whom Soane greatly relied, was appointed as Inspectress of the museum. After Soane's death, Bailey tried to make a collection to rival the library of the Royal Institute for British Architects by continuing subscriptions to periodicals and adding modern works, but ultimately found this impossible. Also impossible was the idea of the library being of great use to architectural students, as most had to work in their offices during the daytime. In 1904 a trustee revived the idea of transferring some of the antiquities and books to the British Museum, and some of the paintings to the National Gallery, but luckily this too failed. As a result, the Sir John Soane Museum is a fascinating glimpse into the extraordinary career of the architect, while his library provides an important example of a Regency book collection, complete with all the records and trade ephemera. It has been observed that there is much in common here with Frank Lloyd Wright, who left his house and studio, including his octagonal library just outside Chicago, to the American public.[29]

By the 1830s, Soane had become the Grand Old Man of Architecture. When Soane was knighted by William IV in 1831, the auctioneer Peter Coxe celebrated his elevation with thirty-seven verses that included, 'SOANE! All regret is haply past/Thy generous Sovereign owns thy claim;/And gracious binds the laurel fast,/That knighthood yield to deck thy name'.[30] There have always been self-made men – Lackington, Britton and Cobbett have featured in this chapter – but Soane was a true phenomenon. A good friend – he got on well with his workmen and his patrons, and had a large circle of acquaintances – he was also a good foe, his life was littered with quarrels and feuds. Even George Dance and John Britton fell out with him on occasion; Mrs Britton secured a reconciliation through a timely delivery of Wiltshire ale and Portuguese onions.

Born two years before the accession of George III, Sir John Soane died in January 1837, just six months before the accession of Queen Victoria. By this time he had become an anachronism, both in his Regency dress and in his architecture. The obituaries were muted in their admiration of his work and his family did not regret his passing, but he must have been sincerely mourned by his booksellers.

CHAPTER 6

A LITTLE LIGHT READING?

Fact and Fiction in Georgian Britain

In Richard Brinsley Sheridan's play of 1775 *The Rivals,* Sir Anthony Absolute talked to Mrs Malaprop of 'an ever-green tree, of diabolical knowledge!' The audience at the Covent Garden Theatre in London would have had no difficulty in recognising the reference. Where today we may debate concerns about delinquent teenagers or the effects of the European Union on employment, late Georgian society fulminated about the twin evils of novel-reading and circulating libraries. And it was women who inspired these attacks.

The tradition of disapproval of the reading of romances and novels was a long one, with two main strands. The first was the idea that fictional works stimulated the imagination, and could lead to all kinds of dangers. The second was the belief that women should be subservient in all spheres of life. Lady Elizabeth Langham, who died in 1664, was known for her rare intellect and her command of Latin, French and Spanish. Yet her male biographer was anxious to point out how she avoided the 'inconveniences, which some have fancied, do necessarily accompany a *Learned Wife*; for even herein she would always lower her Sails to him [her husband] as to her Lord and Head'.[1]

In the sixteenth century, works of fiction were usually described as romances, recounting the life and adventures of a hero of chivalry. They were often Italian, French or Spanish in origin though they were increasingly available in English translations. Baldassare Castiglione's prose dialogue *Il libro del cortegiano*, translated by Sir Thomas Hoby as *The Courtyer* in 1561, included appropriate behaviour for gentlewomen at court. A home-grown work of this genre was Sir Philip Sidney's *Arcadia*, written originally for the private entertainment of his sister, but published with her permission after his early death. A version of *Arcadia* is depicted in Lady Anne Clifford's *Great Picture* (Plate I), along with Ovid's *Metamorphoses* and the works of Geoffrey Chaucer and Edmund Spenser. These works, sometimes known as 'recreational literature', were considered suitable reading for ladies of appropriate rank and education. Women of lower status were expected to eschew works of fiction and concentrate on the Bible and other devotional works, or books of a practical nature.

According to the *Oxford English Dictionary*, the term novel first appears in English in the mid-sixteenth century to describe one of the short stories contained in works such as Boccaccio's *Decameron*. By the time Elizabeth Pepys was reading her novels in her native French, they were far from short. On 31 January 1660 Samuel Pepys records in his diary, 'Home and so to bed, leaving my wife reading in *Polexandre*'.[2] This story of a queen who inhabits an inaccessible island and sends her knight to punish aspiring suitors was told in no less than five volumes by an academician, Marin Le Roy de Gomberville. Pepys's biographer Claire Tomalin remarks with feeling how it is hard going to read now.

Disapproval of the reading of romances and novels is a constant refrain throughout the centuries and from all levels of society. Plays seem to have occupied a middle ground as far as attitudes were concerned, less erudite than the courtly works of Spenser and Sidney, less difficult to understand than Chaucer, but more substantial and reputable than corantos, the early newspapers, and ballads and chapbook romances. The publication of William Shakespeare's plays in the First Folio edition in 1623 proved a great success, and the Second Folio followed within a decade. Awaiting execution, Charles I read both Shakespeare and Ben Jonson. For the deeply religious, however, even Shakespeare was anathema. Edmund Gosse writing of his parents in the nineteenth century related how his mother would have neither novels nor Shakespeare in the house, though his minister father felt that this was going too far.

For the poor in the seventeenth and eighteenth centuries, fiction came in the form of chapbooks bought for a few pence from itinerant sellers. The subject matter ranged from pious tales to stirring histories, respectively classified by Pepys as 'Penny Godlinesses' and 'Vulgaria', while the poet John Milton referred to them as 'countryman's arcadias'. However, they were not only the reading matter of the poor: schoolboys found them the inspiring start of their ventures into fiction.

Into this arena in 1740 came the publication of what is considered by some as the first modern English novel, Samuel Richardson's *Pamela*. Richardson, born in 1689, was the son of a joiner who, like Tom in William Hogarth's series of prints of 1747 charting the upwardly mobile 'Industrious 'Prentice', moved from the margins of the printing trade to marry his master's daughter and become Master of the Stationers' Company. Indeed, one of Richardson's earlier publications was *The Apprentices' Vade Mecum*, a book of advice on morals and conduct. Another of his activities, aged thirteen, was to write letters for young lovers, thus providing him with plenty of experience when his fellow printers encouraged him to write on the concerns of everyday life. These letters grew into *Pamela*, the first part of which was published in 1740, and followed the next year by *Letters to and for Particular Friends*.

Acting as the 'editor' with the story developed by six correspondents, Richardson tells the tale of Pamela Andrews, an unusually literate servant girl of fifteen who suffers all kinds of misfortunes, including attempted rape and mock marriage, before she wins over her seducer through her goodness and accepts his hand in a genuine marriage. In 1741 Richardson produced the second part of the novel; with a heavy dose of moralising he related Pamela's life as a perfect wife. *Pamela* received considerable acclaim, with Richardson hailed as 'a salutary angel in Sodom' and clergymen preaching sermons extolling the theme set out on the title page, a story designed 'to cultivate the principles of religion and virtue in the minds of the youth of both sexes'. As with modern soap operas, for his audience fiction often merged with reality, so that the church bells of Slough were pealed to celebrate Pamela's wedding when the village blacksmith reached that particular part of the story in his public readings. The book, however, also provoked ridicule: even as the second part was produced, a satirical parody appeared entitled *An Apology for the Life of Mrs Shamela Andrews* by 'Conny Keyber'. This was almost certainly the writer Henry Fielding, who went on to deride *Pamela* openly in his novel *The History of Joseph Andrews* which chronicled the adventures of Pamela's equally virtuous brother, a footman who resists the advances not only of the house-keeper but also of his mistress. Richardson, who tended toward the pompous, was deeply upset by Fielding's actions and never forgave him.

Almost exactly contemporaneous with the publication of *Pamela* came the circulating library. The Revd Samuel Fancourt is regarded as the founder of the first circulating library, which he opened in Fleet Street in London around 1740. Offering primarily theological and technical books, he soon ran into financial trouble and turned his institution into a subscription library. The history of libraries is a complicated one, for they come in all shapes and sizes, from cathedral libraries to tiny collections in parish churches, from national institutions to informal reading groups, and with every nuance of organisa-tion and regulation. This chapter concentrates on what might be described as 'non-institutional' libraries – subscription and circulating.

The subscription or proprietary library that developed in the early eigh-teenth century consisted of a group of individuals getting together to buy books, using their joining fee plus a subscription, usually payable on an annual or quarterly basis. Some called themselves libraries, others reading groups, societies of reading, or book clubs. Some were organised on a joint-stock basis with members buying shares. Some kept standing collections, while others sold off the books at the end of each year. One antecedent of this kind of institution was the coffee-house club of the previous century. Writing about Oxford in 1668, Anthony Wood recorded: 'A little before Christmas, the Christchurch men, young men, set a library in Short's coffee house in the study there, viz Rabelais, poems, plays etc. One scholar gave a book of l shilling and chain 10 pence.'[3] A century later, the Irish traveller Dr Thomas Campbell wrote that the Chapter Coffee-house in Paternoster Row in London was 'remarkable for a large collection of books and a Reading Society'. Subscribing a shilling for the right to a year's reading, he 'found all the new publications I sought and I believe, what I am told, that all the new books are laid in'.[4]

Other subscription libraries held their meetings in taverns. The Birmingham Book Club, for instance, was founded in 1775 and met at the Leicester Arms, a tavern belonging to John Freeth at the corner of Lease Lane and Bell Street. The members were of the radical tendency, so that by the 1790s they were known by their political opponents as the Jacobin Club. A painting of 1792 by Johannes Eckstein, now in the Birmingham Art Gallery, shows members of the club, some with tankards of beer, others goblets of wine

45 A meeting of the Birmingham Book Club at the Leicester Arms, painted by Johannes Eckstein in 1792. Not a book in sight, so presumably the members have auctioned them off in the annual sale of stock, and are now enjoying their drinks and tobacco. The tavern owner, John Freeth, is seated second left; on his left, holding a clay pipe is Jeremiah Vaux, one of the first surgeons at Birmingham's General Hospital; the man with a tall hat standing on the right is James Bisset, publisher of the Magnificent Dictionary of the city, which listed the principal manufacturers and social leaders; to his left, gesturing with his pipe is Joseph Fearon, tin merchant.

and churchwarden pipes, and clearly this was a social club as well as a library. John Freeth, acting as both host and member wrote:

> Due regard let the hammer be paid
> Ply the glass, gloomy care to dispel;
> If mellow our hearts are all made
> The Books much better may sell[5]

Here he is referring to the annual sale of stock.

These libraries and groups were scattered right across Britain. At Clavering, a village in Essex, the Society of Reading was established in 1786, with monthly meetings in rotation at homes of members and an annual dinner at the Clavering Inn. A daring departure was instituted four years later when ladies were admitted as members at half rates. Debates were held: one such was entitled, 'Is there any just ground for the censure usually cast up on old maids and old bachelors?' The minutes recorded: 'From the various bad dispositions the old maids commonly discover, there appears just reason for censuring them, while the old bachelors, on these accounts and on others not generally known, deserve even severer censures than those which are usually cast upon them!'[6]. At a time when travelling by night was hazardous and artificial lighting an expensive luxury, the Huntingdon Book Club Society recorded in 1742 that the dinner in the George Inn that accompanied their monthly meetings should be on the table at three o'clock, summer and winter, on the Tuesday before the full moon.

Villages and small towns may have had their subscription libraries and clubs, but London was remarkably poorly served, probably because there were so many alternative institutions and bookshops. The London Library was founded in 1785, and moved several times before being amalgamated with the Westminster Library. It offered a wide range of books for a joining fee of one guinea, and a guinea annual subscription to a membership of about 121, including 10 women. Although the library closed within twenty years, it was revived in 1840 as the London Library in St James's Square, perhaps the most distinguished of subscription libraries, still going strong. This was founded through the determination of Thomas Carlyle, who much preferred taking books home to sitting in a library, such as the Reading Room in the British Museum, in formidable combination with other distinguished men of letters, such as Charles Dickens and William Ewart Gladstone.

The annual subscription for libraries was usually one guinea, putting them out of the financial reach of poorer members of society. The register of the Huntingdon Book Club Society for 1742 shows a membership of eight clergymen, seven attorneys, a surgeon and a physician, while Charles Shillito's poem dating from 1788 entitled 'The Country Book Club' describes the various members of a village society, including the vicar, a draper, a surgeon and the barber, with the squire, of course, taking the chair.[7] Where women were permitted to be members they formed a tiny minority, four or five in a hundred. These must have been brave souls – possibly the stately relicts of the leading merchants of a town, or of a clergyman or squire in the village. Of course many women availed themselves of books through the subscriptions of their fathers, husbands and brothers, and thus remain the hidden readers.

Marginalised by subscription libraries, women found no such attitudes in the circulating libraries. Books had been lent, sometimes for a fee, by book-shops and coffee-houses since the late seventeenth century. In the 1720s Allan Ramsay, poet and father of the portrait painter of the same name, instituted such a service in his Edinburgh bookshop, incurring the wrath of the Revd Robert Wodrow, former librarian of Glasgow University: 'all the villainous profane and obscene books and playes printed at London by Curle [Edmund Curll, a bookseller who courted controversy] and others, are gote doun from London by Allan Ramsey, and lent out, for an easy price, to young boyes, servant weeman of the better sort, and gentleman, and vice and obscenity dreadfully propagated'.[8]

Wodrow's vivid fulminations are an early example of the opprobrium heaped on circulating libraries. In 1765, the author of *Village Memoirs* declared that 'turnpike roads and circulating libraries are the great inlets of vice and debauchery', a denunciation of the physical and mental modes of escape suddenly available to people living in rural communities. The spread of circulating libraries during the second part of the eighteenth century was indeed remarkable. Paul Kaufman identified over 100 such institutions in London, and a further 268 in 119 locations around the rest of the country by 1800. Moreover, he believed it possible that the *Monthly Magazine* for April 1801 was correct in saying that there were at least 1,000 such libraries.[9]

One of the first large establishments in London was the circulating library run by the Noble brothers. Francis had established his publishing business in St Martin's Court, Leicester Fields, where he was joined by his brother John in 1744. Great self-publicists, they produced engravings of the elegant interiors of their library. James Raven describes them as the literary equivalent of managers of Ranelagh Gardens or the master of ceremonies at assembly rooms in one of the fashionable spa resorts.[10] By 1780 the Nobles were trading at the Pope's Head in Carnaby Street, near Golden Square. Their printed cata-logue, priced 6d sewn, 1s bound, offered several thousand volumes in English, French and Latin, at 12s per annum or 4s a quarter. Their opening hours were generous, 8am to 8pm on weekdays (but no longer, the catalogue warned). Two books at a time could be borrowed, and there were fines for keeping

46 An engraving by James Hulett of Wright's Circulating Library in Exeter Court, the Strand. The library was established in 1740, and was probably the second of its kind in London; the first had been opened by the Reverend Samuel Fancourt ten years earlier. Subscribers appear to have had direct access to the shelves, rather than obtaining their books through a librarian.

books over time, causing them damage, and so on. Their great rival was Thomas Lowndes, who had his circulating library in Fleet Street. Fanny Burney is believed to have based the miserly and rough-speaking Briggs on Lowndes in her second novel, *Cecilia*, published in 1786.

Later the Nobles and Lowndes were challenged in the circulating-library stakes by Thomas Hookham, who traded at various smart addresses around New and Old Bond Street and Hanover Square. But perhaps the most famous, or notorious, library proprietor was William Lane of the Minerva Press. The son of a London poulterer, he began selling books from his father's shop. This unlikely start was the subject of many subsequent lampoons, which featured him as a 'chicken-butcher' and a 'scribbling poulterer' who paraded in splendid carriages and brandished gold-headed canes.[11] The carriages and canes were paid for through his highly profitable enterprises; by 1784 he had established a press at his shop in Leadenhall Street in the heart of the City of London, ran a new afternoon newspaper, and expanded to establish the Minerva Press, a large workforce with at least four presses and a celebrated circulating library. His practices were sharp, and he became so famous for his potboilers and lack of quality that people talked about his imprint, the Minerva Press, rather than the titles themselves. Lane divided his readers into four classes: the Historian, the Gay and Volatile, the Sedate, and the Theatrical Amateurs – an early example of marketing classification.

The significant feature of the Nobles, Lowndes, Hookham and Lane was that they all combined publishing businesses with their circulating libraries, with the first providing the novels for the second. They, with other publishers, also supplied independent libraries in the provinces, in North America and in India. Naturally circulating libraries opened in the main cities – Allan Ramsay's early enterprise in Edinburgh was followed by Joseph Barber's circulating library set up at Amen Corner in Newcastle-upon-Tyne around 1740. By the late 1750s he had over 2,000 volumes in stock, charging readers 2s 6d per quarter. He provided a printed catalogue with a verse on the cover:

> Where useful, Entertaining and Polite,
> Collected, join the curious to invite;
> As Sermons, Comments, Pray'rs, religious misteries,
> Lives, Geography, Memoirs, Tracts, and Histories;
> Voyages and Travels, where'er sea or shore is;
> With num'rous of the Muse's raptrous lays,
> From good Eliza's down to George's Days
> Which will be lent to read, by Week or Quarter
> At Joseph Barber's shop in Amen-Corner[12]

The burgeoning fashion for taking the waters, both in spa towns and seaside resorts made these ideal locations for circulating libraries. Margate, on the Kent coast within relatively easy reach of London, boasted no fewer than four – Champion's, Silver's, Hall's and Garner's, all very close to each other. Hall's could contain up to four hundred people, with seats in a piazza. An engraved print of this library, made in about 1790, showed that it was not merely a lending library but also an important place for assembly and promenade. The customers depicted were clearly people of means who could afford holidays: according to records, there were many clergymen among the customers requiring substantial stocks of divinity books.

Bath had three circulating libraries, including Samuel Hazard's and that of James Marshall, who kept a register of his clients that featured the Prince of Wales, clergymen, members of the armed forces of Bath and female readers. In his novel *Humphry Clinker*, published in 1771, Tobias Smollett has Lydia Melford writing to her friend in Gloucester about the libraries and bookshops of Bath. A house by the Pump Room was arranged as a kind of female coffee-house, away from the general assemblies where ladies could read the news and enjoy each other's conversation. Lydia reports that the young are not admitted to this coffee-house, 'inasmuch as the conversation turns on politics, scandal, philosophy, and other subjects above our capacity; but we are allowed to accompany them to booksellers' shops, which are charming places of resort; where we read novels, plays, pamphlets and news-papers, for so small a subscription as a crown a quarter'.[13]

The establishments in Bath, Margate, and their ilk were large and prosperous with plenty of customers in season. Many smaller circulating libraries had to combine lending and selling books with other goods and services, as shown by their trade cards. The traditional association with patent medicines continued, but in addition Webb's Circulating Library in Bedford sold wallpapers and offered a paperhanging service. Curson's Library, opposite St Leonard's Church in Exeter, Devon, could provide blotting paper, playing cards, portable desks, a state lottery office and pianos for sale or rent along with Daffy's Elixir and Oxley's Essence of Ginger. Croydon's of Teignmouth, also in Devon, sold groceries such as Hervey's sauce, olives and an intriguingly named concoction, Zoobditty Mutch.

To stock the shelves of the circulating libraries, a veritable industry was developed. Clara Reeve, chronicling the history of the novel in *Progress of Romance*, published in 1785, described how a huge range was being published, not all good: 'the press groaned under the weight of Novels, which spring up like Mushrooms every year'.[14] Authors comprised men and women in equal numbers, from sea captains to prostitutes, destitute widows and even ambitious adolescents. Annual figures for new titles, numbering 40 in 1770, had reached 74 in 1790, and 99 in 1800. William Lane's Minerva Press produced the biggest crop, followed by the Robinsons, trading from Addison's Head, 25 Paternoster Row, although their productions were much more interesting and above the level of potboilers. In 1774 the Robinson family bought a share in the *Critical Review*, one of the principal vehicles for reviewing novels in the late eighteenth century.

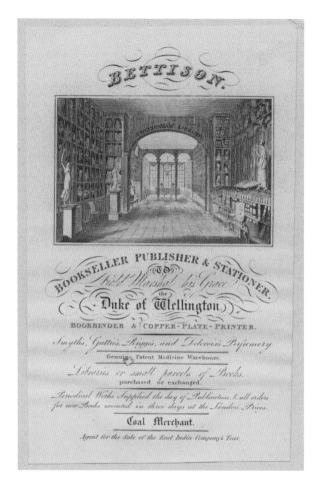

47 Early nineteenth-century trade card for Bettison of Cheltenham, who combined a circulating library with bookselling, publishing, stationery, book-binding, and the sale of patent medicines, coal and East India Company tea.

The idea of writing book reviews possibly came from the practice of Huguenot scholars, scattered across Europe with Louis XIV's Revocation of the Edict of Nantes in 1685, exchanging ideas and providing critiques of recent publications. Addison and Steele included reviews of plays in the *Spectator* and the *Tatler*, but did not do the same for books. The palm for the first popular reviewing journal cannot be given with certainty, but is usually awarded to Edward Cave, the publisher of the *Gentleman's Magazine*. Cave began his magazine in 1731, producing it from his printshop in the gateway of the former priory of St John of Jerusalem in Clerkenwell, in the same building that had housed Richard Hogarth's ill-fated 'Latin' Coffee-house. An image of the gateway became Cave's trademark, reproduced on his plate, on his coach, and on the title page of each edition of the *Gentleman's Magazine.*

In his varied early career, Cave had worked first as a sorter, and later as inspector of franks in the Post Office's inland office in Lombard Street. As a result of this, he was able to gain excellent and cheap distribution of his magazine throughout Britain and North America, to the fury of his competitors. He carried abridgements of recently published books and pamphlets, which again aroused fury, but escaped legal action by various means, including printing letters from readers who claimed to have bought the whole book because of reading extracts. Thus on 31 May 1740 he published a letter from 'W.P.V' of 'Com.W': 'In your Magazine for April last, p.183, you desire any Gentleman to inform you whether he has purchased Père Bougeant's *Amusement, etc.,* upon Occasion of its Extracts you have given it, – I cannot say that: but I can, and do say, that I bought Mr Harte's *Sermon on the Union and Harmony of Reason, Morality and Revealed Religion,* purely because of the Extract I found in your Magazine . . . ; for I love to know something of a Book before I buy it . . .'. Samuel Johnson, who was later to work on the magazine, wrote to Cave on 25 November 1734 suggesting that he might produce for him 'short literary dissertations in Latin or English, critical remarks on authours ancient or modern, forgotten poems that deserve revival or loose pieces . . . By this method, your literary article, for so it might be called, will, he [Johnson] thinks, be better recommended to the publick than by low jests, awkward buffoonery, or the dull scurrilities of either party.'[15]

A review of Samuel Richardson's second novel, *Clarissa,* appeared in June 1749, said to be a translation from the Dutch by Albrecht von Haller. As the book ran to over a million words and had only just been published in its complete form in England, the Dutch reviewer may well have been another ploy of Cave's to avoid legal action especially as the name is identical to that of an eminent German botanist. The review compares *Clarissa* favourably not only with *Pamela* but also with Marivaux's *La Vie de Marianne* published between 1731 and 1741, and seizes the chance to aim a sally at the Old Enemy:

Very large impressions of this work [*Clarissa*] have been impatiently bought up in *England,* and all the readers whom we know concur in giving it the first rank among romances. This expression probably may be resented by the *French,* who have written so many, and imagine they have succeeded so well; but perhaps they will acquiesce in our opinion, if the following observations be considered. The *French* romances are generally no more than representations of the illustrious actions of illustrious persons . . . . *Marianne* amuses, *Clarissa* not only amuses but instructs, and the more effectually as the writer paints nature, and nature alone.

Thanks to Cave's distribution advantages, the *Gentleman's Magazine* proved an enormous success, soon achieving a circulation of around 9,000. He took as his editorial pseudonym Sylvanus Urban, reflecting the fact that he was providing information on the London scene for gentlemen – and ladies – throughout the kingdom. By printing reviews and, perhaps even more usefully, lists of recently published books, periodicals and pamphlets, and

48 The title page of Edward Cave's *The Gentleman's Magazine* for March 1749, with the gate of the priory of St John's Clerkenwell, where he had set up his printing office. He provided reviews and lists of newly published books.

charging only 6d per issue, he performed an invaluable service to the 'world of books'. Cave died in 1754, but the magazine continued to prosper, only ceasing publication in 1922.

Where Cave, Samuel Johnson and the *Gentleman's Magazine* led, others soon followed. Their main rival was the *London Magazine*, but two other journals concentrated on books: the *Monthly Review* established in 1749 and the *Critical Review* in 1756. They developed rather different styles, the *Critical* employing scathing humour, while the *Monthly* was blander. Both contained a few long reviews, usually running to about five pages, with a fairly comprehensive list of other new novels. Archibald Hamilton, the proprietor of the *Critical*, also owned the *Town and Country* and the *Lady's* magazines, both of which were aimed at novel-reading young ladies. Not only did these magazines carry reviews, but also novels in serialised form. John Murray I began his career in books not as a publisher but as the author of a fictional romance, *The History of Sir Launcelot Edgeville*, which appeared over a four-month period from late 1767 in the periodical *Court Miscellany*. An undistinguished sentimental tale, running to about 10,000 words, it was never completed, for Murray admitted to 'being conscious of my inability to bring it to a conclusion'.[16] In his account of his childhood in a remote Wiltshire village, John Britton recalled the impact of newspapers and magazines on the community. None were purchased until 1780, when the Gordon Riots in London were wondered at. A few years later, the *Lady's Magazine* was taken by one of the farmer's daughters, who lent it to Britton's sister as she was fond of reading.

Many book reviewers lived out of London and worked hard for their fees, which, like those for authors, were far from generous. Review copies provided free by the publisher do not appear to have been the norm, so Ralph Griffiths, the editor of the *Monthly*, for instance, expected his reviewers to return the books so that he could sell them back to the original booksellers. Carriage costs were paid by the review editor, but reviewers had to pay for the return of the books to London. Fees were usually calculated per sheet, amounting to sixteen printed pages in octavo: the poet Robert Southey was paid 3 guineas for his work; the philosopher and writer William Godwin received 2 guineas. Critical reviews were not attributed, and the review editors strove to guard this anonymity. However, it is possible to work out the names of reviewers to the *Monthly* during Griffiths's editorship as he made note of their initials. Thus the pre-eminent reviewer from 1778 to 1786 was Samuel Badcock, a Dissenting minister based in South Molton in Devon, who wrote *Monthly* reviews for at least 110 novels. Another of Griffiths's reviewers was William Enfield, again a Dissenting minister who held the rectorship of the eminent Warrington Academy from 1770 until its closure in 1783, whereupon he moved to Norwich, combining preaching with writing. John Trusler even managed to write a review of the second edition of his own book *Modern Times* in 1786 for John Murray's *English Review*, while John Murray like Ralph Griffiths also reviewed novels.

Reviewers' comments could be devastating. Andrew Becket predicted in the *Monthly* that the future of *Emma Dorvill* 'by a Lady' published in 1789 should be as a paper supplier to pastry cooks, while the *Critical* reviewer described Regina Maria Roche's *Maid of the Hamlet*, 1793, as a possible distraction for a toothache. Complaints were made about the language and construction of novels; one reviewer in the *Critical* in 1795 begged novelists to avoid corrupting the language with 'a confusion of words, resembling a wilderness of flowering weeds, which it would be impossible to separate or disentangle'.

On the basis that any publicity was good, the Noble brothers deliberately provoked a longstanding confrontation with Robert Baldwin, proprietor of the *London Magazine*. In January 1769 they issued an 'Advertisement to the Public', accusing Baldwin of damning every novel they produced, and suggesting that he never read most of the books that were reviewed in his magazine. The quarrel dragged on, with the Nobles challenging Baldwin to withdraw accusations that they underpaid authors. William Lane meanwhile even accepted derogatory refences to his own Leadenhall enterprises in Anna Maria Bennet's novel, *The Beggar Girl*, which he published in 1797.

Publishers found that advertising was becoming increasingly important. The cost of advertising in local, regional and London newspapers was not cheap, and represented a remarkably high proportion of investment. Thomas Hookham advertised one of his novels, *Constance* by Eliza Mathews, in the *St James's Chronicle* in 1785 by taking three columns of single words to catch the eye of readers. Some advertisements were placed pre-publication to announce that the novel was in the press and about to be published – Thomas Lowndes was particularly keen on this strategem – others included reviews to act as puffs.

The processes of publishing, marketing and reviewing at this period are very well documented by Fanny Burney's experience with her first novel, *Evelina*. Ironically we know so much because she adopted subterfuges to keep her identity anonymous. The daughter of the distinguished music historian Dr Charles Burney, Fanny destroyed her early literary efforts in a bonfire in 1767. These included an almost complete novel, *The History of Caroline Evelyn*. In secret, lest she be considered to be wasting time on idle and dangerous fictions, she rescued from oblivion Caroline Evelyn's infant daughter and brought her back as Evelina.

As she acted as her father's secretary, her writing was familiar to the printers of Fleet Street, so she wrote the entire manuscript in a feigned hand. In 1776 she offered it to various publishers. James Dodsley, whose firm had published

Samuel Johnson's *Rasselas*, refused to look at the manuscript unless the author's name was revealed. She turned therefore to Thomas Lowndes, publisher of many novels including Horace Walpole's *The Castle of Otranto*. In a letter of 26 December, she wrote: 'The plan of the first Volume is the Introduction of a well educated but inexperienced young woman into public company, and a round of the most fashionable Spring Diversions of London. I believe it has not before been executed, though it seems a fair field open for the Novelist.' She went on to explain, 'such is my situation in Life, that I have objections unconquerable to being known in this transaction', and therefore asked for a reply to be directed via her brother Charles under the pseudonym of 'Mr King' to be collected from the local coffee-house. Lowndes agreed, saying: 'now is the time for a Novel'.[17] Fanny had wanted to have two volumes published, with a gap before the final two, as she thought it wise to feel the pulse of the public before completing the text, but Lowndes insisted on producing the book all in one go. After some negotiation, a fee of 30 guineas was agreed.

The book was duly published in spring 1778 in three volumes, each priced at 9s bound, 7s 6d sewn, in duodecimo, the small format adopted for novels at this period so that they could easily be carried in a pocket or a muff. Such was the cavalier way that publishers treated their authors that Fanny did not realise that the book was out until her stepmother, who was not let into the secret, pointed out over breakfast that *Evelina, or a Young Lady's Entrance into the World* was being advertised in the *London Chronicle*, tucked between a trial of an armed robber in Bristol, and an advertisement for salt of lemons. The book was also available at Bell's Circulating Library at 132 Strand for 3d. After a secret visit to the library, Fanny wrote, 'I have an exceeding odd sensation, when I consider it is now in the power of *any* and *every* body to read what I so carefully hoarded even from my best friends, till this last month or two – and that a work which was so lately lodged, in all privacy, in my bureau may now be seen by every butcher & baker, cobler & tinker, throughout the 3 kingdoms, for the small tribute of 3 pence.'[18]

The reviews were good: indeed, uncommonly good for a first novel by an anonymous author. The *Monthly Review* gave it a short notice, but declared *Evelina* 'sprightly, entertaining and agreeable'. The *London Review* considered: 'There is much more merit as well respecting stile, character & Incident, than is usually to be met with in modern Novels.' By June the first edition of 500 copies had sold out, and Lowndes wrote to Fanny to report that all the polite world were sending to him to buy the book, including one 'Lady of Fashion', who reckoned herself quite unfashionable for not having read it. Translations were being planned in German and Dutch.

Fanny had confided her secret to her father, who now proudly read the book out to friends, declaring, 'I wish I may die, if I do not believe it to be the very best Novel in the Language, except Fielding's! for Smollet's, with all their Wit, are quite too gross.'[19] He let the secret out to the world at dinner with Dr Johnson's great friend, Hester Thrale. Mrs Thrale, one of the 'bluestocking' hostesses of the period who prided themselves on conversing on important subjects rather than idle gossip, was delighted to steal a march over her rivals, Mrs Cholmondeley and Mrs Montagu. She gave the first volume of *Evelina* to Dr Johnson to read on his way home, and he protested that 'there were passages in it which might do *honour* to Richardson'.[20] This praise must have seemed like nectar to Fanny, for Dr Johnson was regarded as the very acme of literary taste; she danced around the mulberry tree when news of his approval was brought to her, and was still talking about it fifty years later when Sir Walter Scott visited her in London.

* * *

In the famous quotation from *The Rivals*, Sir Anthony Absolute not only describes novels from circulating libraries as the 'ever-green tree, of diabolical knowledge' blossoming through the year, but goes on to utter the frightful warning that 'they who are so fond of handling the leaves, will long for the fruit at last'. The reaction to novel-reading in certain quarters was quite astonishing in its vehemence. Thomas Gisborne in *Enquiry into the Duties of the Female Sex*, first published in 1777, suggested that the passion for reading romances 'frequently creates a susceptibility of impression and a premature warmth of tender emotions, which . . . have been known to betray young women into a sudden attachment to persons unworthy of their affection'.[21]

Along with words came pictures. As early as 1736, William Hogarth in his engravings of a seduction scene, *Before* and *After*, depicted a book inscribed 'Novels' in the open drawer of the desk of the endangered lady, signifying her corrupt imagination that would cause her downfall. In an apparently respectable engraving made by Robert Pranker *c.* 1764, a lady is shown reading a novel, while her greyhound sits bolt upright next to her, rigid with alarm at her activity. It was suggested too that visiting a circulating library exposed women to the risqué prints that might be seen in the window. Printsellers took the opportunity to alter plates and inscriptions in response to an evident clientele, gliding into semi-erotica with hints that reading novels could lead to self-abuse or the path to sexual indiscretion.

But were these denunciations and responses, that sometimes bordered on the hysterical, really fair? Were the circulation libraries full only of novels? Did only women read light fiction? Paul Kaufman in his book *Libraries and their*

49 William Hogarth's engraving, *Before*, 1736. Novels and Lord Rochester's poems can be glimpsed in the open drawer of the dressing table, suggesting that the lady's moral decline has led to seduction.

Users, published in 1969, entitled his last chapter 'In Defence of Fair Readers'. Using as his primary source the original account books dating from 1793 to 1799 of James Marshall's Circulating Library in Bath, he showed that of the 1,800 patrons, women constituted less than 30 per cent of the total. He then examined the proportion of fiction offered by three of the Bath libraries and

50 A woman reading a novel, an apparently respectable scene, but one that has alarmed her canine companion. An engraving by Robert Pranker, *c.*1764 from *The Draftsman's Assistant* published by Robert Sayer in 1786.

found that the average came to 20 per cent. Gibbons had the largest stock of fiction, at 45 per cent, while Marshall's was 8 per cent. In the years since Kaufman's analysis, other researchers have found similar results. Using the archives of the Midlands booksellers, Clay's, along with the ledgers of the Cirencester bookseller Timothy Stevens, Jan Fergus has recently concluded that 'Taken together the Clay and Stevens records offer no evidence for a largely female reading public for fiction in the provinces; in fact, they demonstrate a primarily male audience'.[22]

These findings, moreover, are corroborated when the reading habits of some women and the contents of surviving personal libraries are examined. Anna Margaretta Larpent, the daughter of a diplomat, began to keep a diary in 1773 at the age of fifteen.[23] This started as a methodised journal in which she kept all kinds of lists, of people met, excursions made, sermons listened to, and books read. At a tender age when women were considered in particular moral danger from novel reading, Anna was enjoying a wide range of books, over four hundred titles, of which only one tenth were English novels; these included Horace Walpole's *The Castle of Otranto*, and Samuel Richardson's *Clarissa* and *Sir Charles Grandison*. Novels by Rousseau, Marmontel, Voltaire and Marivaux were among those that she read in French. Her reading of drama was extensive in both languages. She listed Milton, Pope, Thomson, Young and Gray among her favourite poets. And she consumed many histories, including Gibbon's *Decline and Fall*, Hume's *History of England*, and Robertson's *History of America*. Sermons by, among others, Tillotson, Blair and Sherlock are included in her lists, along with pious tracts.

In 1782 Anna became the second wife of John Larpent who had been appointed Examiner of Plays four years earlier. All plays during this period required licences before performance and thus were vetted by examiners who sent their recommendations to the Lord Chamberlain. Anna, with her interest in drama, helped Larpent with his work, and unofficially became a deputy examiner. She championed the playwright Elizabeth Inchbald, who translated from German Kotzebue's *Lovers' Vows* in 1798. This was the drama that Jane Austen chose to symbolise the moral downfall of the Bertram family in *Mansfield Park*, but Anna could not find 'the least immorality' in the play.

The Larpents set up house in Newman Street, just north of Oxford Street, with a country retreat at Ashstead in Surrey. A devout Anglican, Anna began her day with prayers and by reading the Bible or a work of piety alone before breakfast. These she would study in depth, or 'in a followed manner', as she put it. She also read serious secular works alone, with what she described as 'humble attention', putting aside about two hours each day for the purpose. Later she might discuss these with her family and friends. Novels and lighter works were enjoyed while out walking, or when her maid dressed her hair. She also took several newspapers and magazines, including the *Gentleman's Magazine*, the *Spectator*, the *Monthly* and *Critical Reviews* and the *European Magazine*. She was thus well informed on the latest books, and the novels that she mentions are recent publications. For example, in May 1790 she recorded reading *The Self-Tormentor*, written 'by a lady' and published the previous year. The *Critical Review* adjudged that 'the language, as well as the conversations, show the author to be much above the tribe of hackneyed novel-writers', and that the work was written in the style of *Evelina*. At the same time Anna was also reading *Hartley House, Calcutta*, by Phebe Gibbes. William Enfield in the *Monthly Review* wrote: 'These volumes contain a lively and elegant and, as far as we are informed, a just picture of the manners of the Europeans residing in the East Indies.' As a respectable, married middle-class lady, Anna Larpent was well aware that novels were regarded with mixed feelings. She describes her novel reading as dissipating 'her mind, now and then'. In February 1790 she received a visit from 'a distressed widow with a large family'. This was Eliza Parsons, author of several novels, regarded by Anna Larpent as 'not without genius though without correctness'. Interestingly she adds, 'she writes Alas! For bread.'

With her marriage, Anna acquired a stepson, Seymour, and had two sons of her own, George and John. Her diary therefore tells us not only the kind of reading that she undertook, but also provides a record of the help she gave to Seymour while he was at school, as well as the books she thought appropriate for George and John. The traditional idea that children should be given a stiff diet of catechistical books was being eroded by the influence of the Enlightenment. Rousseau's famous *Émile*, published in 1762, had laid down the principles for a new scheme of education, where the individual development of the child was encouraged in natural surroundings, to form an independent judgement and stable character. On New Year's Day, 1793, Anna records reading with George *The History of Sandford and Merton*, the novel for young readers written by Thomas Day as a result of his admiration for Rousseau (p. 99).

Anna Larpent often read aloud to her husband, who in turn read to her, to their servants and their friends. Joseph Priestley's comments on *The Origin of Government* were read 'rather to lead to conversation & observation than as a followed reading'. At a country-house party in 1780, Anna and other guests read aloud extracts from Rollin's *Histoire Ancienne*, Marivaux's *La Vie de Marianne*, and *School for Wives*, a comedy by Henry Kelly. As John Brewer points out, this was an eighteenth-century cultural phenomenon 'made possible by publishers and libraries, authors and book clubs . . . . It is impossible to imagine someone in the seventeenth century, regardless of their social position, being able to live this kind of literary life. No matter how well educated and no matter how readily they had access to books, they could not have obtained the number and variety of printed materials which Larpent secured with such apparent ease.'[24]

The Soane household was not dissimilar. John Soane's books ran to many thousands, and his wife Eliza as a well-educated and literate person would have made good use of the collection (pp. 114 and ff). The books definitely belonging to her make up a mere handful, but are similar in subject matter to those noted by Anna Larpent. Soane was a profound religious sceptic, but his wife owned a bible, books of common prayer, the *Devout Christian's Companion*, published in 1715 and inherited from her uncle George Wyatt, Christoph Christian Sturm's *Reflections for every day in the year*, 1810, and the ubiquitous *The Whole Duty of Man*. Another very popular title in her collection was Robert Dodsley's *The Oeconomy of human life*, translated from an

Indian manuscript written by a Brahmin and first published in 1751. This had run to two hundred editions, more than any other book in the eighteenth century apart from the Bible. Like Anna Larpent, Eliza also owned Gibbon's *Decline and Fall of the Roman Empire*.

There are no novels that can be assigned to Eliza Soane; those that are in the library at Lincoln's Inn Fields reflect the conservative tastes of her husband, the works for example of Sterne and Smollett, and his favourite, *Gil Blas*. Trenchant as ever, he once told his son John, 'I was never fond of romances and novels; such works I was early taught to look upon as trash for silly girls.'[25] Eliza kept a journal in tiny notebooks, and these have survived for the years from 1804 to 1813. At the back of two of the books she noted a reading list of books, a mixture of fiction and non-fiction. For 1805, alongside a life of Agrippina and the letters of Lady Mary Wortley Montagu, she lists three novels, including *Mysterious Visit* by the indigent widow, Eliza Parsons. In 1806 she notes two novels just published, Mrs Opie's *Simple Tales* and *The Novice of St Dominick* by Miss Owenson. These were almost certainly borrowed from circulating libraries: an entry in February 1804 records returning books to the library of James Henderson, at 14 Tavistock Street in Covent Garden, another for October 1805 notes paying 12s for half a year's subscription.[26] Eliza also used the circulating libraries in Margate, where she rented lodgings during the summer season to get away from the grime of London, made worse for her by Soane's refurbishment work on their home in Lincoln's Inn Fields.

Turning to personal libraries that have survived from this period, A la Ronde would seem an ideal example to consider. Situated in the seaside resort of Exmouth in Devon, it is a *cottage ornée* built *c.* 1795 for Jane Parminter, the daughter of a Barnstaple wine merchant, and her orphaned cousin, Mary. The Parminter cousins, having spent eleven years touring the Continent, chose the house to have sixteen sides like the Byzantine church of S. Vitale in Ravenna, but the overall effect is more of a gingerbread cottage. Jane died in 1811, but Mary lived on until 1849 when she stipulated in her will that the house should be inherited only by unmarried women. A la Ronde does have a library, but books are also distributed all over the house, some alongside shells and other curiosities in cases. The eighteenth-century books seem to have belonged to Jane and Mary, and consist of standard literary works in English and French, and historical works. Despite being an all female household, there are no 'modern' novels. Either the Parminters had no taste for them, or used a circulating library in Exmouth, just as Eliza Soane did in London and Margate.

Calke Abbey in Derbyshire is a rather plain Baroque mansion built between 1701 and 1704 by the Harpur family. As its name suggests, it is built on the site of an Augustinian priory, in a dip in the land so that it peers rather furtively at the visitor, and this shyness extends to the Harpurs. Until 1789 the baronets were well-to-do Derbyshire gentry, energetic in their public duties, keen on horse-racing and other country sports, and described by William Woolley, writing in the eighteenth century, as 'the best landed Family of any Commoners in this or any of the neighbouring County's'. But then Sir Henry Harpur, the 7th Baronet, inherited and withdrew from all conventional contacts so that his mother was obliged to tell a friend that he refused to be a man of the world. Harpur added fuel to the fire by acquiring as his mistress a lady's maid, Nanette Hawkins, whom he then married. For the rest of his life he maintained a self-imposed seclusion at Calke, becoming known as the 'isolated baronet'.

In 1805 Sir Henry converted a drawing room on the first floor of the east front into the library. It is a comfortable room, retaining the original Regency furniture supplied by Marsh & Tatham: *bergère* armchairs and a chaise longue as well as a library table and steps. One interesting feature is the rolling maps,

51 The early nineteenth-century library at Calke Abbey in Derbyshire, showing fixed to the book-shelves two of the spring rollers that could be dropped down to display maps. This is a comfortable room, with *bergère* chairs and sofas where the Harpur family might relax and read.

showing the various counties of England and Wales, attached to the book-cases. The bookcases rise to ten tiers, and seem to have been added piecemeal when more space was required. Above them hang some of Calke's fine collection of horse paintings. Unlike the early eighteenth-century library at Dunham Massey (p. 67), this is a room in which the family might gather to relax.

Although there does not appear to have been a library before this period, Sir Henry inherited a sizeable collection of books. To this he proceeded to add both fiction and non-fiction, old as well as new titles, many in French, and bound sets of magazines and journals. Some of the books may have been acquired from booksellers in Ashby-de-la-Zouch and Derby, others during the visits he made to London with Nanette. They would rent a country house in the Home Counties from which they could make forays to the shops, to the theatre and to exhibitions in London without taking on the social obligations of a regular residence in the capital. Some of the books in the library carry the labels of circulating libraries, probably acquired when the latter were selling off stock. From the fashionable library of Hookham's in Bond Street comes George Greene's *Relation of Several Circumstances which occurred of the province of Lower Normandy*, published in 1802; from Silver's Circulating Library in Margate, *The Miscellaneous Works of Jean-Jacques Rousseau*, in four volumes, 1767; and from Garner's Library, also in Margate, Sherlock's *Practical Discourse*, 1725, autographed by a member of the family in 1817. None of these books could be remotely described as light fiction.

Like the Larpents, the Harpurs were evidently fond of the theatre. In the Library is a set of several dozen play-scripts published in London between 1780 and 1810, specially bound up into volumes. The plays have wonderful titles, such as *To Marry or Not to Marry*, *Too Many Cooks* and *Love amongst the Locksmiths*. Here, too, is Mrs Inchbald's infamous *Lovers' Vows*, the play featured in *Mansfield Park*. Sir Henry and Nanette had eight children, and so amateur theatricals and play readings may have lightened their winter evenings at Calke, especially if the company also included house guests. One play-script, *The Farm House: A Comedy in Three Acts* by John Philip Kemble, has initials marked in pencil next to the dramatis personae. The male lead of Modeley was taken by H.H., presumably Sir Henry, while one bit part has been deleted, suggesting that there were eight people, six men and two women, available to take part.[27]

Turning from drama to novels, the collection made by Sir Henry Harpur and his family in the 1790s and early 1800s reflects the latest developments in fiction. One of the alterations at Calke at this time was the creation of a Caricature Room with cartoons dating from 1791 through to 1827 pasted on the walls. This was probably the work of Sir Henry's eldest surviving son,

George Crewe: he took the new surname as a result of his father's claim to a dormant barony that had been possessed by one of his ancestors. In 1819 George inherited Calke when his father was killed in an extraordinary accident. Driving his phaeton, he had almost reached his destination in Hertfordshire when he accelerated the horses and drove into a post. George had endured a strange childhood, often away from home, and his letters include a pathetic request that he be allowed back to Calke for Christmas. As squire of Calke, he led a conventional and very pious life, but the strain of shy eccentricity was to return with renewed vigour in his Harpur Crewe descendants.

One of the caricatures at Calke is James Gillray's *Tales of Wonder!*, published in February 1802, showing four ladies sitting around a table in their drawing room frightening themselves rigid by reading a Gothic novel. Gillray is here poking fun at the literary vogue of the time. The real *Tales of Wonder* was a harmless anthology, including for instance a ballad by Sir Walter Scott and a poem by Robert Burns, edited by Matthew Gregory Lewis. Lewis had earlier written a spectacular bestseller, *The Monk,* published in 1797. The monk in

52 James Gillray's *Tales of Wonder!*, published in 1802. One of the ladies seated around the drawing-room table is reading from *The Monk*, the Gothic bestseller by Matthew Gregory Lewis. The horror of the story is echoed by the ornaments on the mantelpiece, while a picture on the wall shows a girl being carried off to rape and slaughter.

question was Ambrosio, a worthy superior of the Capuchin order in Madrid. Falling to the temptations of a fiend-inspired woman disguised as a boy in his monastery, he was so depraved that he pursued one of his penitents and killed her to avoid detection. The book ended dramatically with him being hurled to destruction and damnation by the Devil. The nineteen-year-old author was known thereafter as 'Monk' Lewis.

This genre had begun forty years earlier with Horace Walpole's *The Castle of Otranto*. All the ingredients of the classic Gothic horror story were there – mysterious manuscript, ancestral portrait, usurper, persecuted heroine, noble peasant, hermit, monk, castle in ruins – and Walpole's successors built upon this, gradually pushing aside the epistolary and sentimental novels in terms of popularity. Genteel lady writers joined in the horror: Eliza Parsons, for instance, in *The Castle of Wolfenbach* featured a wicked Count forcing the heroine to watch her lover being tortured to death before being locked up in a dark windowless chamber with the headless body. It was Ann Radcliffe's similarly horrific tale, *The Mysteries of Udolpho* that inspired Jane Austen to pen her burlesque Gothic novel, written in 1798 but eventually published as *Northanger Abbey* in 1818 after her death.

Jane Austen was an avid reader of novels, enjoying access to her father's library. At the age of thirteen, she wrote an essay for *The Loiterer*, a literary magazine begun by her brothers at Oxford: 'You must know, sir, I am a great reader, and not to mention some hundred volumes of novels and plays, have in the past two summers, actually got through all our most celebrated period-ical writers.'[28] She belonged to a book society in Chawton, the village in Hampshire where she lived with her mother and her sister Cassandra after the death of her father. This must have been like a modern reading group, with members exchanging books and commenting on them.

What we know of Jane's taste in novels has been filtered by her clergyman brother writing after her death: he emphasised her liking for moral writers, although in fact she enjoyed what he considered improper novels, such as Fielding's *Tom Jones* and Laurence Sterne's *Tristram Shandy*, and was a connoisseur of Gothic shockers like *The Castle of Otranto*, *The Monk* and *The Mysteries of Udolpho*. She was also an admirer of Fanny Burney, acquiring the title of her most famous novel, *Pride and Prejudice*, from the last sentence of *Cecilia*. In *Northanger Abbey*, which she originally entitled *Susan*, Austen has her heroine, Catherine Morland, declaring, 'Oh! It is only a novel! . . . It is only *Cecilia* or *Camilla*, or *Belinda*; or, in short, only some work in which the greatest powers of the mind are displayed, in which the most thorough knowl-edge of human nature, the happiest delineation of its varieties, the liveliest effusions of wit and humour are conveyed to the world in the best chosen language.'[29] Here she is contrasting Burney's stories with the fantasies of

Radcliffe. The whole plot of the book is a gentle spoof, with Catherine Morland, her head filled with *The Mysteries of Udolpho*, imagining that her host at Northanger Abbey, General Tilney, has done away with his wife.

At the beginning of *Northanger Abbey* Austen lists nine 'horrid' novels that have excited the scheming Isabella Thorpe. Of these, six were from William Lane's notorious Minerva Press, including Mrs Parsons' tale of torture and cruelty, *The Castle of Wolfenbach*. Two others were translations from the German: *The Necromancer, or the Tale of the Black Forest* by Karl Friedrich Kahlert, published in England in 1794, and *Horrid Mysteries* by Karl Friedrich August Grosse, 1796. Interest in all things German had replaced the vogue for the Romance languages of France, Italy and Spain. John Soane's younger son, George, studied German rather than Italian or French, one of the many bones of contention between father and son. The author of a Gothic novel, *The Eve of San Marco*, George later translated plays by Schiller and Goethe's *Faust* with the approval of the latter.

And this interest was two way. Many novels were translated into German, while a large collection of Gothic novels in English are to be found in the Princely Library at Schloss Corvey near Höxter in Germany. Victor Amadeus, Landgrave of Hesse-Rotenburg, and his second wife, Elise, were prodigious collectors so that the library contains 25,000 titles in 73,000 volumes, mainly in German, French and English. The English novels, numbering around 2,500 and published between 1790 and 1834, probably came through a German bookseller, Dr Moller from Gottingen, who specialised in this trade. He would have kept up to date with what was going on in the world of novels in England through reviews and trade catalogues. The collection has recently been catalogued by the University of Paderborn, and has revealed titles that are not known anywhere else, because the huge output of this kind of novel resulted in short shelf lives.

The collection of Gothic novels at Calke is miniscule in comparison with that at Corvey, but interesting in its selection. Missing are both *The Monk* and *Northanger Abbey*, but the Library does contain a whole set of the *Tales of Wonder*, and Monk Lewis's *Romantic Tales* in four volumes. In *The Castle of Otranto* Horace Walpole hides behind the pseudonym of Onuphrio Muraeto, as he wanted an escape route if the book proved a disaster. *The Old English Baron: 'A Gothic Story'* by Clara Reeve is at Calke in a 1789 edition. When it was published in 1777, the *Critical Review* likened it to *Otranto*. The Harpurs owned two of Ann Radcliffe's 'shockers', *The Mysteries of Udolpho* and *The Italian*, both in their first editions, and *A Tale of Mystery or Celina*, translated from the French of Ducray-Duminil by Mrs Meeke, and published at the Minerva Press in Leadenhall Street in 1803.

By the time *Northanger Abbey* was published in 1818, the craze for the Gothic had fallen away, with a brief resurgence following Mary Shelley's *Frankenstein*. Indeed, back in 1804 Mary Goldsmith had published a moral domestic fiction, *Casualties: A Novel*, whose title page declared: 'No Subterranean Caverns – Haunted Castles – Enchanted Forests – Fearful Visions – Mysterious Voices – Supernatural agents – Bloody Daggers – Dead Men's Skulls – Mangled Bodies – Nor Marvellous Lights, form any part of the present Work; but will be found on Perusal, to arise out of Natural Incidents.' Four years later, what has been described as the moral rearmament of the upper classes was on the move with the publication of Hannah More's *Cœlebs in Search of a Wife*. Mrs More, a pious evangelical dubbed 'the Old Bishop in Petticoats' by William Cobbett, decided that the best way to deal with improper novels was to write a proper one herself, as the subtitle suggests, 'Comprehending Observations on Domestic Habits and Manners'. The book sold very well, though probably among the like-minded, and also spawned all kinds of improper parodies, such as *Cœlebs in Search of a Mistress*, published anonymously by the roguish Thomas Tegg in 1810. *In Search of a Wife* was owned by the Harpurs as volume seven of an eleven-volume set of the *Works of Hannah More*.

A year later Maria Edgeworth published the first part of her *Tales of Fashionable Life*. This proved such a successful book that the opportunistic publisher Henry Colburn brought out *Tales of Real Life forming a Sequel to Miss Edgeworth's Tales*, obliging Maria Edgeworth's publisher, Joseph Johnson to publish in the press an assertion of his authoress's work. Such was the desire of her public for the next book that eight thousand copies of *Patronage* were sold on the day of publication in 1814, and one of those eagerly awaited copies is to be found at Calke. Sadly it received poor reviews and never had the continuing success of *Tales of Fashionable Life*.

Colburn, however, must have recognised the commercial potential of the doings of the rich and famous, for he was to be the purveyor of a genre popular in the 1820s, known as 'silver fork novels'. This name was coined by William Hazlitt in his essay, 'The Dandy School', in which he describes a popular author, Theodore Hook, as an *arriviste*, so enamoured of the elite and their manners that he 'considers it a circumstance of no consequence if a whole country starves' and informs readers only that those of quality 'eat their fish with a silver fork'. Although Hazlitt raged against these books, they did sell, helped greatly by the marketing efforts of Henry Colburn, who also published Burke's *Peerage* and, rather incongruously, the transcribed diaries of Samuel Pepys. He advertised widely, paying newspapers and journalists to insert pieces in their gossip and society columns. An ideal author for him was Lady Charlotte Bury who had not only contracted two romantic marriages, but was also the beautiful daughter of a duke and lady-in-waiting to the Queen. For the advance publicity for her novel *Flirtation* in 1828 he suggested that this was a *roman à clef*, thus getting a mention in the 'High Life and Fashionable Chit Chat' column of the *World of Fashion*. Although it was a conventional tale, lacking wit and sparkle, the circulating libraries loved it, and it ran to three editions in the first year. The novel also had a moral element, and this rather than excitement over the high life of London was probably what attracted the Crewes. *Flirtation* is to be found at Calke, along with *A Marriage in High Life*, which is attributed to Lady Scott with the help of her relative, Lady Charlotte Bury.

Maria Edgeworth has also been credited with being the forerunner of the regional historical novel with her tales of Irish life, beginning with *Castle Rackrent*, published in 1800. Her work was greatly admired by Sir Walter Scott who was to acknowledge his debt to her in his preface to *Waverley*. Scott had built up a considerable reputation with his poetry but he sensed that the literary future lay with novels, and in 1805 began quietly to work on *Waverley; or, 'Tis Sixty Years Since* about the Jacobite uprisings in Scotland. Meanwhile, he followed the trends in novels, writing as an anonymous reviewer for the *Quarterly Review*. The *Quarterly* was the younger of two periodicals that had an important influence on readers' tastes. The *Edinburgh Review*, owned partly by the publisher Longmans and launched in 1802, took a Whiggish view, thus irritating John Murray II, who brought out the *Quarterly* to convey his Tory opinions. Unlike the earlier *Critical* and *Monthly Reviews*, these carried much longer reviews of fewer books, and concentrated very heavily on non-fiction, although they provided listings of 'novels and romances' in their appendices of new publications. A distaste for 'female' novels was evident in both, so that Fanny Burney's last novel, *The Wanderer*, published in 1814 got short shrift from the review in the *Quarterly*, which declared it could hardly 'claim any very decided superiority over the thousand-and-one volumes with which the Minerva Press inundates the shelves of circulating libraries, and increases, instead of diverting, the ennui of loungers at watering places'.

Scott, reviewing in the *Quarterly* for May 1810 looked with jaundiced eye at the current crop of fiction. The scandalous doings of the Prince of Wales and his friends had encouraged a fashion for accounts of the lifestyle of the beau monde wrapped up in fiction, with titles such as Mary Julia Young's *Summer in Brighton*. Scott mourned 'our Winters in London, Bath and Brighton, of which it is the dirty object to drag forth the secret history of the day, and to give to Scandal a court of written record'. Moving on, he decried various Gothic novels in the style of Ann Radcliffe and 'Monk' Lewis, among which the book he was supposed to be reviewing, Charles Robert Maturin's *The Fatal Revenge*, stood out as the work of an unusually gifted but misdirected author.

From the outset with his Waverley novels Scott determined to create a superior form of fiction, to appeal to the readers of the *Edinburgh* and *Quarterly
Reviews*. However, neither he nor his publisher, Archibald Constable, could
have envisaged the incredible success that was to follow. In 1814, shortly
before printing *Waverley*, James Ballantyne consulted Constable on how much
paper to order – enough for 750 copies or 1,000? Most novels at this period
had a first print run of 500, and the vast majority never went to reprint.
Constable boldly chose 1,000, but had rapidly to reprint and to go for five
more reprints within three years.

Scott insisted that *Waverley* be published anonymously, so that his subsequent novels were described as by 'the author of *Waverley*'. By the time *Rob
Roy* was published in 1818, this marketing strategy ensured that it was a bestseller from the off, with an initial print run of 10,000. Much speculation was
expressed as to identity of the author of these famous books, and Scott finally
confessed on 23 February 1827 at an official dinner, declaring 'the joke has
lasted long enough, and I was tired of it'.[30] In fact, Jane Austen had guessed
back in September 1814, two months after the publication of *Waverley*,
writing in a letter, 'Walter Scott has no business to write novels, especially

53 *Four Specimens of the Reading Public*, a print by George Cruikshank after Alfred Crowquill,
published by John Fairburn in 1826. The lady, possibly a housekeeper, is asking for a romantic novel
in five volumes; the ageing roué for the lurid revelations of the famous courtesan, Harriet Wilson; the
dust-man for the works of the radical William Cobbett; and the dandy for the new Waverley novel.

good ones. It is not fair. He has Fame and Profit enough as a Poet, and should not be taking the bread out of people's mouths.'[31]

The sales figures for the Waverley novels were huge compared to what had hitherto constituted a best-seller. In *The Reading Nation in the Romantic Period*, William St Clair provides estimated sales figures for varoius books from publication up to the mid-1830s. Sales for *Waverley* were 40,000, for *Guy Mannering* 50,000, compared with 4,000 for Fanny Burney's *Camilla* and between 2,000 and 3,000 for Jane Austen's *Pride and Prejudice*.[32] Although he had already built up a reputation as a poet, Scott was now catapulted into being a national celebrity, frequently featuring in caricatures, a sure indicator of fame. His books were eagerly sought in North America and in the British Empire in the East, particularly in India where Scots were hungry for literature to transport them back in their imaginations to their native land.[33] In Europe too his books sold phenomenally well: between 1820 and 1851, 20 editions of his complete works were published in France alone, in all selling 45,000 copies. The demand for *walterscottamanie* is reflected in the catalogues of French lending libraries. Tartan became the fashion for ladies' clothes while gentlemen had to sport *cravattes à la Walter Scott*. Donizetti composed the opera *Lucia de Lammermoor*, Balzac and Hugo paid him the joint compliments of reverence and imitation, while Goethe said of him, 'I know what he is after and what he can do. He would always entertain me.'[34]

Why was Scott so successful? Despite his reservations about the fiction of the time, his stories drew upon the thrills of the Gothic and the themes of sentimental tales, and from the traditional romances of earlier centuries. Combining Scottish folklore with a wide range of European literature, he attracted both cultural elites and popular audiences. Thomas Carlyle credited him with being the timely rescuer of British literature, which 'lay all puking and sprawling in Werterism, Byronism, and other Sentimentalism tearful or spasmodic (fruit of internal wind) . . . these Historical Novels have taught all men this truth . . . that the bygone ages of the world were actually filled by living men, not by protocols, state-papers, controversies and abstractions. . .'[35]

The dominance of Scott in late Georgian fiction is clearly shown at Calke Abbey where there are several sets of his Waverley novels, alongside works of poetry. The same is to be found in the library of Springhill in County Londonderry, Northern Ireland. The late seventeenth-century whitewashed house has the air of a North American colonial house, which is perhaps not surprising as William Conyngham built his home in hostile territory. His father, a Presbyterian Scot from Ayrshire, was part of the Ulster plantation of James I, driving the native Irish from their homes. Although successive generations of Conynghams and later of Lenox-Conynghams added to Springhill, it is not large, and the library is also modest, with plain bookcases on one wall and parts of two others. More books are housed in low Regency bookcases in the drawing room beyond. The quarters may not be as grand as in English country houses of the time, but the Lenox-Conynghams loved their books, inscribing them with their names and introducing bookplates. Those currently on display date from the seventeenth through to the early nineteenth centuries, with many hundreds of late nineteenth- and twentieth-century books stored away in the attics. A catalogue of the book collection compiled in the 1920s shows that books were scattered all over the house, with some of the devotional books kept in a bible box.

As Ireland was excluded from the 1710 Copyright Act, its book trade differed from that of the rest of Britain, with printers and publishers exploiting this with cheap reprint editions of English works, much to the fury of London booksellers. On the other hand, leading Irish writers, such as Jonathan Swift and Oliver Goldsmith, wanted their books to be published in London. John Murray I, who did a lot of business in Dublin, explained to a friend in 1770: 'In Ireland the booksellers without ceremony reprint upon the English; and the English have the privilege in their turn to reprint upon the Irish. The former however come off with the Loss as it is in London only where the most esteemed English books are first printed.'[36] Two late Georgian cash books at Springhill show that in the 1820s the family bought their books from Mullins and Mahon in Dublin, and Harrison in Belfast. Later they also did business with booksellers nearer to home, Campbell in Londonderry and Dunlop in Coleraine, as well as subscribing directly with publishers in London.

The late eighteenth-century books at Springhill are what might be called polite literature, including French and Italian works, novels, plays, poetry and music, along with periodicals such as the *Annual Register* and a Dublin edition of the *Gentleman's Magazine*. The novels, however, do not reflect a roller-coaster ride of light and sentimental fiction. Smollett, Fielding, Richardson and Le Sage are the authors of choice for the eighteenth century, and in the nineteenth century two novelists stand out above all others: Maria Edgeworth and Sir Walter Scott. The Irish author Maria Edgeworth is represented in an eighteen-volume set published in 1832, as well as individual novels. Alongside his poetical works are ranged Scott's Waverley novels, many carrying Harrison's label: *Rob Roy, Red Gauntlet, Quentin Durward, Ivanhoe, Peveril of the Peak* and *Kenilworth*. The Lenox - Conynghams must have bought them in their three - volume sets from Harrison and others as soon as they were published. In 1821 Scott's publishers, Archibald Constable in Edinburgh and Thomas Longman in London, decided to set the price of *Kenilworth* at the extravagant level of a guinea and a half, or 31s 6d, setting the trend for 'three-deckers' for the rest of the century, but such was the popularity of Scott that customers paid up.

At Springhill there are no Gothic horrors: a series of books mentioned in the 1920 catalogue featuring a hermit – *The Hermit Abroad, The Hermit in London* and *The Hermit in the Country* – were in fact prose sketches on fashionable life by the Irish writer, Felix MacDonogh, published in multi-volumes by Henry Colburn. There are no novels by Fanny Burney, nor by Jane Austen – the only editions of the latter date from the twentieth century and are packed away in the attic. One book from the notorious Minerva Press sits on the shelves, Regina M. Roche's *Munster Cottage Boy*, published in 1820. Its Irish theme may have persuaded the Lenox-Conynghams to make its purchase from Harrison of Belfast, whose label appears on the endpaper.

The libraries at Calke and Springhill, and the diaries of Anna Larpent all support the conclusions drawn by Kaufman and Fergus and others who have investigated the archives of the book trade. Readers were buying a mixture of fiction and non-fiction, indeed very much more of the latter. Pious devotional books mingled with the so-called impious novels. And men were readers of novels. Jane Austen sums this up admirably in *Northanger Abbey* in a conversation between Catherine Morland and Henry Tilney. Catherine suggests that Tilney never reads novels, 'because they are not clever enough for you; gentlemen read better books'. To which he responds, 'The person, be it gentleman or lady who has not pleasure in a good novel, must be intolerably stupid', and goes on to declare that he has read hundreds and hundreds.[37]

The absence of Austen's novels from both Calke and Springhill is striking, but not unusual. The literary critic Leigh Hunt, for instance, never mentioned her. There was a copy of *Emma* in the early nineteenth-century library at Saltram in Devon, but this had been presented by the author to Lady Morley. The audience remained small until the publication of a memoir of Jane Austen by her nephew in 1870. As in Aesop's fable, Sir Walter Scott was the hare, Jane Austen the tortoise. Today Scott is not widely read, and editions of the Waverley novels adorn many a second-hand bookshop shelf. Thanks to television and films, Jane Austen is known the world over, her novels voted the all-time favourites of men and women, young and old, rich and poor. Literary Parnassus must be astonished.

CHAPTER 7

RARE AND CURIOUS

The Books of Charles Winn

Life must have been full of surprises for the young Charles Winn. Born in 1795, he was the younger son of Esther Winn, daughter of the fine house of Nostell in West Yorkshire, and John Williamson, a Manchester baker. The marriage of Esther and John in 1792 had outraged the Winn family: it was described later as a 'moral cloud'.[1] When Charles was born, the Winn estates belonged to his uncle, Sir Rowland, 6th Baronet, 'a gay fox hunter taking pleasure chiefly in his hounds and horses'.[2] He became guardian of Charles and his older brother John at their mother's death in 1803. The boys lived with Shepley Watson, a local solicitor who managed the Winn family estates, at Cold Hiendly, a few miles from Nostell Hall. Since Sir Rowland was not married, John was being groomed to inherit and the two boys would have made frequent visits to their uncle. In 1805 Sir Rowland died, aged only thirty, and his nephews and niece took the surname of Winn. Watson ensured both boys completed their education with Charles destined for the Church. The 'Kind Hearts and Coronets' story continued with the unexpected death of John Winn in Rome in 1817 while on the Grand Tour. Charles then came into the Winn inheritance.

Two years later he married his cousin, Priscilla Strickland. He had wanted to do so earlier, but her father, Sir William Strickland of Boynton Hall near Bridlington, had opposed the match until Charles became heir to Nostell. With this marriage, Charles not only acquired a wife, but also a social circle that shared his own interests. Sir William was scholarly and a keen collector of coins and books, while Charles's diaries show that he was close to Priscilla's brothers and sisters, in particular Eustachius Strickland, a name worthy of a character from a Trollope novel.

What was the inheritance that Charles Winn had so unexpectedly acquired? Nostell Hall had been built in the 1720s in grand Palladian style by his great-grandfather, with Robert Adam brought in by his grandfather to remodel the house and decorate the interior in the most sumptuous style. When Sir Rowland, the 5th Baronet, was killed in a carriage accident in 1785, the family finances were in a parlous state, so Adam and his craftsmen were laid off, leaving Nostell as 'an overgrown and yet unfinished modern house'. The grand London house was sold, and Shepley Watson shrewdly used the family's assets to recover their fortunes, most notably exploiting the coal reserves that lay under the Nostell estates. Charles also acquired an estate at Appleby in Lincolnshire. With these resources, he was able to indulge his passion for collecting books.

In his choice of books, he reflected a long tradition of English bibliophiles, traced back by Thomas Frognall Dibdin to the fourteenth century and one of Edward III's tutors. Dibdin attributed his own early interest in books to his schoolmaster in Reading, John Man, and his father-in-law, William Baker, and he, like John Soane, was given run of their library. In 1802 he published *An introduction to knowledge of rare and valuable editions of Greek and Latin*

54 Charles Winn of Nostell Priory, clergyman, antiquary and bibliophile.

classics which brought him to the attention of George John Spencer, 2nd Earl Spencer, an avid book collector who was building up a magnificent library at Althorp in Northamptonshire. In 1809 Dibdin wrote the first version of his famous, or infamous, *The Bibliomania*. This took the form of a letter to his friend Richard Heber, 'containing some account of the History, Symptoms and Cure of this Fatal Disease'.[3]

Dibdin was not the first to coin the term bibliomania, which was in use in England as early as 1734 when Thomas Hearne remarked on the low prices fetched by manuscripts at the sale of Thomas Rawlinson's library: 'had I been in place I should have been tempted to have laid out a pretty deal of money, without thinking myself at all touched with Bibliomania'.[4] Thomas Jefferson confessed to a friend in 1789 that he 'laboured grievously under the malady of Bibliomanie', and therefore took care to buy only at reasonable prices.[5] Isaac D'Israeli, whose fine collection of antiquarian books is still to be seen at Hughenden Manor in Buckinghamshire, the home of his son Benjamin, wrote in 1807: 'The BIBLIOMANIA, or the collecting an enormous heap of Books, without intelligent curiosity, has, since Libraries have existed, been the rage with some, who would fain pass themselves on us as men of vast erudition. Their motley Libraries have been called the *Mad-houses of the human Mind*; and again, the *Tomb of Books*, when the possessor will not communicate them, and coffins them up in the cases of his Library.' D'Israeli was making various points. First he was distinguishing serious book collectors from avid trophy hunters. Secondly he was noting the 'library miser', who never let anybody see his treasures. He then went on to note the 'library show-offs' who 'place all their fame on the *view* of a splendid Library, where volumes arrayed in all the pomp of lettering, silk linings, triple gold bands, and tinted leather are locked up in wire cases . . . dazzling our eyes like Eastern Beauties peering through their jealousies!'[6]

Dibdin, however, once he had warmed to his theme could not stop, so that *Bibliomania* expanded from the 92 pages of 1809 to an extravagant 796 pages by 1811. Some of the book collectors he introduces did indeed show signs of madness. John Leland, the Tudor antiquary, suffered from manic depression, aggravated by his passion for collecting and the immense task that he set himself in trying to produce a topographical survey of England and Wales. According to a friend, 'he fell besides his wits' and died insane in 1552. Many more, however, were so addicted to books that they faced financial ruin. Perhaps the most spectacular of these was Edward Harley, 2nd Earl of Oxford. In 1724 he inherited not only Wimpole Hall in Cambridgeshire, but also his father Robert's magnificent collection of books. He took over the mantle, amassing a collection of 8,000 volumes of manuscripts, 50,000 printed books, over 350,000 pamphlets, 41,000 prints and dozens of albums of drawings. To

55 Frontispiece of the auction sale catalogue of the collection of paintings, drawings, prints and antiquities of Edward Harley, 2nd Earl of Oxford. The sale was conducted over several days by Christopher Cock in Covent Garden in March 1742. The engraving was taken from George Vertue's drawing that showed the wide range of Harley's collection.

house the greater part of this collection, Edward Harley commissioned James Gibbs to build the fine double cube library at Wimpole, but by 1740 he was bankrupt and his estates were put up for sale. So heavy was the blow that by the following year Edward Harley was dead. His widow sold the vast book collection to the bookseller Thomas Osborne for only £13,000, while his manuscripts were bought for the nation for £10,000, and formed the basis for the British Library.

D'Israeli also observed that bibliomania had never raged more violently than in his day, the first years of the nineteenth century. Opportunities to buy rare and curious books were legion. The suppression of the Jesuits in the 1760s and 1770s, together with the upheavals of the French Revolution had caused the break-up of many fine religious and aristocratic libraries and picture collections. The British were able to exercise immense purchasing power, just as their American counterparts were to do at the end of the nineteenth century. For example, Dibdin's patron, the 2nd Earl Spencer, came from one of the mighty Whig families, 'a class then richer than many sovereign princes'.[7] Spencer began his serious rare-book collecting with English black letter printing, acquiring his first Caxton in 1789, and from there he developed an interest in all kinds of early and fine printing. With the help of his librarian Dibdin, and London booksellers such as Thomas Longman, he bid in the chief auction sales. To prove that Whig blood was no thicker than water, he prevented his nephew, the 6th Duke of Devonshire, from purchasing Caxton's *Book of divers ghostly matters* by putting in an unbeatable bid of £200, with the option of going higher. The apogee of bibliomania came in 1812, when he was in competition with his cousin, the Marquis of Blandford, for the purchase of Boccaccio's *Decameron* in a 1471 edition by Valdarfer of Venice, at the sale of the Duke of Roxburghe's library. Leigh Hunt later recalled the scene: '[Spencer] sat at the farther end of the auctioneer's table, with an air of intelligent indifference, leaning his head on his hand, so as to push up the hat a little from it . . . It was curious, and scarcely pleasant to see two Spencers thus bidding against one another, even though the bone of contention was a book.'[8] After 112 bids, Valdarfer's *Decameron* was sold to Blandford for £2,260, the highest paid price for a printed book to that date, sending shock waves through the salerooms of Europe.[9] When Dibdin acquired for Spencer the first book to be printed in Oxford, this time for a bargain £150, he claimed that it helped to cure an attack of gout: 'in my illness black letter is more efficacious than black doses'.[10] By the time of his death in 1836, Spencer's library comprised over 40,000 volumes, including 55 Caxtons, accommodated in five adjoining rooms at Althorp, where Dibdin rather whimsically suggested that a Shetland pony might be kept 'to carry the more delicate visitor from one extremity to the other'.[11]

Not all book collectors were so flamboyant, or so wealthy as Lord Spencer. Many were serious scholars, acquiring books to further their studies. One such in the eighteenth century was Sir Richard Ellys of Nocton Hall in Lincolnshire. At his death in 1742, his library passed to his distant kinsman, John Hobart, 1st Earl of Buckinghamshire, and most of his books are still be seen at Blickling Hall, the Hobarts' family home in Norfolk. The library contains many wonderful books, but also a collection of Ellys's catalogues and bibliographical publications that show how a discerning collector found out about and acquired books. Ellys began to buy books in earnest after he inherited his father's estates in 1727. When in London, he was a member of Dr Edmund Calamy's 'Congregation of Protestant Dissenters' in Westminster. Dissenters were prohibited from holding public office, and excluded from university libraries and those belonging to the Church, such as the Archbishop of Canterbury's library at Lambeth Palace. Their response was to create libraries of their own and to offer these facilities for research to fellow Dissenters: the library of Dr Williams in Gordon Square is a surviving example. They also sustained themselves by correspondence with Dissenters throughout Europe and in North America, exchanging ideas and the latest information on books in journals. The *Journal des Scavens* was the earliest of these, begun in 1665. Similar journals in English were the *History of the Works of the Learned,* 1699, and the *Republick of Letters,* 1728.

Among the books in Ellys's library are surveys of the historical development of libraries, such as Johannes Lomeier's *De Bibliothecis,* printed in Utrecht in 1680. Lomeier, a Professor of Zutphen Academy, combined general advice about forming and managing libraries with an account of the most important collections in various countries. Ellys also owned a range of printed catalogues of libraries, including that of Harvard College in Massachusetts, dating from 1723. The first to be published by any library in North America, it listed around 3,000 titles acquired since the college's foundation in 1636. It served a dual purpose, providing important information with fund-raising, for it was sent out to potential benefactors, especially among the dissenting community. Ellys's copy, however, is uncut, so Harvard's appeal in this case went unanswered (see p. 85).

As Ellys purchased rare books and manuscripts, he made use of more specialist catalogues and booksellers' lists. These were available in Latin or French from the Continent during the late seventeenth century, and began to appear in English in the early eighteenth century. One that survives at Blickling is *Catalogus universalis librorum, in omni facultate, linquaque insignium, & rarissimorum,* compiled by the bookseller John Hartley in 1699. This represents the first attempt to pull together valuable and rare books from a wide range of sources for the developing English market. Hartley made use of a series of catalogues published by libraries such as the Bodleian in Oxford and the universities of Leiden and Utrecht, together with private European libraries.

Ellys was buying at a time that has been described as a heroic era of book collectors, and attended many sales both in England and on the Continent.[12] One catalogue in his collection lists some of the manuscripts from the library of Thomas Rawlinson, compiled by Thomas Ballard in London in 1734 for an auction to be held at St Paul's Coffee-house in the Churchyard. Rawlinson had built up a great collection of medieval manuscripts and first editions of classical and early English texts totalling more than 50,000 books. When he died in debt in 1725 his brother Richard organised their dispersal. This particular catalogue, priced 1s, describes the contents of the last of sixteen sales. The proceedings are known in detail, for Richard Rawlinson kept detailed accounts of the room hire, payment to porters to carry the books hither and thither, the purchase of candles, snuffers, ink, wine and chairs. A ham was purchased for book buyers at the end of this, the last auction, conducted by Ballard over sixteen days. Ellys acquired several books at this sale, and hopefully enjoyed eating some of the ham.

Charles Winn found out about his books in much the same way as Ellys had done a century earlier – through booksellers, catalogues and sales. Not all the books in his collection are rare and curious. Like many Victorian gentlemen, he owned a set of Scott's Waverley novels. He also subscribed to light fiction; still in the library is a single instalment from *Harry Coverdale's Courtship, and all that came of it* by F.E. Smedley with illustrations by Phiz. There are several books bearing the label of the fashionable circulating library, Hookhams of New Bond Streeet, which he may have acquired in one of their sales to reduce stock, others have the label of Meggitt's & Sons, a circulating library in nearby Wakefield. He purchased a whole series of periodicals, including the *Annual Register*, *Quarterly Review* and the *Edinburgh Magazine*, all of which would have kept him abreast of the latest publications.

One of his London booksellers would seem not to be connected with his antiquarian interests. In 1831 he stayed with William Henry Dalton, at his bookshop at 26 Cockspur Street, Charing Cross, paying him £7 3s 9d for books, and £4 6s for rent. Dalton is not a well-known bookseller, and his imprints are mostly on religious books. In 1843, for instance, he published for the Protestant Association, along with Hatchard and Rivington, *The Church of Rome proved to have the marks of Antichrist*, a work written by Hugh McNeile. Three years later, he issued George Stanley Faber's *Letters on the Tractarian Secession to Popery*. Charles Winn had continued with his studies to become a clergyman, and was the rector of Wragby Church within the grounds of Nostell Priory. He is known to have opposed the emancipation of Roman Catholics, so this may have been the common ground with Dalton. In addition, Cockspur Street was close to the Bull and Mouth Inn, the terminus for the stagecoach up to Doncaster and Edinburgh, so ideal for Winn's arrival in London.

Winn also inherited a substantial collection of books built up by successive generations of his family since the seventeenth century. To these had been added the library of the d'Herwarts, the aristocratic Swiss forebears of his grandmother, Sabine. In an inventory made in 1806 it was estimated that there were 2,133 volumes, housed in the richly appointed library at Nostell commissioned by the 5th Baronet in 1766. Robert Adam's original colour scheme was light green, pink and white, with paintings of philosophers and poets on the upper walls and bookcases surmounted by pediments and classical busts. In the centre of the room stood a magnificent library table, ornamented with lion's heads and paws, designed by Thomas Chippendale, who also supplied six library chairs, an artist's table fitted with cupboards and drawers, and a 'metamorphic' stool that could turn into steps. The eighteenth-century appearance of the room can be seen in Hugh Douglas Hamilton's painting of Charles Winn's grandparents. Leaning against Chippendale's library table, Sir Rowland is resplendently dressed in a red flannel coat over a satin waistcoat decorated with gold lace. Sabine wears a casual gown of oyster satin with an over-dress trimmed with fur. Their cultural credentials are shown by the drawing he supports on a chair, by the book she carries, and the classical female bust who gazes at them in stony admiration.

Their grandson, with his interest in books and in the history of his family, was far too respectful to disperse the collection. However, fashions had changed, so he commissioned Thomas Ward in the 1820s to strip the green paintwork from the bookcases and lightly grain them to resemble bird's-eye maple, along with the lower walls. In the 1830s, as his own collection began to grow, he retained the most interesting antiquarian books from the historic family collection in the library, moving the others to the adjoining Billiard Room where he installed Gillow bookcases bought from a sale at a neighbouring house. In 1875, the year after Charles's death, his son found that piles of books had been built up under the billiard table, and he therefore added a second tier of bookcases, providing shelves right up to the ceiling. Books at the highest level were reached by long library steps, which must have proved terrifying to housemaids sent up to do the dusting.

Charles Winn's first forays into collecting were of a classical nature. At some time in 1816 or 1817 he joined his brother John on the Grand Tour in Italy with their tutor Richard Harrison, a medical student with antiquarian tastes. From the Abbé Campbell in Naples the brothers bought a collection of Greek vases. Harrison remarks in a letter to Charles after John's death that while the Abbé had the vases with the laudable but sole ambition of embellishing his

56 Hugh Douglas Hamilton's double portrait of Sir Rowland Winn, 5th Baronet, and his Swiss wife Sabine, painted in 1767. The Winns are shown in their magnificent Robert Adam Library at Nostell Priory in Yorkshire.

house with objects of real value, 'for you, who have a taste for antiques, these vases must be inestimable and will always reflect credit on the possessor'.[13] This comment is echoed by Thomas Frognall Dibdin, who on a visit to Nostell in the 1830s credited Charles with 'a cultivated eye for the antique'.

John Winn's diary also reveals that Charles was beginning to develop his passion for collecting coins while on the Grand Tour. Back in England, and enjoying his inheritance, he was certainly encouraged in his numismatic interests by his father-in-law, and when the family decided to dispose of Sir William Strickland's notable collection of books and coins at his death in 1834, Winn took the opportunity to enrich his own collection. The books included descriptions of great museums, cabinets and numismatic collections from all over Europe together with works placing the coins and medals in their historical contexts. It is reckoned that as a result of the Strickland purchase, Nostell has one of the finest collections in Britain, and Charles Winn got a great bargain, for he paid 4s a book. He was able, moreover, to keep his coins in an exquisite medal cabinet that had been made by Thomas Chippendale for his grandfather, the 5th Baronet.

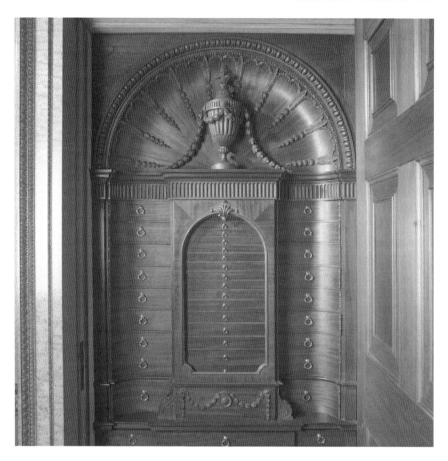

57 Medal cabinet designed by Thomas Chippendale for the 5th Baronet; it was later used by Charles Winn for his collection of ancient coins and seals.

Winn carried on adding to his collection, and in 1842 he acquired from Horace Walpole's library at Strawberry Hill three numismatic books, lot 128 of the first day's sale. Robert Withy's *Twelve Plates of English Silver Coins*, London, 1756, 'principally designed for the use of Young Collectors', contains the bookplates of both Walpole and Winn. John Glen King's *Nummi Familiar: Roman*, 1787, has only Winn's plate, but alongside the appropriate Strawberry Hill shelfmark. The third title, Francis Perry's *Series of English Medals*, London, 1762 is no longer at Nostell. Nor is lot 63 of the seventh day's sale, described in the catalogue as, 'A collection of 52 vols. In folio, 4to and 8vo of manuscripts of that indefatigable Artist and Antiquary, Mr George Vertue . . . are highly interesting to the Antiquary, and well worthy a place in the British Museum'. Fittingly they now repose in the British Library.

The Strawberry Hill sale marked the end of one of the great British eighteenth-century book collections. Horace Walpole, born in 1717, was the fourth son of the first 'Prime Minister', Robert Walpole. In 1747 Horace purchased Strawberry Hill on the Twickenham riverside, later describing it as 'a baby-house full of playthings for my second childhood'.[14] Over the next four decades, with the help of friends known as the Committee of Taste, he transformed the unpretentious little villa into a castle, taking details of Gothic buildings as illustrated in topographical books and adapting them to his requirements. This method can clearly be seen in his description of the Library: 'The books are ranged within Gothic arches of pierced work, taken from a side-door case to the choir in Dugdale's St Paul's. The doors themselves were designed by Mr Chute. The chimney-piece is imitated from the tomb of John of Eltham earl of Cornwall, in Westminster-abbey; the stone-work from that of Thomas duke of Clarence, at Canterbury.'[15]

Walpole's collection of books has been described as an illustration of the transition from the taste for classical texts to one for Gothic.[16] English topography, antiquity and poetry were the books he valued most, and turned to most frequently. His Latin classics were school texts bought in his youth, his Greek authors had significant gaps, no Aristotle or Plato, for instance. He was scathing about Italian writers who were much admired at this time: Dante was 'extravagant, absurd, disgusting', Tasso showed 'a thousand puerilities'. But unlike his antiquarian contemporaries, Horace Walpole held no enthusiasm for black-letter texts. Thus, when he was offered a sixteenth-century edition of Chaucer, he declined, saying, 'I am, though a Goth, so modern a Goth that I hate the black letter, and I love Chaucer better in Dryden and Baskerville, than in his own language and dress.'[17]

Charles Winn's marked-up copy of the Strawberry Hill sale catalogue remains in the family archives.[18] He put pencil notes against many items in the sale, not only of books, but also of portrait miniatures and pieces of furniture. His agent would appear to have been an under-bidder in all of these, as none of them has been recorded at Nostell. However, his selection is interesting. The portraits are of Tudor and early Stuart figures, such as Isaac Oliver's miniature of Robert Cecil, Earl of Salisbury. The furniture has sixteenth-century connections, for example, carved solid ebony chairs of the Elizabethan period with pierced backs and twisted rails. Winn was particularly interested in the origins of his family, and proud of the descent from Sir Thomas More through his daughter, Margaret Roper. One of the treasures of Nostell, now hanging in the Lower Hall, is the portrait of the family of Sir Thomas. The original version, painted by Holbein in 1527, was lost in a fire, and the large-scale copy was made fifty years later. Winn also inherited the seventeenth-century books that had belonged to Katherine Rooper or Roper. It would seem likely, therefore

58 Horace Walpole in his Gothic Library at Strawberry Hill, a drawing by J.H. Muntz, late 1750s.
Walpole is seated in front of one of the bookcases designed by his friend John Chute.

that he considered adding to this connection through purchase of appropriate pictures and furnishings. The description of the chairs is very like the 'black and white' furniture in the Library at Charlecote Park in Warwickshire. Charlecote was an Elizabethan house with Shakespearean associations that was refurbished in Tudor style by George Hammond Lucy and his wife, Mary Elizabeth, in the 1820s and 1830s. The library furniture was bought in London in 1837 in the belief that it had been presented by Elizabeth I to her great favourite, Robert Dudley, Lord Leicester. In fact, this was seventeenth-century ebony inlaid with ivory brought to England by the East India Company, but the idea of a Tudor provenance had been fostered by Horace Walpole.

Charles Winn no doubt deeply appreciated inheriting Nostell, but his anti-quarian heart must have harboured regrets that it was Palladian in style and age, rather than Tudor like Charlecote. The development of his bookplates reflect this harking back to romantic times. He begins with 'Charles Winn, Nostell' in unadorned roman type, but then moves on to 'Charles Winn, Nostell Priory' in gothic black lettering surrounding his coat of arms. The latter recalls the Augustinian priory that had been founded in the early twelfth century on a site very close to the present house. The religious community was abolished at the time of the Dissolution of the Monasteries in the 1530s, although some priory buildings survived and had been converted into a manor house known as Nostall Hall when the Winn family first acquired the estate in 1650. Just as Catherine Morland thrilled to the idea of Northanger Abbey, so Charles Winn chose to emphasise the ancient origins of his estate by using the name Nostell Priory.

Many of his books were bought from antiquarian booksellers in London. His accounts show that Winn had a regular account with Willis and Sotheran. The Sotherans had long been booksellers in York, but Thomas Sotheran trav-elled south in 1801 at the end of his apprenticeship and worked for the Quaker booksellers and publishers, John and Arthur Arch at 61 Cornhill. When he set up on his own, Thomas moved out of the City to the more fash-ionable West End, and his business rapidly expanded with the arrival of his son Henry and the acquisition of George Willis as a partner. By 1860s they had opened several branches and could offer stock of over half a million books, advertising themselves as specialists in 'Architectural books & works connected with the Fine Arts. Libraries & Parcels of books bought or exchanged'. A letter of 4 April 1863 from Mr Willis at 136 the Strand refers to an exchange of books, and is annotated by Charles Winn to say that he agrees.[19]

John and Arthur Arch also employed another fledgling antiquarian book-seller, William Pickering. The circumstances of William's birth in 1796 are both shadowy and romantic. The story went that his father was a book-loving

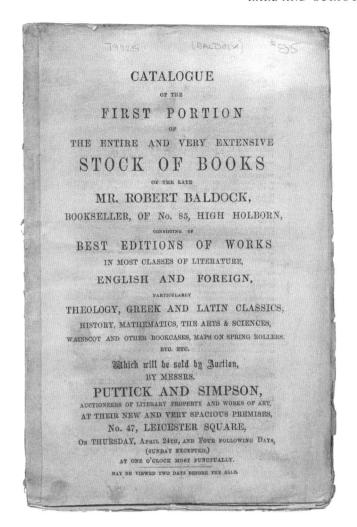

CATALOGUE
OF THE
FIRST PORTION
OF
THE ENTIRE AND VERY EXTENSIVE
STOCK OF BOOKS
OF THE LATE
MR. ROBERT BALDOCK,
BOOKSELLER, OF No. 85, HIGH HOLBORN,
CONSISTING OF
BEST EDITIONS OF WORKS
IN MOST CLASSES OF LITERATURE,
ENGLISH AND FOREIGN,
PARTICULARLY
THEOLOGY, GREEK AND LATIN CLASSICS,
HISTORY, MATHEMATICS, THE ARTS & SCIENCES,
WAINSCOT AND OTHER BOOKCASES, MAPS ON SPRING ROLLERS,
ETC. ETC.
Which will be sold by Auction,
BY MESSRS.
PUTTICK AND SIMPSON,
AUCTIONEERS OF LITERARY PROPERTY AND WORKS OF ART,
AT THEIR NEW AND VERY SPACIOUS PREMISES,
No. 47, LEICESTER SQUARE,
ON THURSDAY, APRIL 24TH, AND FOUR FOLLOWING DAYS,
(SUNDAY EXCEPTED,)
AT ONE O'CLOCK MOST PUNCTUALLY.
MAY BE VIEWED TWO DAYS BEFORE THE SALE.

59 Sale catalogue of the effects of a mid-nineteenth-century bookseller in High Holborn, London. Among the list of furnishings are maps on spring rollers, as installed in the library at Calke Abbey (p. 157).

earl, his mother a lady of title, but not married to each other. His surname came from a tailor called Pickering, whose wife acted as his wet nurse. In 1820 he set up on his own account at 31 Lincoln's Inn Fields, and began publishing reprints of classics, well produced and moderately priced. As a tribute to the sixteenth-century Venetian publisher, Aldus, Pickering adopted the device of the dolphin and anchor, and produced several series under the Aldine imprint. However, it was for his antiquarian publishing and bookselling that Pickering became so well known. When George Hammond Lucy was looking for appropriate books to fill his new Tudor-style Library at Charlecote Park, he turned to William Pickering. In the winter of 1838 he spent no less than £331 8s 6d at his bookshop; his purchases included Shakespeare's *The Merry Wives of Windsor*, Isaak Walton's *The Compleat Angler*, the works of John Britton, Horace Walpole's *Anecdotes of Painting* and Guillim's *Heraldry*. Charles Winn was also a customer of Pickering, who moved in 1841 to 177 Piccadilly where his reputation as the doyen of antiquarian booksellers was established. *Archaeologia Cambrensis* declared in 1848: 'An antiquary without books is like a steamer without paddles – no progress, no work – lost and floundering in sand and mud . . . we would therefore recommend our readers, who may wish to furnish themselves with antiquarian books to do as we do, and to resort to the old-bookshops of London . . . Mr Pickering, 177 Piccadilly – a sort of Golconda to him who looks for diamonds of antiquity. You may spend two or three hundred pounds there in a morning and come home with a cart load of folios, quartos, and miniature duodecimos.'

The extensive catalogues of Willis & Sotheran, and of William Pickering are still at Nostell, along with those of Bernard Quaritch. Quaritch arrived in London from Germany in 1842 as cataloguer and assistant to the distinguished publisher, Henry George Bohn. Five years later Quaritch announced that he was going to become the 'first bookseller in Europe', establishing himself at 16 Castle Street, Leicester Square. His early stock was learned and second-hand at moderate prices, but by the mid-1850s he had also moved into the field of fine and rare books. His domination both of London salerooms and country-house sales earned him from the press the soubriquet 'Napoleon of Booksellers', much to his horror, as he regarded Bonaparte as cruel and selfish and would own no books associated with him. From 1860 he traded from 15 Piccadilly, but his principal method of distribution was through catalogues. Beginning with broadsheets, he moved on first to octavo pamphlets, then to plump specialised catalogues, and finally to massive general catalogues. Quaritch's catalogue available in the year of Winn's death in 1874 was a double-decker, with over 44,000 entries representing 200,000 volumes. Not all the books mentioned were available for purchase: he was also providing guidelines for standard prices for antiquarian and out-of-print books.

Charles Winn also kept abreast of what was going on in the world of antiquarianism and archaeology by subscribing to the *Gentleman's Magazine*. At the death in 1754 of Edward Cave, the magazine's founder, his sister and her husband continued publishing, selling a share of the business in 1778 to John Nichols. The son of an Islington baker, Nichols had an extremely lucky break when he entered the printing office of William Bowyer. The learned Bowyer took Nichols under his wing, setting him Latin exercises and escorting him to science lectures. In 1766 Bowyer made Nichols a partner in his very large printing practice, which included contracts for both the Royal Society and the Society of Antiquaries. By 1792 John Nichols was in entire control of the *Gentleman's Magazine*. Although his printing office was in Red Lion Passage, off Fleet Street, he retained on the title page Cave's familiar trademark of the gatehouse of St John's Priory in Clerkenwell. However, he made some important changes, doubling the size, providing longer reviews and increasing the space for literary and antiquarian contributions. A knowledgeable and keen antiquarian himself, he would put in footnotes questioning the accuracy of articles in order to inspire debate and response from readers. With his great friend, the antiquary Richard Gough, Nichols travelled around the country visiting ancient sites and collaborated on ambitious publishing projects such as the *Bibliotheca Topographica Britannica*, which ran to 52 numbers between 1780 and 1790.

John Nichols' work was continued by his son, John Bowyer Nichols, and grandson John Gough Nichols. They were both active members of the Society of Antiquaries and John Bowyer regularly hosted feasts for the Noviomagians, the Society's convivial dining club. Charles Winn, despite his antiquarian interests, eschewed the Society of Antiquaries. Instead he was a member of the Camden Society, founded in 1838, with John Bowyer and John Gough Nichols taking leading roles. Named in honour of William Camden, the sixteenth-century historian, it was established to publish early historical and literary materials, both unpublished manuscripts and new editions of rare printed books. Charles Winn would appear to have been a retiring person, preferring the society of his own family circle and living the quiet life of a country landowner, with entries in his diary about shooting and problems with drainage alongside those about organising his books in the library.[20] In the 1830s, when he travelled up to London he did so by stage, sleeping at Newark and Hatfield en route, but later would have taken advantage of the train that made the journey in hours rather than days. Once in the capital he stayed at Thompson's Hotel in Cavendish Square or the United Universities Club, from which he could make his forays to bookshops, salerooms and art exhibitions.

The London bookshops and salerooms were not Winn's only source of books for his library. He was on good terms with several booksellers in York, including Alexander Barclay. When the library of Mark Masterman Sykes of Sledmere was dispersed in 1824, Winn bid at the sale itself, and acquired books indirectly through booksellers, a pattern that continued in the ensuing years. Alexander Barclay, whose bookshop was in Low Ousegate in York, was assiduous in his acquisition of whole libraries. It was most probably through him that Winn obtained a collection of religious and political pamphlets that had belonged to William Robert Hay, vicar of Rochdale and rector of Ackworth, who died in 1839. The collection is huge – 2,500 printed items

Oliver amazed at the Dodger's mode of "going to work"

60 The perils of browsing in second-hand bookshops: a gentleman having his pockets picked in an illustration by George Cruikshank for Dickens' *Oliver Twist*, published in 1837.

bound in some 300 volumes – and would seem an odd choice of subject for Winn. However, he was always interested in tracts, noting collections of them in the Strawberry Hill sale catalogue, and as an opponent of Catholic Emancipation shared the views of Hay, though in a much quieter way. Hay was much loathed as chairman of the Salford and Manchester magistrates who called in the troops in the 1819 Peterloo Massacre.

Charles was close to all the brothers and sisters of his wife Priscilla, but with Eustachius, eight years his senior, he also shared an interest in local history. When Eustachius died in 1840, the Yorkshire Philosophical Society's obituary described him as 'a valued friend long and earnestly devoted to English antiquities' and recorded his bequest of money and of the collections he had made towards a history of St Mary's Abbey in the city. Charles Winn owned a range of books about Yorkshire and in his collection are two books on similar subjects, but totally different in style. In 1733 Thomas Gent published in York his *Antient and Modern History of the Loyal Town of Ripon*, in duodecimo with woodcuts. Three years later, Francis Drake published in London his *Eboracum: or the History and Antiquities of the City of York* in two volumes in folio format with illustrations in copper plate.

Remarkably, we have much detailed background concerning these two works as Thomas Gent wrote an account of his life in 1746 which was discovered among family papers and published in 1832.[21] Gent arrived in England from Dublin in 1710, having broken his apprenticeship as a printer, though in his autobiography he is rather slow in admitting this. He began working for Edward Midwinter, publisher of ballads and chapbooks at the Looking Glass on London Bridge. Although a quarrelsome fellow, who complained about the long hours that he was obliged to work 'through our hurry with hawkers', Thomas Gent was also clearly intelligent. Mrs Midwinter set him to writing pamphlets when one of their hack writers was confined in various prisons for debt. He was also interested in history, visiting the Tower of London, Westminster Abbey and travelling upriver to the palace at Hampton Court.

Eventually Gent established himself as a bookseller and printer in a house in Petergate in York. In 1729 he published a proposal for a book relating to the antiquities of York to attract subscriptions. His research was thorough: 'I took, indeed, great pains in every church, having many of the sepulchral monuments washed and cleansed, to come as perfectly as I could to the characters, many of which were almost delible, and diurnally conveyed them to my press.' He ascended 'the most lofty dangerous places' to explore the stained glass, 'as well as into gloomy cemeteries, to restore the long dead to recent memory'. The book was published in 1730 with great success, although he was conscious of critics who scoffed at his obscure background, and at the humble monuments that he had included. When Drake published his book in 1736, he dismissed Gent's work as a small printed tract, and felt it necessary to point out that he had borrowed nothing from it. Gent meanwhile justified the format of his books on York and Ripon as pocket companions that could be read by gentlemen and ladies in their carriages on the road, or as 'an entertainer in their closets'.[22]

In his national survey of antiquities written in 1768, Richard Gough described Gent's history of York as 'a useful compendium, the work of an industrious printer, containing some things not in larger histories'.[23] He regarded Gent's final book, *The Most Delectable, Scriptural and Pious History of the Famous and Magnificent Great East Window . . . in St Peter's Cathedral, York*, however, as providing little information of value, suggesting that by 1762 he was sinking under age and necessity. Instead, he recommends Drake's work, which he found so sophisticated, in contrast to Gent's work that led directly back to his youthful employment with the chapbook seller, Edward Midwinter. The comparison can be drawn between these books and Gothic architecture itself: Gent reflects the Gothic survival seen well into the eighteenth century in work by country master masons, while Drake resembles the Gothic revival of Horace Walpole's Strawberry Hill. It is significant that by the mid-nineteenth century, antiquarians like Charles Winn should value both and have them in his collection.

It was a book about the topography and history of Yorkshire that brought the young antiquary James Orchard Halliwell to his attention, when Winn received a letter seeking his subscription. This was a moment of serendipity, as Winn was becoming interested in collecting Shakespeareana, while Halliwell had recently published a life of the bard, and was working on *A New Boke about Shakespeare and Stratford upon Avon*, where he codified hundreds of records both genuine and false. In 1854 Halliwell helped to found the Warton Club, producing over the next decade an ambitious project of sixteen volumes of *Works* lavishly illustrated and limited to 150 copies. These scholarly reprints in limited editions were precisely the kind of publications that appealed to Winn, who subscribed to them all. However, when Halliwell followed these with an even more expensive lithographic reprint of known Shakespeare quartos in 48 volumes, priced at 5 guineas apiece, caution tempered Winn's enthusiasm, and he asked to see a volume before he

61 Thomas Gent's woodcut illustration of the ruins of Fountains Abbey in Yorkshire, in a style that he had learnt when working for the chapbook publisher, Edward Midwinter.

embarked on the considerable outlay. But this met with his approval and in March 1862 he agreed to subscribe to two facsimiles a year to be 'sent to me merely bound in boards and uncut'.[24]

For Halliwell, Winn was the ideal client, accepting the many limited editions that he offered, and their correspondence shows the mechanisms and costs of subscription publications at this period. In July 1863 Halliwell offered him *The Calendar of the Shakespeare Records*, 'printed on beautiful paper which cost me £4 a ream . . . If I printed 500 copies at a guinea, I should have endless trouble & before a year was over, they would be on stalls at half price'.[25] The following September he offered Winn 'my large folio edition of Shakespeare, eleven volumes are ready, & it will be completed in fifteen volumes. Only 150 copies are printed. I have a second hand copy as good as new I could send you at four guineas a volume, & the subscription, which altogether will amount to £63'.[26]

Among the many books of and about Shakespeare there is a facsimile of the First Folio of 1623, nicely bound and produced in the 1820s. There is also a two-volume, grangerised edition. The Revd James Granger had published in 1769 *A Bibliographical History of England* in which he left blank pages for the reception of engraved portraits cut from other books. Winn appears to have liked this custom for he owned several grangerised books. Not only did this mean the ruin of other books, but in the Shakespeare volume he places nineteenth-century whimsical metal engravings next to seventeenth-century type. In 1870, however, Halliwell acquired for him the real thing, an original Shakespeare First Folio. Along with the Gutenberg Bible, a First Folio had become the most prized of all printed books: until the 1780s, it was not greatly valued, and could be bought for £5 or £10 depending upon condition. However, by the early nineteenth century the price was rising steeply, with Thomas Grenville paying £121 16s, to the amazement of Dibdin, and John Britton securing a copy for John Soane at 100 guineas in 1825. The cheque paid to Halliwell by Winn on 16 December 1870 was for only 15 guineas. It may be that the book was not in good condition – it has subsequently been sold out of Nostell – or else Halliwell was giving his generous patron a very good deal.

Behind the study of Shakespeare and other sixteenth-century writers and scholars, James Orchard Halliwell led a tumultuous personal life. In 1839 he had begun to correspond with Sir Thomas Phillipps in the hope that he would buy some scientific manuscripts to extricate him from financial diffi-culties. Phillipps was a prodigious and extravagant collector of manuscripts and antiquarian books who described himself as a Vello-maniac. He also had a reputation for irascibility. In 1842, after Halliwell sought to marry his elder daughter, Phillipps's refusal resulted in the couple eloping. In the ensuing quarrels, he tried to ruin Halliwell in print, accusing him of sharp practice, which carried more than a grain of truth. A simmering feud continued between them over the following decades, with Phillipps moving out of his Worcestershire home in an attempt to prevent his son-in-law inheriting his collection through the complexities of a family trust. Years of negotation also ensued over who might have his great collection of 60,000 manuscripts, with the Bodleian Library and the British Museum as possible contenders. In 1861 Phillipps became a trustee of the British Museum, but resigned in a huff when some of his very sensible recommendations for modernisation were rejected. When he died in 1872, his collections were sold off by his younger daughter through deals with foreign governments and private collectors. Halliwell did not therefore get his hands on the books and manuscripts, but he did adopt his father-in-law's name, becoming James Orchard Halliwell-Phillipps.

Charles Winn must have known of Sir Thomas's uncertain temper when he decided to approach him in 1843 about some manuscripts in his collection that gave details of the medieval priory of Nostell. Wisely he did this through a mutual acquaintance. Sir Thomas's shrewd reply ran: 'If Mr Wynn would have no objection to an interchange of MSS on <u>loan</u> I wd lend him one of my books for one of his & so successively or all at once . . . Each of us to return Book for Book as soon as done with.'[27] The intermediary provided a vivid description of the domestic life of the baronet, and a warning about the perils of exchanges on loan: 'he lives in a labyrinth of books, the walls of his house totter from the weight of accumulation & his unfortunate wife and daughters are exhausted with the fatigue of transcribing and copying – you must judge for yourself of the proposal . . . In one respect it is <u>safe</u> as you would have a hold upon him, by exchange – but his neighbours say he is not to be trusted with anything valuable – as a <u>loan</u>, it being not easy to reclaim what is once in his possession. . .'[28] When news of Phillipps's death reached Winn in 1872, he was obliged to write to the family asking for the return of his manuscripts.

This unfortunate experience was an exception, and Winn lent to and borrowed books from scholars, and opened his library to visitors. In 1824 the antiquary Joseph Hunter asked permission to peruse a fifteenth-century manuscript for his forthcoming book, *South Yorkshire*. Winn not only agreed, but provided a picture of the park and extra information on his family pedigree. This began a correspondence that continued for many years. Winn's diary entry for 1829 noted a visit from the architect and artist William Fowler, who gave him a copy of his book of coloured engravings of mosaic pavements. A subsequent entry reads: 'Engaged from breakfast till lunch in looking over the book of tessellated pavements left by Old Fowler.' Not every visitor was an antiquarian scholar. The family doctor recorded how he was given full use of the library in the summer of 1842 when his family had moved into a house next to Nostell.

The range of Charles Winn's interests was wide. He kept in the library his various collections of ethnography and natural history, alongside his medal collection: in this he was harking back to the cabinets of curiosity of seventeenth-century scholars. He also owned some particularly fine books of natural history. His copy of John James Audubon's *Birds of America* is no longer at Nostell, but three of the books of John Gould remain one of the library's treasures. John Gould was the son of the foreman gardener at Windsor Castle, in charge of 'the Slopes', and Gould himself worked in the gardens at Kew and Ripley Castle in Yorkshire before setting up a taxidermy shop in London in 1825. One of his early customers was the King himself, who commissioned him to preserve a Thick-kneed Bustard, and he went on to stuff the first giraffe to arrive in England, a present from Mehemet Ali of Egypt. Gould joined the Zoological Society as an animal preserver, and became superintendent of their ornithological department. When a consignment of Himalayan mountain birds arrived at the Society, he conceived the idea of publishing a volume of hand-coloured lithographical prints in imperial folio of the eighty species along with figures of a hundred birds. A friend, N.A. Vigors, wrote the text, and Gould's wife Elizabeth made the drawings and transferred them onto the litho stones. When he failed to find a publisher, John Gould very bravely decided to produce the book himself in twenty monthly parts, with four pictures for each part.

This was the method of publishing that he adopted thereafter, producing in all fifty imperial folios. He acted as the collector, purchaser of specimens, taxonomist, author of the text, publisher and distributor. After his wife's death, he commissioned various artists, including Edward Lear, and gave them rough sketches for reference. In 1836 Gould was given the birds that Charles Darwin brought back from the Galapagos, and was able to furnish him with the crucial evidence to come to his theory about island speciation. For Darwin and other friends he ran off introductions to the various books in octavo, and also published in a smaller size for those who could not afford the imperial folios.

To get each publishing project off the ground, Gould drew up a list of subscribers. For the pioneering *A Century of Birds Hitherto Unfigured from the Himalaya Mountains* that Gould produced between 1830 and 1832, the list is headed by William IV and Queen Adelaide, followed by European royalty, dukes down to esquires, with institutions like the Zoological Society and the Subscription Library of York. Although Charles Winn did subscribe, he does not appear on the list. He also ordered *The Birds of Europe* (1832–7) and *The*

62 A Swallow-tailed Kite from John Gould's *The Birds of Europe*, published in complete form in 1837.

Birds of Australia (1840–8). However, he was not happy with Gould's binding for these two volumes and wrote to him, 'I cannot help again stating how much I regret that my wishes with reference to the binding of your two works on European & Australian Birds have not been more strictly attended to and the more so as the books are not only extremely conspicuous in the Library but their gaudiness gives rise to remarks from my friends, which are certainly not complimentary to what is supposed to be <u>my</u> taste for book binding.'[29] Winn's taste was subdued and plain, so Gould's books went off to the London binders Clyde for a more acceptable garb. The friendship between Winn and John Gould survived this binding affront, and their letters are personally affectionate.

* * * *

In many ways Charles Winn does not qualify for D'Israeli's definition of a *bibliomane*. He was not a library miser, allowing his friends and scholars use of his library. Nor was his the collection of a library show-off. He had some trophies, such as the 1493 Nuremberg Chronicle acquired from the library of Mark Masterman Sykes and sold by the family in 1962, and Shakespeare's First Folio, sold in 1971, but the huge majority of his books were bought to read and refer to. Nevertheless there was a touch of bibliomania. Like modern book collectors with their easy access to the internet, he bought compulsively and had difficulty keeping up with all his acquisitions. At Nostell are packages of unbound books still in their wrappers, and some where the string has not even been untied.

63 The Billiard Room at Nostell, with Charles Winn's book collection in shelves reaching right up to the ceiling.

In 1871 Priscilla Winn wrote to her son Rowland that his father had suggested abandoning the Library and Billiard Room to take three rooms in one wing of the house and lay them together to make one large Library.[30] Charles Winn died in 1874 before this threat was put into practice, and instead his son coped with the overwhelming piles of books by adding the precipitous shelves. Although Rowland and his descendants added to the collection, they did so at a greatly reduced rate, keeping their books in the family's other properties. Thus Charles Winn's library remained almost totally intact, an unusual fate. The great Harleian Library had been dispersed, with books sold and manuscripts given to the British Museum. Horace Walpole's collection was likewise scattered, although partially reassembled and taken to America as the Lewis Walpole Library in Farmington, Connecticut. Spencer's library from Althorp was sold in 1892 by the 5th Earl who, finding the estate heavily encumbered, decided that the future lay in agriculture. It was bought by Mrs John Rylands for £210,000 and is now housed in the main hall of the John Rylands Library in Manchester. Thus, with his library still at Nostell, and all his correspondence, bills and catalogues surviving, Charles Winn provides a unique record of a Victorian bibliophile.

CHAPTER 8

THE COMMON READER

Books for Working Men and Women

While commenting on Thomas Gray's poem 'Elegy Written in a Country Churchyard', Samuel Johnson invoked the term 'common reader', whom he commended for natural common sense, untouched by literary fashion and prejudices.[1] Although not a term now in favour because of its catch-all description of a group that is far from homogeneous, it does describe a readership constrained by economic factors.

For the common reader, the struggle to enjoy books has at times resembled an obstacle race. First, there was the issue of literacy. Estimates of the percentage of people in Britain who could read and write at different periods have been frequently adjusted when traditional means of calculation are shown to be misleading. For example, it has been demonstrated that the fact that a person marked a legal paper with an X rather than a signature is not always a sign of illiteracy. Richard Altick in *The English Common Reader* reckoned that one-third of the population of late sixteenth-century London was illiterate, with a higher proportion in the countryside.[2] By the mid-nineteenth century, for the population right across the nation, the proportion is estimated to be 40 per cent illiteracy among men, slightly higher for women. It is disputed whether the proportion was higher in rural areas.

Only in 1870 with Forster's Education Act was it possible for all children to be provided with a rudimentary education. At the time it was judged that there were four million children of school age, but nearly half of these were not provided for, a situation that was far inferior to those pertaining in other parts of Europe and in the United States. W.E. Forster introduced a bill giving extra funds for the retention of voluntary schools that were already providing a sufficiently good standard of education, and for board schools under the control of local elected boards maintained by a combination of government grants, parents' fees and local rates. Of course, the provision of education is no guarantee of literacy. Many a bone-headed youth has been given a first-class education but never opened a book thereafter. Those who could neither read nor write could enjoy the pleasures of literature by being read to. Dickens's biographer, Edgar Johnson, describes how an old charlady lodging over a snuff shop attended a subscription tea on the first Monday of every month, so that she might listen to the landlord reading the latest number of *Dombey and Son*.[3]

Secondly, there is the matter of money. Altick made a comparison of the average wages of various workers against the price of books from the sixteenth century onwards. In late Elizabethan times, London artisans were paid 16d per day, with schoolmasters earning an annual salary of around £6 and clergymen between £10 and £20. In 1600 William Cavendish's most expensive purchase was Hakluyt's *Principal Navigations, Voyages, Traffiques and Discoveries of the English Nation* an illustrated folio in three volumes costing £1 2s. Most of his books cost 3s or 4s, though he did buy pamphlets costing between 1d and 1s (p. 25). By the early eighteenth century, a shopman just out of apprenticeship could expect to earn between 4s and 16s per week, while clerks in a London merchant's office received £1 Folios at this period cost between 10s and 12s, octavos 5s and 6s, small novels 2s to 3s, and pamphlets between 6d and 1s 6d. The price of books rose abruptly after 1780, so that a quarto could command 2 guineas, an octavo between 12s and 14s, and a duodecimo between 5s and 6s. When Walter Scott's *Kenilworth* was published in 1821 as a three-decker costing a guinea and a half, this was approximately the same as the weekly earnings of a skilled London artisan, while a Glasgow carpenter brought home 14s per week, and a handloom weaver a meagre 5s 6d.[4] Books were luxury items.

Thirdly there are physical constraints. Those who worked in the fields started at sunrise and ended their labour at sunset. Those who laboured in the factories of the Industrial Revolution might work even longer hours, and in monotonous, mind-numbing activities. By the time these labours came to an end, reading a book was probably the last thing that many workers wanted to do. And the light to enable them to make out the page was not available. Samuel Pepys, his nose in a book, tripped after a link boy carrying a flame through the dark streets of London, and read into the night with the aid of a candle. Readers of more modest means used firelight, or the light of the moon, or a tallow candle that would require constant trimming of the wick to provide any kind of flame. Pepys's eyesight suffered to such an extent that he was obliged to cease writing his diary. A fascinating link between reading and poor sight is revealed in the customs accounts for London in the late fifteenth century, when the ownership of printed books began to develop. More than thirty gross of spectacles with ground lenses were imported from the Low Countries in 1480–1, along with twenty-six gross of spectacle cases.[5] Like books, these were luxury items.

Next there is the question of attitude. Although Samuel Johnson called upon the common reader with approbation in the quote given earlier, he also expressed distrust of the same in *Rasselas*, while Virginia Woolf looked down on what she described as 'middle brows', both intellectually and socially.[6] Even champions for the provision of opportunities for working-class readers, such as W.E. Gladstone and Charles Dickens, were concerned that literacy should bring with it discernment. Others believed that to encourage the poor man to read and think, thus making him conscious of his misery, would be to fly in the face of divine intention, 'the great law of subordination' as Daniel Defoe described it. At the end of the eighteenth century, the outrageous Revd Dr John Trusler attributed the political problems in France to the spread of printing and feared the press in England would bring about political catastrophe: 'I am bold to say that the more untaught the labouring part of mankind are, the more humble are they and modest and the better servants they make'.[7] This attitude is encapsulated in the cartoon reproduced as Plate IV.

Lastly there is the matter of opportunity. In his autobiography, James Lackington describes how as young men he and his friends were thirsty for knowledge, but 'we were ashamed to go into the booksellers' shops'. Speaking from his position as an established bookseller in 1791, he wrote with feeling: 'there are thousands now in England in the very same situation; many, very many, have come to my shop, who have discovered an enquiring mind, but were totally at a loss what to ask for, and who had no friend to direct them'.[8]

Despite all these obstacles, working men and women *did* acquire books, and often felt passionate about their reading matter. Autobiography after autobiography of working men and women in the eighteenth, nineteenth and early twentieth centuries relate how reading liberated them. Alison Uttley described the hopes of her heroine, based on her own experience of applying for a scholarship in the 1890s, that 'the golden gates would fly apart and she would step into that world of books and language'.[9]

As ever, James Lackington gives some idea of what might constitute the books of a humble eighteenth-century household. In 1760, at the age of fourteen, he was apprenticed to a shoemaker in Taunton in Somerset. 'My master's whole library consisted of a school-size bible, Watts' Psalms and Hymns, Foot's Tract on Baptism, Culpepper's Herbal, the History of the Gentle Craft, an old imperfect volume of Receipts in Physic, Surgery, etc., and the Ready Reckoner'.[10] Lackington's master was an Anabaptist, a member of a Dissenting community that believed in re-baptism for adults as infants could not commit to religious faith, hence the presence of an edition of William Foot's *A Plain Account of the Ordinance of Baptism*. Isaac Watts was a former Dissenting minister who published collections of verse including *Hymns and Spiritual Songs*, 1707, and *The Psalms of David Imitated*, 1719.

The 'gentle craft' was shoemaking, and the book an edition of Thomas Deloney's *Pleasant and Princely History of the Gentle Craft*. Deloney was a silk weaver who wrote broadsides and ballads, but was best known for four works of prose fiction published in the last years of the sixteenth century that celebrated the self-advancement of hardworking craftsmen. The subtitle to the book provides a synopsis of its contents: 'a discourse containing many matters of delight; very pleasant to read. Shewing what famous men have been shooemakers in times past in this land, with their worthy deeds and great hospitality. Set forth with pictures, and variety of wit and mirth. Declaring the cause why it was called the gentle-craft. And also how the proverb first grew "A shooe-maker's son is a prince-born".' The book also features the story of Simon Eyre, who died in 1459, a shoemaker's apprentice who became Lord Mayor of London and founder of Leadenhall as a public granary and market: Dick Whittington in leather.

The other three titles were practical. Nicholas Culpeper was a nonconformist apothecary who campaigned against the monopoly of the College of Physicians in London, publishing in 1649 an English version of *Pharmacopoeia* thus giving access about remedies to the poor. His *Herbal*, first issued in 1653, sold in huge quantities and remains available today. The *Ready Reckoner* was a book of tables enabling calculation of the price of goods bought and sold, vital for a craftsman.

The Somerset shoemaker's 'library' accords with evidence of the books of other common readers. John Dawson was an exciseman who left his collection of books to his local church, St Leonard's in Shoreditch, just north of the City of London, in 1765. By the time of his death, Dawson had built up a substantial library of nearly nine hundred books, but in his youth, when he served both as a soldier and a sailor, he owned only ten books. Two had been inherited from his father: the perennial best-seller, *The Whole Duty of Man*; and John Holwell's *A Sure Guide to the Practical Surveyor*.

The Midlands booksellers, the Clay family, who had shops at various times in Daventry, Rugby, Lutterworth and Warwick, kept records that show the purchases of fifty servants between 1746 and 1784.[11] Although they represent a very small proportion of the Clays' customers, about 2 or 3 per cent, they provide valuable information on individuals who have left no other trace of their reading preferences. These individuals were indoor servants, in a better position to enjoy books than most of their peers. They had more leisure, access to better artificial lighting, and their wages were more substantial: a footman in the mid-eighteenth century would be paid between 5 and 16 guineas per annum, plus board and livery; a housemaid would earn between 6 and 10 guineas. Thirty-six of the Clays' servant customers were male and fourteen were female. Although women are in the minority, they constitute a much higher proportion than the figures for non-servant customers, possibly due to being single or widowed: most female purchases are hidden within the accounts of their husbands. Also, of course, these fifty names represent a tiny proportion of the number of servants that might come into the catchment area of the Clays. Most, if interested at all in books and periodicals, would obtain them elsewhere, at markets and fairs, and from itinerant chapmen and stationers.

Sixty per cent of books bought were of practical use: religious works such as bibles and catechisms, guides and reference books, almanacs and pocket books. For instance, a manservant in 1747 paid 1s 6d for a dictionary, *Glossographica Anglicana Nova*, 'a dictionary interpreting such hard words of whatever language, as are at present used in the English tongue, with their etymologies, definitions, etc.' The preface goes on to explain that the book 'shou'd be useful even to the lowest sort of illiterate, yet I have chiefly consulted the advantage of such as are gently advancing to Science; and for want of opportunities of Learned Helps have the misfortune to be their own Conductors, or have not Money Sufficient to lay in the necessary Furniture of Learning'. The manservant of an attorney ordered *The Complete Letter-Writer; or, Polite English Secretary. Containing familiar letters on the most common occasions in life*, appearing in its thirteenth edition in 1770. An attorney's maidservant ordered *The Complete Servant Maid: or, Young Woman's Best Companion. Containing full, plain and easy direction for qualifying them for service in general*, also published in 1770 – clearly she was a girl who wanted to go far.

Clays kept lists of subscribers to serial publications and to magazines. David Prowett, the son of an innkeeper, and probably the servant of a draper, subscribed to *A la Mode Magazine* for two months in 1777, then switched to the *Lady's Magazine* which he ordered until 1780, a faithfulness that was rare among most subscribers. This might seem an odd choice of reading for a young man, but these magazines provided him with fiction, for they contained novellas and short stories that were both cheap and easily available in towns and villages beyond the reach of London. Prowett also bought poetry by James Thomson, Edward Young and Jonathan Swift. The last was probably as published in John Bell's low-price edition of *British Poets* (see p. 206).

By the 1770s, books and periodicals for entertainment were being ordered at Clays by servant and non-servant customers alike. The most popular play for both was Isaac Bickerstaffe's comic opera of 1762, *Love in a Village*, with a plot involving the heroine disguised as a chambermaid to escape her father's marriage plans, then falling in love with the gardener, who was the very person her father had intended for her. The coming together of upstairs and downstairs here mirrors the popularity enjoyed by Richardson's *Pamela*. Richardson had published his guide on writing letters for servants before using the epistolary style in *Pamela*, whose heroine was a servant girl. Lackington in his autobiography records that poorer country people who used to spend their evenings 'in relating stories of witches, ghosts, hobgoblins, &c, now shorten their winter nights by hearing their sons and daughters read tales, romances &c', and goes on to describe Dolly returning from market with a copy of 'The History of Pamela Andrews'.[12] Lackington is sometimes dismissed as painting too rosy a picture of humble readers, but Clays' records bear him out in the example of *Pamela*, for Richardson is the only novelist to have attracted purchases from servants.

A rather different scenario offering the crossover between servant and employer is also provided by Clays' records. Elizabeth Hands was a poet and a servant who probably enjoyed access to the library of her employers, the Huddesford family who lived at Allesley in Warwickshire. Although Hands herself never bought from Clays, the Huddesfords did, and when in 1789 she published a book of poems entitled *The Death of Amnon*, the network of patrons provided by the bookseller made a major contribution towards the subscription of 5s per person, raising the considerable sum of £300. Hands also wrote a wry verse describing a household's reaction to a notice appearing in the morning paper about the publication of a volume of poems by a maidservant:

> 'A servant write verses!' says Madam Du Bloom:
> 'Pray what is the subject – a Mop, or a Broom?'
> 'He, he, he' says Miss Flounce: 'I suppose we shall see
> An Ode on a Dishclout – what else can it be?
> Says Miss Coquettilla, 'Why, ladies, so tart?
> Perhaps Tom the footman has fired her heart'.

A subsequent character, Miss Prudella could stand in for the Revd Trusler, for she notes:

> 'If servants can tell
> How to write to their mothers, to say they are well,
> And read of a Sunday, *The Duty of Man*,
> Which is more I believe than one half of them can;
> I think 'tis much *properer* they should rest there,
> Than be reaching at things so much out of their sphere'.

A second poem describes the reaction at the tea-table after the volume has been read, including 'The Death of Amnon', the poem that provided the title, and which dealt with the subject of incestuous rape, albeit biblical.[13]

Hands married a blacksmith and retired into obscurity, but another poetic servant enjoyed a remarkable career. Robert Dodsley was employed as a footman in the household of Charles Dartiqueneave, a friend of Jonathan Swift and Alexander Pope and a regular contributor to the *Tatler*. While in Dartiqueneave's service, he published *Servitude,* a poetic countering of Defoe's rants about offending servants. His next employer, Mrs Lowther, organised her influential friends to subscribe to his collection of poems, *A Muse in Livery, or The Footman's Miscellany*, published in 1732. The subscription list included the Prime Minister, Sir Robert Walpole, and no less than three duchesses. With the backing of Pope, Dodsley opened a bookshop at the sign of Tully's Head in Pall Mall, and became the highly respected publisher of a whole list of poets and literary figures, including Pope himself, Edward Young and Thomas Gray. Appropriately he issued Swift's subversive *Directions to Servants,* and suggested to Samuel Johnson that he should compile a dictionary.

Dodsley is completely out of the ordinary, but by their close proximity to their employers and their friends, household servants could enjoy privileged access to books. There are many examples of employers teaching their servants to read and write, and giving them and their children the freedom of their library. The writer H.G. Wells was the son of Sarah, employed in the 1870s as the housekeeper at Uppark, a charming Queen Anne house perched high up on the South Downs. In his autobiographical novel *Tono-Bungay* he describes how his mother allowed him access to the books at Uppark, disguised as Bladesover. Many of the older books had been banished to a closet during what he described as 'the Victorian revival of good taste and emasculated orthodoxy . . . So I read and understood the good sound rhetoric of Tom Paine's *Rights of Man* and his *Common Sense*, excellent books, once praised by bishops and since sedulously lied about. Gulliver was there unexpurgated, strong meat for a boy perhaps, but not too strong I hold – I have never regretted that I escaped niceness in these affairs.'[14] While Wells was enjoying the delights of the closet, the book that dominated the servants' quarters was a peerage, several copies of which were scattered around, enabling accurate application of social precedence when, for instance, seating guests at dinner or visiting servants at meals below stairs.

Proximity could also have its down side, for employers might dictate the reading matter of their servants. In his *Hints and Observations Seriously Addressed to Heads of Families*, published in 1816, the Revd H.G. Watkins provided a list of basic titles suitable for the kitchen library of servants. These ran as follows: the Bible, Jones's *Scripture Directory*, Biddulph's *Prayers for the Morning and Evening of Every Day Through the Week, The Pilgrim's Progress*, Beveridge's *Private Thoughts*, Doddridge's *Rise and Progress of Religion in the Soul* and Scott's *Sermon on the Fatal Consequences of Licentiousness.* In addition to this daunting and dreary list, he suggested tracts from the various societies for promoting Christian knowledge, including some written by himself. This presents a total contrast to Leigh Hunt's spirited account written in 1829 of the 'mobile library' of a maidservant arriving in a new town house. In the kitchen she keeps an old volume of *Pamela* and a sixpenny play, such as an adaptation of Aphra Behn's *Oroonoko*. Upstairs in her garret bedroom she has the Bible, but in her trunk are 'two or three song books consisting of nineteen for the penny; sundry tragedies at a halfpenny a sheet; the *Whole Nature of Dreams Laid Open,* together with the *Fortune Teller* and the *Account of the Ghost of Mrs Veal; the Story of the Beautiful Zoa, who was cast away on a desert island.*[15] These were the successors of the chapbooks and romances collected by Samuel Pepys in the seventeenth century, now often known as 'penny dreadfuls'. Little wonder then that the evangelical Hannah More, who started schools to teach girls sewing, knitting and spinning to 'train up the lower classes in habits of industry and piety' and recorded 'I allow of no writing for the poor', had revenge visited upon her in her old age by her servants, who threw parties when she was safely in bed.

In its many country houses, the National Trust has few records of below-stairs reading matter. At Dunham Massey there are sets in identical sheepskin bindings of a work entitled *The Knowledge and Practice of Christianity*: seven of the 1781 edition, and thirteen of the 1787 edition. These would seem to have been bought in bulk for the edification of the servants, or possibly of tenants on the estate. However, there is one collection of books for servants that does not go down the road of piety. Cragside in Northumberland was the country home of William, lst Lord Armstrong. Having made his fortune through engineering and arms manufacturing, in the early 1860s he built a country house at Rothbury, thirty miles north of Newcastle-upon-Tyne. The Servants' Library at Cragside, consisting of more than two hundred books, would appear to date from the time of William Watson-Armstrong, Lord Armstrong's great-nephew, who inherited the estate in 1900. However, the spirit of the lst Lord Armstrong lingers, as he provided libraries and reading rooms for the workers at his engineering works, as well as supporting the facilities for education and literature local to Cragside.

Sixty-three books are inscribed 'Servants' Hall', forty-eight have 'Housekeeper's Room' and a few indicate 'Housemaids' Room'. The majority in the first category were novels, such as a complete set of Sir Walter Scott's *Waverley*, Charles Dickens's *The Pickwick Papers* and *The Old Curiosity Shop*, H. Rider Haggard's *Maiwa's Revenge* and R.M. Ballantyne's *Silver Lake*. As the indoor servants would have been mainly women, it is not surprising that books intended for female readership are strongly represented: light novels such as Annie S. Swan's *The Ne'er Do Well,* Maria Crommelin's *Love Knots* and a Plain Woman's *My Trivial Life and Misfortune*, all inscribed 'Housemaids' Room'. There are also bound sets of periodicals, such as *Sunday at Home, Good Words* and *Sunday Magazine*. Non-fiction is represented by biography such as Francis Darwin's *Life and Letters of Charles Darwin* and Queen Victoria's *Leaves from the Journal of Our Life in the Highlands*.[16]

The kinds of books and periodicals in the Servants' Library at Cragside are close in subject and style to a library run for employees at Loveclough Printworks, which printed cotton, on the fringe of the Rossendale Valley in Lancashire. In 1870 the owner of the works provided a club house with a collection of 700 books. Although there were some works of moral education and enlightenment for apprentices, there were also books of recreation such as *The Boy's Handy Book of Games*. As at Cragside the majority of books were novels, whole sets of Dickens, Mrs Henry Wood, Conan Doyle, Ballantyne, and light romances by Dora Russell, Hesba Stratton and Annie S. Swan. A good supply of magazines was provided including *Tit-bits, Comic Cuts* and *Cassell's Saturday Journal*. From October 1894, subscriptions for a new set of magazines was added: *Sylvia's Journal*, the *Queen* and *Home Notes*, possibly as a result of requests from female workers.[17]

Several of the books in the collection at Cragside provide evidence of their provenance. Some came from Mawson, Swan and Morgan, a local bookseller in Newcastle, others from circulating libraries, notably Mudie's Select. Mudie's was a Victorian phenomenon. Charles Edward Mudie, who ran a stationer's shop in Bloomsbury in London, began to lend books in 1842. His staple business was the loan of three-decker novels, priced at a guinea and a half, that had become fashionable with the publication of Scott's *Kenilworth* in 1821. Despite efforts by various publishers to break this very high price for new fiction, three-deckers sailed in a stately manner through the rest of the century. In 1870 Anthony Trollope declared in a lecture, 'We have become a novel-reading people from the Prime Minister down to the last-appointed scullery-maid'.[18] But men and women enjoying good incomes, let alone scullery-maids, baulked at the price and borrowing became the norm for new fiction.

Mudie cleverly made his rates cheaper than most of his rivals, at a guinea per annum, and he offered a very wide range of books including the latest American poetry, biography and travel. He also emphasised that his library was select, excluding titles on moral grounds, so that parents could rest easy in their beds knowing that a bright yellow cover with the Pegasus label, the Mudie trademark, might lie on the parlour table ready for any family member to read aloud. The business expanded hugely, with a large establishment on the corner of New Oxford and Museum Streets opening triumphantly in December 1860 and described by Trollope as 'Mudie's great flare-up'. Branches

64 The label of Mudie's Select Library, which adorned many a novel in the nineteenth century. This particular romance, published in 1888, is *A Breton Maiden* by a French Lady, author of '*Till My Wedding Day*.

were opened in Birmingham and Manchester, and book clubs, societies and provincial libraries all over the country were supplied with books. Tin-lined boxes that could survive shipwrecks were dispatched across the world to Russia, China, India and South Africa.

However, as the novelty of the books wore off, and cheap reprints began to challenge, stocks were piling up in catacombs under the London headquarters. The *Spectator* recorded in 1863 a holding of over one million books so that even the collection 'of the famous Bodleian sinks into the shade, and that of the Vatican becomes dwarfish'. To try to cope with the huge stocks, Mudie's began to sell off three-deckers so that, for instance, George Eliot's *The Mill on the Floss*, published in 1860, was quickly marked down from 31s 6d to 7s. Bulk lots, a hundred at a time, were sold off to provincial libraries, and the Mudie books at Cragside were probably acquired in this way, as the labels of other circulating libraries are pasted over the original yellow stickers. The beginning of the end came in 1894, when Mudie's allied with W.H. Smith to kill off the three-decker. This bold move did not in the end save Mudie's, which was too old-fashioned and centralised in approach, and the Select Library closed in 1937, with the remaining stock bought by Harrods.

While the Mudie books at Cragside were probably acquired by the Armstrongs, it is possible that other books were brought in by the servants themselves. One volume, *Doctor Antonio* 'by the author of Lorenzo Benoni', is marked with the label of W.E. Franklin, who ran the station bookstall in Newcastle-upon-Tyne on contract from the North Eastern Railway. The great expansion of the railways took place in the 1840s; by 1850, with locomotives reaching speeds of more than 50mph, the number of passengers using the railway annually was estimated to be a staggering sixty million. At first the stalls on the stations were run by former railway employees or their widows as a kind of working pension arrangement, but complaints were raised about standards: 'Cheap French novels of the shadiest class, and mischievous trash of every description which no respectable bookseller would offer, found purchasers.'[19] The opportunity to do something about this was irresistible to William Henry Smith. His father's business, established in Mayfair in the 1790s, had been a newswalk, selling, hiring and distributing newspapers. By 1821 the firm had moved to the Strand, close to both Fleet Street and the coaching inns from which newspapers would be sent out all over the country. Diversifying into bookselling, it opened a reading room where a wide range of publications were available, including papers and magazines.

In 1848, having acquired exclusive rights to over a thousand miles of railway routes, W.H. Smith opened his first stall on Euston Station. This sold all the things a traveller might need, such as rugs and candles, maps and newspapers, but also books. Although Samuel Pepys had apparently read in his carriage, books and coaches were not ideal bedfellows – stagecoaches were often crowded, lumbering and ill-lit, so that only at coaching inns could books be enjoyed. Now, however, there was a mode of transport that made possible reading on the move. W.H. Smith, having offered Charles Edward Mudie the chance to have a different kind of circulating library and having been strangely declined, seized the hour and set up his own system. For an annual fee of one guinea per volume, travellers could register at one of the major bookstalls and borrow from its stock, returning the book to the same stall. By 1861, 177 such bookstalls operated this system. Space, however, was key, so most books were ordered from printed catalogues, delivered by train for collection the next day. The headquarters in the Strand organised all the subscriptions and surplus stock which was sold off cheaply, as with Mudie's.

Space considerations, and the profile of his clientele, also meant that W.H. Smith disliked the three-decker novels, preferring cheaper, single volumes. He was careful in his market research, discovering that women liked fiction that was not too serious, schoolboys liked gory historical tales, such as those by Harrison Ainsworth, Yorkshire did not buy poetry, Liverpool didn't care for religion, and the American writer Washingon Irving went down well everywhere.

Samuel Phillips wrote: 'The Universities are exclusive, but the "rail" knows no distinction of rank, religion or caste. We cannot promise to instruct by steam or to convey knowledge by express speed, but we may at least provide cheap and good books for willing purchasers.'[20] One publisher who took speedy advantage of this new market was George Routledge. From 1848 he began to produce novels priced at one shilling in what he called his Railway Library. He was able to do this by dodging the copyright laws and reprinting American titles, beginning with James Fenimore Cooper's sea yarn, *The Pilot*. As the series took off, he negotiated terms with British authors, such as Captain Marryat and Benjamin Disraeli. One of his most successful books was *Romance of War*, James Grant's novel about his father's experiences in the Peninsular War, which sold over 100,000 copies by 1888, the year of Routledge's death. But the really successful title was Harriet Beecher Stowe's *Uncle Tom's Cabin*, which put even the novels of Sir Walter Scott and Charles

65 The railway station bookstall run by W.H. Smith at Blackpool North, photographed in 1896.

Dickens in the shade. Following a magnificent review in *The Times* in 1852, one spectator wrote: 'flaring placards were to be seen in the booksellers' windows announcing its publication in various forms, sizes and prices. No collector in the trade at this time will forget the scramble there was to obtain copies.'[21] Routledge, having observed six first-class passengers reading the book in one railway compartment on the Brighton line, decided to bring it out in a variety of formats, from 6s to 6d, often sending out 100,000 copies in one day. In all, he sold over half a million.

Routledge produced his railway novels in glazed colour covers over boards with eye-catching pictures on the front and advertisements on the back. The spines were yellow, so that the genre became known as 'yellowbacks'. Genuinely keen to foster a taste in literature among 'common readers', he strove to make the books as attractive as possible, with illustrations by Walter Crane reproduced in colour through the skills of the printer, Edmund Evans. In this he was following in a fine publishing tradition. Three-quarters of a century earlier, John Bell, trading from the British Library in the Strand, had produced a whole raft of first-class books at very cheap prices. He was an extraordinary combination – a great letter founder, publisher, binder, owner of newspapers and periodicals, bookseller and a popular educator. The long

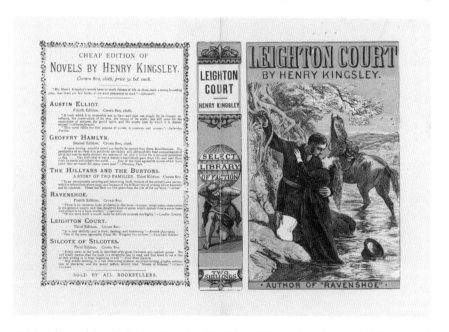

66 Printer's proof for a 'yellowback', produced by Edmund Evans. Evans learnt his skill as a wood engraver during his apprenticeship to one of Thomas Bewick's assistants. His hallmark was a combination of wood engraving with bright colours on a glazed yellow paper. *Leighton Court,* by the brother of the Revd Charles Kingsley of *Water Babies* fame, was first published in 1866.

'f's in type, which now seem so quaint, were dropped by him first in books, then in newspapers. He founded several newspapers, including *The Morning Post* launched in 1772, and realising that newspapers were read at speed and for information, he broke up the solid setting, giving prominence to the paragraphs, and setting the production style that is still used.

Taking advantage of a judgement in the House of Lords that upheld the abolition of perpetual copyright, John Bell produced cheap reprints of classical works, beginning with his edition of Shakespeare in 1774, followed by *The British Theatre* in 21 volumes in 6d weekly parts from 1776 to 1778, and *Poets of Great Britain from Chaucer to Churchill*, in a staggering 109 volumes each priced at 1s 6d and published between 1777 and 1782. He had refused to join the conger of London publishers who financed a similar series with prefaces by Samuel Johnson. Although Johnson's *Lives of the Poets* represents a height of English literary criticism, the series failed commercially while Bell's proved a triumph. Perhaps the secret of his success was that he passionately believed in the value of his project, whereas Johnson was sceptical of all cheap editions, comparing their publishers with Robin Hood, robbing the rich to give to the poor.

Another publisher who was passionately supportive of popular education was John Cassell. Born in 1817, the son of a Manchester publican, he became a child labourer in a local cotton mill before being apprenticed to a joiner in Salford. According to legend, of which there are several, he took to drink but signed the temperance pledge and set off for London, lecturing on the sins of alcohol. Known as the Manchester Carpenter, he presented a striking sight, gaunt with fanatical eyes, wearing his joiner's apron and speaking in a strong Lancashire accent. His wife's patrimony enabled him to set up business in London, first selling shilling bags of coffee and tea, and later producing part-publications. Using the small press that printed his tea and coffee labels, he began his publishing career with *Teetotal Times*. A fervent opponent of stamp duty on newspapers, he explained to the select committee in 1851: 'I entered into the publishing trade for the purpose of issuing a series of publications which I believed were calculated to advance the moral and social well-being of the working classes.'[22] He then proceeded to produce a whole range of publications, including the *Working Man's Friend, Cassell's Illustrated Family Paper, Cassell's Magazine* and *Cassell's Popular Educator*. The last, offering an encyclopedic self-instruction course in the arts and science at one penny a number, enjoyed a huge circulation and great influence – the poet Thomas Hardy for instance, taught himself German with the help of the *Educator*.

The tradition continued with Joseph Malaby Dent, born in 1849 the son of a house painter from Darlington, who first became a bookbinder, then a publisher. He hated the idea that cheap publications should be equated with shoddy production and poor type. As secretary of the William Shakespeare Society at the settlement of Toynbee Hall in the East End of London, he saw how members had to cope with a confusing variety of editions that lacked good critical apparatus. As a result, he launched in 1894 his forty-volume Temple Shakespeare, edited by Israel Gollancz with title pages designed by Walter Crane, priced at a shilling per volume. Over five million copies were sold over the next forty years. At the age of fifteen, J.M. Dent had given a talk at the mutual improvement society of his Methodist Chapel on Boswell's *Life of Samuel Johnson*. When he decided to produce a uniform edition of world literature, this was the book he chose to begin his famous Everyman Library.

One source of cheap books was the second-hand market. Henry Mayhew, in his survey of 1851 of London street sellers, interviewed those who specialised in books, and found them particularly knowledgeable about what

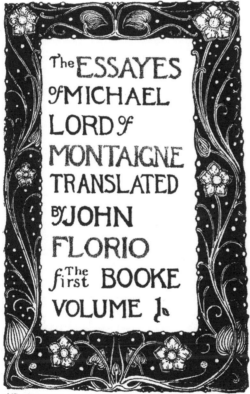

67 Title page of Montaigne's *Essays*, published by J.M. Dent in his Aldine editions, 1897.

sold and to whom.[23] Stalls were set up market style in well-frequented thoroughfares such as the City Road and the Old Kent Road. If the stock was plentiful the books were displayed spine upwards, with a paper attached giving price and a rough-and-ready category such as poetry, religion or French. When stock was scant, then their front covers were shown. Sometimes several books were bound together, with bizarre results: 'Lord Mount Edgecumbe's *Opera, What is Currency,* Watts's *Scripture History, Thoughts on Taxation,* only 1s 3d'. Others would be consigned to the 1d or 2d box. For a penny, one could buy the *Letters of the Rt. Hon. Lord John Russell on State Education,* or a *Pastoral Letter to the Clergy and Members of the Protestant Episcopal Church in the United States of America,* or *Friendly Advice to Conservatives.*

Mayhew describes how the customer base for these bookstalls was wide – bank clerks on their way to the City, ladies looking for novels such as Fenimore Cooper's *The Pilot* or Lewis's *The Monk.* Mechanics were good customers for scientific and trade books: 'I know many such who are rare ones for searching into knowledge', while 'Boys very seldom buy of me, unless it's a work about pigeons, or something that way'. One stallholder reported how he did well out of English classics, such as Johnson's *Rasselas* or Goldsmith's *The Vicar of Wakefield,* but not Butler's *Hudibras* or Milton. The one thing that was not likely to appear was an undiscovered printing treasure, such as black-letter books. Anything 'rare or curious' would have been picked up speedily by second-hand booksellers to put in their antiquarian catalogues. Stallholders also directed those in search of pornography to the booksellers' rows in Holywell Street, off the Strand.

Mayhew reported that the sale of new books by street auction was by the mid-nineteenth century irregular and dwindling. Such sales were rough and ready, with windows and doors removed from buildings, and the auctioneer set up at a counter, with bidders standing in the street. He described one such auction that had taken place a few years earlier in Stoke Newington, to the north east of the City. Here the patter was good but the product less so – poorly printed with illustrations pirated from other books, possibly by the rather doubtful publisher Thomas Tegg. The successful bidder for Young's *Night Thoughts* at two shillings was dismayed to find that the frontispiece, of a man on a tombstone, was the same as in his copy of Hervey's *Meditations Among the Tombs,* but the auctioneer would have none of it.

Although three-decker novels at a guinea and a half were way beyond the means of working-class readers, some could afford weekly or monthly instalments of novels. In 1836 Charles Dickens produced 'a monthly something' for his publisher Chapman & Hall, which grew into *The Posthumous Papers of the Pickwick Club.* This proved so popular that by the time the final instalment appeared, the print run had risen from 1,000 to 40,000 copies. Dickens reversed this method for his subsequent works of fiction, mapping them out as full-length stories, which he then worked into instalments. At one stage he considered abandoning the practice, concerned that he was making himself too cheap and spoiling the chances of novels by other writers, but soon changed his mind. The working up of the instalments so that he could finish on a cliff hanger perfectly suited his style.

Just as modern 'soaps' on radio and television so capture the imagination of listeners and viewers that they believe the characters are real people and part of their lives, Dickens created a cast of personalities that held thousands in their thrall. Over the weekend of 30–1 January 1841 it was estimated that half a million people in Britain were reading or hearing instalment number 44 of *Master Humphrey's Clock*, in which Dickens told of the death of Little Nell in *The Old Curiosity Shop*, while crowds gathered on the quayside in New York to receive copies in their familiar pale blue wrappers.[24]

Anthony Trollope described Dickens as 'Mr Popular Sentiment', with the real power to engage public opinion and thus promote social reform. Dickens strongly supported the working-man's interest in, and access to literary culture. On a visit to Birmingham in 1853, he was told of the plans for a new Industrial and Literary Institute, and offered to read *A Christmas Carol* at a fundraiser. Three readings were given that December, with working people admitted free to all parts of the hall to ensure no segregation of the audience. Such was the success of these events that Dickens's career as a public reader was launched.

Reading aloud had been an integral part of culture for centuries in a domestic environment, while celebrated writers such as Thackeray and Trollope gave public lectures, but did not read their own work. It was Dickens who brought these strands together in the most extraordinary way. Although he was keen that working men and women should be able attend his readings, the price for unreserved seats was a shilling, the price of a monthly instalment of one of his novels, and a lot of money for a labourer. In 1865 Edward Brotherton of the Manchester and Salford Education Aid Society reckoned that three shillings per head per week was the minimum subsistence income, exclusive of rent, and a penny was charged for most concerts. But for those who could afford it, the experience of a Dickens reading was unforgettable. The stage would be set up with a maroon-coloured backcloth. In front of this, twelve feet off the ground, was a horizontal row of gas-jets with a tin reflector, supported by two lateral rods, each carrying a small gas-jet. In the centre of this softly lit, warm frame was a little reading desk covered in red. Each programme would have one long item that was both demanding and dramatic, followed by a short, comic piece which Dickens hoped would appeal to the lower classes in his audience. Such were his acting abilities that specta-tors at a reading from *Nicholas Nickleby* noted how monstrous he looked as Squeers, the sadistic schoolmaster, and that he even managed in a scene between Nicholas and Fanny Squeers to take on their identities on each side of his face.

The demand for performances was huge. In the winter of 1867, Dickens travelled to America to provide a series of readings. Long queues built up in freezing weather outside the Steinway Hall in New York, with over 5,000 people by 8 o'clock on the morning that tickets went on sale. One group who braved a ferocious snowstorm declared: 'Why, we wouldn't have come over

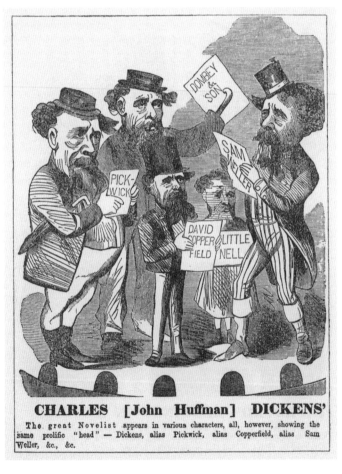

68 An American cartoon, probably dating from February 1868, demonstrating how Charles Dickens was able to take on the various characters in his public readings, even down to Little Nell.

from Brooklyn on such a night as this to hear the Apostle Paul . . . but we came to hear Dickens'.[25]

Three years after Dickens had given his first performance in Birmingham, penny readings were begun in 1854 in Hanley in Staffordshire, where Samuel Taylor, a clayworker, read excerpts from William Howard Russell's dispatches from the Crimea for *The Times*. These took place in the market square, but he then moved his 'Literary and Musical Entertainments for the People' into the town hall, where a penny was charged. The idea took off, and penny readings became a nationwide institution, held in village and town halls, schoolrooms, and Literary and Mechanic Institutes. Anthologies were published, as well as advice on establishing and conducting such occasions. An evening might consist of songs, instrumental solos, and a recitation, the most popular authors being Scott, Tennyson, Lord Byron, Thomas Hood and Dickens himself. In *Lark Rise to Candleford*, Flora Thompson describes a penny reading in Candleford Green, a village on the borders of Oxfordshire and Northamptonshire, in the 1890s. The schoolroom was lent free of charge, so the pennies went towards heat and light. Whole families would attend, enjoying the excitement of going out after dark into a warm room full of neighbours. The star turn was Old Mr Greenwood from a neighbouring village, who had heard Dickens reading his own works. Comic passages, featuring Mr Pickwick, Dick Swiveller or the nurse, Mrs Gamp, would be punctuated with bursts of laughter. Oliver Twist asking for more, and the deathbed of Little Nell drew tears from the women, throat-clearing from the men. Interestingly, Thompson recalled that although they loved the Dickens readings, the villagers would not be likely to borrow his novels from the parish library – 'they were waiting, a public ready made, for the wireless and the cinema'.[26]

* * * *

For those who could not afford to buy books, even second hand, if they were lucky, there were 'free libraries'. It really was a matter of being in the right place at the right time, and being deemed worthy of borrowing books. For instance, William Smart, draper, portman and Member of Parliament for Ipswich in Suffolk, in 1599 bequeathed his books to a library for the use of the Common Preacher and other preachers at the civic church of St Mary-le-Tower. Twenty-eight volumes were kept in a chest until 1611 when one of the preachers persuaded the Corporation of Ipswich that he and his Puritan colleagues had need of a working library. The collection was duly installed in the former dormitory of the Friar Preachers and gifts of books and money were received from local benefactors. Later in the century it moved to the grammar school, where the headmaster arranged the books fore-edge facing, with diagonal lines and symbols painted in white, green or black, to provide guidance for unlettered assistants to return volumes to their correct positions.[27]

The great founder of parochial libraries was Thomas Bray, whose determination to bring books, especially the Gospel, to the North American colonies is described in Chapter 4. As the founder of the Society for Promoting Christian Knowledge he set out to help the clergy in preaching and catechising children lest their parishioners fall into the errors of dissent or Roman Catholicism. His vision was a library in every deanery, with lockable bookcases, so that books could be borrowed and returned on, say, market day. He moved from rural to urban with his *Bibliothecha parochialis*, written in 1697, with a list of books on subjects including philosophy, mathematics, antiquities and civil law, which he considered essential for clergy and for the edification of their parishioners. More down to earth was the form of book club operated in the parish library at Measham in Leicestershire. Consisting of only six books, it was established by the minister John Jackson in 1635 to raise the consciousness of the works of God among his parishioners. His plan, written in a flyleaf of one of the works, was that the first six families with a literate member would take a book, keep it for three months, then return it to the minister and churchwardens so that it could be passed to the next six families until the whole parish was covered.

That the library at Ipswich is still with us is remarkable, but perhaps the most extraordinary survival is the library at Innerpeffray, near Crieff in Perthshire. It was founded by David Drummond, 3rd Lord Maddertie, and accommodated in an upper chamber in the chapel of his family's burial ground. In his mortification, or will, written in 1680, he specified that the books should be used for the benefit of young students, but by 1762 when the collection was moved to a purpose-built home hard by the chapel, it was open to all. The move was made by Robert Hay Drummond, Archbishop of York, who added his own considerable collection of books. Innerpeffray still has the ledgers of borrowers kept from 1747 through to 1969, and these provide a rare insight into the reading tastes of the local community.

Borrowers were required to write in the ledger their name, occupation and place of residence, followed by the book or books that they had taken. On the return of the books, they signed by the entry, which was then crossed out by the librarian. A page of the register beginning 11 December 1756 opens with the declaration of 'Thomas Thomson student of Philosophy in Crieff grant me to have borrowed forth of the Library Stow's Chronicle of England'. His entry is followed by a wide cross-section of borrowers, the teacher from the school at Kinkell, the minister of the church at Trinity Gask, but also a weaver, a mason, a dyer's apprentice, a flax dresser and a glover. Some entries use the word 'lent', suggesting that a servant had come to collect the book and the entry was made by the librarian. The entry for 24 July 1756 declared that the borrower, John Robert, a weaver from Lonhead, could not write. Only seventeen women in over half a century were recorded as acquiring books, and again the librarian made the entry, describing the titles as lent, which also suggests that it was deemed improper for them to come and collect the books in person.[28] Women were all sent books of a religious nature, apart from Mrs Mary Drummond, who broke the mould with a collection of travels and Clarendon's *History* in 1765, and Catherine Preston, who borrowed a volume of Shakespeare's plays in 1794.

It is exciting to find that all the books borrowed from December 1756 to June the following year are still in the library. James Sharp of Innerpeffray borrowed a life of James Drummond of Hay and Patrick Abercromby's *Martial Achievements of the Scots Nation*, published in Edinburgh in 1709;

69 The opening page for 1757 in the borrowers' register for Innerpeffray Library in Perthshire. Readers wishing to take out books would make a declaration, counter-signing this when they returned them, at which point the librarian would cross out the entry. Some entries commence 'lent' indicating that the borrower did not come to the library in person.

Donald Foaze the flax dresser from Crieff took Robert Cleaver's *A Plaine and Familiar Exposition of the Ten Commandments*, published in 1632; Ebenezer Clement, the apprentice dyer, borrowed the first volume of George Mackenzie's *Lives and Characters of the Most Eminent Writers of the Scots Nation*, published in Edinburgh in 1708. In his analysis of the number of loans for books, Paul Kaufman found that the most popular by far during the period from 1747 to 1800 was the *History of Charles V* by William Robertson, Principal of Edinburgh University and one of the leading figures of the Scottish Enlightenment. Although sermons by Tillotson, Sherlock and Atterbury all appear in the top category of loans, so too do Buffon's *Natural History* and the works of John Locke.[29] The one category of books notable by its absence was lighter literature, showing that the citizens of Crieff and surrounding villages took their reading seriously. Only in the nineteenth century is there an increase of loans for secular over religious titles, and for more pleasures of the imagination.

The taste for serious reading is reflected too by the contents of the Miners' Library at Leadhills in Lanarkshire. For centuries miners had travelled up into the Lowther Hills to work the lead-mines during the summer months, spending their winters down in the valleys, an existence matching Thomas Hobbes's famous description, 'nasty, brutish and short'. All this was transformed by the remarkable James Stirling, who fled to Italy following the failure of the Jacobite rising in 1715, only to escape from Venice with a price on his head when he showed too much interest in the city's glass-making techniques. He was engaged as manager at Leadhills in 1734 by the Scots Mining Company with an annual salary of £200, a new house to be designed by William Adam, and a coach and pair. In turn he cut the miners' working hours from twelve to six per day, encouraged them to build sturdy stone houses and to cultivate gardens, started a health insurance plan and improved the schooling for their sons and daughters. All this is thought to have provided the prototype for Robert Owen to found his enlightened community at New Lanark. Stirling also encouraged the miners to set up a library and a reading society in 1741, and this model was copied fifteen years later by neighbouring Wanlockhead, and in 1792 by Westerkirk.

These three miners' libraries were community or subscription institutions, once common in Scotland. The members clubbed together to pay entrance fees with a subscription to be spent on books. While the wealthy laid out guineas to join subscription libraries with large stocks of books, these workers paid shillings for a much more modest range of reading matter, though this was enlarged by subsidies from the mining companies and donations from benefactors. The members' roll for Leadhills has survived, showing that the original membership on 15 April 1743 was made up of twenty-one miners, the minister and the schoolmaster. Stirling was not a member, for the miners were always determined to maintain their own control over their books – even the local landowner, the Earl of Hopetoun, was firmly excluded from any interference with the management of the Reading Society. The conditions of membership were set down in the 'Articles and Laws': a prospective candidate was required to apply in writing to the 'Preses' or president, and attend a quarterly meeting where he would be admitted or rejected, the decision indicated by the placing of white or black balls in a ballot box that is still in the library. It was a case of 'he', for women were not admitted at Leadhills until 1881, though the miners at Wanlockhead were more enlightened and had women members from the 1780s. Once admitted, the member received a certificate and would pay an annual subscription of two shillings.

Leadhills lost some of its early documents in fires, though the bargain books have survived. These are not the remaindered books now offered on many a high street, but records of the bargains struck between teams of workers and mine owners in pre-union days. Wanlockhead does have its original declaration, which states its purpose to be 'purchasing a collection of books for our mutual improvement'. Many of these early books were religious in nature, such as the ubiquitous *The Whole Duty of Man*, Scougal's *The Life of God in the Soul of Man* and DuPin's *History of the Church*. History was a popular area with the full set of *The Universal History* and works by David Hume. Science was represented by the *Philosophical Principles of Universal Chemistry* by Georg Stahl and, unsurprisingly, Robert Jameson's *System of Mineralogy*. Buffon's nine-volume *Natural History*, published by William Creech of Edinburgh, was also acquired. The first books for the library may have been obtained from London by James Stirling, but the letterbooks of the Edinburgh-based bookseller, Charles Elliot, record that he was supplying books in the 1770s for both Leadhills and Wanlockhead via Dr James Williamson of Glasgow University.[30] A letter from Elliot to Williamson dated 18 September 1777 refers to a request for Hugh Blair's *Lectures on Rhetoric and Belles-Lettres*, which Elliot could not supply as Dr Blair was trying to suppress them. A copy of the *Lectures* is still to be seen on the shelves at Leadhills. The reading matter of the miners was diverse and profound. Little wonder that when Dorothy Wordsworth, on a walking holiday with her brother William in 1803, asked a Leadhills miner in astonishment, 'What! Have you Shakespeare?', he replied, 'Yes we have that, and all sorts of books.'[31]

Once a month, the miners gathered in the library, forming an orderly queue to request the books they wanted, having studied the printed catalogue of the collection or been recommended a title by a colleague. Each member might choose six books, and once this preliminary selection had been made, they could take as many more as they wished from the books remaining. Six

70 The bookplate that was put on the inside cover of books in the Leadhills Miners' Library. The image was produced some time between 1760 and 1790 by a prominent Edinburgh engraver, Andrew Bell. The pillar represents wisdom, the dove peace, and the Society's motto, 'and leave the rest to Heaven', is a quotation translated from the work of Corneille.

inspectors on the committee would examine the returned books to detect any damage, and were, moreover, empowered to enter members' houses at any time to make a similar examination. The rules decreed punishment by fines for members guilty of obstinate behaviour, and any member not residing in Leadhills itself had to provide a bag sufficient to keep out the rain. This was all good sense, for the minute books surviving from 1821 record considerable expenditure for the repair and rebinding of books that were in constant use. The minutes also record the purchase of 1 stone 4lbs of candles from McCall & Smith of Lanark; at a cost of 7s 8d per stone, they were probably of wax and of a quality that could aid reading on long winter nights.

Leadhills Library, having survived the threat of closure in the 1970s, remains as a Reading Society, with a membership of about fifty, meeting regularly in the large room that houses the books on their original shelves. The library of Wanlockhead, now part of the Mining Museum, has been reconstructed to show what a reading room would have looked like in the nine-teenth century. Westerkirk is a parish library, with the borrowing of books restricted to persons living in surrounding parishes. This remarkable group serves as a reminder of the love of books of mining communities all over Britain, and especially those of the coalmines of South Wales. It is reckoned that in the 1930s there were over 200 such libraries in the valleys, with an average stock of about 3,000 volumes, though the largest, Tredegar, where the Labour politician Aneurin Bevan headed the book selection committee, had a circulation of 100,000. Richard Booth, the self-styled 'Emperor of Hay-on-Wye', describes in his autobiography how the libraries were the spiritual heart of the valley towns: a bar licence was not forthcoming without a reading room. Tipped off in the early 1970s that these libraries were being closed down and their contents dispersed, Booth bought up many books, rescuing some from scrap heaps of waste paper. Public libraries took their place, but Booth makes the point that the stock in a public library is chosen for the people, not by them, and the erudition of the miners' libraries has been eradicated.[32] Only two Welsh miners' libraries remain today, one at Cwmaman, the other at Trecynon.

The Scottish miners' libraries are often described as progenitors of the mechanics institutes. The idea for the latter began in Glasgow following the appointment of George Birkbeck as Professor of Natural Philosophy at Anderson's Institution in December 1799. In addition to his lectures to under-graduates, he offered extra-curricular lectures on popular science, known as 'mechanics classes'. Birkbeck left Scotland in 1804 but the Glasgow Mechanics Institute developed and became the prototype for many hundreds of similar organisations. In December 1823 Birkbeck inaugurated the London Mechanics Institute in association with Lord Brougham, the flamboyant lawyer who gained much popularity by his protest at the treatment meted out to Caroline of Brunswick, George IV's estranged wife.[33] Brougham was a Utilitarian who believed that the imparting of elements of scientific knowl-edge through classes, lectures and libraries would make for better workers and, by strengthening religious belief, ideas of revolution would be damped down. In 1826, therefore, he founded the Society for the Diffusion of Useful Knowledge, supported by the publications of Charles Knight. Knight produced a series of books and journals, including the *Working Man's Companion*, the *Quarterly Journal of Education*, most notably the *Penny Magazine* and most bravely the *Penny Cyclopaedia*. In the last venture, launched in 1833, Knight included many illustrations that made use of the latest printing techniques for steel engravings and lithography. His good intentions imperilled finances and in 1846 he became bankrupt, along with the Society.

Mechanics institutes provoked much debate. William Cobbett, writing in the *Political Register*, poured scorn on the 'brilliant enterprise to make us "*a'enlightened*" and to fill us with "*antellect*", brought, ready bottled up, from north of the Tweed', being neatly offensive both to Birkbeck with his Glasgow connexion and Brougham whose birthplace was Edinburgh. The Scottish leadminers had fiercely guarded the selection of books for their libraries, and the question of who was in control soon caused a split in the London Mechanics Institute, with working-class members breaking away to found their own mutual improvement clubs. The Liverpool Mechanics and Apprentices Library, established in 1824, was run by middle-class directors, while the Sheffield version, founded the year before, was run by its working-class members. Ironically it was Sheffield which tried to ban what might be considered unsuitable books such as novels, while Liverpool operated a much more open system.

The lectures too caused difficulties. After a long day working day, many labouring men wanted to relax and drink, and found both the subjects boring and the levels of the lectures too hard. Charles Dickens reflected his hostility to the ideology of hard facts in his novel *Hard Times* with the character of Mr Gradgrind, who states 'Now, what I want is Facts . . . Facts alone are wanted in Life.' Gradually the working-class audiences gave way to those of the aspirational middle classes, while courses on the 3 Rs to supplement inadequate elementary education attracted increasing numbers, including women and young people. Nevertheless, mechanics institutes represent some of the largest and longest-lived libraries for the working classes, with 610 in operation in 1850, owning 700,000 volumes and a circulation of 2 million. While the larger often became middle-class institutions, the smaller ones stayed true. For example, Daniel Hudson, a cottage lacemaker in Ilkeston in Derbyshire, ensured that the best books were ordered in his local institute, and got them early, reading them propped by his loom.

Many mechanics institutes were transformed into public libraries following the Act of 1850 guided through Parliament by the radical MP, William Ewart. This was a landmark piece of legislation, but hampered by the limitation of its powers. Municipal boroughs with a population of over 10,000 were *permitted* to become library authorities and establish public libraries funded from the rates. They could, however, only do this if they charged ratepayers no more than one halfpenny in the pound for the purpose, limited their spending to facilities and not books, and received permission of two-thirds of the ratepayers in a special poll. In Scotland in 1854 the rate was raised to one penny to allow expenditure on books, and eventually England followed suit, reducing the population qualification to 5,000, and extending the act to include parish vestries.

Unsurprisingly, the Act was slow to take off: by 1868 only twenty-seven English local authorities had taken the decision, half of them in the industrial and commercial centres of the Midlands and the North. Thomas Carlyle was moved to ask, 'Why is there not a Majesty's library in every county town? There is a Majesty's gaol and gallows in every one.'[34] This question was taken up by Thomas Greenwood, a commercial traveller for a Sheffield hardware firm who, while on the road, sought out public libraries for personal reading, eventually becoming a publisher of technical books and earning himself a large fortune. His *Free Public Libraries*, first published in 1886, urged municipal councils to place libraries higher up the agenda. An effective publicist, he used quotations from leading figures, dead and alive. Thus, from Charles Dickens: 'The Free Library is a great Free School, inviting the humblest workman to come in and be a student'; and from Joseph Chamberlain: 'It is absolutely necessary that [the student] should have access to books, many of which are costly, many of which are very difficult to obtain even to the richest of single individuals, *but which it is in the power of a community to provide for all its members alike.*'[35]

Gradually Greenwood and other champions of public libraries prevailed, though London in particular remained bereft. The chief cause was the hostility of ratepayers from both the working and middle classes, sceptical of the assurance that the rates for libraries would never rise over a penny in the pound,

[*Designed by Mr. J. Williams Benn.*]

71 The frontispiece to Thomas Greenwood's *Free Public Libraries: Their Organisation, Uses and Management*, published in 1886. Greenwood argued that by providing free libraries and reading rooms the working man would avoid the temptations of the public house and thus escape the workhouse.

recalling how the school board rate had risen to sixpence after only eight years. The well-to-do, able to afford their own books, resented being taxed for a service they would not use, and libraries did not fall into the same category of necessary evils as workhouses, prisons, wash-houses and even schools. In Hackney in 1871, for instance, the ratepayers defeated a motion to establish a public library by 4,389 votes to 631 after a riotous meeting in the Town Hall, with further efforts failing in 1891 and 1893. In neighbouring Stoke Newington on 5 February 1890, however, the Public Libraries Act was adopted without a poll because the majority present at the meeting was in favour. Thomas Greenwood in his address bedazzled his audience with statistics concerning rates and spoke of the gifts being made by philanthropists like Andrew Carnegie and John Passmore Edwards.

Both Carnegie and Passmore Edwards rose from poverty to prosperity. Carnegie was born in Dunfermline in Fife in 1835, the son of a damask linen weaver who took his family to the United States in 1848. Carnegie's first job was as a bobbin boy in a cotton factory in Pittsburgh on a weekly wage of $1.20. By the time he was sixty-five he was able to retire to 30,000 acres at Skibo Castle in Sutherland, having made a colossal fortune from steel, railroads and newspaper publishing. Taking his motto as 'the man who dies rich, dies disgraced', he set up trusts that eventually founded 2,811 free libraries, 1,946 in America and 660 in Britain. John Passmore Edwards was born in 1823, the son of a Cornish carpenter. He recalled in his autobiography how he read by the light of a single candle in the midst of his family: 'Hundreds and hundreds of times I pressed my thumbs firmly on my ears until they ached, in order to read with as little distraction as possible.'[36] Passmore Edwards tried various publishing enterprises in newspapers and magazines, before striking rich with the *Echo*. With the profits from his publishing, he gave money to schools, hospitals, museums and libraries, in particular to Cornwall and poorer parts of London. In 1884 Carnegie bought into the *Echo*, but the partnership of the two philanthropists did not flourish.

The library at Stoke Newington was opened in July 1892, with a new building provided by Passmore Edwards, along with 1,000 books towards the total capacity of 40,000. Into this library went a Cotgreave indicator, bought directly from the inventor Alfred Cotgreave, local resident and chief librarian at West Ham. This large contraption was the cause of considerable dispute in its day, for readers at public libraries did not enjoy open access to the bookshelves. The concept of browsing, so much part of modern experience, was not considered appropriate either in libraries or in shops that sold books. The reader or customer had to make a specific request and be given it by a librarian or a shop assistant. Gentlemen could browse in their own libraries, privileged customers might be allowed to roam the shelves of bookshops and circulating libraries if the illustrations to trade bills are to be believed, but it was a luxury not accorded to all. Printed catalogues giving shelfmarks or reference numbers had to be consulted. There were various kinds of indicators, but Cotgreave's was the most popular. It consisted of tiny drawers, one for each book, and was kept on or by the counter. The drawers were coloured blue at one end, red at the other. Armed with the shelfmark or reference, the reader would check the drawer facing them. If blue, then the book was available, and a request made to the librarian; if red, it was out. The librarian, having collected the book from the closed shelves, would fill in the details of the borrower and the date of the loan, and put them into the drawer.

An example of a Cotgreave indicator is still installed, though not used, in the library at Edzell in Angus, on the east coast of Scotland. Edzell Library was opened in 1898 to celebrate Queen Victoria's Diamond Jubilee through the generosity of Robert William Inglis, son of the manse who had made his fortune on the London Stock Exchange. It was housed in a memorial hall in the Scottish baronial style, and furnished with over 5,000 books specially bound along with a printed catalogue by the London booksellers, Henry Sotheran & Co. Number 1 in the catalogue was Ainsworth's melodramatic novel, *The Tower of London*; number 5001, *Silk of the Kine* by L. McManus; and these were coordinated with the Cotgreave indicator which had sufficient drawers for 6,000 titles.

Four years before the opening of Edzell Library, James Duff Brown had introduced the concept of open access at his library in Clerkenwell in London. He was able to do so by inventing a new system of subject classification using letters for different categories of non-fiction. This system was adopted by many libraries in Britain before being superseded by the Dewey or Universal decimal classifications, ushering in a spirited debated about open versus closed access.[37] Cotgreave, not surprisingly, maintained that his indicator had transformed chaos into efficiency, but it was criticised as a clumsy and unsightly object that provided a handy shelter for librarians to hide behind. It also was an intimidating system, especially for the reader who turned up in hob-nailed boots or a tattered shawl. The deep-seated mistrust of the masses once more reared its head. Thomas Greenwood's biographer, writing in 1949, observed: 'The "Gentle Reader" of today, browsing from shelf to shelf, would be amused at the picture then drawn of hundreds of hooligans rushing in, throwing books about, or alternatively thieving them.'[38]

Into the fray came the *Sun* newspaper with an article on 9 September 1897 entitled 'The Battle of the Books: The Bitter War in the Library'. It ran: 'There is a war in the library world. Some readers would scarcely credit its vehemence. But it rages and probably will rage for days to come.' The public had real wars to worry about, and the debate died down, but indicators were

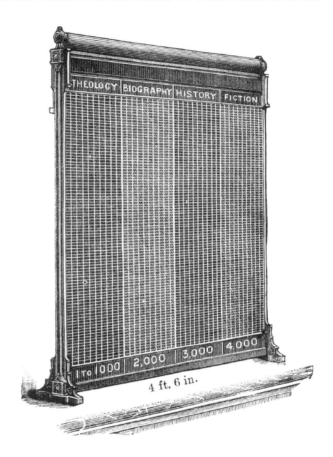

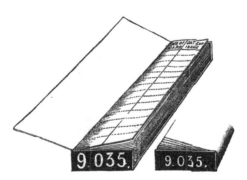

72 & 73 The Cotgreave indicator, reproduced in Greenwood's *Free Public Libraries*. In the example shown here there was room for 4,000 titles. Each title was allotted a book or ledger measuring 3 × 1 inch attached to a slide, coloured red at one end and blue at the other to indicate availability. There were various kinds of indicator produced, but Alfred Cotgreave's was the most widely used.

gradually removed from public libraries over the following decades. Haggerston, just down the road from Duff Brown's pioneering Clerkenwell, finally went over to open access in 1936. One of the last to hold out was Charles Goss, the librarian at the Bishopsgate Institute which provided education to the very poor areas on the eastern fringes of the City of London. From a deprived background himself, Goss believed that the knowledge provided in books at the public library should be rendered accessible to all, developing a descriptive cataloguing method that made visible the contents of his library through annotated entries. His opposition to open access was grounded in his belief that there was no system so effective as a helpful and approachable librarian, knowledgeable about his collection. This argument of course is entirely contingent on the abilities of the librarian, and in the end open access did prevail without the end of civilisation as we know it.

If access was a battle, then the debate about the quality of books provided by libraries was a long drawn out war. Stoke Newington Library, having opened in 1892 with John Passmore Edwards' donation of 1,000 books, had reached a stock of 9,000 by 1900, with a registered membership of 3,800 borrowing at an annual rate of 90,000 issues. This huge rate of activity was intriguingly attributed by the local library commissioners to the practice of cycling among the young. But the books on offer to Stoke Newington cyclists and non-cyclists alike were predominately non-fiction: in 1908 only 16.3 per cent of the total stock was fiction. This low figure was satirised in *Punch* on 8 July of that year, with a whimsical account of novelists meeting in Hyde Park to protest against Stoke Newington's reluctance to buy more novels. Demonstrators, led by the creator of the Scarlet Pimpernel, Baroness Orczy, captured the parish at the point of quills aided by the army of San Marino. In fact, the imbalance was the result of a high number of donations of non-fiction, together with determination on the part of the Stoke Newington Library commissioners to provide 'worthwhile' literature.

'Unworthwhile literature' could be offered by the circulating libraries that catered for the common reader. In 1898, at the instigation of Florence Boot, the pharmaceutical company decided to take advantage of the company's network of high street shops to open the Boot's Book-lover's Library. This offered mostly fiction, much of it stock from the surplus lists of other institutions, at a highly competitive price. By 1907 there were 256 branches, with a million books bought in each year. At the other end of the scale were the tiny village shops where a few books might be bought, and others lent. The artist Edward Burne-Jones paints a vivid picture of one such in the village of Rottingdean on the Sussex coast in the last years of the nineteenth century: 'Nothing in the shop is worth half a farthing – it sells balls of string, and potatoes, and sand boots and galoshes, and geraniums in pots, and occasionally a cucumber, and

Cassells popular reader, and newspapers, and it has a circulating library of as many as eighteen volumes which sit on the shelf from year to year and never circulate.'[39]

* * * *

The 'non-circulating' library has disappeared from British life, leaving only evocative descriptions like that of Edward Burne-Jones, and just as surely we can only imagine the library of a common reader from the eighteenth or nineteenth centuries. Two collections of books do, however, give some idea, although both Thomas Bewick and James Ramsay MacDonald by their achievements became very uncommon readers, and thus the concentration here is upon the period of their straitened circumstances.

Thomas Bewick was born in August 1753 at Cherryburn, a farmstead on the banks of the Tyne, eleven miles west of Newcastle. He was the eldest of eight children born to John Bewick, tenant farmer and colliery manager, and his wife Jane. Their little farmhouse has survived, with its kitchen, the main living room of the house, refurbished by the National Trust using a sketch made by Thomas's son Robert in 1844. No books are shown, but they might have been accommodated on shelves next to the kitchen range and, apart from the Bible, would have consisted mostly of chapbooks bought from pedlars, such as 'Jack the Giant Killer' and an abridged version of Defoe's *Robinson Crusoe*. A particular favourite was *Aesop's Fables* in the edition published by Samuel Croxall in 1722 with illustrations by Elisha Kirkall: Thomas Bewick kept this crumpled copy all his life.

In 1800 William Wordsworth expressed his admiration for Bewick in a manuscript addition to his poem 'The Two Thieves': 'Oh! Now that the boxwood and graver were mine/Of the Poet who lives on the banks of the Tyne,/Who has plied his rude tools with more fortunate toil/Than Reynolds e'er brought to his canvas and oil.' Wordsworth, however, was romantic but wrong if he believed that Bewick was an untutored genius. Thomas himself later put the record straight: 'my education was not so scanty as many imagine; I was sent early to a good school and regularly kept there'.[40] He was a strong-minded child, who often played truant and filled his Latin primers with drawings of the countryside around Cherryburn, but he was well taught by the Revd Christopher Gregson in the book-filled schoolroom at nearby Ovingham. Moreover, the villages around Cherryburn were not isolated intellectually. A turnpike road linking Newcastle to Hexham ensured that the local inns had newspapers, and a large proportion of the cottagers were literate. In his autobiography, Bewick describes one of his childhood neighbours Anthony Liddell, the 'village Hampden', who read the Bible with such care that 'the whole cast of his character was formed'. 'Besides the Bible, Josephus was his next favourite author; next The Holy Wars, and these and Bishop Taylor's sermons composed his whole library, and his memory enabled him nearly to repeat whatever he had read.'[41]

At the age of fourteen, Thomas Bewick left Cherryburn to be apprenticed to Ralph Beilby, engraver of Newcastle, whose workshop was located in Amen Corner. Here he found himself in the very heart of the city's publishing activities, reckoned to have been the most important after London and Oxbridge at the time. In 1800 there were 20 printers, 3 engravers, 13 binders and 12 booksellers, including the shop and circulating library of Joseph Barber immediately next door to Beilby. Bewick's thirst for books completely outstripped the modest wages that he earned as an apprentice engraver, but he was able to use the library and guidance of the bookbinder Gilbert Gray, who had worked with Allan Ramsay, the Edinburgh poet and bookseller, and was fired with the ideas of the Scottish Enlightenment. Bewick also persuaded the servant girl in the Beilby household to give him access to his master's books so that he could enjoy Smollett's *A Complete History of England*. One particular advantage that accrued from his trade was his access to the bookbindery of William Gray, Gilbert's son, where 'his workshop was often filled with the Works of the best Authors, to bind for Gentlemen – To these, while binding, I had ready access – for which purpose I rose early in the morning . . . & there I remained with him 'till my work hour came.'[42]

Although most of the work that went through Beilby's workshop was metal engraving, Thomas Bewick began to develop his skills as a wood engraver. Recognising the crudity of the woodcuts in the chapbooks that he had as a child, he acquired illustrated books such as Gerard's *Herbal* with its engravings of plants, and a book of woodcuts of the Passion by the great German engraver, Albrecht Dürer. Although he already owned Croxall's *Aesop's Fables*, he now bought a book of fables in Latin, *Fabulae Variorum Auctorum, Aesopi, etc* published in Frankfurt in 1660, and Edward Topsell's *Foure-footed Beastes*, an English translation made in 1607 of the pioneering work of the great Swiss naturalist Conrad Gesner with woodcut illustrations of the animals described.

Using close-grained boxwood, Bewick started to cut emblematic blocks for children's books. The very concept of fun books aimed at children was a comparatively recent innovation; the earliest in Britain was probably *A Little Book for Children*, published in 1712, using pictures to teach letters and words. The London bookseller John Newbery, having made a fortune from selling patent James's Powders, produced all kinds of children's books, priced at sixpence or a shilling, and some of these were pirated by the Newcastle bookseller Thomas Saint. Through Beilby, Saint commissioned Bewick to provide the illustrations for his own books of fairy tales and for a reworking of the fables of Thomas Gay. Bewick, recalling the oval vignettes that Elisha Kirkall had produced for Croxall's *Aesop*, made charming little engravings for the beginning of each fable. One surreal scene depicts an elephant conversant in ancient Greek encountering a bookseller who wishes to commission a book from him on the senselessness of men.

Having completed his apprenticeship and spent a brief and uncongenial time in London, Bewick went into partnership with his former master Ralph Beilby. Their business prospered as his skill as a wood engraver grew, but Bewick wanted to move beyond providing illustrations for other people's works. One of his childhood books, Thomas Boreman's *Description of Three Hundred Animals*, had particularly offended him because of the crude copperplate pictures. Slowly he developed the idea of a survey of four-footed animals for which he produced the illustrations, and worked with Beilby on the text. His *A General History of Quadrupeds* was begun in 1785 and completed five years later, with representations and descriptions of 199 animals. The

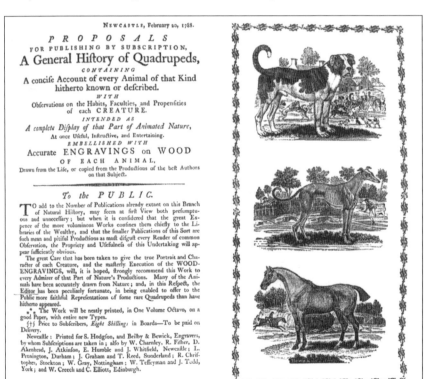

74 Thomas Bewick's advertisement for publishing by subscription his great work, *A General History of Quadrupeds*, 1788.

first printing of 1,600 copies sold out in months, and the book went through eight editions in his lifetime. In a letter written in 1819 Bewick wrote: 'I date the Quadrupeds to be my commencement of Wood Engraving worthy of attention.'[43]

Bewick was now a man of means, very much part of the intellectual scene of Newcastle. As the member of a book group that met regularly at the Cannon, a tavern owned by Sam Alcock, he could enjoy the company of fellow tradesmen, drink ale, eat cake and discuss books. He was also a founder member of a Philosophical Society that debated literature, philosophy and politics, and in 1799 he joined the Newcastle Literary and Philosophical Society, where he was able to use the library. He began to build up his personal library: at his death in 1828, his collection numbered almost 700 volumes, which must have been unusually extensive for a craftsman of the period. This collection was dispersed in a series of sales, but references in his autobiography, auction catalogues and descriptions by his children have all helped to build up a picture of what he bought. He used local booksellers to acquire both new and second hand titles. He also bought copies of the works that he had illustrated; today, book illustrators would expect to be given these for free by the publisher. Like many a keen book collector, he responded to catalogues, as shown in a letter to an un-named bookseller: 'I recd one of your sales Catalogues last night for which . . . thanks . . . I had not an opportunity of looking at it till this morning – then not in time to send you this by post. If Buffon No. 390 is not sold – I wish much to have it.'[44] Many of the books that he acquired were to help him in his work, hence his interest in Buffon's *Natural History of Birds*, but he also enjoyed poetry and ballads, and books of history and biography feature in the library lists. Although the library was dispersed, admirers of Bewick have reassembled some of the books in the library of the Natural History Society of Northumbria and in the Pease Collection in Newcastle City Library. A handful have returned to Cherryburn, where an exhibition of Bewick's life and work are shown in the nineteenth-century farmhouse next door to his much smaller birthplace.

James Ramsay MacDonald was born just over a hundred years after Bewick, in October 1866 in Lossiemouth on the Moray coast of Scotland. His mother was Annie Ramsay, who worked as a housekeeper on a farm where his father, John MacDonald, a Highlander from the Black Isle, was the head ploughman. The couple did not marry, and Ramsay MacDonald was brought up by his mother and grandmother, Bella Ramsay. Lossiemouth was a grim village of fishing and farming, where Bella lived in a squat two-roomed cottage, known as 'but and ben', with a thatched roof, flagged floor and tiny windows of bottle glass. Not the easiest start in life, yet there were patches of blue sky in this louring cloud. MacDonald occupied the centre of attention of two strong-minded, intelligent women. The passing of the 1870 Education Act would have ensured an adequate basic education, but as a Scot, he benefited from a system that was traditionally finer than that on offer south of the Border. At a cost of 18d per month, he was sent to the parish school in nearby Drainie, where 'The machinery was as old as Knox; the education was the best ever given to the sons and daughters of men'.[45]

James MacDonald, the dominie at Drainie, had a profound influence on the young boy. For formal education, he used Bain's Sixteenpenny Grammar before moving on to Latin and Greek, but James MacDonald's literary heroes were Sir Walter Scott and George MacDonald. When Ramsay MacDonald asked to borrow a copy of Scott's *Tales of a Grandfather*, the dominie asked him what his grandmother's library consisted of, to which the response was 'A great three-volumed Brown's Bible in sheepskin, a huge Life of Christ which I could not lift but whose back in green polished leather always attracted me, some collections of Sermons and a few books bound in black on theology and Church history, a volume or two of the classics in their original, and some tattered odds and ends'.[46] The reference to classics in the original shows the remarkable venue in which Ramsay MacDonald was nurtured.

On his visits to Elgin, a walk of ten miles each way, MacDonald stood outside the windows of booksellers, 'stealing from the pages of the books exposed to view what delight they could give me . . . When I was the proud possessor of a penny, it was not to the booksellers I went, however. Their prices, even at their lowest were not for me. There was a pawnbroker in the city, and he sold me his "rubbish" for next to nothing'. At school, one of *Chambers' Readers*, an anthology of great writers, introduced him to 'the music, the colour, and the dignity of words', while an encounter with a ragman who read from a book perched on his barrow of crockery, resulted in the acquisition of Thucydides in translation. When a consumptive watchmaker returned to Lossiemouth to die, he introduced Ramsay MacDonald to Dickens, lending him volumes that would be returned wrapped in a clean white towel.[47]

It was clear to the dominie that this was no ordinary youth, and after a brief spell as a farm labourer, MacDonald became a pupil teacher with an annual salary of £7 and access to his master's library, where he enjoyed the works of Hazlitt, Carlyle and Ruskin. At a dinner party much later in his life, he was asked what had been his university, to which his reply was Cassell's *Popular Educator*. The three-volume work, subtitled 'A Complete Encyclopaedia, or Elementary, Advanced and Technical Education' is among the collection of his books, inscribed 'James MacDonald, Allan Lane, Lossiemouth, 26 March 1884'. At this time, he began to take Joynes's monthly *Christian Socialist* and acquired Henry George's *Progress and Poverty*, published in 1883. The latter is also in the collection of his books, dated 20 July 1883, so he clearly bought it new. Henry George dedicated his book, 'To those who, seeing the Vice and Misery that spring from the unequal distribution of wealth and privilege, feel the possibility of higher social state, and would strive for its attainment'. MacDonald was one of the many who was converted to the Socialist cause by this important work.

After a brief period in Bristol, MacDonald moved to London where he took a job addressing envelopes at 10s a week, rising to 15s when he became an invoice clerk. He had always been interested in science and was founder of the Lossiemouth Field Club, so he nurtured the idea of taking a scholarship at South Kensington, with many hours spent in the Guildhall Library, the Birkbeck Institute and the Reading Room of the British Museum. Near to a breakdown through overwork, he found employment as secretary to the radical politician Thomas Lough, who was standing as a Liberal candidate for West Islington. Not only did Lough pay him an annual salary of £75, but he also provided him with contacts, both among Socialist politicians and journalists. MacDonald joined the Fellowship of New Life, a group founded in 1883 by disciples of Thomas Davidson, a Scotsman who had emigrated to the United States, and took lodgings in the household of the Fellowship in Doughty Street, which included Sydney Olivier, Secretary of the Fabian Society. In 1892 he left Lough and launched himself into freelance journalism and lecturing, the kind of existence described by George Gissing in his novel, *New Grub Street*. Indeed, MacDonald began to write a novel of his own, highly derivative of Gissing's earlier book, *Workers in the Dawn*. MacDonald's central character was a Socialist journalist who, out of misplaced social conscience, marries an unlettered servant girl before finding true companionship in love with an emancipated schoolteacher. The servant girl commits suicide on the shores of Moray Firth. The title of this novel has perished, though a draft of the text remains in MacDonald's papers.

Despite the Gissing gloom, MacDonald's life was blossoming. He joined the Independent Labour Party in 1896, and in the following year married Margaret Gladstone. Margaret, whom MacDonald met in the Reading Room of the British Museum, was a high-minded East London charity worker, distantly related to William Ewart Gladstone. With her private income the young couple were able to buy an apartment in Lincoln's Inn Fields, which became a cross between an office and a salon for supporters of the Labour movement. These were the first rungs of the political ladder that led to Ramsay MacDonald becoming the first Labour Prime Minister of Great Britain, and to accusations of betrayal that ultimately left him a disappointed man. Certainly he was no longer a common reader. After his death in 1937 his children gave his books to the National Library of Scotland. Although this

75 Advertisement for William Sugg & Co. inserted into Greenwood's *Free Public Libraries*. Sugg had produced in 1874 the 'Christiania' burner, which was commended as a great leap forward in the quality of gas lighting, especially when combined with the white 'Albatrine' shade. Compared to light from candles, or even oil lamps, gas lighting provided for readers a steady light of great illumination without shadow.

collection reflects his interests, in politics, in science, in poetry, in songs and in ballads especially of Scotland, very few of the books date from his youth, no doubt because they had been discarded with his growing prosperity, or because the family did not think that they were worthy of retaining.

Can conclusions be drawn by comparing the experiences of Thomas Bewick and James Ramsay MacDonald? The north east of England and Scotland were both known for providing good basic education. MacDonald's grandmother and mother chose to send him to a school that charged fees, albeit modest ones, but they did have the opportunities provided by the passing of Forster's Education Act in 1870. The range of books that MacDonald enjoyed as a child

EDUCATION'S FRANKENSTEIN—A DREAM OF THE FUTURE.

(*Dedicated to the School-Board.*)

76 *Punch* cartoon for 1884 lamenting the passing of Forster's 1870 Education Act, showing Frankenstein supporting education and thus good careers for the working classes while the genteel were suffering from lack of work and income.

was much greater than that offered to Bewick, who had to rely almost entirely on chapbooks for leisure reading. Indeed, it was Thomas and his brother John Bewick who were to enliven books for children by their illustrations. Technological developments such as the invention of the steam printing press, improvements in the manufacture of paper and of bindings, along with the determination of publishers like Cassell and J.M. Dent ensured that for MacDonald and his generation the classics and general knowledge were available at affordable prices. Bewick enjoyed the social pleasures of Cooke's Book Club and the Literary and Philosophical Society in Newcastle, but MacDonald had access to free municipal libraries, the Birkbeck Institute that had developed from the London Mechanics Institute, and the Reading Room of the British Museum, developed into a national research library during the mid-nineteenth century by its Keeper of Printed Books, Antonio Panizzi. The long hours of working on illustrations for his books by the light of a candle led to eye strain so that Bewick was obliged to seek assistance in this task. A century later MacDonald could light his oil lamp or work in a library furnished with the latest gas lamps from Sugg & Co.

Yet when the common reader has overturned all the hurdles in their path, one may remain standing – prejudice, whether it be social or intellectual. In its almanack for 1884, *Punch* published a cartoon, 'Education's Frankenstein – A Dream of the Future'. A hideous monster, clutching a purse of money bears on his mortar board a group of blithe young students that have benefited from Forster's Education Act, while at his feet are desperate figures such as a barrister, a poet, an artist and a governess, all out of work. The law of subordination remained alive and well.

CHAPTER 9

CHILDREN OF THE REVOLUTION

The Books of Denis and Edna Healey

There have been many different types of revolution discussed in this book: technical, political, intellectual, but this chapter title refers to a social revolution. Three nineteenth-century pieces of legislation have had a profound effect upon the lives of generations of Britons, and on their relationship with books. The first two were the Public Libraries Acts, of 1850 and 1855, which had extremely slow-burning fuses. This slowness was due to the fact that the acts permitted rather than obliged municipal boroughs to fund a library, so that by 1918, 566 local authorities had made this move, but there was still a long way to go. Forster's Education Act of 1870, on the other hand, produced a result that was instantaneous, and by the 1890s 90 per cent of children were attending school.

For people like Denis and Edna Healey, born into modest circumstances in the second decade of the twentieth century, the opportunities provided by these three pieces of legislation were enormous. Denis, now Lord Healey of Riddlesden, has had a distinguished political career. Described as the finest Prime Minister that the British never had, he held major offices of state in the Labour governments of the 1960s and 1970s, including Defence Secretary and Chancellor of the Exchequer. He has written several books, including a compilation of the literary influences on his life, *My Secret Planet*.[1] For over sixty years he has been married to Edna, and together they have built up a library of over 17,000 books, now accommodated in their house in Sussex. Edna has been a teacher, a political wife, mother, lecturer, and at the age of sixty began her very successful writing career.[2]

Denis Healey was born on 30 August 1917. The accident of war meant that his birthplace was near to Woolwich Arsenal in south-east London, though his family very soon returned to the West Riding of Yorkshire where he spent his childhood. His father, Will, had won an engineering scholarship to Leeds University, and subsequently taught engineering, becoming in 1922 Principal

77 Denis and Edna Healey in the library of their Sussex home.

of Keighley Technical College. Denis's mother Winnie was the daughter of a signalman and stationmaster at the village halt at Newnham-on-Severn in Gloucestershire. She had attended teacher training college in Cheltenham, where she had several Suffragette friends. Her influence on her son was strong, and from her he gained his love of reading. In particular she was inspired by the radio broadcasts of Harold Nicolson. These began in 1929, with a series of ten talks entitled 'The New Spirit in Modern Literature', but ended in a quarrel with the Director-General of the BBC, Sir John Reith. With his Presbyterian views he was shocked by Nicolson's introduction of the novels of D.H. Lawrence, and refused to let him mention the forbidden novel, James Joyce's *Ulysses.* Nicolson declared that Reith's 'head is made entirely of bone and it's impossible to talk to him as an intelligent human being . . . Wants me to induce illiterate members of the population to read Milton instead of going on bicycle excursions.'[3] Elitist as this sounds, Nicolson was in fact a regular and very popular broadcaster, who went on to give a series 'People and Things', where he discussed a whole range of subjects from 'Smells' to 'Is the Broadcaster Sincere?' The last went out on air in April 1931, with Nicolson claiming an audience of 15 million, of whom Winnie Healey was one devoted listener.[4]

The Healey home in Keighley was a terraced house, the kind described over half a century earlier by Elizabeth Gaskell: 'Grey stone abounds; and the rows of house built of it have a kind of solid grandeur connected with their uniform and enduring lines.'[5] Denis began his education at Drake and Tonson's kindergarten in Keighley, but when he won a scholarship to Bradford Grammar School the family moved to Riddlesden. From here, there were views across the moors to Haworth. Denis particularly identified with the Brontë family as his Healey grandfather was a tailor from Kiltyclogher in Ireland, who had settled in Todmorden, a similar journey to that made by Patrick, father of the Brontë sisters and of Bramwell.

Bradford was one of the great northern grammar schools, and Denis received a first-class education, stimulating a love of classical literature. A pupil of Leavis taught him English, and the magazine *Scrutiny* became his bible. He particularly appreciated Leavis's cutting away of the undergrowth of Georgian poets and revealing the later poems of Yeats. For private reading, Denis enjoyed the Father Brown stories of G.K. Chesterton, who had modelled his hero on Father O'Connor, a Keighley priest. He later took to Virginia Woolf, first her novels and then her essays. He was also drawn to the historical novels of Merejkowski and the works of Dostoevsky, Tolstoy and Turgenev. The discovery of *Murphy* led to a lifetime devotion to the writing of Samuel Beckett.

Much of Denis's reading matter was acquired from the excellent public library in Keighley. This had been opened in 1904, helped considerably by a gift of £10,000 from the philanthropist, Andrew Carnegie. The idea of assisting had been put to Carnegie over dinner at Skibo Castle by Sir Swiro Smith. The latter may sound like a Regency villain from the novels of Georgette Heyer, but Sir Swiro was in fact interested in the promotion of adult education and mechanics institutes. He pointed out that Keighley students were winning national prizes, but had no access to books in their own town. Carnegie offered to help with what became one of many libraries that he helped to establish in the United Kingdom.

In 1936 Denis won a scholarship to Balliol College, Oxford, to read Mods & Greats, or *Litterae Humaniores*, a combination of classical literature, ancient history and philosophy that particularly appealed. Many northern grammar schoolboys took scholarships to the Queen's College, but Denis chose Balliol as a result of his admiration for the college's great nineteenth-century Master, Benjamin Jowett. Edna's path to the dreaming spires was perhaps more strewn with obstacles. She was born on 14 June 1918 in Coleford in the Forest of Dean in Gloucestershire. The original derivation of the word 'forest' is 'outside' rather than 'a place of trees'. The idea of a Royal Forest came to England in the eleventh century with the Norman kings, who set aside an area of rough land where deer might be kept and killed exclusively by themselves or their magnates. These areas were outside the common law; here the forest laws prevailed. The idea of 'outsideness' can still be felt in the Forest, but was even more marked when Edna was growing up there. Her father, Edward Edmunds, worked in a stone quarry as a crane driver. With five children to feed, money was very tight, especially when he lost his job during the Slump. Eventually he became the engineer in charge of a pumping station in a village two miles away from Coleford.

Home was a terraced house with gas lighting in the kitchen only; oil lamps were used for homework. There were just two shelves for books, for Ted Edmunds and his wife Rose enjoyed music more than reading, and their social life revolved around the Baptist church. All the books on these shelves were prizes, most of them from Sunday School – Kipling's *The Jungle Book* and George MacDonald's *At the Back of the North Wind*, along with lives of missionaries such as David Livingstone and Mary Slessor, whose biography *The White Queen of the Okajong* was later to inspire one of Edna's television documentaries. Not only were they prizes, but prized: handsome products, beautifully bound in soft leather, or even covered with lace. They were always kept in brown paper wrappers for protection. The one link with the outside world was the radio, and Edna recalled sitting with her siblings, each with their headphones, 'like cherries on a stalk', listening to 'Uncle Mac'.

The public library may have reached Keighley half a century after the passing of the Libraries Acts, but Coleford had no such facility, nor were there bookcases at Edna's infant and junior schools. Books would arrive in wooden boxes from Gloucester and the musty smell of copies of the novels of Dickens was an abiding memory for Edna. At the age of eleven, she gained a place at Bell's Grammar School in Coleford, originally endowed when Robert and Jane Greyndour left money for the education of poorer children of the parish under a discreet priest 'sufficiently learned in art of grammar'. These children were of course boys; girls only began to attend the school at the beginning of the twentieth century. Again, the school had no library, so the teachers transported the books in their cars from the public libraries in Gloucester and Cheltenham.

Edna was particularly inspired by two of her teachers: Robert Noble the history teacher, who brought his own books from Gloucester, including *Mother India* which he thought might cause embarrassment because it contained descriptions of childbirth, and Joan Davis, the English mistress, who convinced Edna's mother Rose to let her go in for the Oxford entrance examination. Despite concerns by people who thought that, coming from a humble background, she might not be able to cope, she applied for a place to read English at St Hugh's College, and won it in 1936.

Edna describes the libraries, bookshops and museums of Oxford as doors opening to an undiscovered country. Having a grant of £12 per annum to buy books, she was dependent on the libraries, and particularly loved the Upper Bodleian, with its smell of ancient books, providing her with a combination of the first real sense of the 'world of books' and a meeting place with the young men of the university. One of her tutors was Edmund Blunden, who showed her a new attitude to books. She would watch entranced as he took books off the shelf and offered to lend them to her, and as he read, she could hear Samuel Johnson's voice booming out. Denis, too, was inspired by his tutor, 'Sandy' Lindsay, Master of Balliol in succession to Benjamin Jowett. Lindsay went beyond the philosophy curriculum, which stuck at Kant and Hegel, and introduced the undergraduates to the ideas of Georges Gurdjieff, Reinhold Niebuhr and Lev Shestov.

For Edna and Denis this was a time of increasing political consciousness, with the outbreak of civil war in Spain, the rise of Fascism in Italy and Nazism in Germany. Both joined the Communist Party and, as candidates of the Popular Front, were involved in the famous Oxford by-election of 1938 when Denis's tutor, Sandy Lindsay, was put up in opposition to the government candidate, Quintin Hogg, in protest at the Munich Agreement. Lindsay's supporters among the undergraduates crossed the traditional party lines, so Denis and Edna campaigned side by side with Roy Jenkins, Edward Heath and Nigel Nicolson, son of Winnie's hero, Harold. In the event, Hogg squeezed home, but the message delivered to Neville Chamberlain's government was clear. Both Denis and Edna were also members of the Left Book Club – Edna recalled with nostalgia the orange covers of books like George Orwell's *Road to Wigan Pier*, while the first book produced by the Club, Clement Atlee's *Labour Party in Perspective,* is still in Denis's library.

The Left Book Club was the brainchild of Victor Gollancz. VG, as he was known, was an ebullient character who had started his own publishing house, based at 14 Henrietta Street in Covent Garden, in 1928. His particular strength lay in creating adventurous book jackets and advertisements. Until the late nineteenth century, books were protected by plain dustcovers, but letterpress jackets were then introduced as part of the promotion of the book. Comparatively early examples of these were wrapped around two series produced by J.M. Dent, 'Temple Classics' and 'Temple Shakespeares'. Significantly both were edited by the Shakespearean scholar, Israel Gollancz, VG's uncle. 'Picture' jackets soon began to appear, much to Gollancz's disapproval; he later described their introduction as one of the worst days in the world for the British book trade. Setting aside afternoons, he visited all the

London termini to look at the railway bookstalls and find the most effective background colour, which he decided was yellow. Stanley Morison, one of the finest typographers of the period, designed for him a plain front cover with the title, contents and purpose of the book in black and bright red (later changed to magenta). Intended to surprise and startle the reader, these were condemned by some as crude, but Raymond Mortimer put his finger on their importance by pointing out that as a reviewer he was faced with fifty or more novels every fortnight and could not 'fail to choose at least for examination those that are clad in attractive raiment'.[6]

Until the 1920s, publishers' advertisements in newspapers were discreet, traditionally placed next to patent medicines and more recently drawings of ladies' underwear. VG proceeded to splash literary pages of the *Observer* and the *Sunday Times* with huge spreads, shouting his wares: today we would describe them as 'in your face'. In the spring and Christmas supplements of the *Observer*, he monopolised the whole front page, announcing his forthcoming plum titles. At a time when book reviews ran for several pages, he took a double column down each side of the main book page, and emphasised his advertisements with all kinds of printers' ornaments, including the pointing hand. As Sheila Hodges points out in her account of the publishing house, he made the public considerably more book conscious.

Although Victor Gollancz held strong political views, he realised that he must put his publishing house on a strong financial footing and build up a good list of writers before embarking on political books. These were traditionally difficult to publish successfully: both the press and booksellers avoided them, while the public were generally indifferent to them. However, these were different times, with high unemployment, widespread poverty and the rise of right-wing extremism in Europe. In 1932 Gollancz published John Strachey's *The Coming Struggle for Power*, describing it in his catalogue as 'an extremely dangerous book . . . and those who wish to keep their eyes tight shut and in particular those who regard Russia with horror should under no circumstances read it'. The book proved a best-seller and is regarded as one of the most effective catalysts in converting members of the British middle classes to socialism. In 1935 Strachey was invited by the Worker's Bookshop, the leading Communist bookshop in London, to sit on a committee of a club that would select left-wing books from publishers' lists. Gollancz was the only publisher who responded to their proposal, and over lunch with Strachey and the lawyer Stafford Cripps during the following January, he proposed that he should start the club himself. A month later the first advertisement for the Left Book Club appeared as a double-page spread in the *New Statesman*, proposing to 'help in the struggle *for* world peace and a better social and economic order, and *against* fascism', shortly followed by a similar advertisement in the *News Chronicle*.

The Observer
CHRISTMAS LITERARY SUPPLEMENT.
LONDON, SUNDAY, NOVEMBER 29. 1931.

78 The front page of the *Observer* Christmas Supplement, 29 November 1931, filled with advertisements for VG's titles.

The response was amazing. More than 6,000 people signed up within the month, and by the end of the year the membership had reached 40,000. Club books were supplied only to registered members; full members undertook to buy the monthly choice for a minimum of six months, and before long there were additional books that could be bought if the member wanted to. The price was uniformly set at 2s 6d, whatever the length of the book, and members received free the monthly magazine, originally called *Left Book News*, and later, *Left News*. After some trial and error, the books were bound in limp orange cloth, and Stanley Morison designed the device that appeared on the front with the initials LBC slightly to the left of centre, reflecting the spirit of the Club. The books were distributed to members via bookshops. The reaction of booksellers was initially lukewarm as the administration was complex with small returns, but they soon realised that new customers were being brought into their shops. Non-members could buy the titles, but would pay 7s 6d, three times the price paid by members.

Titles for the Club were chosen by a committee of three: Victor Gollancz, John Strachey, and Harold Laski, Professor of Political Science at the London School of Economics. One of the first titles chosen was Strachey's own *The Theory and Practice of Socialism*, which became the bible of the Club. Orwell's *Road to Wigan Pier* was the choice for March 1937 and proved to be one of the most popular. The fine strata of opinions within the Communist Party at this time meant that Gollancz turned down Orwell's next book, *Homage to Catalonia*, and it appeared instead under the imprint of Secker. The print run for *Homage* was 1,500 copies, while that of *Road* was 42,000 – a clear indication of the power of the Left Book Club.[7]

Book clubs, of course, were a common phenomenon of literary circles in eighteenth-century Britain, but these were informal groups, not large organisations spread across the country. VG modelled his club on the Book Society that had been formed by Alan Bott, with a selection committee chaired by the novelist, Hugh Walpole. Publishers were invited to propose books to the committee, and if they were chosen then they would be offered to members of the club at no discount, the theory being that members could rely on the sound judgement of Walpole and his colleagues. Gollancz had been so successful in getting choices that he was suspected of having a secret tie-up with the Book Society. Several clubs sprang up in imitation of the Left Book Club, including a Right Book Club, administered by Foyles Bookshop. The cartoonist David Low, who was a LBC supporter, produced a 'Book Club War' cartoon with the caption: 'A fierce battle is now taking place on the reading front, the Blimp Book Club advancing strongly against the Left. Heavy casualties are reported, including twenty-nine unconscious and General Gollancz's spectacles blown up.'

The Left Book Club became a way of life for many, especially after the outbreak of war in Spain. Local groups were formed to discuss the monthly choices; by 1939 there were over 1,200 of these. Denis Healey and Edna Edmunds belonged to the Oxford group, which held its meetings in the Left Bookshop by the railway station. Here young men returning from the battle front sang Spanish war songs, and Denis gave some of his first political talks. Club Groups could be organised on particular lines, such as clerical workers, bus drivers, sixth formers, London Indian residents, and some had their own premises. In London, the Camden Town branch furnished theirs with 'two tables, a typewriter, a gramophone and a couple of banjos', while the Wolverhampton group could manage only a gloomy loft in a barn, approached by a ladder, where members could play table tennis or obtain 'brightly coloured Soviet posters'.[8]

This extraordinary phenomenon drew to a close with political developments in 1938. Recognising the strong possibility of war, VG came to argue that even a non-socialist Britain would be justified in fighting Germany. He also realised that the Communist Party was having a controlling influence over many Club branches. The signature of the Nazi-Soviet Pact on 23 August 1939 posed a major moral and intellectual dilemma for all Communists and, with the outbreak of war shortly afterwards, the great days of the Left Book Club were over. Nevertheless the millions of Left Book Club books in circulation and the many thousands of club members who could talk about them were to make an enormous impact on attitudes both during the Second World War and on the general election of 1945.

If Victor Gollancz through his publishing brought about a social revolution in the 1930s, he was not alone; Allen Lane with his Penguin paperbacks can be seen as a fellow mover and shaker. In some ways they were alike, with their creative energy and their treatment of their staff – low wages coupled with bouts of great generosity. In others, they were quite different. While Gollancz was larger than life and noisy, those that knew Lane in the 1960s remember a dapper man, beautifully dressed, standing silently in the corner at parties.

Allen Lane was in fact born Allen Williams: his family all dutifully changed their name so that he might join the firm of his uncle, John Lane, who published at the sign of the Bodley Head in Vigo Street off Piccadilly. This styling harked back to the signs before streets were numbered, and Lane adopted the Bodley Head because Sir Thomas Bodley was, like him, a Devon man of books. When John Lane died in 1925, Allen Lane became the managing director. The legends surrounding the invention of Penguins are legion, but it is generally accepted that Lane was driven to action by the dearth of cheap reading material on the bookstall at Exeter railway station while returning from a weekend visit to the mystery writer, Agatha Christie, and her archaeologist husband, Max Mallowan. He therefore proposed to his fellow directors at the Bodley Head that they should produce a series of paperback books that were attractive to look at, thus encouraging good display, that the sales should extend beyond traditional outlets, and that a large print run should be envisaged to keep down the price. He proposed that the last should be sixpence, the price of a packet of cigarettes.

The idea of publishing in paperback was an old one that has been traced back to the books produced by the Venetian printer, Aldus Manutius, in the early sixteenth century. Initiatives were constantly being developed for low-price paperbacks, but quality and cheapness rarely went hand in hand, so that George Hutchinson might initiate Sixpenny Blacks, but his son Walter developed instead rubbishy thrillers and romances in lurid covers. By the early twentieth century, hardback fiction was usually priced at 7s 6d, with popular non-fiction such as travel and biography at 12s 6d. Most publishers reissued these titles in cheaper hardback editions, sometimes at 3s 6d, sometimes lower, depending on the copyright situation. Victor Gollancz decided in 1930 to set up a subsidiary company, Mundanus Ltd, to publish original novels in paper covers, aimed at a mass circulation, priced at 3s. Stanley Morison was commissioned to produce uniform covers in the style of French and German editions, and the paper chosen was thin so that the books might 'slip comfortably into the pocket'. The career of Mundanus was brief, despite support from the novelist Arnold Bennett in his role as the highly influential book reviewer on the *Evening Standard*. Only nine books were published, put out at long intervals.

Allen Lane noted the lessons learnt from Mundanus, among others, when considering his options. Perhaps one important lesson was to find a catchy name: Mundanus was not likely to capture the imagination. The idea of Penguin came from one of Lane's secretaries, Joan Coles. Edward Young, then an office junior, was dispatched to London Zoo to sketch the penguins in their pool, complaining about the stink when he returned. He proceeded to organise the design of the front covers in three horizontal stripes, with the upper and lower colour coded according to the category of the book: orange for fiction, green for crime, blue for biography. The central white panel contained the author and title in black, in Gill Sans Serif. The first Penguins had printed dustjackets like conventional hardbacks.

The initial reaction of fellow directors to the proposal by Allen Lane was so negative that with his two brothers, Richard and John, he decided to market the books as if from the Bodley Head, but using family capital. The first of many hurdles Lane had to jump was to persuade publishers to release paperback rights to the titles he wanted. Gollancz reacted with the sulks, in fact refusing to do business with Lane until 1950. Lane must have rubbed salt in the wound by acquiring the rights from Benn of *The Unpleasantness at the Bellona Club* by Dorothy Sayers, an author whom Gollancz considered particularly his own. Another publisher who declined to sell his titles was Harry Raymond at Chatto who was concerned that Penguins would harm his cheap editions, but once he saw how good the Penguins looked, he came round to the idea. Lane's first list consisted of ten titles, six of which came from Jonathan Cape, who was considered to have the finest literary list in London. Lane had been round to Cape's offices in Bedford Square and some hard bargaining had ensued.

Hurdle number two was to convince booksellers, and this turned out to be a tough proposition. The old order was changing rapidly, but not everybody wanted to embrace the new. For instance, WH Smith, which had been such a force for innovation in the nineteenth century, had become resistant to new initiatives. Book tokens, suggested by Harry Raymond in 1928, were initially opposed because Smith's and other booksellers were worried about parents using tokens to buy children's school textbooks. In 1929 P.R. Chapell in the advertising department of Smith's made the radical suggestion of a line of cheap shops selling cheap books: 'This is an age of cheapness, and all classes – even the Queen herself – have patronised Woolworths. There is a limit to the amount of business to be obtained from the cultured classes to whom our handsome shops mainly appeal, and we want more people to venture further than the bookstall – which they do not do in sufficient numbers other than at Christmas time'.[9] The idea was swiftly rejected by his superiors.

Newspapers, whose circulations were rapidly shooting up, were offering books at a reduced price in exchange for coupons in order to win new readers. The *Daily Mail*, for example, offered a full set of Shakespeare's works for 5s 9d, plus six coupons cut from the paper. Bernard Shaw, who had a special deal with his publishers in that he retained all publishing rights, negotiated with the *Daily Herald* to offer a full set of his plays for 3s 9d plus coupons as opposed to the 12s 6d price of the Constable version. To the fury of the trade, three extra plays were added to this special edition. Shaw, relishing this confrontation, wrote to the Oxford bookseller and publisher, Basil Blackwell: 'I can do nothing for the booksellers but tell them not to be childish . . . Have you no bowels of compassion for the millions of your fellow-countrymen who can no more afford a twelve-and-sixpenny book than a trip round the world? I am really surprised at you. When we met at Bumpus's [the London bookshop] you seemed quite an intelligent youth.'[10]

This was the climate in which Allen Lane sought his first sales for his baby Penguins. Although Selfridges offered him a window and John G.Wilson at Bumpus's was supportive, most booksellers refused to take them, saying the margin was too small or that the books would get torn and grubby, or threatened to consign them to a bin outside the shop. WH Smith and the huge wholesaler Simpkin Marshall showed no interest. Just as Lane was despairing, he paid a Saturday visit to the headquarters of Woolworths, then also known as the Sixpenny Bazaar, the highest price of anything sold in the stores. Books were ordered for the store by Clifford Prescott, buyer for the haberdashery department. He was unconvinced by the Penguins, pointing out that there were no pictures on the jackets, and that Woolworths' own Readers' Library seemed better value. His judgement was reversed, however, when his wife appeared wanting lunch after a morning shopping and, swayed by Lane's good looks, persuaded Prescott to take the books. An order for 63,500 duly arrived, and the future for Penguins was assured. Some say that Lane embellished this story, but it shows how close defeat and victory can be.

The first ten Penguins were published on the Tuesday before August Bank Holiday, 1935. On the Friday, Lane stepped off the bus at Selfridges on his way to his office, to be told by the bookbuyer that the initial 100 copies of each title had almost sold out, and he needed 1,000 more. When he reached the office, the phone was constantly ringing with booksellers demanding copies. The press loved the new books. J.B. Priestley wrote to Lane: 'These Penguin Books are amazingly good value for money. If you can make the series pay for itself – with such books at such a price – you will have performed a great publishing feat.'[11] The *Observer* called them 'perfect reading for sixpence a time, in the jolliest coloured paper bindings. Perfect for seashore, wood, moorland, and even the train or aeroplane.'[12] In the first four months, according to the *Evening Standard*, a million books had been sold.

The impact on the book-buying public was immense. Denis Healey, for instance, was bowled over by them, while they were the first books, apart from textbooks, that Edna actually bought. Significantly Denis had bought other paperback books before – maroon bindings from Woolworths, he recalls – but couldn't remember who published them. The great achievement of Allen Lane, much to his own annoyance, was to create something that has become generic, like Biros and Hoovers. Imitations soon appeared including sixpenny Toucans, published by Hutchinson, and Crime Club Sixpennies from Collins.

Allen Lane, like a firework, began to produce sparks in every direction. Once more the railway station proved a useful pointer to the marketplace. This time Lane was standing by the bookstall at King's Cross when he over-heard a lady asking for 'one of those Pelican books'. Given the predatory arrival of Toucan, he decided to snap up the use of Pelican, inaugurating a new non-fiction list, pale blue in colour. The first title to be published was a new, enlarged edition of Bernard Shaw's *The Intelligent Woman's Guide to Socialism, Capitalism, Sovietism and Fascism*. Other series followed including Penguin Specials, which dealt with the developing political issues of the time,

79 Allen Lane with his Penguincubator, a slot-machine that dispensed his paperbacks at 6d a time. The more conservative members of the book trade were shocked by such an innovation, so he set the machine up outside the Bomb Shop at 66 Charing Cross Road. This shop, which reflected socialist-anarchist views, was renamed Collet's in 1934.

beginning with Edgar Mowrer's *Germany Puts the Clock Back*, published in November 1937, Shakespeare Plays, County Guides, and illustrated King Penguin hardbacks. Lane was determined to communicate directly with his readers, keeping them informed of forthcoming titles with his magazine, *Penguins Progress.* He shocked the conservative trade with his 'Penguincubator', a slot-machine book dispenser which he installed in the Charing Cross Road, and by putting business reply cards in some of his books, offering a direct mail service. Books were dispatched from the crypt of Holy Trinity Church, Marylebone, designed in 1828 by John Soane. Empty tombs fitted with metal doors were employed for the petty cash and invoice books. Books were hurled down chutes from the churchyard, packed in brown paper parcels and sent upwards in an ancient lift formerly used for bodies.

Lane's activities did not cease with the declaration of the Second World War, in fact his creative outburst gave him a distinct advantage over more conventional publishers. The effect of war on Britain's reading habits was star-tling. Winnie Healey greeted news of the declaration by running up to her son and crying, 'Put away your books!' but this was not how the nation reacted.

80 Every cloud has a silver lining. Boots Booklovers Library seized the opportunity offered by the privations of the Second World War to recruit new members.

During the First World War, WH Smith reported how their staff in Swanage in Dorset were obliged to lock themselves in an empty carriage in the station for protection, selling newspapers through the windows, such was the demand for reading matter.[13] In the Second World War, the problem was the lack of supplies of paper, with rationing introduced in March 1940. Quotas were based on the percentage of paper used by a publishing firm between August 1938 and the same month in 1939. For many this was a serious problem, but

THE FIRST BIG FIVE OF THE WAR

LIGHT ON MOSCOW
by D. N. PRITT, K.C., M.P.

THE CASE FOR FEDERAL UNION
by W. B. CURRY

WHY BRITAIN IS AT WAR
by HAROLD NICOLSON

THE PENGUIN POLITICAL DICTIONARY
by WALTER TYMER

TRAVELS OF A REPUBLICAN RADICAL
IN SEARCH OF HOT WATER
by H. G. WELLS

These Specials with the exception of H. G. Wells have been specially written since the outbreak of war

PENGUIN SPECIALS

81 The outbreak of the Second World War provided an impetus for Allen Lane's publishing programme beginning with his Penguin Specials.

Lane had published so much in this period that he had access to a large proportion, as did Victor Gollancz. In addition Lane was able to call upon all kinds of extra resources. One of his best-selling wartime titles was G.H. Goodchild's *Keeping Poultry and Rabbits on Scraps*, and Goodchild proved doubly useful when he was able to get extra paper because 'the Government attach great importance to Rabbit Breeding'.[14] More significantly, one of the leading editors at Penguin, W.E. Williams, played a leading role in the Army Bureau of Current Affairs. This enabled Lane's books to be distributed in large quantities to Allied soldiers across the world. Penguins formed a substantial proportion of the books sent via the Services Central Book Club from 1940, while two years later a Forces Book Club was set up to print editions of books for distribution through the army's own channels. Even the format of Penguins proved ideal: a Golden Section rectangle, 7⅛ × 4⅜ inches, that conveniently fitted into the battledress pocket. Thus Denis Healey and his generation went to war armed with Penguin books.

The great demand for books was dealt a terrible blow on 29 December 1940. On a clear night, the Luftwaffe made a raid over the City of London, destroying the area around St Paul's Cathedral. Miraculously the cathedral survived, but the winding streets that had for centuries been a centre of book publishing did not. The City bookseller Hubert Wilson writing under the pseudonym Petrel in the *Bookseller* vividly described the scene:

> It is the eve of the new year – and the hub of the English book trade lies in smoking ruins. Such a scene of destruction I have never seen or imagined ... With many others Simpkin's, Whitaker's, Longman's, Nelson's, Hutchinson's, and, further afield Collins and Eyre & Spottiswoode, are gutted shells.... As I picked my way gingerly across from brick to brick, hot gouts of sulphurous fumes from buried fires seeped up between my feet: desultory flames played in the remains of a rafter here or a floor joist there, and on either side of the smoking causeway fell sharply away into cavernous glowing holes, once basements full of stock, now the crematories of the City's book world.[15]

These words recall those of the diarists John Evelyn and Samuel Pepys following the Great Fire of London in 1666. But while the book trade returned to the shadow of the new-built cathedral in the seventeenth century, it was never to do so in the twentieth century. A brave new book world was to spring up all over London and the rest of the United Kingdom. Meanwhile Bernard Shaw wryly commented: 'The Germans have done what Constable's never succeeded in doing. They have disposed of 86,701 sheets of my work in less than twenty-four hours.'[16]

* * * *

The end of the war marked a new beginning for Denis Healey and Edna Edmunds. They were married on 21 December 1945, with the groom wearing his major's uniform. Edna had taken a teaching post in Bromley, while Denis, having unsuccessfully contested the safe Conservative Yorkshire constituency of Pudsey and Otley, was appointed International Secretary at Labour Party Headquarters (he became the MP for South East Leeds in 1952). Now that they were based in London, Denis could indulge his passion for second-hand books. Edna had quickly realised that to love Denis was also to love old bookshops. He bought from venerable antiquarian Piccadilly booksellers, such as Henry Sotheran & Co and Bernard Quaritch, but the heartland of the more modest second-hand trade lay in the Charing Cross Road.

This street, described by a local councillor in 1902 as one of the ugliest thoroughfares in London, had become a mecca for bookshops after the 'old booksellers' row' in Holywell Street was demolished at the end of the nineteenth century to make way for the Aldwych. One of Denis's haunts was Marks & Co, at 84 Charing Cross Road, made famous by Helene Hanff in her story of a brash New Yorker winning over a staid London establishment, published in the States in 1970. Many feel this is not a true picture of Marks & Co, which was characterful rather than staid. With an unchanging window display featuring a large tabby cat, the ground floor offered cloth-bound books for browsers, presided over by Ben Marks reading a copy of *The Times*. The basement held library bindings, the first floor contained first editions and bound sets, the second freemasonry and Rariora, the third topography and unpriced items. Marks' partner Mark Cohen would attend major London auctions in the company of Jack Joseph, bookseller at 48a, where they focussed on sets of the *Encyclopaedia Britannica*, with Joseph going for the immaculate and Cohen for the slightly damaged.[17]

Almost all the second-hand bookshops on Charing Cross Road have now gone, making way for stores selling new books and remainders, along with fast food cafés and a few music shops around Tin Pan Alley. One survivor is Foyles Bookshop, which continues to do business at 119–125. When brothers

82 Marks & Co. at 84 Charing Cross Road, immortalised by Helene Hanff in her book published in the United States in 1970.

William and Gilbert Foyle failed their civil service examinations in 1904, they discovered a market for second-hand text books and began to trade from the kitchen of their parents' house in Hoxton. After several moves, they opened their first shop in the Charing Cross Road in 1906, originally with second-hand and antiquarian books, but introducing new titles in 1912. The business expanded rapidly, with an enlarged shop opened seventeen years later, when William's redoubtable daughter Christina joined the firm. The brothers used strong advertising methods: one scam was to send a cable to the anti-British mayor of Chicago, 'Big Bill' Thompson, reading 'Can offer high price for all English books from the Chicago Public Libraries'. Christina followed this up ten years later by sending a telegram to Adolf Hitler offering to buy Jewish books that were destined for burning. She is also famous for creating a sales system that has been compared to those of Communist Eastern Europe, and for hiring underpaid foreign assistants, who might run the antiquarian department if they understood Roman numerals. Nevertheless, she also instituted the famous Foyles literary lunches after recommending *The Forsyte Saga* to one customer who turned out to be the author, John Galsworthy. Realising that there was a market for opportunities for readers to meet their favourite authors in surroundings less formal than a lecture hall, in October 1930 Christina began holding lunches at the Holborn Restaurant, with 250 diners paying 4s 6d a head. Subsequently she founded the Foyles Book Club, opened an art gallery and created a lecture service. Edna Healey, wanting to be more than just 'a Parliamentary wife', signed up as a Foyles lecturer in the 1950s, and found herself talking about the changing role of women to members of the Rotary Club and the Round Table.

In his 1936 essay, 'Bookshop Memories', George Orwell described working in Booklover's Corner, on the corner of South End Green, Hampstead. This combined selling second-hand books with running a lending library of about 500 volumes, all fiction, that could be borrowed for 'two penny no deposit'. He provides a vivid record of the clientele, including a 'decayed person smelling of old breadcrusts who comes every day, sometimes several times a day and tries to sell you worthless books'. All too soon he lost his love of books: 'Nowadays I do buy one occasionally, but only if it is a book that I want to read and can't borrow . . . The sweet smell of decaying paper appeals to me no longer. It is too closely associated in my mind with paranoiac customers and dead bluebottles.'[18]

More stylish establishments that did not suffer from these olfactory problems were three bookshops catering for what was known as the carriage trade. Both Hatchards in Piccadilly and Bumpus's in Oxford Street started business in the eighteenth century, while Heywood Hill Bookshop in Mayfair's Curzon Street was founded in 1936. The most famous booksellers of the eighteenth century, such as Thomas Longman and John Murray, turned to publishing, abandoning their retailing business, but Hatchards did the opposite. Edna was particularly drawn to the shop in Piccadilly, especially when she discovered that one of the early partners had been John Wedgwood, son of the famous potter, and that what became the Royal Horticultural Society had its beginning in the shop's back room. The history of the shop at 10 Curzon Street has been well recorded by Heywood Hill's wife Anne, by Nancy Mitford who worked in the shop during the war ,and more recently by the long-term manager,John Saumarez Smith.[19]Hill,who carried both old and new books,did not believe in selling off the counter, but displayed books informally on round tables as in a private drawing-room. It is interesting that this style has recently been taken up by bookstore chains such as Waterstones. A long-term relationship with the customer was what Hill sought, and this sometimes involved the bookshop staff in providing all kinds of errands. Anne Hill described one customer, Harry Clifton, who constantly asked for non-bookish tasks to be undertaken, including bidding at Sotheby's, harking back to the requests made to his booksellers by Sir William Boothby in the late seventeenth century. The personal touch was taken even further by John G. Wilson at Bumpus's. One trainee later remembered Wilson standing at the door of the shop handing out copies of the newly published *Some People* by Harold Nicolson, telling bemused customers, 'I'll charge it to your account'.[20]

Heywood Hill sent out quarterly lists with recommendations of new titles on subjects likely to be of interest to customers, and also catalogues of second-hand books, a tradition that has continued under Saumarez Smith. Antiquarian books were not only acquired from the sale of private libraries, but also from 'runners', who made their living by buying from provincial shops and reselling in London. One of the Heywood Hill runners was A.W. Howlett who would appear carrying his books in 'two cardboard boxes and, whatever their weight, he supported them with lengths of old-fashioned string'. Howlett's itinerary was to take the early train from Tunbridge Wells in Kent to London, pick a destination such as Brighton in Sussex or Guildford in Surrey, and trawl the secondhand bookshops, filling his boxes and bringing them back to London. Because he knew the taste of both the staff and the customers at Heywood Hill bookshop, he could thus refresh the shelves and make himself a modest living.[21]

Frank Ward claimed that he had the first 'modern bookshop' in London, which he opened at 3 Baker Street in 1931. This challenged the image of the traditional bookshop that had window displays to obscure the inside of the shop. Instead he had light oak shelves, a fitted carpet and a low, open window. However, the first establishment to be designed from the outset as a bookshop was for Francis Edwards at 83 Marylebone High Street in 1912. If Heywood

Hill's shop was like a drawing room, Edwards's bookshop resembled the library of a country house, with a gallery running round the main room to allow for further shelving. Francis Edwards was an antiquarian bookseller, so filled up the space in front of the shelves with cabinets, but the elegance of the shop returned when it was taken over in 1989 by Daunt Books.

The idea of a chain of bookshops nationwide came with WH Smith. The company faced a crisis in 1905 when contracts for railway bookstalls were cancelled in bulk. Within ten weeks 200 shops had been opened as close as possible to railway terminals and to Underground stations in London. In 1933, WH Smith took over the Truslove & Hanson chain, with three shops in the capital's fashionable West End, and by 1949 had more than 500 bookstalls and bookshops that not only sold books but functioned as branches of a circulating library. Its main circulating library rival in the high street was the chemists, Boots. When Florence Boot instigated the libraries in 1898, she intended the stock to appeal to the less well-educated reader who needed guidance on what to choose, with a high proportion of fiction. Boots based their stock on Ernest Baker's *Descriptive Guide to the Best Fiction: British and American*. Baker was a librarian who used as his criteria, 'the best prose fiction in English, including, not all that interests students, but all that the ordinary reader is likely to come about, with as much description of matter and style, for the guidance of readers, as can be condensed into a few lines of print for each book'.[22] This, inevitably, brought the library into the Great Fiction Debate and incurred the wrath of Queenie Leavis. Stationing herself in the library department of a branch of Boots, she observed the books selected by readers as part of the research for her book, *Fiction and the Reading Public*, published in 1932. In this she looked back nostalgically to sixteenth-century England, when 'the common reader' enjoyed the works of William Shakespeare and Christopher Marlowe. The Fall came in Victorian times, when tastes polarised, so that in the twentieth century the reading public enjoyed the trivia of crime fiction and romances, leaving the 'real literature' of writers such as D.H. Lawrence and Virginia Woolf to a coterie of highbrow readers. However, most of the British public remained unmoved by such judgements and were enthusiastic users of the Boots Booklovers Library, enjoying the competitive terms offered, an annual subscription of 10s 6d or 1 or 2d per title with a returnable deposit. The libraries were located either at the back of the shop or on an upper floor, acting as loss leaders to draw customers past the array of toiletries.

A third national circulating library of the early twentieth century was run by *The Times*. The newspaper had run into trouble with publishers through offering to sell the books featured in their library catalogue at below net price, and John Murray won a court case against them in 1907. Already in financial difficulties, the newspaper thus fell into the hands of Harmsworth, who signed up to the Net Book Agreement the following year.[23] From 1914 the Times Book Club gave direct public access to its shelves, which was more than most municipal libraries offered to their readers. But this was the twilight of the circulating library. The great Victorian institution, Mudie's, survived as a shadow of its former self until 1937. After making regular losses, WH Smith closed its library in 1961, and Boots followed in 1966, selling off its vast stock so that many a personal library contains the familiar green label. These closures echoed down the line, so that the end came for the last private circulating library in Bath in the same year as Boots.

There were three catalysts that were effecting this change: cheap paperbacks in bookshops, the impact of television, and the comprehensive range of books, fiction and non-fiction, available in public municipal libraries. In 1924 the national stock in public libraries was estimated at 15 million books; by 1949 this had risen to 42 million with 123 million borrowers taking out 300 million books each year. Access was also being given to communities that had previously been excluded. The roots of the mobile library system could be said to lie with the 'itinerating libraries' introduced by Samuel Brown, a minister in East Lothian who circulated collections of books, most religious, in boxes around the villages, and by 1830 he was operating fifty such collections. The first recorded use of a mobile vehicle to deliver books was in Warrington in 1859, when the Mechanics Institute acquired a van, a horse and books to the value of £275, a considerable outlay. Their investment was worth it, for within the first year there were 12,000 borrowings. The County Libraries Act of 1919 empowered county councils to set up library services and many used a system of boxes. Gloucestershire sent theirs by the Great Western Railway, as Edna Healey vividly recalls. After the Second World War not only were mobile vans touring remote country areas, but they also provided a service to the huge council estates that were built as a result of the devastation of inner cities. These estates often had no shops or other facilities, so the mobile library came as a godsend to mothers cut off from the advantages of metropolitan life.

Like circulating libraries, commercial book clubs were also going through bad times. Most of the clubs that had sprung up around Gollancz's Left Book Club had closed down, though Reader's Union, founded in 1937 by John Baker, was still going strong. Baker offered books at a reduced price, for instance titles at 13s 6d in the shops would have a special club price of 2s 6d, but members would have to wait for a period after publication. In the United States, however, the book clubs were much more aggressive, offering books at the time of publication. The Book of the Month Club (BOMC) had been founded by Henry Scherman in 1926, based on the book guilds that sprang up in Germany at the end of the First World War. Only months after BOMC,

Literary Guild was launched by Samuel Craig and Harold Guinzburg, founders of the publishing house the Viking Press. The American book-buying market at the time was reckoned to be a mere 200,000, but Scherman was convinced that the potential was much higher if mail order were used. His early slogan ran: 'Handed to you by the Postman, the New Books you intend to Read', and he was right, the market was vast. The other vital ingredient for both BOMC and Literary Guild was an editorial board of literary experts and celebrities, who could provide the reassurance that readers required in the absence of a bookseller or a librarian to guide them. In 1966 WH Smith and the New York publishers Doubleday combined to launch Book Club Associates in England, based on the American model.

The arrival of the book club based on mail order played an important part in the development of the illustrated book. Before the Second World War, Anton Zwemmer, based in the Charing Cross Road, had begun publishing fine art books that he acquired through the agency of Albert Skira in Geneva. However, he found the British public were not ready for these: when he produced a monograph on Henry Moore, his home trade subscription amounted to 36, with most of the edition going to Japan. By the early 1950s, times had changed. After the bleakness of the post-war years, the coronation of Elizabeth II sparked off an interest in Britain's history. Although the nation watched the ceremony on tiny black-and-white televisions, if they had such a luxury, they could also go to the cinema and see it all in glorious technicolour, and began to expect the same visual treats from their books. At first publishers found it hard to secure the fine art paper required for illustrated books to meet this demand.

Just as the production of books had benefited from Louis XIV's Revocation of the Edict of Nantes in 1685, sending to Britain skilled Huguenot artists and craftsmen, so post-war publishing gained from the technical skills and cultural knowledge of refugees from Nazi Europe. Phaidon Press was founded by Bela Horovitz and Ludwig Goldscheider in Vienna in 1923. When Hitler annexed Austria in 1938 the two men fled to London, having sold their stocks and assets to the English publishing house of Allen & Unwin for a nominal sum, so that Phaidon Press officially had no Jewish connection when the Nazis arrived. Also from Vienna came Walter Neurath, whose idea for a Britain in Pictures series was taken up by William Collins. Later he began his own firm specialising in illustrated books, Thames & Hudson, and yet another Viennese refugee George Weidenfeld, having worked for the BBC in London during the war, linked up with Denis Healey's Oxford friend Nigel Nicolson to found the publishing house of Weidenfeld & Nicolson. Paul Hamlyn was born in Berlin but was brought to England in 1933 because of the Nazi threat by his Jewish parents, whom he used to describe as 'Middle European

Melancholics'.[24] He worked for Zwemmer before starting his own publishing in 1949, using Czechoslovakia for printing. His first efforts at illustrated books were not very beautiful because of the quality of the printing and paper, but they were cheap, and he was able to prove that the British would buy illustrated books at the right price.

To get highly illustrated books of quality off the ground, publishers had to find partners from other countries, and once more Frankfurt became an important trading centre. The medieval fair that dominated European publishing had faltered with the increasing religious intolerance of the Austro-Hungarian Empire, so that the baton passed to Leipzig. After the Second World War, with Leipzig behind the Iron Curtain, Frankfurt seized the opportunity to resurrect the international book fair, despite the fact that the city was almost totally devastated. The first fair in 1948 was attended by a handful of British publishers, taking tables in a hall, but each October the fair increased in size, so that today it is a huge industry, accommodated in several halls, with publishers from every country in the world attending to make important rights deals. From the 1950s onwards, the Frankfurt Book Fair presented the ideal opportunity for illustrated book publishers to sell co-editions to houses in America and Australasia and, if possible, foreign rights deals to Europe and the Far East. This kind of operation reached hitherto unimagined heights with the development of the Dorling Kindersley imprint. In 1974 Christopher Dorling and Peter Kindersley set up first as book pack-agers (producers of the text and pictures of a book that is then sold to a publisher), before becoming publishers themselves twelve years later. Their reference books had a distinctive style, with white covers and copious illustra-tions, and such was their success that they were able to sell rights into every conceivable international market. Like Allen Lane, they produced a publishing imprint that became a brand.

Where a book had a strongly national subject, and therefore could not attract international co-editions, then the book club could play a vital role. An example of this is a series that was first published by Weidenfeld & Nicolson in the early 1970s. Although there were a lot of biographies of English and British monarchs on the market, the editorial director responsible for illus-trated books, Christopher Falkus, had the idea of producing short texts by respected academics on the life and times of kings and queens. Having worked on the highly successful illustrated part-works produced by Purnell, such as the *History of the English-Speaking Peoples*, Falkus recognised the power of pictures, so the books were well illustrated. Lady Antonia Fraser who had just written an acclaimed biography of Mary, Queen of Scots, was brought in as general editor, thus reassuring readers who were not specialist historians that the books were authoritative as well as accessible. Book Club Associates became the major partner with Weidenfeld, and the first two volumes, *Edward VII* by Keith Middlemas, then Lecturer in Modern History at the University of Sussex, and *Charles II* written by Falkus himself were produced in 1972. Over the next few years, millions of copies were bought by book club members, while the bookshop editions have sold steadily ever since.

The impact of television on the worlds of publishing, bookselling and book-buying has been enormous. *The Forsyte Saga*, John Galsworthy's tale of three generations of a London middle-class family, sold between 2,000 and 3,000 copies each year following publication in 1922. When, however, it was dramatised in twenty-six episodes for television in black and white from January 1967, the nine novels began to sell in huge quantities, reaching 1.9 million copies by the end of 1970. With the advent of colour television, the opportunities to translate what was seen on the screen into what were known as coffee-table books were endless. For the arts, there was Lord Clark's *Civilisation*, for natural history David Attenborough's stunning programmes and books.

83 Publishers have been producing part-works since the seventeenth century, but they were particularly popular in the twentieth. 'The Story of the British Nation' was produced in 1923 by Walter Hutchinson, an enthusiastic part-work publisher. A vital ingredient of this kind of publishing was to emphasise the authority of the text with an impressive editorial board.

Cookery programmes on television and tie-in books have had an interesting history. The first TV cook was Moira Meighn, who made her appearance in 1936 having written *The Magic Ring for the Needy and Greedy*, the magic ring being a primus stove. Post-war austerity was represented by Philip Harbin, obliged to use his own food rations, joined by Marguerite Patten fresh from the Ministry of Food. Her many cookery books, selling in huge quantities, were produced in colour by Paul Hamlyn, but were not directly connected with her TV programmes. Then in 1955 Fanny Cradock arrived, a splash of vibrant colour on black-and-white television, with the long-suffering Johnnie, to whom she was not actually married. With each of Fanny's series came a printed booklet giving detailed accounts of the recipes demonstrated. However, the ultimate blissful marriage between TV and tie-in books came with Delia Smith. Dr Johnson declared that while women can spin, they cannot write books on cookery, a comment not borne out by experience. In 1835 when Eliza Acton approached the publisher Thomas Longman with her book of poems, he advised her that cookery was now the thing, so she went away and ten years later presented him with *Modern Cookery for Private Families* that turned into a Victorian bestseller. The twentieth-century version of Eliza Acton was Delia, and now the bestseller charts are full of books by TV cooks and chefs.

With increasing competition among publishers, marketing became of major importance. In May 1967 Allen Lane had a major and very public dispute with his chief editor, Tony Godwin. Penguin was finding that other paperback firms were creeping up on them, notably Pan Books, which held the paperback rights to the novels of James Bond. Godwin felt that the old banded designs of the Penguin family were now looking tired and old-fashioned, and introduced illustrated paperback covers. In an interview with Anne Batt of the *Daily Express*, under the heading 'A Book is not a Tin of Beans', Lane declared that great literature was something to be handled with loving care, not wrapped up in the most commercial pack and flogged like toothpaste in supermarkets and petrol stations. He had conveniently forgotten the marketing schemes of his youth.

The National Book League had been established in 1924 to help publishers to promote their books, with headquarters in Albemarle Street where there was a café and an information service for the public. New life was breathed into the organisation with the appointment in 1970 of the former bookseller Martyn Goff as director. The following May, with a committee of publishers that included André Deutsch and Tom Maschler, editorial director of Jonathan Cape, he held a Book Bang in Bedford Square, home to several publishing houses in London. With a tiny budget, mail-outs were made to schools and colleges, and an impressive array of writers was assembled to meet their readers. The event lasted for two weeks, with splendid spring weather for the first few days, but what everybody now can remember was the deluge of rain in the second week, which made the Book Bang the literary equivalent of the music festival at Glastonbury. Barbara Cartland's fuchsia pink stiletto heels got stuck in the wet gravel, Queen Frederica of Greece's shoes sunk deep in the mud, though she assured Martyn Goff that she had another thirty-six pairs back in her hotel. Sometimes the encounter between author and reader could be unexpected: the first person to approach the distinguished biographer Michael Holroyd asked him if he could return his damaged copy of the life of Augustus John. Despite the weather the event was a great success with packed audiences listening to their favourite authors talking about their books. A forerunner of the many literary festivals today, it showed that marketing books could be effective and fun.[25]

The small firm of Sidgwick & Jackson, with the Earl of Longford as its chairman, was making a name for itself with high profile authors and publicity campaigns. The Conservative Prime Minister Edward Heath resigned in March 1974 having lost the general election. In the political doldrums, he was persuaded by Sidgwick & Jackson to write about his passion for sailing, which brought him both success in the bookshops and popularity with the public, pleased to find that a politican had what Edna Healey refers to as 'hinterland'. He went on to write about his interests in music and in travel, and was provided by Sidgwick's sales director Stephen du Sautoy with a train to take him round the country as he signed copies of his books. It was said that the copies of value were the ones that Heath had *not* signed.

When Edna Healey decided to turn her hand to writing a book, it was Sidgwick & Jackson who commissioned her to produce a biography of Angela Burdett-Coutts. She had become fascinated by Angela while living in the grounds of her former home in Holly Lodge, Highgate. In 1837, at the age of twenty-three, Angela had inherited the vast fortune of her banker grandfather, Thomas Coutts, making her one of the richest and thus potentially powerful women in Victorian England. She moved in the highest social circles, falling in love with the Duke of Wellington, entertaining the rising stars of the political scene, Disraeli and Gladstone, and pursuing her philanthropic work with Charles Dickens. Yet she remained throughout her life a shy and supremely private person, which is why the book was entitled *Lady Unknown* – a risk as negative titles are thought to be unsaleable. Despite this, the book proved a great success when it was launched in 1978, and Edna in turn went on an author's tour. After promoting the book in Edinburgh, she returned to London by British Rail rather than a special train *à la heath*. As compensation the owner of her hotel dispatched a Highland piper to accompany her down to Waverley Station and pipe 'Will ye no come back?' as she sat in her carriage.

In 1986 Sidgwick & Jackson published Edna's second book, *Wives of Fame*, about three Victorian ladies who married celebrated men: Mary Livingstone, Jenny Marx and Emma Darwin, and this too enjoyed *succès d'estime* so that she was subsequently invited to act as one of the judges for the Booker Prize. The Booker, originally called the Booker-McConnell after the company that sponsored it, was established in 1968 at the suggestion of Tom Maschler and administered by the National Book League. The prize was to be awarded for the 'best full length novel written in the English language by a citizen of either the Commonwealth of Nations or the Republic of Ireland'. This type of prize may be traced back to 1903 with the first of the awards by the Académie Goncourt to the French author of 'the best and most imaginative prose work of the year'. The Prix Goncourt not only brought the winner literary prestige, but also a significant boost to sales of their books, and Booker Prize winners have had the same experience. Thus when Anita Brookner won the prize in 1984 with *Hotel du Lac*, her publishers, Cape, found that her previous track record of sales of between 2,000 and 3,000 copies shot up to bestselling levels. Such is the free publicity engendered that publishing houses even find it worth their while to add 'long listed' to the cover of books nominated for Booker, which might seem like damning with faint praise. There is now a whole range of prizes for various categories of books, but the Man Booker retains the highest profile. One bookseller bravely predicted that the 2007 long list was 'full of the literary giants of the future', but Aesop's fable of the tortoise and the hare has to be borne in mind.[26]

Edna found that being a Booker judge was very hard work, for it involved reading about 130 books and then having meetings gradually to whittle these down with a final showdown, all dressed up ready for the formal dinner, to choose the winner from a shortlist of six. She noticed that many of the books had a patch two-thirds through, where the plot fell off, just like Beechers Brook in the Grand National, which is often compared to the Booker Prize with all the betting and excitement engendered. In 1986, Edna's personal favourite was *What's Bred in the Bone* by the Canadian writer Robertson Davies, but the winner was Kingsley Amis's *Old Devils*. According to Denis, she learned more about sex in the weeks of reading modern novels than in more than forty years of marriage.

When Edna published her autobiography, *Part of the Pattern*, in 2006, this time with the publisher Hodder Headline, she discovered that much had changed since the marketing of *Lady Unknown* back in the 1970s. Today publishers encourage, indeed require their authors to be, if not media stars, good communicators. Once the book has been published, the hard work begins with promotional tours, lectures and signing sessions in bookshops, interviews with local radio stations and, if lucky, on national radio and television. In 1978 the one annual literary festival to attend was held in early October in Cheltenham, Gloucestershire, a tradition that dated back to 1949. Now there are dozens of literary and arts festivals all over Great Britain, including an international book event linked with the Edinburgh Festival, and another based in Hay-on-Wye, the little market town on the Welsh Marches which in 1977 was declared an independent kingdom by the second-hand bookseller, Richard Booth, and has become a mecca for bibliophiles. What has struck Edna about these festivals is not only their popularity, but the pleasure derived by authors, the eminent and the not-so-eminent, in attending and meeting their readers.

At the first book festival held at Hexham in Northumberland in 2006, one of the events was a forum of reading groups, another phenomenon that has become very popular in the last few years. This covered a whole range of groups, including mothers who got to know each other through their children attending the same school, enthusiastic cooks combining the discussion of the chosen book with a fine meal, and readers brought together by librarians and bookshops. What fascinated those who attended the forum was the variety of ways in which the groups organised themselves and the different directions they had taken. They were united by the benefit of having their reading horizons widened and discovering pleasure in books that they would never have considered reading without such an impetus. Such groups have a fine literary tradition, for in the eighteenth century book groups flourished in towns and villages all over the country, so that Thomas Bewick and his friends foregathered at the Cannon tavern in Newcastle while Jane Austen and her sister were members of the book society in their Hampshire village of Chawton.

An opportunity for a reading group to talk directly to the author would have seemed as impossible to Bewick, Austen and their contemporaries as the odds of a man walking on the moon. With modern technology this has been made possible, with the radio programme 'Book Club' where readers can ask questions of the author, and discuss details of particular books with him or her. The latest technology has enabled the Canadian novelist Margaret Atwood to use the Longpen, a machine that allows the author to communicate directly with an individual reader by employing a screen, microphone and earphones together with a tablet on which she can write with a electronic arm and pen. Atwood has both been praised for being greener than the authors who fly round the world, by creating a 'carbon-neutral' book tour, and criticised by those who feel that the very special face-to-face experience of meeting an author, sometimes after hours spent queuing, has been lost.

A new kind of book club has been provided by television. In the United States Oprah Winfrey, who has the highest rated talk show in television history, runs a hugely popular book club. She started the club in 1996 by selecting a new book each month, and such was 'the Oprah effect' that many hitherto obscure titles became bestsellers, increasing sales by as many as a million copies. In Britain this power lies in the hands of Richard and Judy. Amanda Ross, executive producer and managing director of the company that makes the Richard and Judy Show, decided to run a ten-week book club series, focusing on a recently published book that was 'a cracking read'. When Joseph O'Connor's novel about Irish refugees in 1847, *Star of the Sea*, was published in paperback in 2004, the publisher's hopes for it were modest. However, as the second book to feature in Richard and Judy's book club its fortunes changed overnight, climbing from 337 in the UK bestseller chart to the top spot, with sales of over quarter of a million within a month. As the *Guardian* reported, 'It is as though a new demographic of readers has suddenly sprung into being – all of them galvanised into reading by one of the most derided couples on TV.'[27]

Yet again the old problem of prejudice rears its head. Jonathan Franzen, author of *The Corrections*, asked for his book to be removed from Oprah's list allegedly because he felt that his novel was part of the high-art literary tradition, while some of her earlier choices could not be so described. Richard and Judy face the same reaction, with some declaring they would not read anything recommended on the show; shades of Queenie Leavis can be detected here. Yet many of the titles chosen for Richard and Judy, such as *Toast*, the culinary memoir of the food critic Nigel Slater, Victoria Hislop's *The Island*, a novel about Spinalonga, a Greek leper colony, and William Dalrymple's *White Mughals*, about the British in India, suggest a list of breadth and depth. It is sometimes considered surprising that people watching an early evening television programme should be so inspired by the books recommended. But they are in many ways the descendants of earlier generations who found the formality of bookshops and libraries intimidating, and needed guidance from somebody with whom they felt an affinity.

* * * *

The overwhelming impression that one has about books in Britain in the early twenty-first century is of the enormity of the range on offer. It is estimated that about 100,000 new titles are published each year. Publishers vie with each other to market these titles, so that the potential customer is bombarded with information through reviews and advertising, through authors giving lectures and talking about their books on television, radio, in newspapers and magazines. A reader may purchase a new book at one of the large book chains, at an independent bookshop, in the supermarket or at a specialist outlet such as a garden centre or a local museum. If unable or reluctant to leave the house, they can buy online, and in any language and from any part of the world. For second-hand books, not only are there bookshops real and virtual, but also charity shops and ubiquitous boxes of books at markets, county shows, bring-and-buy sales. Where Foyles may have boasted to have been the largest book-shop in the world in the 1930s, now Amazon can make that claim. The Strand Bookstore in New York may have offered miles of second-hand books, but AbeBooks can currently make the connection with scores of miles of titles.

The men and women who have appeared in this book often encountered the lack of books, of ways of buying them and of finding out about them. Now the problem facing readers is an excess of choice. This brings with it an interesting dilemma, for in the highly competitive market, it is the enterprises without economic muscle that appear to be suffering: small independent publishers, independent booksellers, municipal libraries. Yet the large publishing houses have to feed the machine, and often the safest way to do that is to go for the tried and tested. Recent reports suggest that small publishers can survive through producing exciting and innovative new books and ideas, and that some authors much prefer to stick with this kind of publishing rather than be a very small cog in a large machine.[28] It is the inde-pendent booksellers and public libraries that can provide personal advice and help to the bewildered customer, advice and help that are disinterested at a time when the 'personal recommendations' of staff in large bookstores have been shown to be purchased by publishers at a price, along with inclusion in their catalogues. Perhaps the most threatened of all is the municipal library, where the holding of stock becomes a burden, and the temptation is to throw out the books and concentrate on offering cds, dvds and coffee.

It has been said that the book trade displays a death wish in the face of each new invention.[29] The one certain prediction is that nothing is certain as far as books is concerned. Two men of talent, both born and bred in the world of print, have ventured to look into the future and been proved wrong. Dr Johnson pronounced in 1759, 'the trade of advertising is now so near perfec-tion that it is not easy to propose any improvement'.[30] He would be astonished to see how J.K. Rowling's publishers have made her a very rich woman, and her Harry Potter books famous throughout the world. In the early 1990s, Peter Kindersley announced the death of the book with the development of the CD-Rom. In fact, it was his ownership of Dorling Kindersley that was in jeopardy, for with crippling debts partly caused by over-enthusiastic investment in the latest technology, he was obliged to sell his company to the Pearson Group in 1999. The wise person should keep their counsel and watch as the world of books transforms itself yet again.

APPENDIX

Equivalent Values of the Pound

This statistical series shows changes in the value of money since the fifteenth century, giving the amount of money required at November 2007 to purchase goods bought at £1 at the dates shown on the table.

The figures, provided by the Bank of England, are derived from the Retail Prices Index, based at January 1987 = 100. Data in the period up to 1914 has been taken from E.H. Phelps Brown and S.V. Hopkins, 'Seven Centuries of the Prices of Consumables, compared with Builders' Wage-rates' in *A Perspective of Wages and Prices*, London, 1981.

The Retail Prices Index is based on the combined cost of a number of specified goods and does not, for example, take into account the cost of real property or the level of wages.

Unit	Date	Equivalent in 2007
£1	1450	£551.03
£1	1500	£535.09
£1	1550	£220.72
£1	1600	£110.78
£1	1650	£83.18
£1	1700	£85.96
£1	1750	£93.75
£1	1800	£35.41
£1	1850	£64.43
£1	1900	£62.81
£1	1930	£36.79
£1	1950	£25.08
£1	1980	£3.14
£1	2000	£1.23

NOTES

Introduction

1. 'Nam et ipsa scientia potestas est', Sir Francis Bacon, *Religious Meditations: Of Heresies*, London, 1597.
2. Jonathan Rose, *The Intellectual Life of the British Working Classes*, New Haven and London, 2001, pp. 393 and ff.
3. Robert Darnton, *The Kiss of Lamourette: Reflections in Cultural History*, London 1990, p. 110.
4. Kevin Jackson, *Invisible Forms: A Guide to Literary Curiosities*, London, 1999, p. 273 and ff.

Chapter 1 – Books Do Furnish a Room

1. I was given to understand that this was said by Ernest Bevin, but as it was quoted to me by one of his contemporaries, I cannot confirm this.
2. The monetary equivalent today is £1 = £440, so the daughters' bequests would have been approximately £3,880 apiece.
3. Calendar of State Papers: Letters & Papers 24 Henry VIII, pp. 621–2.
4. Devonshire Mss, CHA, Hardwick Mss, Bess and Earls Misc. Box 2, Sir William St Loe's accounts, 1560, fol. 21.
5. British Library, C.132.i.26 – there is another copy, published in 1584, still at Chatsworth, but this is inscribed by Christopher Abdy, a fellow commoner of Pembroke Hall, Oxford/Cambridge.
6. *Diary of Lady Margaret Hoby*, ed. D.M. Meads, London, 1930, p. 95.
7. A detailed analysis of the different sources used by Bess and her craftsmen is given in Anthony Wells-Cole, *Art and Decoration in Elizabethan and Jacobean England*, New Haven and London, 1997. This has been supplemented by Santina M. Levey in her monumental catalogue of the embroideries and textiles, *The Embroideries at Hardwick Hall*, National Trust, 2007.
8. Devonshire Mss, CHA, Hardwick Mss, Bess and Earls Misc. Box 2. The inventory was signed off by Bess herself, probably when Northaw, a dissolved monastic house near St Albans in Hertfordshire, was sold in 1550 so that the Cavendishes could concentrate their property holdings in Derbyshire. Three English books are recorded in the New Parlour: 'scilt [to wit] Chaucer Froissart cronicles and a book of French and English [presumably a dictionary or grammar]'. Levey identifies the Chaucer as the edition printed by Thomas Godfray in *The Embroideries at Hardwick Hall*, p. 16.

9. There is no evidence of the price of prints in London before the seventeenth century. The cost of engravings from Plantin is taken from Jan van der Stock, *Printing Images in Antwerp: The Introduction of Printmaking in a City, Fifteenth Century to 1585*, Rotterdam, 1998, p. 207, n.12. According to the *Oxford English Dictionary*, a stuiver was the equivalent of an English penny.

10. 'There is likewise at the east end of the Chauncell a Comon privie taken awaie, whereunto the schollers of Powles schoole, and all the inhabits there aboutes used to resorte where by the Churche Yarde nere aboute the Crosse lyeth more like a laystall than a Churche yarde to the great offence of many.' Guildhall Library, Ms. 9, 537/9, fol. 55r.

11. The modern equivalent of £1 in the 1560s is £196; inflation had caused the value of the pound to fall dramatically since the beginning of the sixteenth century (see n.2).

12. This custom was referred to by John Aubrey in a letter of 1693 to Anthony Wood about the recent publication *Athenae Oxoniensis*, Bodleian Library Ms. Wood 51, fol. 6.

13. Quoted in David Hall's introduction to *A History of the Book in America*, Vol. 1: *The Colonial Book in the Atlantic World*, eds Hugh Amory and David D. Hall, Cambridge, 2000, p. 3.

14. Translated from the Latin by Graham Pollard in *The Distribution of Books by Catalogue: From the Invention of Printing to AD 1800*, eds Graham Pollard and Albert Ehrman, Cambridge, 1965, p. 47.

15. Translated from Latin by Graham Pollard in *The Distribution of Books by Catalogue*, Pollard and Ehrman, eds, p. 75.

16. Calendar 148, Doc.16 in W.W. Greg, *A Companion to Arber*, Oxford, 1967.

17. Nicholas England's order from the Plantin-Moretus Archives, Antwerp, 44 fol. 44v. The titles are: 25 Plautus 16°; 12 flores Terentij triglingues; 50 Virgilius 8°; 50 Apophthegmata Erasmi 8°; 25 Epistole famil.Cicer; 50 Epistole selecte Ciceroni 8°; 12 Sententie Ciceronis 16°; 25 Terentius sine annotat.; 5 Annotationes in eundem; 25 Grammatica greca Clenardi; 12 Hesiodi opera et dies.

18. His books are now in Cambridge University Library.

19. Norfolk Record Office KNY 678, 372X5.

20. Desiderius Erasmus, *De Pueris Instituendis*, Basel, 1529. English version from *Collected Works of Erasmus*, Toronto, 1985, Vol. 26, pp. 305–6.

21. Richard Mulcaster, *Positions*, London, 1581, p. 177.

22. Margaret Cavendish, *Philosophical and Physical Opinions*, 1655, fol. B2v. Quoted in Elaine Hobby, *Virtue of Necessity: English Women's Writing, 1649–88*, London, 1988, p. 190.

23. Sarah Gristwood, in her biography, *Arbella: England's Lost Queen*, London, 2003, has investigated this theory, and finds that Marlowe's dates fit the facts, but that there is no conclusive proof.

24. Quoted by Gristwood, *Arbella*, p. 76.

25. Identified by Nicolas Barker in *The Devonshire Inheritance: Five Centuries of Collecting at Chatsworth*, Virginia, 2003.

26. Fox's account remains in manuscript form in the library at Chatsworth, Hardwick Mss 45A. It has been published as *Mr Harrie Cavendish his Journey to and from Constantinople by Fox, his Servant*, ed. A.C. Wood, Camden Miscellany 17, London, 1940.

27. Devonshire Mss, CHA, Hardwick Mss, 10A, Book of Accounts for 1597–1601.

28. Entry for 28 January 1617 in *Diary of Lady Anne Clifford*, ed. Vita Sackville-West, London, 1923, p. 52.

29. As far as I can ascertain, this is the first time that John Norton has been proposed as the bookseller to the Cavendish family. The purchase of a catalogue from Frankfurt would be a very early English example, along with that of Dr Dee referred to on p. 13.

30. Devonshire Mss, CHA, Chatsworth Hobbes Mss, E1A. Bess's books are recorded as *Calvin upon Job*, folio English, *Bunnie's Resolution*, 8o, and *Saloman's Solaces*, 4o.

Chapter 2 – Enjoyment of All that's Worth Seeking After

1. *The Diary of Samuel Pepys*, eds R.C. Latham and W. Matthews, London, 1983, vol. IX, pp. 160–1. Unusually this entry is in the form of rough notes.
2. John Evelyn, *A Character of England. As it was lately presented in a letter, to a Noble Man of France*, London, 1659, p. 28.
3. *Diary*, vol. V, 14 December 1664, p. 344.
4. *Diary*, vol. VIII, 11 November 1667, p. 526.
5. *Diary*, vol. VIII, 8 April 1667, p. 156.
6. *Diary*, vol. IX, 24 April 1668, p. 173.
7. *Diary*, vol. IX, 23 October 1668, p. 335.
8. See Mark Purcell, 'Useful Weapons for the Defence of That Cause: Richard Allestree, John Fell and the Foundation of the Allestree Library', *Library History*, 6th series, 21:2, 1999.
9. *Diary*, vol. IX, 31 May 1669, p. 365.
10. *The Distribution of Books by Catalogue: From the Invention of Printing to AD 1800*, eds Graham Pollard and Albert Ehrman, Cambridge, 1965, p. 164.
11. *The Tangier Papers of Samuel Pepys*, ed. E. Chappell, London, Naval Records Society 73, 1935, p. 108.
12. *Pepys Library Catalogue*, vol. IV, Cambridge, 1989, Introduction to Maps, p. 83.
13. Gabriel Naudé, translated by John Evelyn as *Instructions concerning erecting of a library*, London, 1661, sig. A4ᵘ.
14. Adrian Johns, 'Science and the Book' in *The Cambridge History of the Book in Britain*, vol. IV, 1557–1695, eds John Barnard and D.F. McKenzie, Cambridge, 2002, p. 302.
15. *Diary*, vol. VIII, 11 December 1667, p. 575.
16. *Diary*, vol. III, 2 December 1662, p. 273.
17. *Diary*, vol. V, 3 February 1664, p. 37.
18. *Diary*, vol. IX, 8 February 1668, p. 58.
19. *Essayes by Sir William Cornwallis*, ed. D.C. Allen, Baltimore, 1946, p. 50.
20. Quoted in Margaret Spufford, *Small Books and Pleasant Histories: Popular Fiction and its Readership in Seventeenth-Century England*, London, 1981, p. 73.
21. *Diary*, vol. IV, 4 September 1663, p. 297.
22. *Diary*, vol. VI, 22 November 1665, p. 305.
23. *Pepys Library Catalogue*, vol. IV, Calligraphy, p. 1.
24. *Diary*, vol. I, 25 September 1660, p. 253.
25. Letter to Dr Charlett, 5 November 1700, *Private Correspondence and Miscellaneous Papers of Samuel Pepys, 1679–1703*, ed. J.R. Tanner, London, 1926, vol. 2, p. 105.
26. *Diary*, vol. IV, 15 May 1663, p. 140.
27. Pepys Library 520. I am grateful to Dr Richard Luckett for pointing this out to me.
28. *Diary*, vol. VIII, 23 July 1666, p. 214.
29. These are now in the Bodleian Library.
30. *Private Correspondence*, vol. 2, pp. 247–8.
31. Quoted by Anthony Hobson, *Great Libraries*, London, 1970, p. 220.
32. Letter, 28 March 1692, *Letters and the Second Diary of Samuel Pepys*, ed. R.G. Howarth, London, 1932, p. 228.
33. Quoted by Claire Tomalin, *Samuel Pepys: The Unequalled Self*, London, 2002, p. 373.
34. Nathanael Jacob Gerlach, quoted by Hobson, *Great Libraries*, p. 220.
35. Letter, 29 August 1692, *Letters*, p. 230.

Chapter 3 – Distance Learning

1. Johnson made the remark on 20 September 1777, during a tour of Derbyshire.
2. In the back of the last of Sir William's letter-books (see n.3 below) is a loose leaf on which his son Brooke made a note of his expenses for his first two journeys to London

in October and November 1702. He records setting off from Ashbourne on a Friday, stopping at Coleshill, Croperdy, Windover and Uxbridge, and reaching London the following Tuesday.

3. Boothby's personal diary, running from 29 September 1676 to 23 March 1677, together with letter-books from 29 March 1683 to 17 September 1686, and 26 March 1688 to 28 September 1689 are now in the British Library, Add Mss 71689–71692.

4. The Clavell *versus* Starkey quarrel with interventions from other booksellers is detailed by Graham Pollard in *The Distribution of Books by Catalogue: From the Invention of Printing to AD 1800*, eds Graham Pollard and Albert Ehrman, Cambridge, 1965, pp. 129–131.

5. Markman Ellis, *The Coffee House: A Cultural History*, London, 2004, p. 158.

6. Richard Steele, 'Dedication', the *Tatler*, vol. 1, nos 1–50 (London 1710), ed. Donald Bond, I, p. 8.

7. The *Spectator*, no. 10.

8. Quoted in J.E. Hodgson, 'Romance and Humour of the Auction Room', *Connoisseur*, June 1939.

9. For analyses of the twists and turns of copyright, see John Brewer, *The Pleasures of the Imagination: English Culture in the Eighteenth Century*, London, 1997, pp. 132 and ff, and James Raven, *The Business of Books: Booksellers and the English Book Trade, 1450–1850*, New Haven and London, 2007, pp. 128–9, and pp. 230–2.

10. *The Letters of Samuel Johnson*, ed. R.W. Chapman, Oxford, 1984, vol. 2, p. 608, 13 April 1779.

11. Edward Potten, 'The Books of Henry Booth, lst Earl of Warrington', unpublished paper.

12. *The Works of the Rt. Hon. Henry, late L. Delamer and Earl of Warrington*, London, 1694, pp. 1; 17–18; 10; 19.

13. *The Life and Errors of John Dunton*, first published in London, 1705, republished by Garland Publishing, London and New York, 1974, pp. 115; 299; 289; 287; 237.

14. Dedication to *The Works of the Rt. Hon. Henry*.

15. John Murray to John Haslington, 29 September 1779, John Murray Archives, National Library of Scotland, Ms. 41903.

16. John Murray to William Creech, 4 November 1782, John Murray Archives, Ms. 41904.

17. John Murray to William Smellie, 10 August 1779, John Murray Archives, Ms. 41903.

18. Ned Ward, *A Fair Step to Stir-Bitch-Fair: with Remarks upon the University of Cambridge*, London, 1700.

19. *The Life and Errors of John Dunton*, p. 299.

20. *Post-Man*, 1704.

21. Mark Purcell, 'Books and Readers in Eighteenth-century Westmorland: The Brownes of Townend', *Library History* 17, 2001.

22. Kendal Record Office, WD/TE/Box 2/V/104. The copy of Thomas Wood's *An Institute of the Lawes of England* (In the Savoy, 1724) is still at Townend.

23. Kendal Record Office, WD/TE/Box 2/V/108.

24. Kendal Record Office, WD/TE/Box 2/V/86.

25. Kendal Record Office, WD/TE/Box 8/3/34.

26. Dunham Massey papers, John Rylands University Library, Manchester, EGR 7/15.

27. Dunham Massey papers, John Rylands Library, EGR 3/7.

Chapter 4 – A Founding Father

1. In a letter of 10 June 1815, from *The Adams-Jefferson Letters*, ed. Lester J. Cappon, Chapel Hill, 1959, [2] 2:441–3.

2. For details of the sources, see David D. Hall, 'The Chesapeake in the Seventeenth Century', in *A History of the Book in America*, vol. 1: *The Colonial Book in the Atlantic World*, eds Hugh Amory and David D. Hall, Cambridge, 2000, p. 539, n.49.

3. 'Journal of the Meetings of the President and Masters of William and Mary College', *William and Mary Quarterly*, 1st series, vol. 2 (1893), 51. Quoted and annotated by Calhoun Winton, 'Eighteenth-Century Southern Book Trade' in *A History of the Book in America*, eds Amory and Hall, p. 229.

4. Letter of 19 October 1748, *Papers of Benjamin Franklin*, ed. Leonard W. Labaree, New Haven, 1961, vol. 3, p. 322.

5. *Jefferson Papers*, ed. Julian P. Boyd, Princeton, New Jersey, 1950, 1:33.

6. John Mair, *Book-keeping Methodiz'd*, Edinburgh, 1760, p. 332.

7. John Murray Archives, National Library of Scotland, letter-books 1772–1774, Mss 41898 and 41899.

8. John Murray to Robert Miller, 26 March 1773, John Murray Archives Ms. 41898.

9. *Jefferson Papers*, 1:34.

10. *Jefferson Papers*, 1:76–81.

11. E. Millicent Sowerby, *Catalogue of the Library of Thomas Jefferson*, Library of Congress, Washington, 1953, vol. III, pp. 254–5.

12. Quoted in Arthur Herman, *The Scottish Enlightenment: The Scots' Invention of the Modern World*, London, 2002, p. 222.

13. Jefferson met de Buffon in Paris, and they corresponded frequently thereafter.

14. *Notes on the State of Virginia*, Baltimore, 1800, p. 69.

15. Quoted in Henry Steele Commager's essay, 'Thomas Jefferson and the Character of America', in *Thomas Jefferson's Garden Book*, ed. Robert Baron, Colorado, 1987, p. 30.

16. Letter from Charles Elliot to Colebourn Barrel, John Murray Archives, Ms 43092, letter 1118.

17. John McCall to Dilly, 14 January 1786, letter 38, Charleston Library Society letter-book.

18. Letter 53, 14 September 1792, Charleston Library Society letter-book.

19. Letter to Samuel Harrison Smith, offering the library to Congress, 21 Sept 1814, *Jefferson Papers*, 18:35n.

20. To James Monroe, 26 May 1795, cited Sowerby, *Catalogue*, vol. V, p. 189.

21. Quoted in F.A. Mumby and Ian Norrie, *Publishing and Bookselling*, London, 1974, p. 208.

22. *Jefferson Papers*, 8:301.

23. To William Stephens Smith, 28 September 1787, *Jefferson Papers* 12:193.

24. *Diary of John* Adams, ed. L.H. Butterfield, Harvard, 1961, 3:189.

25. *Jefferson Papers*, 11:183.

26. Letter from Benjamin Franklin, 24 October 1788, *Jefferson Papers*, 14:36.

27. Quoted in Fawn M. Brodie, *Thomas Jefferson: An Intimate History*, London, 1974, p. 336.

28. To John Langdon, 2 August 1808, *Writings of Thomas Jefferson*, eds Andrew Lipscomb and Albert Bergh, Washington, 1903, XVI:310.

29. Letter to Abraham Baldwin, 14 April 1802, *Jefferson Papers*, 19:128.

30. I am grateful to Anthony Hobson for this analysis.

31. Text from Hearne's *Johannis Glastionensis Chronica II*, 490–5: Calendar of Treasury Papers 1556/7–1696.

32. Letter of 8 August 1759 to James Brown, *Correspondence of Thomas Gray*, eds Paget Toynbee and Leonard Whibley, vol. 2, Oxford, 1935, pp. 632–3.

33. Quoted in *America's Library: The Story of the Library of Congress, 1800–2000* by James Conaway, New Haven, 2000, p. 30.

34. Letter of 10 June 1815, *Adams-Jefferson Letters*, [2] 2: 441–43.

35. Letter to William Roscoe, 27 Dec 1820, *Writings of Thomas Jefferson*, XV: 303.

36. Quoted by Douglas L. Wilson in *Jefferson's Books*, the Thomas Jefferson Foundation, Monticello, 1995, p. 46.

Chapter 5 – Building a Library

1. The *Encyclopaedia Britannica*, edited by Colin Macfarquhar and Andrew Bell, was published first in instalments from 1768 to 1771, and then as a quarto set of three volumes. John Soane owned a set of this edition.
2. William Cobbett, *The Autobiography of William Cobbett: The Progress of a Plough-boy to a Seat in Parliament*, ed. William Reitzel, London, 1947, p. 18.
3. Richard Altick, *The English Common Reader: A Social History of the Mass Reading Public 1800–1900*, Chicago and London, 1957, p. 31.
4. *The Life of James Lackington, Bookseller, 1746–1815*, abridged by Peter Hopkins for the Merton Historical Society, Morden, 2004.
5. Lackington, Letter III.
6. John Britton, *Autobiography*, London, 1850, p. 35n.
7. E.W. Brayley, *History of Surrey*, vol. 2, London, 1841. Ironically this volume was compiled with the help of Soane's great friend John Britton, himself from humble origins.
8. From the anonymous essay, pp. 14–15, quoted by Pierre de la Ruffinière du Prey in *John Soane's Architectural Education 1753–80*, New York and London, 1977, p. 29.
9. Du Prey, *John Soane's Architectural Education*, p. 30.
10. Farington Diary typescript, British Museum, Prints & Drawings, vol. I, p. 235, 3n5u4y, 10 October 1794.
11. Soane often quoted this line, which is probably from a poem composed by his friend Barbara Hofland.
12. Laurence Sterne, *A Sentimental Journey through France and Italy*, London, 1775, vol. 2, pp. 12–13.
13. Du Prey, *John Soane's Architectural Education*, p. 140.
14. John Soane, *Memoirs of the Professional Life of an Architect*, privately printed, 1835, p. 16.
15. *William Blake's Writings*, ed. G.E. Bentley, Oxford, 1978, vol. 2, p. 582.
16. Britton, *Autobiography*, p. 200.
17. Britton, *Autobiography*, p. 229.
18. *Lackington*, Letter XXI.
19. *Lackington*, Letter XXXIII.
20. *Lackington*, Letter XXXV.
21. *Lackington*, Letter XXXIX.
22. Soane archives, Spiers Box.
23. Ibid.
24. David Watkin, *Sir John Soane: Enlightenment Thought and the RA Lectures*, Cambridge 1996, pp. 12–13.
25. Letter from Britton to Soane, 4 June 1825, Soane archives.
26. Pitshanger, or Pitzhanger as it is now known, is in the care of the London Borough of Ealing, which is planning to restore Soane's library to its former glory.
27. Quoted in Gillian Darley, *John Soane: An Accidental Romantic*, New Haven and London, 1999, p. 207.
28. Arthur Bolton, *The Portrait of Sir John Soane, R.A.*, London, 1927, pp. 205–6, a transcript from Soane's notebook.
29. Watkin, *Sir John Soane*, p. 3.
30. Peter Coxe, 'To Sir John Soane, Royal Academician', privately printed in 1837.

Chapter 6 – A Little Light Reading?

1. Samuel Clark, *The Lives of Sundry Eminent Persons*, 1683, p. 202.
2. *The Diary of Samuel Pepys*, eds, R.C. Latham and W. Matthews, London, 1970, vol. I, p. 35.

3. *Life and Times of Anthony Wood, 1632–1695*, ed. Andrew Clark, Oxford, 1891–1900, vol. 2, p. 147.
4. *Diary of a Visit to England*, ed. J.L. Clifford, New York, 1947, p. 58.
5. Account by E. Vaughan Tomey, President of the Birmingham Book Club, 1926, quoted by Paul Kaufman, *Libraries and their Users: Collected Papers in Library History*, London, 1969, p. 52.
6. Hubert Collar, 'An Eighteenth-Century Book Society', *Essex Review*, vol. 44, 1935, pp. 109–12, quoted Kaufman, *Libraries and their Users*, p. 53.
7. Kaufman, *Libraries and their Users*, p. 36.
8. Robert Wodrow, *Analecta, or Materials for a History of Remarkable Providences mostly relating to Scotch Ministers and Christians*, first published in 1728, reprinted for the Maitland Club, Edinburgh, 1843, vol. 3, p. 515.
9. Kaufman, *Libraries and their Users*, p. 192.
10. James Raven, 'The Novel comes of Age', p. 75 in *The English Novel, 1770–1829: A Bibliographical Survey of Prose Fiction Published in the British Isles*, ed. Peter Garside, James Raven and Rainer Schrölering, vol. 1, Oxford, 2000.
11. *Reminiscences and Table Talk of Samuel Rogers*, ed. G.H. Powell, London, 1903, p. 108.
12. A copy of this catalogue is in the John Johnson Collection, Bodleian Library, Oxford.
13. Tobias Smollett, *The Expedition of Humphry Clinker*, Wordsworth Classics edition, Ware, Herts, 1995, p. 35.
14. Clara Reeve, *Progress of Romance*, Colchester, 1785, vol. 2, p. 7.
15. *Boswell's Life of Johnson*, ed. Edward Fletcher, London, 1938, vol. 1, p. 48.
16. John Murray to William Gordon, 19 May 1767, John Murray Archives, National Library of Scotland, Ms. 41896.
17. *The Early Journals and Letters of Fanny Burney, 1768–91*, eds Lars E. Troide *et al*, Oxford, 1988, vol. 2, pp. 215 and 291.
18. *Evelina*, ed. A. Bloom, Oxford University Press edition, Oxford, 1990, vol. 1, p. xv.
19. *The Early Journals*, vol. 3, pp. 28–9.
20. Original letter from Mrs Thrale to Charles Burney was found in a grangerised edition of the *Diary and Letters of Mme d'Arblay, 1778–1840* and quoted in Kate Chisholm, *Fanny Burney: Her Life*, London, 1998, p. 58.
21. Thomas Gisborne, *Enquiry into the Duties of the Female Sex*, 4th edition, 1797, p. 217.
22. Jan Fergus, *Provincial Readers in Eighteenth-Century England*, Oxford, 2006, p. 15.
23. Her diaries are now in the Huntington Library, San Marino, California, Mss 31201. They are available on microfilm, 'A Woman's View of Drama, 1790–1830', published by Adam Matthew Publications, Marlborough, Wiltshire, 1995.
24. John Brewer, *The Pleasures of the Imagination: English Culture in the Eighteenth Century*, London, 1997, p. 196.
25. Quoted in Gillian Darley, *John Soane: An Accidental Romantic*, New Haven and London, 1999, p. 207.
26. Her notebooks are in the Soane archives, MrsSNB, 1,3, 4 and 6.
27. In the National Trust report on Calke Abbey Library, Peter Hoare points out that this is the only known copy of Kemble's *The Farm House*. This suggests that, as with novels during this period, the print runs for plays were small and reprints depended upon possibilities of revivals.
28. *The Loiterer* no. 9, 28 March 1789. Austen wrote under the pseudonym 'Sophia Sentiment'.
29. *Northanger Abbey*, Novel Library edition published by Hamish Hamilton, 1948, p. 25.
30. Quoted in *The Journal of Sir Walter Scott*, ed. W.E. Anderson, Oxford, 1972, p. 319.
31. Quoted in Claire Lamont's introduction to *Waverley*, Oxford World Classics edition, 1998, p. ix.
32. Table 12.4 on p. 222 in William St Clair, *The Reading Nation in the Romantic Period*, Cambridge, 2004. But, as Jan Fergus has subsequently pointed out in *Provincial*

Readers, p. 4, Maria Edgeworth's *Patronage* achieved sales of 8,000 copies on publication day alone.

33. The market for Scott in India is illustrated by 'A new Scotch novel called Waverley: an appreciation from Madras' by Iain Gordon Brown, *The Bibliotheck,* vol. 23, 1998.
34. Quoted in Georg Lukács, *The Historical Novel,* London, 1962, p. 66.
35. Thomas Carlyle's review of Scott's memoirs, originally in the *London and Westminster Review,* no. 12, 1837, quoted by Donald Sassoon, *The Culture of the Europeans,* London, 2006, p. 149.
36. John Murray to John Cunningham, 13 February 1770, John Murray Archives, Ms. 41897.
37. Jane Austen, *Northanger Abbey,* Novel Library edition, London, 1948, p. 95.

Chapter 7 – Rare and Curious

1. In a letter from Catherine Cappe to Lady Strickland, 29 January 1819: 'that moral cloud which unhappily so long obscured the prosperity and happiness of a family which . . . was so justly and honourably distinguished', West Yorkshire Archive Service, Leeds, A1/8/12.
2. T.G. Wright, 'Reminiscences of Nostell', 1887, Ms 803, Yorkshire Archaeological Society, Leeds.
3. *The Bibliomania; or, Book-madness; containing some account of the history, symptoms and cure of this fatal disease. In an epistle addressed to Richard Heber,* London, 1809.
4. T. Hearne, *Remarks and Collections,* ed. H.E. Salter, Oxford Historical Society, 72, Oxford, 1921, vol. ii, p. 389.
5. Letter to Lucy Ludwell Paradise, 1 June 1789, *Jefferson Papers,* ed. Julian P. Boyd, Princeton, New Jersey, 1950, vol. 15, pp. 162–3.
6. Isaac D'Israeli, *Curiosities of Literature,* London, 1807, 5th edition, vol. 1, pp. 10–11.
7. Anthony Hobson in the chapter on John Rylands Library, *Great Libraries,* London, 1970, p. 268.
8. *The Autobiography of Leigh Hunt,* London, 1859, ch. 6.
9. Ironically, Spencer was able to acquire the *Decameron* for £918 in 1819 when Blandford sold his library.
10. John Rylands University Library of Manchester, Rylands Eng. Ms. 71, fol.125.
11. Quoted by Hobson, *Great Libraries,* p. 273.
12. Giles Mandelbrote and Yvonne Lewis, *Learning to Collect: The Library of Sir Richard Ellys (1682–1742) at Blickling Hall,* London, 2004, p. 17.
13. 30 April 1818, quoted in Christie's sale catalogue, 1975.
14. Letter to George Nicol, 6 July 1790, *Correspondence of Horace Walpole,* ed. W.S. Lewis, New Haven, 1980, vol. 42, p. 285.
15. Horace Walpole, *A Description of the Villa of Mr Horace Walpole, youngest son of Sir Robert Walpole, Earl of Orford, at Strawberry Hill near Twickenham Middlesex with an inventory of the Furniture, Pictures, Curiosities &c,* Strawberry Hill, 1784. He refers to Sir William Dugdale's *History of St Paul's,* 1658 and to John Chute of The Vyne, one of the Committee of Taste.
16. Arnold Hunt, 'Private Libraries in the Age of Bibliomania', *Cambridge History of Libraries in Britain and Ireland, Vol II, 1640–1850,* eds Giles Mandelbrote and K.A. Manley, Cambridge, 2006, p. 445.
17. Letter to William Mason, 13 November 1781, *Correspondence,* ed. W.S. Lewis, New Haven, 1955, vol. 29, p. 165.
18. West Yorkshire Archive Service, Leeds 1352/A1/8/19.
19. WYAS1352/A1/8/16/1. The books in question were five volumes of *Histories of Durham,* by Surtees and Raine, priced at £36, sent to Winn by rail.

20. WYAS1352/A1/8/26/9.
21. *The Life of Mr Thomas Gent, Printer of York, written by himself,* printed by Thomas Thorpe, London, 1832.
22. *The Life of Mr Thomas Gent,* pp. 176, 178 and 189.
23. Richard Gough, *Anecdotes of British Topography,* London, 1768, p. 550.
24. WYAS/A1/8/16/2: letters 10 and 14 March 1862.
25. WYAS/A1/8/16/2: letter 22 July 1863.
26. WYAS/A1/8/16/2: letter 23 September 1863.
27. WYAS/A1/8/16/1: letter from Phillipps to Mrs Lowndes, 18 July 1843.
28. WYAS/A1/8/16/1: note from Mrs Lowndes to Charles Winn.
29. WYAS/A1/8/16/1: undated letter.
30. WYAS NP/A1/10 (1808), 18 December 1871.

Chapter 8 – The Common Reader

1. 'In the character of his Elegy I rejoice to concur with the common reader; for by the common sense of readers uncorrupted with literary prejudices, after all the refinements of subtilty and the dogmatism of learning, must be finally decided all claim to poetical honours. The *Church-yard* abounds with images which find a mirrour in every mind, and with sentiments to which every bosom returns an echo.' Samuel Johnson, *Lives of the Most Eminent English Poets,* London, 1781, vol. 4, p. 485.
2. Richard Altick, *The English Common Reader: A Social History of the Mass Reading Public, 1800–1900,* Chicago and London, 1957, pp. 15 and ff.
3. Edgar Johnson, *Charles Dickens: His Tragedy and his Triumph,* London, 1953, vol. 2, p. 613.
4. Altick, *The English Common Reader,* pp. 22, 51–2.
5. I am grateful to Hazel Forsyth at the Museum of London for this information.
6. 'Middlebrow' in Virginia Woolf's *Collected Essays,* London, 1966, vol. 2, pp. 196 and ff. Although Woolf produced two collections of essays entitled 'The Common Reader' in 1925 and 1932, this essay began life as a letter to the *New Statesman* that was never sent.
7. 'Memoirs of the Life of Revd Dr John Trusler', vol. 2, ch. 34, fol. 337, unpublished mss, Lewis Walpole Library, Farmington, Connecticut.
8. *The Life of James Lackington, Bookseller, 1746–1815,* Merton Historical Society, 2004, Letter XIII.
9. Alison Uttley, *The Farm on the Hill,* London, 1941, p. 180.
10. *Lackington,* Letter VI.
11. Jan Fergus, 'Provincial Servants' Reading in the Late Eighteenth Century', chapter 11 in *The Practice and Representation of Reading in England,* eds James Raven, Helen Small and Naomi Tadmor, Cambridge, 1996.
12. *Lackington,* Letter XXXIX.
13. *Eighteenth-Century Women Poets,* ed. Roger Lonsdale, Oxford, 1989, 'A poem, on the supposition of an advertisement appearing in a morning paper, of the publication of a volume of poems, by a Servant-Maid', p. 425; 'A poem, on the supposition of the book having been published and read', p. 427.
14. H.G. Wells, *Tono-Bungay,* London, 1946, p. 24.
15. His unsigned contribution appeared in William Hone's *Every-Day Book.* It is quoted in E.S. Turner, *What the Butler Saw,* London, 1962, p. 101.
16. Felicity Stimpson, 'Servants' Reading: An Examination of the Servants' Library at Cragside', *Library History,* vol. 19, March 2003.
17. P.R. Catcheside, 'Loveclough Printworks Library', *Library History,* vol. 2, 1970. The books passed to Rawtenstall Public Library in 1969.

18. Anthony Trollope, lecture delivered 28 January 1870 in Edinburgh and reproduced as 'On English Prose Fiction as a Rational Amusement', *Four Lectures*, ed. Morris L. Parrish, London, 1938.

19. Sir Herbert Maxwell, *Life of W.H. Smith*, London, 1894, p. 29.

20. Samuel Phillips, 'Literature of the Railway', *The Times*, 9 August 1851.

21. Quoted by F.A. Mumby, *The House of Routledge: 1834–1934*, London, 1934, p. 53.

22. S. Nowell-Smith, *The House of Cassell, 1848–1958*, London, 1958, p. 22.

23. Henry Mayhew, *London Labour and the London Poor*, London, 1861–2, vol. 1, pp. 289 and ff.

24. Dickens's friend Wilkie Collins also had readers clamouring outside his publisher's offices, demanding more of *The Woman in White*. His instalments were bound in yellow wrappers.

25. Malcolm Andrews, *Charles Dickens and his Performing Selves*, Oxford, 2006, p. 5.

26. Flora Thompson, 'Penny Reading' in *Candleford Green*, the third part of the trilogy, *Lark Rise to Candleford*, London, 1973, pp. 433–47.

27. The books are still housed in this way in Ipswich School.

28. 'An Investigation of Records Available at the Library for the Evidence of the Spread of Enlightenment in the Second Half of the Eighteenth Century', a thesis by Cairns Mason, 2007, held in Innerpeffray Library.

29. Paul Kaufman, *Libraries and their Users,* London, 1969, pp. 155–6.

30. Charles Elliot's letter-books, Mss. 43090 and 43091, in the John Murray Archives, National Library of Scotland.

31. *Journals of Dorothy Wordsworth*, ed. E. de Selincourt, London, 1941, vol. 1, p. 209.

32. Richard Booth with Lucia Stuart, *My Kingdom of Books*, Talybont, 1999, p. 82.

33. The London Mechanics Institute later became the Birkbeck Literary and Scientific Institution, and in 1907 Birkbeck College.

34. Quoted by Thomas Greenwood, *Public Libraries*, 4th ed., London, 1891, p. 9.

35. Pamphlets for *Free Public Libraries* are in the John Johnson Collection, Bodleian Library.

36. John Passmore Edwards, *A Few Footprints*, London, 1906, p. 6.

37. Duff Brown's system is still apparently in use in the Manx Museum Library on the Isle of Man.

38. Grace Carlton, *Spade-work: The Story of Thomas Greenwood*, London, 1949, p. 125.

39. Letter to May Gaskell, quoted by Josceline Dimbleby, *A Profound Secret*, London, 2004, p. 145.

40. In his preface to the edition of *A History of British Birds*, published in June 1826.

41. Thomas Bewick, *My Life*, ed. Iain Bain, Folio Society edition, London, 1981, p. 47.

42. Bewick, *My Life*, p. 69.

43. Quoted in John Brewer, *Pleasures of the Imagination: English Culture in the Eighteenth Century*, London, 1997, p. 500.

44. This letter was found tipped in William Smellie's translation of Buffon's *Natural History of Birds* and is described in David Gardner-Medwin's essay, 'The Library of Thomas Bewick' in *Bewick Studies, Essays in Celebration of the 250th anniversary of the Birth of Thomas Bewick, 1753–1828*, ed. David Gardner-Medwin, Newcastle-upon-Tyne, 2003, p. 59.

45. James Ramsay MacDonald, *Wanderings and Excursions*, London, 1932, p. 24.

46. Quoted by Godfrey R. Elton, *The Life of James Ramsay MacDonald, 1866–1919*, London, 1939, p. 24.

47. Elton, *The Life of James Ramsay MacDonald*, pp. 25–6, 28.

Chapter 9 – Children of the Revolution

1. *Healey's Eye: A Photographic Memoir*, London, 1980; *The Time of My Life*, London, 1989; *When Shrimps Learn to Whistle*, London, 1990; *My Secret Planet*, London, 1992. The title of *When Shrimps . . .* comes from Khrushchev's boast that the Soviet Union would abandon its Communist principles only 'when shrimps learn to whistle'.

2. Her books are: *Lady Unknown*, London, 1978; *Wives of Fame*, London 1986; *Coutts & Co: The Portrait of a Private Bank*, London, 1992; *The Queen's House: A Social History of Buckingham Palace*, London, 1997; *Emma Darwin, The Inspirational Wife of a Genius*, London, 2001; *Part of the Pattern*, London, 2006.

3. Harold Nicolson's entry in his diary for 29 June 1931, quoted by Norman Rose, *Harold Nicolson*, London, 2005, pp. 166–7.

4. *People and Things: Wireless Talks*, Harold Nicolson, London, 1931.

5. Elizabeth Gaskell, *The Life of Charlotte Brontë*, vol. 1, p. 2, 2nd edition, London, 1857.

6. Writing in *Nation and Athenaeum*. Quoted by Sheila Hodges, *Victor Gollancz: The Story of a Publishing House, 1928–78*, London, 1978, p. 32.

7. Left Book Club titles, collected by Orwellian scholar Ian Angus, can be seen in their orange-pink glory in the special collections library of University College, London.

8. *Left Book Club Anthology*, ed. Paul Laity, London, 2001, pp. xxii and ff. This was the last non-fiction title to be published under the VG imprint, which is now part of the Orion Group.

9. WHS archives 156/1, 28 June 1929.

10. Quoted by Jeremy Lewis in *Penguin Special: The Life and Times of Allen Lane*, London 2005, p. 80.

11. Letter to Allen Lane, 22 July 1935, in the Penguin archives, University of Bristol Library.

12. *Observer*, 18 March 1935.

13. Charles Wilson, *First with the News: The History of W.H. Smith, 1792–1972*, London, 1985, p. 274.

14. Letter to Allen Lane, 24 November 1942, in the Penguin archives, University of Bristol Library.

15. Quoted by Ian Norrie in *Mumby's Publishing and Bookselling in the Twentieth Century*, 6th edition, London 1982, pp. 87–8.

16. Norrie, *Mumby's Publishing*, p. 87.

17. Memories of the Cecil Court bookseller Norman Storey in Sheila Markham, *A Book of Booksellers*, London, 2004, p. 263.

18. 'Bookshop Memories' from *The Collected Essays, Journalism and Letters* by George Orwell (Copyright George Orwell, 1936) by permission of Bill Hamilton as the Literary Executor of the Estate of the Late Sonia Brownell Orwell and Secker & Warburg Ltd. First published in *Fortnightly*, November 1936. Reprinted in *George Orwell Essays*, Penguin edition, London 1984, pp. 25–9.

19. See *A Bookseller's War: Heywood and Anne Hill*, ed. Jonathan Gathorne-Hardy, Norwich, 1997; *A Bookshop at 10 Curzon Street: Letters between Nancy Mitford and Heywood Hill 1952–73*, ed. John Saumarez Smith, London, 2004; *A Spy in the Bookshop: Letters between Heywood Hill and John Saumarez Smith 1966–74*, ed. John Saumarez Smith, London, 2006.

20. Recollection by Ian Parsons, who became Chairman of Chatto and Windus, in Norrie, *Mumby's Publishing*, p. 73.

21. John Saumarez Smith, 'Doing a Runner' in *Slightly Foxed*, no. 2, 2004.

22. Ernest Baker, *Descriptive Guide*, London, 1903, preface, p. v.

23. The Net Book Agreement that established retail price maintenance was signed in 1900. It collapsed in the 1990s.

24. Quoted by Tim Rix in the entry for Paul Hamlyn in the *Oxford Dictionary of National Biography*.

25. I am grateful for their recollections to Martyn Goff and to Gill Coleridge, who was the publicity manager for the Book Bang.
26. Jonathan Ruppin of Foyles, reported in *The Times*, 7 September 2007.
27. *Guardian*, 26 February 2004.
28. For figures on the bookshops and market share see the *Guardian*, 14 April 2007, financial section.
29. Norrie, *Mumby's Publishing*, p. 94. While I have been writing this book, Amazon have produced an electronic book device, Kindle, which can stand alone without a computer, and thus claims to overcome the objection to reading from a machine on the beach, or tucked up in bed.
30. Quoted Neil McKendrick in John Brewer and J.H. Plumb, *The Birth of a Consumer Society: The Commercialization of Eighteenth-Century England*, London 1982, p. 151.

FURTHER READING

As the range of each chapter is very different, I have indicated my background reading accordingly, rather than present one general list. I hope this will prove the most useful in practice.

1 *Books do Furnish a Room*

Primary Sources

Devonshire Mss CHA: Sir William St Loe's accounts, 1560, Hardwick Mss, Bess and Earls Misc. Box 2; William Cavendish's Book of Accounts, 1597–1601, 10A; Fox's account of visit to Constantinople, 45A; and Chatsworth Hobbes Mss, E1A.

Printed Publications

Barnard, John and D.F. McKenzie, eds, *The Cambridge History of the Book in Britain, Vol. IV, 1557–1695*, Cambridge, 2002.
Blayney, Peter, *The Bookshops in Paul's Cross Churchyard*, London, 1990.
Charlton, Kenneth, *Women, Religion and Education in Early Modern England*, London, 1999.
Durant, David, *Bess of Hardwick: Portrait of an Elizabethan Dynast*, Newark, Notts., 1988.
Girouard, Mark, *Robert Smythson and the Architecture of the Elizabethan Era*, London, 1966.
Gristwood, Sarah, *Arbella: England's Lost Queen*, London, 2003.
Hull, Suzanne W., *Chaste, Silent and Obedient, 1475–1640*, San Marino, CA, 1982.
Levey, Santina M., *An Elizabethan Inheritance: The Hardwick Hall Textiles*, London, 1998.
Levey, Santina M., *The Embroideries at Hardwick Hall*, National Trust, 2007.
Lovell, Mary, *Bess of Hardwick: First Lady of Chatsworth*, London, 2005.
McKerrow, Ronald B., et al, *A Dictionary of Printers and Booksellers in England, Scotland and Ireland, and of Foreign Printers of English Books, 1557–1640*, London, 1968.
McKitterick, David, *The Library of Sir Thomas Knyvett of Ashwellthorpe, c. 1539–1618*, Cambridge, 1978.
McKitterick, David, 'Women and their Books in seventeenth-century England: The case of Elizabeth Puckering', *The Library*, 7th series, 2000.
Meads, D.M., ed., *Diary of Lady Margaret Hoby*, London, 1930.
National Trust (guidebook), *Hardwick Hall*, 1989 edition.
Nevinson, John, 'An Elizabethan Herbarium' in *National Trust Yearbook: Studies in Art History and Nature Conservation, 1975–6*, ed. Gervase Jackson-Stops, London, 1975.

Pollard, Graham and Albert Ehrman, eds, *The Distribution of Books by Catalogue: From the Invention of Printing to AD 1800*, Cambridge, 1965.

Sackville-West, Vita, ed., *Diary of Lady Anne Clifford*, London, 1923.

Sherman, William H., *John Dee: The Politics of Reading and Writing in the English Renaissance*, Amherst, 1995.

Voet, Léon, *The Golden Compasses: A History and Evaluation of the Printing and Publishing Activities of the Officina Plantiniana at Antwerp*, Amsterdam, 1969.

Wells-Cole, Anthony, *Art and Decoration in Elizabethan and Jacobean England*, New Haven and London, 1997.

White, Gillian, '"that whyche ys nedefoulle and necessary": the Nature and Purpose of the Original Furnishings and Decoration of Hardwick Hall', thesis for the Centre for the Study of the Renaissance, University of Warwick, 2005.

Wilson, C. Anne, *Banquetting Stuffe*, Edinburgh, 1989.

2 *Enjoyment of All that's Worth Seeking After*

Printed Publications

Barnard, John and D.F. McKenzie, eds, *The Cambridge History of the Book in Britain, Vol. IV, 1557–1695*, Cambridge, 2002.

Ellis, Markman, *The Coffee House: A Cultural History*, London, 2004.

Heal, Sir Ambrose, 'Samuel Pepys, His Trade Cards', *Connoisseur* XCII, December 1933.

Heal, Sir Ambrose, 'Seventeenth-century Booksellers' & Stationers' Trade Cards', *Alphabet & Image* 8, December 1948.

Hobson, Anthony, *Great Libraries*, London, 1970.

Howarth, R.G., ed., *Letters and Second Diary of Samuel Pepys*, London, 1932.

Latham, R.C. and W. Matthews, eds, *The Diary of Samuel Pepys*, 11 vols, London, 1983.

Myers, Robin, Michael Harris and Giles Mandelbrote, eds, *The London Book Trade: Topographies of Print*, London, 2004.

Pepys Library Catalogue: II *Ballads*, 1994; III *Prints and Drawings*, 1980; IV *Music, Maps, Calligraphy*, 1989; VI *Bindings*, 1984; Cambridge.

Plomer, Henry R., *A Dictionary of the Printers and Booksellers who were at work in England, Scotland and Ireland from 1668 to 1725*, Oxford, 1922.

Pollard, Graham and Albert Ehrman, eds, *The Distribution of Books by Catalogue: From the Invention of Printing to AD 1800*, Cambridge, 1965.

Purcell, Mark, 'Useful Weapons for the Defence of that cause: Richard Allestree, John Fell and the foundation of the Allestree Library', *Library History*, 6th series, xxi, 2, 1999.

Smith, Margaret, *The Title Page*, London, 2000.

Spufford, Margaret, *Small Books and Pleasant Histories*, London, 1985.

Tanner, J.R., ed., *Private Correspondence and Miscellaneous Papers of Samuel Pepys, 1679–1703*, 2 vols, London, 1926.

Tomalin, Claire, *Samuel Pepys: The Unequalled Self*, London, 2002.

3 *Distance Learning*

Primary sources

Dunham Massey papers, EGR, in the John Rylands University Library, Manchester.

The diary and letter-books of Sir William Boothby, British Library, Add Mss 71689–71692.

The letter-books of John Murray, Mss 41903–4, John Murray Archives, National Library of Scotland.

Printed Publications

Barker, Nicholas, ed., *Treasures from the Libraries of National Trust Country Houses*, New York, 1999.

Barnard, John and D.F. McKenzie, eds, *The Cambridge History of the Book in Britain, Vol. IV, 1557–1695*, Cambridge, 2002.

Beal, Peter, 'Books are the Great Joy of My Life: Sir William Boothby, 17th-century Bibliophile', *Book Collector* 46, 1997.

Beckett, J.V. and Clyve Jones, 'Financial Improvidence and Political Independence in the early eighteenth century: George Booth, 2nd Earl of Warrington, 1675–1758', *Bulletin of the John Rylands University Library*, vol. 65, no. 1, 1982.

Booth, Henry, *The Works of the Rt. Hon. Henry, Late L. Delamer and Earl of Warrington*, London, 1694.

Cliffe, J.T., *The World of the Country House in Seventeenth-century England*, New Haven and London, 1999.

Dunton, John, *The Life and Errors of John Dunton*, first published 1705, republished by Garland Publishing, London and New York, 1974.

Ellis, Aytoun, *The Penny Universities: A History of Coffee-Houses*, London, 1956.

Fleeman, J.D., 'Michael Johnson, the "Lichfield Librarian"', *Publishing History*, 39, 1996.

Hodgson, J. E., 'Romance and Humour of the Auction Room', *Connoisseur*, June 1939.

Isaac, Peter, 'The English Provincial Book Trade to 1800', *Transactions of the Lancashire and Cheshire Antiquarian Society*, vol. 97, 2001.

Lillywhite, Bryant, *London Coffee Houses*, London, 1963.

National Trust (library report), *Dunham Massey*, 2003.

National Trust (library report), *Townend*, 2000.

Plomer, Henry R., *A Dictionary of the Printers and Booksellers who were at work in England, Scotland and Ireland from 1726 to 1775*, Oxford, 1932.

Pollard, Graham and Albert Ehrman, eds, *The Distribution of Books by Catalogue: From the Invention of Printing to 1800*, Cambridge, 1965.

Potten, Edward, 'The Books of Henry Booth, 1st Lord Warrington', unpublished paper.

Purcell, Mark, 'Books and Readers in Eighteenth-century Westmorland: The Brownes of Townend', *Library History* 17, 2001.

Raven, James, *The Business of Books: Booksellers and the English Book Trade, 1450–1850*, New Haven and London, 2007.

Uglow, Jenny, *William Hogarth: A Life and a World*, London, 1997.

Zachs, William, *The First John Murray and the Late Eighteenth-Century Book Trade*, Oxford, 1998.

4 A Founding Father

Primary Sources

The letter-books of John Murray, Mss 41898–9, and of Charles Elliot, Ms 43092, John Murray Archives, National Library of Soctland.

Printed Publications

Amory, Hugh and David D. Hall, eds, *A History of the Book in America, Vol.I: The Colonial Book in the Atlantic World*, Cambridge, 2000.

Boyd, Julian P., *Jefferson Papers*, 33 vols, Princeton, N.J., 1950–.

Brodie, Fawn M., *Thomas Jefferson: An Intimate History*, London, 1974.

Conaway, James, *America's Library: The Story of the Library of Congress, 1800–2000*, New Haven, 2000.

Goodrum, Charles A. and Helen W. Dalrymple, *Library of Congress*, Colorado, 1982.

Herman, Arthur, *The Scottish Enlightenment: The Scots' Invention of the Modern World*, London, 2002.

Hobson, Anthony, *Great Libraries*, London, 1970.

Jackson, D., *Thomas Jefferson and the Stony Mountains: Exploring the West from Monticello*, Urbana, IL, 1981.

Mandelbrote, Giles and K.A. Manley, eds, *Cambridge History of Libraries in Britain and Ireland, Vol II, 1640–1850*, Cambridge, 2006.

Raven, James, *London Booksellers and American Customers: Transatlantic Literary Community and the Charleston Library Society, 1748–1811*, Columbia, 2001.

Rice, Howard C., *Thomas Jefferson's Paris*, Princeton, N.J., 1976.

Sowerby, E. Millicent, *The Catalogue of the Library of Thomas Jefferson*, 5 vols, Washington, 1952–.

Stockdale, Eric, *'Tis Treason my Good Man!*, London, 2005.

Wilson, Douglas L., *Jefferson's Books*, the Thomas Jefferson Foundation, Monticello, 1996.

5 Building a Library

Primary Sources

Soane's office account books, journals, notebooks, correspondence and book trade ephemera, Soane Archives, Sir John Soane's Museum.

Printed Publications

Altick, Richard, *The English Common Reader: A Social History of the Mass Reading Public 1800–1900*, Chicago and London, 1957.

Britton, John, *Autobiography*, London, 1850.

Brown, Philip A., *London Publishers and Printers, c. 1800–1870*, London, 1982.

Darley, Gillian, *John Soane: An Accidental Romantic*, New Haven and London, 1999.

Du Prey, Pierre de la Ruffinière, *John Soane's Architectural Education, 1753–80*, New York and London, 1977.

Harris, Eileen, 'O, Books! Ye Monuments of Mind', *Apollo*, April 1990, vol. 131.

Harris, Eileen and Nicholas Savage, *Hooked on Books: The Library of Sir John Soane Architect, 1753–1837*, Sir John Soane's Museum, 2004.

Ingrams, Richard, *The Life and Adventures of William Cobbett*, London, 2005.

Lackington, James, *The Life of James Lackington, Bookseller 1746–1815*, abridged by Peter Hopkins for Merton Historical Society, Morden, 2004.

Maxted, Ian, *The London Book Trades, 1775–1800*, London, 1977.

Mordaunt Crook, Jo, 'John Britton and the Gothic Revival', in John Summerson, ed., *Essays concerning Architecture*, London, 1968.

Soane, John, *Memoir of the Professional Life of an Architect*, printed privately in 1835.

Watkin, David, *Sir John Soane: Enlightenment Thought and the RA Lectures*, Cambridge, 1996.

6 A Little Light Reading?

Primary sources

Anna Larpent's diary, Mss 31201, Huntington Library, San Marino, California; microfilm 'A Woman's View of Drama, 1790–1830', published by Adam Matthew, Marlborough, Wiltshire, 1995.

Eliza Soane's notebooks, 1804–13, MrsSNB, Soane Archives, Sir John Soane's Museum.

Letter-book of John Murray, Ms. 41897, John Murray Archives, National Library of Scotland.

Printed Publications

Adburgham, Alison, *Silver Fork Society: Fashionable Life and Literature 1814–1840*, London, 1983.
Brewer, John, *The Pleasures of the Imagination: English Culture in the Eighteenth Century*, London, 1997.
Chisholm, Kate, *Fanny Burney: Her Life*, London, 1998.
D'Oench, Ellen G., *Copper into Gold: Prints by John Raphael Smith*, New Haven and London, 1999.
Fergus, Jan, *Provincial Readers in Eighteenth-century England*, Oxford, 2006.
Garside, Peter, James Raven and Rainer Schwölering, eds, *The English Novel: A Bibliographical Survey of Prose Fiction Published in the British Isles, Vol. 1: 1770–99, Vol. 2: 1800–29*, Oxford, 2000.
Kaufman, Paul, *Libraries and their Users*, London, 1969.
Mandelbrote, Giles and K.A. Manley, eds, *Cambridge History of Libraries in Britain and Ireland, Vol. II, 1640–1850*, Cambridge, 2006.
National Trust (library report), *Calke Abbey*, 2000.
National Trust (library report), *Springhill*, 2000.
Nokes, David, *Jane Austen: A Life*, London, 1997.
Palmer, Susan, *The Soanes at Home*, Sir John Soane's Museum, London, 1997.
Raven, James, 'From Promotion to Proscription: Arrangements for Reading and Eighteenth-Century Libraries', in *The Practice and Representation of Reading in England*, eds James Raven, Helen Small and Naomi Tabor, Cambridge, 1996.
Rosa, Matthew Whiting, *The Silver-Fork Novels of Fashion Preceding Vanity Fair*, New York, 1936.
Sassoon, Douglas, *Culture of the Europeans*, London, 2006.
St Clair, William, *The Reading Nation in the Romantic Period*, Cambridge, 2004.
Steinberg, S.H., *Five Hundred Years of Printing*, (revised edition by John Trevitt), London, 1996.
Vickery, Amanda, *The Gentleman's Daughter: Women's Lives in Georgian England*, New Haven and London, 2003.

7 Rare and Curious

Primary Sources

Charles Winn's diary, account books, correspondence and notebooks, West Yorkshire Archives Service, Leeds.

Printed Publications

Danckwerts, Peter, ed., *Bibliomania: Thomas Frognall Dibdin*, Richmond, 2004.
D'Israeli, Isaac, *Curiosities of Literature*, 5th edition, 3 vols, London, 1807.
Gent, Thomas, *The Life of Mr Thomas Gent, Printer of York written by himself*, London, 1832.
Gough, Richard, *Anecdotes of British Topography*, London, 1768.
Hobson, Anthony, *Great Libraries*, London, 1970.
Lister, Anthony, 'The Althorp Library of Second Earl Spencer, now in the John Rylands Library of Manchester: Its Formation and Growth', *Bulletin of the John Rylands University Library*, vol. 71, no. 2, 1989.
Mandelbrote, Giles and Yvonne Lewis, *Learning to Collect: The library of Sir Richard Ellys at Blickling Hall*, National Trust, 2004.
Mandelbrote, Giles and K.A. Manley, eds, *Cambridge History of Libraries in Britain and Ireland, Vol.l II, 1640–1820*, Cambridge, 2006.

Myers, Robin, Michael Harris and Giles Mandelbrote, eds, *Under the Hammer: Book Auctions since the Seventeenth Century*, London, 2001.
National Trust (library report), *Nostell Priory*, 2002.
Potten, Edward, 'Charles Winn and his Library', unpublished paper.
Raikes, Sophie, 'A Cultivated Eye for the Antique: Charles Winn and the enrichment of Nostell Priory in the Nineteenth Century', *Apollo*, April 2003.
Wainwright, Clive, *The Romantic Interior*, New Haven and London, 1989.

8 *The Common Reader*

Primary Sources

The letter-books of Charles Elliot, Mss 43090 and 43091, John Murray Archives, National Library of Scotland.
Pamphlets and book trade ephemera in the John Johnson Collection, Bodleian Library.

Printed Publications

Altick, Richard, *The English Common Reader: A Social History of the Mass Reading Public 1800–1900*, Chicago and London, 1957.
Andrews, Malcolm, *Charles Dickens and his Performing Selves*, Oxford, 2006.
Bewick, Thomas, *My Life*, ed. Iain Bain, London, 1981.
Brewer, John, *Pleasures of the Imagination: English Culture in the Eighteenth Century*, London, 1997.
Catcheside, P.R., 'Loveclough Printworks Library', *Library History*, vol. 2, 1970.
Elton, Godfrey. R., *The Life of James Ramsay MacDonald, 1866–1919*, London, 1939.
Fergus, Jan, 'Provincial Servants' Reading in the late Eighteenth Century' in *The Practice and Representation of Reading in England*, eds James Raven, Helen Small and Naomi Tadmor, Cambridge, 1996.
Flanders, Judith, *Consuming Passions: Leisure and Pleasure in Victorian Britain*, London, 2006.
Gardner-Medwin, David, 'The Library of Thomas Bewick' in *Bewick Studies, Essays in Celebration of the 250th Anniversary of the Birth of Thomas Bewick, 1753–1828*, ed. Gardner-Medwin, Newcastle-upon-Tyne, 2003.
Griest, Guinevere L., *Mudie's Circulating Library and the Victorian Novel*, Newton Abbot, 1971.
Hoare, Peter and Alastair Black, eds, *Cambridge History of Libraries in Britain and Ireland, Vol. III, 1850–2000*, Cambridge, 2006.
Johansen, Michael, 'A Fault-line in Library History: Charles Goss, the Society of Public Librarians, and the "Battle of the Books" in the late 19th century', *Library History*, 19, July 2003.
Kaufman, Paul, *Libraries and their Users*, London, 1969.
Ker, N., *The Parochial Libraries of the Church of England*, London, 1959.
Lackington, James, *The Life of James Lackington, Bookseller 1746–1815*, abridged by Peter Hopkins for Merton Historical Society, Morden, 2004.
Mandelbrote, Giles and K.A. Manley, eds, *Cambridge History of Libraries in Britain and Ireland, Vol II, 1640–1850*, Cambridge, 2006.
Manley, K.A., 'Libraries of Stoke Newington', *Journal of Librarianship*, 6, April 1974.
Marquand, David, *Ramsay MacDonald*, London, 1977.
Mayhew, Henry, *London Labour and the London Poor*, 4 vols, London, 1861–2.
Morgan, Kevin, *James Ramsay MacDonald*, London, 2006.
Mumby, F.A., *The House of Routledge: 1834–1934*, London, 1934.

Rose, Jonathan, *The Intellectual Life of the British Working Class*, New Haven and London, 2001.

Sassoon, Donald, *The Culture of the Europeans*, London, 2006.

Small, Helen, 'A Pulse of 124: Charles Dickens and a Pathology of the Mid-Victorian Reading Public', in *The Practice and Representation of Reading in England*, eds James Raven, Helen Small and Naomi Tadmor, Cambridge, 1996.

Steinberg, S.H., *Five Hundred Years of Printing* (revised edition by John Trevitt), London, 1996.

Stimpson, Felicity, 'Servants' Reading: An Examination of the Servants' Library at Cragside', *Library History*, vol. 19, March 2003.

Turner, E.S., *What the Butler Saw*, London, 1962.

Uglow, Jenny, *Nature's Engraver: A Life of Thomas Bewick*, London, 2006.

Wilson, Charles, *First with the News: the history of W.H. Smith, 1792–1972*, London, 1985.

9 *Children of the Revolution*

Primary sources

Book trade ephemera in the John Johnson Collection, Bodleian Library.

Penguin archives, University of Bristol Library.

Printed publications

Baines, Phil, *Penguin by Design: A Cover Story, 1935–2005*, Harmondsworth, 2005.

Brown, Richard and Stanley Brett, *The London Bookshop*, London, 1977.

Crick, Bernard, *George Orwell*, London, 1980.

Healey, Denis, *The Time of My Life*, London, 1989.

Healey, Edna, *Part of the Pattern*, London, 2006.

Hoare, Peter and Alastair Black, eds, *Cambridge History of Libraries in Britain and Ireland, Vol. III*, Cambridge, 2006.

Hodges, Sheila, *Victor Gollancz: The Story of a Publishing House, 1928–78*, London, 1978.

Laity, Paul, ed., *Left Book Club Anthology*, London, 2001.

Lewis, Jeremy, *Penguin Special: The Life and Times of Allen Lane*, London, 2005.

Mandelbrote, Giles, ed., *Out of Print and into Profit: A History of the Rare and Secondhand Book Trade in Britain in the Twentieth Century*, London, 2007.

Norrie, Ian, ed., *Mumby's Publishing and Bookselling in the Twentieth Century*, 6th edition, London, 1982.

Rose, Norman, *Harold Nicolson*, London, 2005.

Stringer, Ian, *Mobile Libraries*, Appleby-in-Westmorland, 2001.

Tebbel, John, *A History of Book Publishing in the United States, Vol. III: The Golden Age between Two Wars, 1920–40*, New York and London, 1971.

Wilson, Charles, *First with the News: The history of W.H. Smith, 1792–1972*, London, 1985.

INDEX

Page numbers in *italic* refer to illustrations

AbeBooks 262
Acton, Eliza 257
Adam, Robert 68, 114, 126, 168, 175
Adams, John 83, *97*, 100, 101, 103, 106, 107–8
Addison, Joseph 59–60, 77, 88, 145
Aesop 2, 34, 167, 225–6, 259
Ainsworth, William Harrison 204, 221
A la Ronde, Devon 156
Allestree, Richard 34, 38, 69, 77, 89, 155, 196, 198, 215, *Plate IV*
Althorp, Northamptonshire 170, 172
Altick, Richard 110, 193–4
Amazon 262, 275n29
Ambleside, Cumbria 80
Amis, Kingsley 259
Amman, Jost 5–6, *15*
Amsterdam 46, 64, 80, 96
Annapolis, Maryland 87, 88
Anne, Princess, later Queen *35*
Anson, George, Admiral Lord 88
Anthony, Anthony 38, *39*
Antwerp 13–14, *15*, 80
Appleby-in-Westmorland 75, 76
Arlington, Henry Bennet, Earl of 33, 47, 57
Armstrong, William, 1st Lord 200
Arundel, Alethea Howard, Countess of 22
Ascham, Roger 2, 21
Ashbourne Hall, Derbyshire 56, 62, 63
Ashby-de-la-Zouch, Leics. 63, 75, 158
Attenborough, Sir David 256
Atterbury, Francis 214
Attlee, Clement 237
Atwood, Margaret 260
Aubrey, John 34
auction sales 60–1, 73–5, 80, 119, 121, 126, 127–8, *128*

Austen, Jane 119, 154, 158, 160–1, 164–5, 167, 260

Baclehouse, John (the Painter) 6, 7
Bacon, Francis xi, 106
Bacon, Nathaniel 64, 66
Badcock, Samuel 148
Bagford, John 42, 53
Bailey, George 134
Baker, Ernest 252
Baker, John 253
Baker, William 111, 169
Baldwin, Robert 149
ballads 43–6
Ballantyne, James 119, 164
Ballantyne, R.M. 200, 201
Balliol College, Oxford 235
Bampton, Cumbria 76
Barbe-Marois, François 94
Barker, Jane 57
Barrow, Dr Isaac *82*
Basildon, Berkshire 109
Bath (circulating libraries) 144, 152–3
Beckett, Samuel 235
Behn, Aphra 57, 200
Beilby, Ralph 225–6
Belfast 166
Belzoni, Giovanni Battista 129
Bennett, Arnold 242
Berquin, Arnaud 100, 101
Bess of Hardwick *see* Cavendish, Elizabeth
Bevan, Aneurin 217
Beveridge, William 69, 199
Bewick, Thomas 117, *205*, 224–7, *226*, 230–2, 260

bibliomania 170–2
Bickerstaffe, Isaac 197
Bicknell, John 99–100
Birkbeck, George 217–18
Birkbeck Institute 229
Birkett, Elizabeth 75, 77
Birmingham 75, 80, 88, 202, 209; book club 139–40, *139*
Bishopsgate Institute 223
Blaeu, Willem 69
Blair, Hugh 122, 154, 215
Blake, William 116
Blickling Hall, Norfolk 173
Blount, Charles 62
Blunden, Edmund 237
Boaden, James 132
Boccaccio, Giovanni 137, 172
Bodleian Library, Oxford 104, 174, 188, 202, 237
Bodley, Sir Thomas 104, 241
Book Bang 257
book clubs 138, 155, 232, 240, 247, 253–4, 260–1
Book Club Associates 254, 255–6
Booker Prize 259
book groups 138, 160, 227, 260
Book of the Month Club 253–4
book prizes 259
book runners 251
booksellers: AMSTERDAM: Van Damme 101; ANTWERP: Cock, Hieronymous 6; Plantin, Christopher 7, 14, 26; Richart, Jean 23; AUGSBURG: Willer, George 13; BATH: Marshall, James (and library proprietor) 144, 152–3; BELFAST: Harrison 166; BIRMINGHAM: John Baskerville 80, 178; CAMBRIDGE: Morden, William 31; CIRENCESTER: Stevens, Timothy 153; COLERAINE: Dunlop 166; COLOGNE: Birckmann family 13–14; DUBLIN: Mullins & Mahon 166; EDINBURGH: Constable, Archibald 164, 166; Creech, William 72, 215; Elliott, Charles 96, 215; Ramsay, Allan (and library proprietor) 141, 225; FRANKFURT: Marni, Claude and Aubri, John 26; GOTTINGEN: Moller, Dr 161; HAY-ON-WYE: Booth, Richard 217, 260; KENDAL: Ashburner, Thomas 80; Cotton, Thomas 80; Harrison, Miles 80; Willan, Thomas 80; KNUTSFORD: Leech, John 82; LICHFIELD: Johnson, Michael 62–3, 75; LONDON: Allestree, James 34; Almon,

John 98, 100; Arch, John and Arthur 180; Asperne, James 122, *124*; Back, John 45, 63; Baker, Samuel 128; Baldock, Robert *181*; Ballard, Thomas 174; Bell, John (and library proprietor) 106, *107*, 150, 197, 205–6; Bent, William 119; Birt, Samuel 90; Blare, Josiah 45; Bohn, Henry George 182; Bomb Shop *245*; Booklover's Corner (Hampstead) 250; Brome, Henry 36, 47–8; Bumpus & Bumpus 243, 250, 251; Cadell, Thomas 63, 90, 91, 100, 122; Caxton, William 21, 42, *43*, 172; Chiswell, Richard 57, 58, 61, 84; Clavell, Robert 36, 37, 57–8, 63, 65; Cock, Christopher *171*; Colburn, Henry 162–3, 167; Cooper, William 61; Dalton, William Henry 174–5; Daunt Books 252; Day, John 11; Debrett, John 98; De Worde, Wynkyn 21, 42; Dilly, Charles & Edward 96, 98. 100; Dodsley, James & Robert 149–50, 155–6, 199; Dulau & Co. 129; Dunton, John 59, *60*, 65–6, 72, 73, 75, 83, 84; England, Nicholas 14; Foyles Bookshop 240, 249–50, 262; Garrett, John 49; Garthwaite, Timothy 38; Hartley, John, 173–4; Harrison & Byshop 4; Harrison, James 117; Hatchard, John (Hatchards) 98, 101, 174, 250–1; Herringman, Henry 41; Heywood Hill 250–1; Hookham, Thomas (and library proprietor) 142, 149, 174; Johnson, Joseph 98, 101, 162; Johnston, William 90; Joseph, Jack 249; Kirkman, Francis 46; Kirton, Joshua 32–3, 65; Lackington, James 100, 111, 119–22, *121*, *123*, 195, 198; Lane, William (Minerva Press and library proprietor) 143, 144, 149, 161, 167; Lawrence, Edward 124; Lawrence, John 65; Longman, Thomas 117–19, 124, 166, 172, 248, 251, 257; Lowndes, Thomas (and library proprietor) 142, 149, 150; Marks & Co. 249, *249*; Martin, John 42; Maunsell, Andrew 26, 62; Midwinter, Edward 185; Millington, Edward 73; Mitchell, Miles & Ann, 31–2; Mortier, David 49; Mount, Richard 39–40; Mudie, Charles Edward (Mudie's Select) 201–3, *202*, 203, 253; Murray, John I 71–2, 90–1, 96, 148, 149, 166; Murray, John II 119, 163; Newbery, John 225; Nicoll, William 96; Noble, Francis & John (and library proprietors) 141–2,

149; Norton, Bonham 26; Norton, John 26; Osborne, Thomas 89, 172; Parkhurst, Thomas 65; Payne, Thomas 101, 106, *107*, 121; Pickering, William 180–2; Playford, John 37, 50; Quaritch, Bernard 182, 248; Rivington, Charles 174; Salusbury, John 66; Sandby, William 71; Sayer, Robert 90; Scott, Robert 53; Shrewsbury, William 28, 33, 42, 66, 75; Simpson, Richard 62; Sotheran & Co. 221, 248; Starkey, John 33, 57–8, 64, 65, 66; Stockdale, John 96, 98–100, *99*, 121; Strahan, William 89, 90, 98; Taylor, Isaac & Josiah 124–5, 126; Tegg, Thomas 162, 208; Tias, Charles 45; Truslove & Hanson 252, Tucker, Roger 49; Vautrollier, Thomas 19; Walker, John 119, 121; Waller, Thomas 90, 92; Watts, Joseph 58; White & Cochrane 123; Wight, Thomas 4; Williams, John 126, *127*; Willis & Sotheran 180, 182; Wilson, Hubert 248; Worker's Bookshop 238; Zwemmer, Anton 254–5; LONDONDERRY: Campbell 166; LYONS: De Tournes, Jean 4; MANCHESTER: Haslington, John 72; Whitworth, Robert 71; MIDLANDS: Clay family 153, 196–8; NEWCASTLE UPON TYNE: Barber, Joseph 143, 225; Mawson, Swan & Morgan 201; Saint, Thomas 225–6; NEW YORK: Strand Bookstore 262; OXFORD: Blackwell, Basil 243; PARIS: Barrois 96–7; Estienne, Robert 12; Froullé, J-F. 96, 101; Pissot 101; Salmon, J. 129; PHILADELPHIA: Byrne, Patrick 101; Dufief 101; Reibelt Roche 101; WARRINGTON: Eyres, William 69; WILLAMSBURG: Hunter, William 89–90; Parks, William 88–9; Royle, Joseph 89–90; *Virginia Gazette* Bookstore 88–90; YORK: Barclay, Alexander 183; Gent, Thomas 184–6, *186*
Book Society 240
Boot, Florence 223, 252
Booth, George, 2nd Earl of Warrington 63, 66, *67*, 80; matrimonial problems 66–7; rebuilding of Dunham Massey 67; furnishing of library 68; science and astronomical books 69; religious and devotional books 68–9; books on Cheshire 68; architectural and horticultural books 70
Booth, Henry, 1st Earl of Warrington 63, 65, 66; political career 64; recommendations of political and constitutional books 64; advice to children on reading 65
Booth, Mary, Countess of Stamford 63, 67, 80–2; devotional reading 69; cookery books 70
Boothby, Sir William 64, 83, 84, 251; his literary circle 56; literary taste 57; his London booksellers 57; political opinions 58; and Michael Johnson 62–3
Boots Book-lovers Library 223, *246*, 252, 253
Boston, New England 66, 72, 84, *85*
Boswell, James 75, 207
Botany Club 59
Bott, Alan 240
Boughton, Edward 77
Boutcher, William 72
Bowyer, William 182–3
Bradford, Andrew 91
Brandon, Frances *see* Grey, Frances
Bray, Revd Thomas 86–7, *86*, 212
Braybrooke, Lord 54
Brayley, E.W. 112, 117
Brettingham, Matthew the Younger 127
Brewer, John 155
British Library, xii, 177
British Museum Library 42, 68, 104, 134, 140, 188, 192, 229, 232
Britton, John 111, 116, 117–9, 128–9, 135, 148, 182, 187
Brontë family 235
Brookner, Anita 259
Brougham, Henry, 1st Lord 217–8
Brown, Lancelot, 'Capability' 114
Brown, Mather 97
Browne, Benjamin (Old); purchases at public auction 75; keeps tally of books lent 79, *79*
Browne, Benjamin (Young) *74*; acquires practical books 77; buys books in London 77; sends books to Lake District 77–8
Buffon, Georges-Louis Leclerc, Comte de 72, 95, 214, 227
Bunny, Edmund 4
Bunyan, John 45–6, 73, 199, *Plate IV*
Burdett-Coutts, Angela 258
Burne-Jones, Edward 223
Burney, Dr Charles 149–51
Burney, Fanny 142, 149–51, 160–1, 163, 165, 167
Burns, Robert 159

Bury, Lady Charlotte 162–3
Butler, Samuel 208
Button, Daniel 59
Byrd II, William 92–3
Byron, George Gordon, 6th Baron 119, 211

Cade, John 31
Calke Abbey, Derbyshire 156, *157*, 160, 165
Calvin, John 4
Cambridge 62, 73, 80
Camden Society 183
Camden, William 18, 24, 183, *Plate I*
Campbell, Colen 70
Carew, Richard 24–5
Carlyle, Thomas xiii, 140, 165, 219, 228
Carnegie, Andrew 220, 235
Carter, Charles 70
Castiglione, Baldassare 25, 136
catalogues (books) 37, 57, 62, 71, *85*, 90–1, 121–2, *123*, 141, 173–4, 182, 227, 251
Catherine of Braganza, Queen 30, *35*, 36, 41
Cave, Edward 145–8, *147*, 182
Cavendish, Charles 5
Cavendish, Elizabeth (Bess of Hardwick) xii, *3*; early life and marriages 1–2; books recorded in chamber 4; use of books and prints in decorative schemes 5–9, *7*, *8*, *10*; education of children and granddaughter 18–21; practical books 21–2; legacy 27
Cavendish, Grace, née Talbot 2
Cavendish, Henry 2, 19, 23–4
Cavendish, Margaret, Duchess of Newcastle 19–21, 57
Cavendish, Sir William 2, 3, 6, 18, 21
Cavendish, William, 1st Earl of Devonshire 2, 19, 194; travel and history books 23–4; books of etiquette 24; pamphlets 25–6; works of fiction 25; London bookseller and European connections 26
Cavendish, William, 3rd Earl of Devonshire 56
Cecil, Sir William, Lord Burghley 2, 14, 23
Cervantes, Miguel 25
Cellarius, Andreas 69
Chamberlain, Joseph 219
Chambers, Sir William 113, 114
chapbooks 43–6, *44*, 137, 224, 232
Charlecote Park, Warwickshire 180, 182

Charles I, King of England 31, 79, 137
Charles II, King of England 29, 30, 32, 35, *35*, 36, 37, 38, *39*, 40, 41, 46, 47, 64
Charleston Library Society 87, 96
Charlett, Dr 38
Chatsworth, Derbyshire 2, 3, 4, 5, 6, *8*, 11, 23, 26, 56
Chaucer, Geoffrey 6, 7, 18, 42, 136, 137, 178, *Plate I*
Chawton, Hampshire 160, 260
Cheltenham, Glos; circulating library *145*; literary festival 260, *Plate VII*
Cherryburn, Northumberland 224–5, 227
Chertsey, Surrey 112
Chesapeake Bay 83, 84, 88
Chester 65, 72, 82
Chesterton, G.K. 235
Chippendale, Thomas the Younger 175, 176, *176*, *177*
Christie, Agatha 241
Christie, James 127, 133
Christie's 120, 126, 127–8
Chute, John 178, *179*
circulating libraries xi–xii, 77, 136, 138, 141–5, *142*, *145*, 156, 158, 174, 223–5, 252, 253
Clarendon, Edward Hyde, Earl of 82, 213
Clark, Kenneth, Lord 256, *Plate VI*
Clavering Society of Reading 140
Clifford, Lady Anne 18, 25, 75, 80, 136, *Plate I*
Cobbett, William 110, 134, 162, *164*, 218
coffee-houses 30, 47, *48*, 58–60, 72–3, 76–7, 139, 141, 144; Bath 144, 152–3; Dublin 73; Liverpool 72; London 30, 40, 41, 59, 76, 90, 116, 174; Margate 143–4, 156, 158; North America 72; Oxford 139; Rome 114
Coke, Sir Edward 64
Coleford, Gloucestershire 235–6
Coleridge, Gill 274n.25
Coles, Joan 242
Comber, Thomas 69
Conduitt, Edward and Sally 129, 134
Conyngham family *see* Lenox-Conyngham
Cooper, James Fenimore 204, 208
Copyright Act, 1710 61, 166
Copyright Act, 1814 104
Corneille, Pierre 41, *216*
Cornwallis, Sir William 43–4
Corrozet, Gilles 25
Cotgreave, Alfred 220–1, *222*

County Libraries Act, 1919 253
Coventry 62
Cradock, Fanny 257
Cragside, Northumberland 200–1, 203
Craig, Samuel 254
Crane, Walter 205, 207
Crewe, Sir George, 8th Baronet 158–9
Cromleholme, Samuel 28–9, 32, 37
Crommelin, Maria 200
Cromwell, Oliver 28, 31, 50
Croxall, Samuel 225–6
Cruikshank, George *164, 184*
Culpepper, Nicholas 79, 195–6
Cwmaman, Monmouthshire 217

Dahl, Michael *67*
Dalrymple, William 261
Dance, George, the Younger 112–3, 120,
   135
Darnton, Robert xii
Darwin, Charles 189
Davies, William Robertson 259
Davis, Joan 236
Dawson, John 196
Day, Thomas 99–100, 155
Dee, Dr John 13, 104
Defoe, Daniel 110, 195, 199
De la Heuze, John 65, 68
Deloney, Thomas 196
De Mendoza, Diego Hurtado 25
Descartes, René 41
De Scuderi, Madeleine 41
Desgodetz, Antoine Babuty *115*
De Villamont, Seigneur 24
De Voragine, Jacques 28, 42
De Vos, Maarten 7
De Vries, Vriedman 23
Dibdin, Thomas Frognall xiii, 111, 169–72,
   176, 187
Dickens, Charles xiii, 140, *184*, 194, 195,
   200, 201, 204–5, 208–11, *210*, 218, 219,
   228, 236, 258
Dickinson, John, 98
Disraeli, Benjamin 94, 98, 170, 204,
   258
D'Israeli, Isaac 98, 101, 170, 172, 190
Dorling, Christopher 255
Douglas Hamilton, Hugh *176*
Downhill, County Antrim 115
Doyle, Arthur Conan 201
Drake, Francis 185
Drelincourt, Charles 89
Drumbleby (flageolet maker) 28

Drummond, David, 3rd Lord Maddertie
   212
Drummond, Robert Hay 212
Dryden, John 41, 42, 50, 57, 59, 61, 178
Dublin 62, 72, 73, 90, 166
Dudley, Robert, Earl of Leicester 2, 5, 17,
   23, 180
Duff Brown, James 221
Dugdale, Sir William 69, 178
Dunham Massey, Cheshire 63, 64, 66, 67,
   68–70, 80–2, *81*, 158, 200, *Plate II*
DuPin, Louis Ellies 215
Du Prey, Pierre de la Ruffinière 114
Dürer, Albrecht 225
Du Sautoy, Stephen 258

East India Company 23, 180
Eckstein, Johannes 139, *139*
Edgeworth, Maria 162, 163, 166
Edinburgh 62, 71, 90, 94, 141, 143, 174,
   213, 214, 215, 218, 225, 258, 260
Education Act, 1870 193, 228, 230, *231*,
   232, 233
Edward VI, King of England 11
Edzell, Angus 221
Egerton, Samuel 68
Elgin, Moray 228
Elizabeth I, Queen of England 1–2, 5, 11,
   21, 23, 25, 180
Elliot, George 202
Ellys, Sir Richard *85*, 173–5
Emmanuel College, Cambridge 84
Enfield, William 148, 154
Enlightenment, the 155; American 94;
   French 72, 94–5, 125–6; Scottish 94–5,
   109, 214, 225
Erasmus, Desiderius 9, *10*, 18
Evans, Edmund 205, *205*
Evelyn, John 30, 31, 33, 36, 38, 49, 50, 52,
   53, 55, 57, 68, 248
Ewart, William 218

Fairthorne, William 49
Falkus, Christopher 255–6
Farington, Joseph 112
Farnham, Surrey 110
Fauquier, Francis 88
Fenton, Edward 38
Fergus, Jan 153, 167
Fielding, Henry 92, 121, 138, 151, 160,
   166
Floris, Frans and Jacob 6, *8*
Floyer, Sir John 63

Foot, William 195
Forest of Dean, Gloucestershire 235–6
Forster, W.E. 193, 230, *231*, 232, 233
Forsyth, Hazel 272n.5
Fortescue, Sir John 64
Fox (Henry Cavendish's servant) 23
Foxe, John 11–12, 19
Frankfurt am Main 13–14, 26, 96, 255
Franklin, Benjamin 89, 91, 98, 101
Franzen, Jonathan 261
Fraser, Lady Antonia 255

Galle, Philips 9
Galsworthy, John 250, 256
Gandy, Joseph 130, *131*, 132
Gardiner, Bishop Stephen 5
Gaskell, Elizabeth 235
Gay, Thomas 226
George III, King of Great Britain 100, 104,
   113
George IV, King of Great Britain 104, 189,
   217
George, Henry 228–9
Gerard, John 18, 22–3, 225, *Plate I*
Gerlach, Nathanael Jacob 266 n.30
Gesner, Conrad xiii, 12, 225
Gibbes, Phebe 154
Gibbon, Edward 154, 156
Gibbons, Grinling 68
Gibbs, James 132, 172
Gilbert, William 25
Gillray, James 159, *159*
Gissing, George 229
Gladstone, William Ewart 140, 195, 229,
   258
Glasgow 90, 94, 215, 217, 218
Godwin, Tony 257
Godwin, William 101, 148
Goethe, Johann Wolfgang von 161, 165
Goff, Martyn 257–8, 274n.25
Goldscheider, Ludwig 254
Goldsmith, Oliver 114, 166
Gollancz, Israel 207, 237
Gomberville, Marin le Roy de 137
Goss, Charles 223
Gosse, Edmund 137
Gough, Richard 185
Gould, John 189–90, *190*
Granger, Revd James 187
Grant, James 204
Gray, Gilbert & William 225
Gray, Thomas 72, 104, 154, 193, 199
Great Fire of London 30, 32–3, 34, 38, 57,
   248

Greenwood, Thomas 218–21, *218, 222*
Grew, Dr Nehemiah 56, 59
Grey, Frances, Marchioness of Dorset
   1, 5
Grey, Henry, Marquess of Dorset 1, 5
Grey, Lady Jane 1, 2, 21
Griffiths, Ralph 148
Grotius, Hugo 65
Guazzo, Stefano 25
Guillim, John 69, 182
Guinzburg, Harold 254

Haggard, Sir Henry Rider 200
Hakluyt, Richard 24, 194
Hall, David 89
Halliwell, James Orchard 186–8
Hamilton, Archibald 148
Hands, Elizabeth 198–9
Hanff, Helene 249
Harbin, Philip 257
Hardwick, Elizabeth *see* Cavendish,
   Elizabeth
Hardwick Hall, Derbyshire (Old and New
   Halls) 1, 3, 4, 5–7, 8, 9, 17, 19, 21, 22, 23,
   26
Harington, Sir John 21
Harley, Edward, 2nd Earl of Oxford 42,
   131–2, 170–2, *171*, 192
Harley, Robert, 1st Earl of Oxford 42,
   131–2, 170, 192
Harpur, Sir Henry, 7th Baronet, and
   Nanette, Lady 157–9
Harrington, James 30
Harris, John 69
Harvard College, Massachusetts 66, 84, *85*,
   173
Hatton, Sir Christopher 23
Hay-on-Wye 217, 260
Hay, William Robert 183
Hazlitt, William 162, 228
Healey, Denis, Lord Healey of Riddlesden
   234; early life and education 233–5; and
   Left Book Club 237; impact of Penguin
   books 244, 247; and second-hand
   bookshops 248–9
Healey, Edna, Lady, neé Edmunds *234*;
   early life and education 235–7; becomes
   a Foyles lecturer 250; as author and
   book prize judge 258–60
Heath, Edward 258
Henry VIII, King of England xi, 12, 38, *39*
Hervey, Frederick, 4th Earl of Bristol and
   Bishop of Derry 114–15, *115*

Hervey, John, 1st Earl of Bristol *60*
Hervey, James 208
Hesse-Rotenburg, Victor Amadeus,
 Landgrave of, and Elise 161
Hewer, William 37, 54
Hexham, Northumberland 224, 260
Hislop, Victoria 261
Hobbes, Thomas 24, 26, 56, 120, 214
Hobson, Anthony 268n.31
Hoby, Lady Margaret 5
Hodges, Sheila 238
Hogarth, William 76, 137, 151, *152*
Hoggart, Richard 76, 145
Holland, Henry 113–4
Hollar, Wenceslas *32*, 35
Holroyd, Michael 258
Hone, William 272n.15
Hood, Thomas 211
Horovitz, Bela 254
Houblon, James 49, 53
Hulett, James *142*
Hume, David 90, 94, 154, 215
Hunt, Leigh 167, 172, 200
Huntingdon Book Club Society 140
Hutcheson, Francis 94–5
Huys, Frans 6, *8*
Hyrde, Richard 19

Inchbald, Elizabeth 154, 158
Innerpeffray, Perthshire 212–14, *213*
Ipswich, Suffolk 211–12
Irving, Washington 204

Jackson, John 49, 53, 54, 55
Jackson, John, minister of Measham 212
James I, King of England 85
James II, King of England 30, 33, *35*, 36,
 37, 47, 48, *51*, 52, 58, 64, 65, 75
Jefferson, Martha 91, 93, 95
Jefferson, Peter 87, 97
Jefferson, Thomas 83, *97*, 116, 121, 170;
 family background and education 87–8;
 his American booksellers 88–90, 101;
 his European booksellers 90, 96–101;
 library at Monticello 91–3, *92*; writings
 93, 94–5; sells books to Library of
 Congress 103–6; and University of
 Virginia 106–7
John Rylands Library, Manchester 192
Johnson, Edgar 194
Johnson, Samuel 56, 62–3, 71, 75, 146, 148,
 150, 151, 193, 194, 199, 206, 207, 208,
 237, 257, 262

Jonson, Ben 41, 137
journals *see* periodicals
Joyce, James 234

Kames, Henry Home, Lord 92, 94
Kaufman, Paul 141, 151–3, 167, 214
Kedermister, Sir John and Dame Mary
 16–17, *17*
Keighley, Yorkshire 235
Kemble, John Philip 128, 158
Kendal, Cumbria 75, 76–7, 80
Kent, Elizabeth Grey, Countess of 22
Kindersley, Peter 255, 262
King, Cyrus 104
King, Daniel 69
Kingsley, Henry *205*
Kipling, Rudyard 236
Kneller, Sir Godfrey *29*
Knyvett, Sir Thomas 16–18

La Calprenède, Gauthier de Costes,
 Seigneur de 41
Lane, Allen 241–5, *245*, *247*, 247–55, 257
Lane, John 241
Langford, T. 70
Larpent, Anna Margaretta 153–5, 167
Laski, Harold 240
Latham, Robert 54
Laugier, Marc-Antoine 126
law of subordination 110, 195
Lawrence, D.H. xi, 234, 252
Lawson & Semple 90
Leadhills, Lanarkshire 214–17, *216*
Leavis, F.R. 235
Leavis, Queenie 252, 261
Lee, Arthur 98
Left Book Club 237, 238–41, 253, *Plate I*
Leland, John 170
Le Nôtre, André 67
Lenox-Conyngham family 165–7
Le Sage, Alain-René 114, 133, 156, 166
L'Estrange, Sir Roger 46–8, 58
Levey, Santina 6
Lewis, Matthew Gregory 132, 159–60, *159*,
 161, 163
Lewis Walpole Library 192
Leycester, Sir Peter 69
Library of Congress, Washington 83, *102*,
 103–6, *105*
Licensing Act, 1695 62, 72, 80
Lichfield, Staffs. 62–3, 75
lighting 31, *76*, 88, 140, 194, *231*, 232,
 236

Lindsay, 'Sandy' 237
literary festivals 260
Literary Guild 254
Liverpool 72, 73–5, 82, 218
Loarte, Gaspar 4
Locke, John 91, 214
Lockey, Rowland *20*
Loggan, David 35
London: CITY: Aldersgate Street 9; Ave
    Maria Lane 9; Blackfriars 19, 26;
    Chiswell Street 112, 120; City Road 208;
    Clare Market 36; Cornhill 30, 31, 122,
    124, 180; Duck Lane 12, 28, 33, 34;
    Exchange Alley 59; Fetter Lane 42;
    Finsbury Place 120; Fleet Street 21, 28,
    32, 33, 50, 59, 65, 71, 98, 116, 119, 149,
    183; Gresham College 40; Guildhall
    Library 229; Leadenhall 143, 144, 149,
    161, 167, 196; Little Britain 12, 33, 73;
    Lombard Street 146; London Bridge *32*,
    44–5, 63, 185; London Wall 49;
    Moorfields 33, *74*, 112; Paternoster Row
    9, 14, 59, 117, 144; Poultry 65, 98; Royal
    Exchange 33, 36, 49, 90; St Paul's
    Churchyard and School 9–11, 13, 14, 26,
    28, 32, *32*, 33, 34, 36, 47, 57, 58, 63, 84,
    98, 101, 116, 248; Seething Lane 32, 37;
    Stationers' Hall 32; Stocksmarket 59;
    Temple 33, 50, 100; Tower of London
    37, 40, 64, 65; Warwick Lane 36, 59;
    West Smithfield 12, 44; WESTMINSTER
    AND WEST END: Albemarle Street 119;
    Axe Yard 30; Bedford Square 243, 257–8;
    Bloomsbury 122, 201; Buckingham
    Street 37; Carnaby Street 141; Charing
    Cross 174, 245, 248–50, 254; Covent
    Garden 33, 41, 59, 116, 127, 156, 237;
    Curzon Street 250; Gordon Square 173;
    Holborn 42, 122, 124, *181*; Leicester
    Fields 101, 141, 182; Lincoln's Inn Fields
    35, 109, 116, 122, 130, 133, 156, 181,
    229; Marylebone 245, 251–2; New and
    Old Bond Streets 142; New Exchange
    33, 36, 41; New Palace Yard 30; Oxford
    Street 116, 154, 250; Pall Mall 36, 116,
    127, 199; Piccadilly 70, 98, 100, 101, 116,
    182, 241, 248, 250; St James's 59, 98, 140;
    Soho 70, 126, 129; the Strand 42, 49, 57,
    90, 112; Westminster Abbey and Hall 21,
    31–2, 47, 178; Whitehall 29, 41, 47;
    ENVIRONS: Clapham 54; Clerkenwell 59,
    76, 145, *147*, 183, 221–3; Dulwich 109;
    Ealing 112, 132; Hackney 220; Highgate
    258; Old Kent Road 208; Shoreditch
    196; Stoke Newington 208, 220, 223
London Library xiii, 140
'London Spy' 73
Longford, Frank Pakenham, 7th Earl 258
Lorrain, Paul 49, 53, 54
Lossiemouth, Moray 227–9
lotteries 34–6
Louis XIV, King of France 33, 47, 67, 145,
    254
Loveclough Printworks, Lancashire 201
Low, David 240
Luckett, Dr Richard 266n.27
Lucy, George Hammond and Mary
    Elizabeth 180, 181–2
Lunar Society, 88, 99
Lyte, Henry 22

MacDonald, George 228, 238
MacDonald, James 228
MacDonald, James Ramsay 224, 227–232
Machiavelli, Nicolò, 65
Madison, James 100
Madison, James, US President 102
Madrid 96, 101
magazines *see* periodicals
Magdalene College, Cambridge 29, 50, 54
Man, John 111, 169,
Manchester 71, 72–3, 82, 168, 192, 202,
    206, 209
Margate, Kent: circulating libraries 143–4,
    156, 158
Marivaux, Pierre Carlet de Chamblain de
    146, 154, 155
Marlowe, Christopher 13, 21, 252
Marmontel, Jean-François 154
Marryat, Captain Frederick 204
Mary of Modena, Queen *35*, 64, 75
Mary Stuart, Queen of Scots 2, 9
Mary I, Queen of England 5, 9, 11, 62, 104
Mary II, Queen of England *35*, 58, 64
Maschler, Tom 257, 259
Matthews, Douglas xiii
Matthews, Prof. William 54
Mattioli, Pier Andrea 9, *10*, 22
Maury, James 87–8
Mayhew, Henry 207–8
MacDonogh, Felix 167
mechanics institutes 211, 217–18, 253
Meighn, Moira 257
Miller, Robert 90–1
Millot, Michel 42
Milton, John 57, 90, 137, 154, 208, 234

miners' libraries 214–17
Minerva Press *see* William Lane
Mitford, Nancy 251
mobile libraries 253
Molière 41
Monmouth, James Scott, Duke of 33, *35*, 65
Monroe, James 96
Montagu, Edward, 1st Earl of Sandwich 28, 29, 32
Montagu, Dr John 53
Montaigne, Michel de 25, 77, *207*
Monticello, Virginia 91, *92*, 94, 105, 106
More, Hannah 162, 200
Morelli, Cesare 50
Morison, Stanley 238, 240, 242
Mortimer, Raymond 238, *Plate VI*
Moxon, Joseph 36, 39, 42, 57
Moyes, James 122, 124
Muddiman, Henry 46, 47
Mulcaster, Richard 18

Napoleon Bonaparte 129, 182
Nash, John 126, 133
National Book League 257–8, 259
Naudé, Gabriel 57
Net Book Agreement 253
Neurath, Walter 254
Newcastle upon Tyne 143, 203, 224, 225–7, 232, 260
New York 72, 209, 210
newspapers 46–8, 72–3, 96, 103;
SEVENTEENTH CENTURY: *Intelligencer* 47; *London (Oxford) Gazette* 35, 47, *48*, 59, 61; *Loyal News* 48; *Mercurius Librarius* 58; *News* 47; *Observator* 47; *Perfect Diurnal* 37; *Protestant News* 48; *Snotty-Nose Gazette* 48; EIGHTEENTH CENTURY: *Kendal Weekly Courant* 80; *Leverpole Courant* 72; *London Chronicle* 150; *Manchester Weekly Newsletter* 72–3; *Maryland Gazette* 89; *Mercury* (Kendal) 80; *Morning Post* 205; *Pennsylvania Gazette* 89; *Post-Man* 48; *Public Occurrences* (Boston) 72; *Reading Mercury* 88; *St James's Chronicle* 149; *Virginia Gazette* 89; NINETEENTH CENTURY: *Champion* 133; *Echo* 220; *Sun* 221; *The Times* 205, 211; TWENTIETH CENTURY: *Daily Express* 257; *Daily Herald* 243; *Daily Mail* 243; *Evening Standard* 242, 244; *Guardian* 261; *News Chronicle* 238; *Observer* 238, *239*, 244; *Sunday Times* 238; *see also* periodicals

Newton, Isaac 41
Nichols family, 182–3
Nicolson, Sir Harold 234–5, 237, *247*, 251
Nicolson, Nigel 237, 254
Noble, Robert 236
Northaw, Hertfordshire 6, 264n.8
Nostell Priory, Yorkshire 168–9, 174, 175, 180, 188, 191, *191*

O'Connor, Joseph 261
Ogilby, John 34–5, *35*, *74*, 77, *78*
Oldenburg, Henry 40
Orwell, George 237, 240, 250, *Plate V*
Ovid 136
Owen, William *115*
Oxford 34, 40, 62, 71, 72, 80, 139, 236–7, 241

Paine, Thomas 98, 101, 199
Palladio, Andrea 23, 70, 91, 114, *115*, 126
Palsgrave, John 2
Paris 12, 36, 42, 80, 95–8, 100, 101, 129
Parminter, Jane and Mary 156
Parsons, Eliza 154–5, 156, 160, 161
Parsons, Robert (also Persons) 4
Pascal, Blaise 41
Passmore Edwards, John 220, 223
Patten, Marguerite 257
Peacock, James 112
Pecke, Samuel 37
Peel, Sir Robert 134
penny readings 211
Pepys, Elizabeth 30, 31, 36, 41, 50, 137
Pepys, Samuel *29*, 59, 63, 65, 66, 137, 162, 194, 200, 203, 248; early life and education 28; marriage 30–1; keeps a diary 31; his booksellers 31–4; books on naval history and maps 38–40; books of plays 41; taste in literature 41–2; collection of incunabula, ballads and chapbooks 42–4; newspapers 47; books of music 50; borrows books 53; bequeaths his library to Cambridge 54
Percy, Henry, 9th Earl of Northumberland 17
periodicals: SEVENTEENTH CENTURY: *Athenian Gazette (Mercury)* 59, *60*, 66; *Flying Post* 66; *History of the Works of the Learned* 173; *Journal des Scavens* 173; *Old Bailey Inquest after Blood* 147; *Philosophical Transactions* 40, 47; EIGHTEENTH CENTURY; *A la Mode Magazine* 197; *American Magazine* 91;

periodicals (*cont.*)
  Court Miscellany 148; *Critical Review*
  144, 148–9, 154, 161, 163; *English
  Review* 149; *European Magazine* 154;
  General Magazine 91; *Gentleman's
  Magazine* 91, 145–8, *147*, 154; *Lady's
  Magazine* 148, 182–3, 197; *London
  Magazine* 91, 148, 149; *London Review*
  150; *Monthly Review* 148–9, 150, 154,
  163; *Philosophical Transactions* 88;
  Republic of Letters 173; *Spectator* 59–60,
  145, 154; *Tatler* 59–60, 145; *Town and
  Country Magazine* 148; *Whitworth's
  Manchester Magazine* 71; NINETEENTH
  CENTURY: *Annual Register* 124, 166, 174;
  Cassell's Illustrated Family Paper 206;
  Cassell's Magazine 206; *Cassell's Popular
  Educator* 206, 224, 228; *Cassell's
  Saturday Journal* 201; *Comic Cuts* 201;
  Edinburgh Magazine 174; *Edinburgh
  Review* 119, 163, 164; *European
  Magazine* 122, *124*, 153; *Gentleman's
  Magazine* 115–16, 166, 182–3; *Good
  Words* 201; *Home Notes* 201; *Monthly
  Magazine* 141; *Penny Cyclopaedia* 217;
  Penny Magazine 217; *Political Register*
  218; *Punch 231*, 232; *Quarterly Journal
  of Education* 217; *Quarterly Review* 119,
  163, 164, 174; *Queen* 201; *Spectator* 202;
  Sunday at Home 201; *Sunday Magazine*
  201; *Sylvia's Journal* 201; *Tit-bits* 201;
  Working Man's Companion 217;
  Working Man's Friend 206; *The World
  of Fashion* 163; TWENTIETH CENTURY:
  Bookseller 119, 248; *New Statesman*
  238; *Punch* 223; *Scrutiny* 235; *see also*
  newspapers
Perkins, Buchanan & Brown 90, 91
Philadelphia 89, 91, 94, 95, 101
Phillipps, James Orchard Halliwell *see*
  Halliwell
Phillipps, Sir Thomas 187–8
Pitshanger Manor, Ealing 112, 132
Platt, Sir Hugh 25, 70
Polyglot Bible 34, 69
Ponet, John 11
Pope, Alexander 59, 88, 199
Potten, Edward 64
Pranker, Robert 151, *153*
Priestley, J.B. 244
Priestley, Joseph 69, 155
Public Library Acts, 1850 & 1855 218, 233,
  236

publishers: Allen & Unwin 254; Benn,
  Ernest 243; Bodley Head 241, 242; Cape,
  Jonathan 243, 257, 259; Cassell, John
  206, 228, 232; Chapman & Hall 208;
  Chatto & Windus 243; Collins, William
  244, 248, 254; Constable 248; Dent,
  Joseph Malaby 206–7, *207*, 232, 237;
  Deutsch, André 257; Dorling Kindersley
  255, 262; Doubleday & Co. 254; Eyre &
  Spottiswoode 248; Gollancz, Victor 38,
  237–41, 242–3, 247, *Plate V*; Hamlyn,
  Paul 254–5, 257; Hodder Headline 259;
  Hutchinson, George & Walter, 242, 244,
  248, *256*; John Murray 251, 252; Knight,
  Charles 217; Nelson's 248; Penguin
  Books 242–5, 245, 257, *Plate VI*;
  Phaidon Press 254; Purnell 255;
  Robinson family 144; Routledge, George
  204–5; Secker, Martin 240; Sidgwick &
  Jackson 258–9; Thames & Hudson 254;
  Viking Press 254; Weidenfeld &
  Nicolson 254
Purcell, Mark 77

Racine, Jean 41
Radcliffe, Ann 121, 160–1, 163
radio 211, 234, 236, 259, 260
railways 203–5, *204*, 252
Randolph, Isham 87
Randolph, Colonel William 87
Rapin, Paul de 88
Raven, James 141
Rawlinson, Richard and Thomas, 170, 174
Raynal, Abbé 95
Readers Union book club 253
Reading, Berkshire 111, 169
reading societies 138, 215, 216
Rees, Thomas 117–19
Reeve, Clara 144, 161
Reid, Thomas 94
Reith, Sir John 234
Repton, Humphry 126
reviews 144–50, 154
Revett, Nicholas 126
Revocation of the Edict of Nantes 145, 254
Richard and Judy Show 261
Richardson, Samuel 89, 92, 114, 137–8,
  146, 154, 166, 197–8, 200
Richmond, Virginia 85, 94
Ripon, Yorkshire 184
Robertson, William 82, 90, 94, 95, 154, 214
Roche, Regina Maria 149, 167
Rome 53, 114

Roper, Katherine 178
Rose, Jonathan xii
Ross, Amanda 261
Rota Club 30
Rousseau, Jean-Jacques 99, 114, 125, 154, 155, 158
Rowlandson, Thomas 98, *99*, *128*
Rowling, J.K. 262
Royal Academy 112, 113, 116, 125
Royal Society 34, 40–1, 47, 54, 59, 88, 116, 183
Ruskin, John 228
Russell, Dora 201
Russell, William Howard 211
Russia Company 23
Rycaut, Paul 33

St Clair, William 165
St Hugh's College, Oxford 237
St Loe, Sir William 2, 14, 19, 23
Salomon, Bernard 4
Sandby, Thomas 113
Sault, Richard 59
Saumarez Smith, John 251
Sayers, Dorothy L. 243, *Plate V*
Scherman, Henry 253–4
Schiller, Friedrich 161
Schloss Corvey, Princely library at 161
Scott, Sir Walter 119, 151, 159, 163–5, *164*, 174, 194, 200, 201, 204, 211, 228, *Plate IV*
Scougal, Henry 215
Seaman, Lazarus 61
Second World War 241, 245–8, *246*, *247*, 255
Selfridges 243, 244
Serlio, Sebastiano 23, 126
Shadwell, Albemarle County, Virginia 83, 87, 91
Shadwell, Dr John 53, 54
Shakespeare, William 42, 45, 77, 88, 114, 128–9, 133, 137, 180, 182, 186–7, 191, 206, 207, 213, 215, 252
Shaw, George Bernard 243, 244, 248
Shelton, Thomas 29, 31, 54
Shenstone, William 90
Sheridan, Richard Brinsley 136, 151
Sherley, Sir Anthony 24
Sherlock, William 74–5, 154, 158, 214
Shillito, Charles 140–1
Short, William 101
Shrewsbury, Earls of *see* Talbot
Shute, John 6, *7*

Sidney, Sir Philip 18, 25, 136, 137, *Plate I*
Simpkin Marshall (book wholesalers) 244, 248
Simpson, Thomas 51, *51*, 54
Skinner, Mary 37, 53
Skipwith, Robert 92, 94, 106
Slater, Nigel 261
Sloane, Sir Hans 42, 54, 59, 68
Small, William 88
Smart, William 211
Smellie, William 72, 273n.44
Smith, Delia 257
Smith, Revd John 54
Smith, Joseph 70
Smith, Robert 70
Smith, William 90
Smith, William Henry 203–5, *204*; *see also* WH Smith
Smollett, Tobias 92, 114, 121, 144, 151, 156, 166, 225
Smythson, Robert 17, 22, 23
Soan, William 112
Soane, Eliza, neé Smith 115–16, 125, 130, *131*, 133, 155–6
Soane, George 116, 130, *131*, 132, 133, 134, 161
Soane, Sir John *115*, 155–6, 161, 169, 187, 245; early life and education 109–14; travels to Italy 114–15; marriage and life in Lincoln's Inn Fields 116, 130; his booksellers 119–125; influenced by the Enlightenment 125–6; buys from auctions 126–9; interest in Shakespeare and Bonaparte 128–9; designs for libraries 130–1, *Plate III*; collapse of family life 133; bequeaths library and house to the nation 133–4
Soane, John (son) 116, 130, *131*, 132, 133, 156
Society of Antiquaries 116, 183
Society for the Diffusion of Useful Knowledge 217
Society for Promoting Christian Knowledge 86, 212
Society for the Propagation of the Gospel in Foreign Parts 86–7, *86*
Sotheby, John 128
Sotheran, Thomas *see* Willis & Sotheran
Southey, Robert 148
Spencer, George John, 2nd Earl 170, 172, 192
Spenser, Edmund 18, 25, *107*, 136, 137, *Plate I*

Sprat, Thomas 40
Springhill, County Londonderry 165–7
Stationers' Company xi, 9, 12, 62, 137
Steadman, Ralph *Plate VII*
Steele, Richard 59–60, 77, 145
Sterne, Laurence 114, 156, 160
Stirling, James 214–15
Stow, John 212
Stowe, Harriet Beecher 204–5
Strachey, John 238, 240
Stradanus, Johannes 9
Stratton, Hesba 201
Strawberry Hill, Twickenham 177–80, *179*, 184, 186
Strickland, Eustachius 168, 184
Strickland, Sir William 168, 176
Stuart, Lady Arbella 19–21, *20*, 26
Stukeley, William 104, 126
Sturbridge Fair, Cambridge 73
subscription libraries 138–41
Sugg, William & Co. *230*, 232
Swan, Annie S. 200, 201
Swift, Jonathan 59, 88, 110, 166, 197, 199
Sykes, Mark Masterman 183, 191

Talbot, George, 6th Earl of Shrewsbury 2, 14, 22, 23
Talbot, Gilbert, 7th Earl of Shrewsbury 2
Talbot, Mary 2, 20–1
Taylor, Jeremy 68–9, 77, 225
Taylor, Samuel 211
television 253, 254, 256–7, 260–1
term catalogues 37, 57, 84
Thevet, André 23
Thompson, Flora 211
Thomson, James 72, 154, 197
Thynne, Sir John 22, 23
Thornton, John, chartmaker 39
Thrale, Hester 151
Ticknor, George 106
Tillotson, John 154, 214
The Times: circulating library 252–3
Tomalin, Claire 30, 137
Topsell, Edward 225
Townend, Troutbeck, Cumbria 75, *76*, 77, 80, *82*
Trecynon, Glamorgan 217
Tredegar, Gwent 217
Trollope, Anthony 201, 209
Trusler, Revd Dr John 148–9, 195, 198
Tuckahoe, Goochland County 87

Uppark, Sussex 199

Usher, John 84
Uttley, Alison 195
Uttoxeter, Staffs. 63, 75

Van Heemskerck, Maarten 7
Victoria, Queen of Great Britain 201
Virginia Company 23, 34, 84, 85
Virginia, University of 83, 106–7
Vitruvius 114, 126
Vives, Juan Luis 19
Voltaire 154

Waghenaer, Lucas Janszoon 38
Walpole, Horace 150, 154, 160, 161, 177–80, *179*, 182, 186, 192
Walpole, Hugh 240
Walton, Brian 69
Wanlockhead, Dumfriesshire 214, 215, 216–17
Warde, W. 22
Warrington Academy 69–70, 82, 148
Warton Club 186
Washington 101, 102, 103, 105, *108*
Waterstone's 251
Watkin, David 125
Watson-Armstrong, William, 2nd Lord Armstrong 200, 203
Watts, Isaac 195, 208, *Plate IV*
Webbe, Edward 24
Weidenfeld, George, Lord 254
Wells, H.G. 199, *247*
Wells-Cole, Anthony 5
Wesley, John 111
Wesley, Samuel 59
West, Captain Thomas 59
Westerkirk, Dumfriesshire 214, 217
Weston, Sir Richard 70
WH Smith 243, 246, 252, 253, 254; *see also* Smith, William Henry
Wightwick, George 133
Willan, Thomas 80
Willett, Deb 41
William & Mary College, Williamsburg 86, 87, 88, 89, 94, 100
William III, King of England 58, 64
William IV, King of Great Britain, and Queen Adelaide 135, 189
Williams, Dr, library of 173
Williamsburg, Virginia 86, 88
Williamson, secretary to Lord Arlington 47
Willoughby, Francis 40
Willoughby, Sir Francis 23
Wilson, John G. 243, 251

Wimpole Hall, Cambridgeshire 131–2, 170, *Plate III*
Winfrey, Oprah 260–1
Winn, Charles *169*; early life and marriage 168–9; his booksellers in London and York 174–5, 180, 182, 183–4; library at Nostell 175; interest in numismatics 176–7; purchases from Strawberry Hill sale 177–80; interest in Shakespeareana 186–7; dealings with John Gould 189–90
Winn, John 168, 175, 176
Winn, Patricia 168, 184, 192
Winn, Sir Rowland, 5th Baronet, and Sabine, Lady 168–9, 175, *176*, *177*
Winn, Rowland, 1st Lord St Oswald 192
Wodrow, Revd Robert 141
Wollstonecraft, Mary 101, 116
Wood, Anthony 139
Wood, Mrs Henry 201
Woolf, Virginia 194, 235, 252

Woolworths 243, 244
Wordsworth, Dorothy and William 215, 224
Worrall, John 71
Wright, Thomas 68
Wythe, George 88, 95, 101

Yale College, New Haven, Connecticut 84
yellowbacks 204, *204*
York 180, 183, 184, 185, 189, 212
York, James Duke of *see* James II, King of England
Yorke, Philip, 3rd Earl of Hardwicke 131–2, *Plate III*
Young, Edward 90, 120, 154, 197, 199, 208
Young, Edward (designer of Penguin logo) 242

Zouche family 1, 9
Zwemmer, Anton 254–5